Navigating the Shifting Landscape of Consumer Behavior

Fatih Sahin
Bandirma Onyedi Eylul University, Turkey

Cevat Soylemez
Kutahya Dumlupinar University, Turkey

A volume in the Advances in Marketing, Customer Relationship Management, and E-Services (AMCRMES) Book Series

Published in the United States of America by
    IGI Global
    Business Science Reference (an imprint of IGI Global)
    701 E. Chocolate Avenue
    Hershey PA, USA 17033
    Tel: 717-533-8845
    Fax: 717-533-8661
    E-mail: cust@igi-global.com
    Web site: http://www.igi-global.com

Copyright © 2024 by IGI Global. All rights reserved. No part of this publication may be reproduced, stored or distributed in any form or by any means, electronic or mechanical, including photocopying, without written permission from the publisher.
Product or company names used in this set are for identification purposes only. Inclusion of the names of the products or companies does not indicate a claim of ownership by IGI Global of the trademark or registered trademark.

Library of Congress Cataloging-in-Publication Data

Names: Sahin, Fatih, 1980- editor. | Soylemez, Cevat, 1987- editor.
Title: Navigating the shifting landscape of consumer behavior / edited by
   Fatih Sahin, Cevat Soylemez.
Description: Hershey, PA : Business Science Reference, [2024] | Includes
   bibliographical references and index. | Summary: "The major goal of this
   book is to offer a thorough knowledge of the quickly changing consumer
   environment in the digital era. It seeks to shed light on how customers
   think, react, and interact with companies in an age of knowledge and
   choice"-- Provided by publisher.
Identifiers: LCCN 2023059479 (print) | LCCN 2023059480 (ebook) | ISBN
   9798369315941 (hardcover) | ISBN 9798369315958 (ebook)
Subjects: LCSH: Consumer behavior.
Classification: LCC HF5415.32 .N378 2024 (print) | LCC HF5415.32 (ebook)
   | DDC 658.8/342--dc23/eng/20231227
LC record available at https://lccn.loc.gov/2023059479
LC ebook record available at https://lccn.loc.gov/2023059480

This book is published in the IGI Global book series Advances in Marketing, Customer Relationship Management, and E-Services (AMCRMES) (ISSN: 2327-5502; eISSN: 2327-5529)

British Cataloguing in Publication Data
A Cataloguing in Publication record for this book is available from the British Library.

All work contributed to this book is new, previously-unpublished material.
The views expressed in this book are those of the authors, but not necessarily of the publisher.

For electronic access to this publication, please contact: eresources@igi-global.com.

Advances in Marketing, Customer Relationship Management, and E-Services (AMCRMES) Book Series

Eldon Y. Li
National Chengchi University, Taiwan &
California Polytechnic State University, USA

ISSN:2327-5502
EISSN:2327-5529

MISSION

Business processes, services, and communications are important factors in the management of good customer relationship, which is the foundation of any well organized business. Technology continues to play a vital role in the organization and automation of business processes for marketing, sales, and customer service. These features aid in the attraction of new clients and maintaining existing relationships.

The Advances in Marketing, Customer Relationship Management, and E-Services (AMCRMES) Book Series addresses success factors for customer relationship management, marketing, and electronic services and its performance outcomes. This collection of reference source covers aspects of consumer behavior and marketing business strategies aiming towards researchers, scholars, and practitioners in the fields of marketing management.

COVERAGE

- CRM and customer trust
- Cases on Electronic Services
- Text Mining and Marketing
- Cases on CRM Implementation
- Mobile Services
- Ethical Considerations in E-Marketing
- Web Mining and Marketing
- Mobile CRM
- Online Community Management and Behavior
- Customer Retention

IGI Global is currently accepting manuscripts for publication within this series. To submit a proposal for a volume in this series, please contact our Acquisition Editors at Acquisitions@igi-global.com or visit: http://www.igi-global.com/publish/.

The Advances in Marketing, Customer Relationship Management, and E-Services (AMCRMES) Book Series (ISSN 2327-5502) is published by IGI Global, 701 E. Chocolate Avenue, Hershey, PA 17033-1240, USA, www.igi-global.com. This series is composed of titles available for purchase individually; each title is edited to be contextually exclusive from any other title within the series. For pricing and ordering information please visit http://www.igi-global.com/book-series/advances-marketing-customer-relationship-management/37150. Postmaster: Send all address changes to above address. Copyright © 2024 IGI Global. All rights, including translation in other languages reserved by the publisher. No part of this series may be reproduced or used in any form or by any means – graphics, electronic, or mechanical, including photocopying, recording, taping, or information and retrieval systems – without written permission from the publisher, except for non commercial, educational use, including classroom teaching purposes. The views expressed in this series are those of the authors, but not necessarily of IGI Global.

Titles in this Series

For a list of additional titles in this series, please visit: http://www.igi-global.com/book-series/

Smart and Sustainable Interactive Marketing
Hamid Reza Irani (University of Tehran, Iran) and Hamed Nozari (Department of Management, Azad University of the Emirates, Dubai, UAE)
Business Science Reference • © 2024 • 320pp • H/C (ISBN: 9798369313398) • US $265.00

Connecting With Consumers Through Effective Personalization and Programmatic Advertising
Jorge Remondes (Instituto Superior de Entre Douro e Vouga, Portugal & ISCAP, Instituto Politecnico do Porto, Portugal) Paulo Madeira (Instituto Superior de Entre Douro e Vouga, Portugal) and Carlos Alves (Instituto Superior de Entre Douro e Vouga, Portugal)
Business Science Reference • © 2024 • 308pp • H/C (ISBN: 9781668491461) • US $250.00

Business Drivers in Promoting Digital Detoxification
Simon Grima (Department of Insurance, Faculty of Economics Management and Accountancy, University of Malta, Msida, Malta & Faculty of Business, Management and Economics, University of Latvia, Riga, Latvia) Shilpa Chaudhary (Lovely Professional University, India) Kiran Sood (Chitkara Business School, Chitkara University, India & Research Fellow at the Women Researchers Council (WRC) at Azerbaijan State University of Economics (UNEC), Azerbaijan) and Sanjeev Kumar (Lovely Professional University, India)
Business Science Reference • © 2024 • 355pp • H/C (ISBN: 9798369311073) • US $265.00

Using Influencer Marketing as a Digital Business Strategy
Sandrina Teixeira (ISCAP, Polytechnic Institute of Porto, Portugal) Sara Teixeira (Polytechnic Institute of Porto) Zaila Oliveira (Unichristus, Brazil & Unifametro, Brazil) and Elnivan Souza (Christus University Center, Brazil)
Business Science Reference • © 2024 • 371pp • H/C (ISBN: 9798369305515) • US $265.00

The Use of Artificial Intelligence in Digital Marketing Competitive Strategies and Tactics
Sandrina Teixeira (Centre for Organizational and Social Studies (CEOS), Porto Accounting and Business School, Polytechnic of Porto, Portugal) and Jorge Remondes (Centre for Organizational and Social Studies (CEOS), Porto Accounting and Business School, Polytechnic of Porto, Portugal)
Business Science Reference • © 2024 • 318pp • H/C (ISBN: 9781668493243) • US $250.00

701 East Chocolate Avenue, Hershey, PA 17033, USA
Tel: 717-533-8845 x100 • Fax: 717-533-8661
E-Mail: cust@igi-global.com • www.igi-global.com

Table of Contents

Preface..xii

Chapter 1
Understanding the Modern Consumer Mindset and the Psychological
Elements Driving It...1
    Astha Singh, PES University, India
    Vedika Bhargaw, PES University, India
    Zidan Kachhi, PES University, India

Chapter 2
Polarization in Consumer Behavior: The Rise of Minimalism in a Materialist
World..23
    Meziyet Uyanik, Istanbul Topkapi University, Turkey

Chapter 3
Consumer Culture and the Paradox of Choice in an Ambivalent Era of
Emancipation of Individual Freedoms..51
    Ondřej Roubal, University of Finance and Administration, Czech Republic

Chapter 4
Multichannel and Omnichannel Marketing: The New Trends in Digital
Retail 86
    Monaliz Amirkhanpour, University of Gloucestershire, UK

Chapter 5
New Marketing Approaches and Consumer Trends in Line With
Technological Developments 113
    Aylin Atasoy, İstanbul Gelişim University, Turkey
    Murat Basal, İstanbul Gelişim University, Turkey

Chapter 6
Where Is Digital Retailing Evolving? An Evaluation From the Perspective of
Digital Retailing Technologies 139
  Cansu Gökmen Köksal, Istanbul Topkapi University, Turkey

Chapter 7
Unleashing the Déjà Rêvé Effect in Marketing: Empowering Customer
Realities...174
  Fatih Sahin, Bandirma Onyedi Eylul University, Turkey

Chapter 8
Can Social Media Be a Transformative Tool for Building a Better Society?
The Case of YouTube Videos on Consumer Sustainability Perception.............207
  Neslihan Paker, Izmir Kavram Vocational School, Turkey

Chapter 9
How Would You Like Your (Sustainability) Influencer? A Cross-Cultural
Discrete Choice Experiment on Preferred Influencer Characteristics 235
  Moritz M. Botts, Turkish-German University, Turkey
  Ömer Hurmacı, Turkish-German University, Turkey

Chapter 10
Novel Forms of Consumption in the Postmodern Era 259
  Myriam Ertz, LaboNFC, University of Quebec in Montreal, Canada
  Walid Addar, LaboNFC, Université du Québec à Chicoutimi, Canada
  Asmaah Sultan, LaboNFC, Université du Québec à Chicoutimi, Canada

Compilation of References 290

About the Contributors 336

Index... 339

Detailed Table of Contents

Preface..xii

Chapter 1
Understanding the Modern Consumer Mindset and the Psychological
Elements Driving It...1
  Astha Singh, PES University, India
  Vedika Bhargaw, PES University, India
  Zidan Kachhi, PES University, India

The chapter delves into the complex world of consumer behaviour, examining the profound impact of cognitive biases and social influences. In terms of cognitive bias, the issue unfolds through an examination of confirmation bias, anchoring bias, availability estimates, and endowment effects. These biases largely define decision-making, affecting how consumers perceive, interact with, and remain brand loyal. Methods for channeling and leveraging these biases have been clarified, enabling marketers to understand consumer behavior and adjust accordingly. Turning to social issues, the chapter reveals the dynamic interactions between peer influence, family traditions, word-of-mouth advocacy, social identity, and social norms and explores the role of social media in this development in the digital age. A thorough understanding of these social forces allows firms to develop strategies that align with customer values, preferences, and social expectations. The chapter emphasizes the importance of education in reducing cognitive biases and moderating social influences.

Chapter 2
Polarization in Consumer Behavior: The Rise of Minimalism in a Materialist
World...23
  Meziyet Uyanik, Istanbul Topkapi University, Turkey

Polarizations in economic and social life caused by increasing income and wealth injustices worldwide also affect consumer behavior. In the polarization of consumers' lifestyles, at one end of the spectrum are the consumerist culture's representatives with ostentatious and exaggerated spending based on materialistic understanding. On the other hand, consumers who adopt an anti-consumption approach sensitive to social, environmental, or individual welfare, regardless of the necessity of economic difficulties or economic factors, are increasing rapidly. This study aims to conceptually evaluate the concepts of minimalist and materialist consumption, which represent two rising values regarding consumer behavior and are mutually exclusive, and to provide readers with a holistic perspective. In this context, in this study, the concepts of materialism, minimalist consumption, and anti-consumption were evaluated from environmental, social, and individual perspectives, and their effects on consumer welfare were discussed.

Chapter 3
Consumer Culture and the Paradox of Choice in an Ambivalent Era of
Emancipation of Individual Freedoms...51
Ondřej Roubal, University of Finance and Administration, Czech Republic

Consumer culture in modern societies is interpreted as a culture that maximizes the freedom of consumer choice. The emancipation of individual freedoms in the form of consumer choice is positively associated with the growth of material standards of living and the affluence of a society. At the same time, an ambivalent situation arises in the form of unintended consequences, whereby customers with increasing freedoms in the areas of consumer choice run into problems making decisions and the paradox of choice, all in a landscape that is becoming less clear and oversaturated with options and opportunities. The goal is to contribute to a deeper understanding of the ambivalent character of contemporary consumer culture in the context of intensified individualization and external options for consumer choice. The authors also seek to propose a theoretical model of consumer mentalities that is more resistant to the negative effects of the paradox of choice. This model is based on the Epicurean consumption pattern of voluntary simplicity, reducing aspirations, and delayed gratification.

Chapter 4
Multichannel and Omnichannel Marketing: The New Trends in Digital
Retail...86
Monaliz Amirkhanpour, University of Gloucestershire, UK

The purpose of this chapter is to investigate the role and importance of using advanced digital marketing communication channels in retail and to analyze how adaptive the marketers are towards smartphone-based mobile technologies. This will be achieved through the synthesis of the findings in digital marketing literature, especially mobile marketing in addition to exploring the significance of adopting a multichannel or omnichannel marketing approach and investigating the role of social media and modern mobile devices such as smartphones in selecting the appropriate marketing strategy. The theoretical considerations from the literature are further conceptually developed to construct a provisional framework for empirical validation. The identified research gaps and inconsistencies are presented within the chapter as a result of systematic review of qualified literature sources.

Chapter 5
New Marketing Approaches and Consumer Trends in Line With
Technological Developments 113
Aylin Atasoy, İstanbul Gelişim University, Turkey
Murat Basal, İstanbul Gelişim University, Turkey

Today, it is clear that brands that want to provide consumers with useful and helpful experiences must use information and technology to positively influence the future process. In the digital age, masses of data about consumers, products and services are coming from many channels. This big data is now being used for customers who expect to be special, through personalization-based marketing approaches such as phygital, data-based and content marketing. Also, data-driven, predictive, contextual, augmented and agile marketing approaches as components of Marketing 5.0 are new marketing trends that increase the performance of brands and their competitiveness in the market. These new technology-enabled marketing trends include augmented reality (AR) and virtual reality (VR), chatbots and digital assistants, influencer marketing, video marketing, location-based marketing, machine learning and artificial intelligence, and content marketing.

Chapter 6
Where Is Digital Retailing Evolving? An Evaluation From the Perspective of
Digital Retailing Technologies 139
Cansu Gökmen Köksal, Istanbul Topkapi University, Turkey

This study delves into the intricacies of digitalization in the retail industry and how it has evolved with the onset of the industrial revolution. It explores the dynamics of this process and proposes several frameworks for categorizing digital retailing technologies. Additionally, the study highlights the core technologies that are integral to this transformation. Moreover, it examines the shift from conventional retail practices to metaverse retailing, showcasing the distinctive attributes of this model. Lastly, the research delves into the factors that are set to shape the future of retailing and offers recommendations for further exploration in this area.

Chapter 7
Unleashing the Déjà Rêvé Effect in Marketing: Empowering Customer
Realities..174
Fatih Sahin, Bandirma Onyedi Eylul University, Turkey

Déjà rêvé, subjective sensation of re-experiencing a past dream, is a key concept in marketing. It involves the sensation of déjà vu, blurring the lines between reality and representation. The concept of simulacra, where replicas surpass their original sources, challenges the conventional understanding of reality. The metaverse, a concept that integrates digital experiences, raises concerns about the replacement of genuine reality with simulated ones. The convergence of VR, postmodernism, and innovative marketing strategies has reshaped how individuals interact with technology and perceive reality. The integration of VR and AR technologies with postmodern influences has led to immersive experiences that evoke a sense of déjà rêvé, blurring the boundaries between reality and the virtual world. This immersive experience can blur the boundaries between digital identities and real-life experiences, offering marketers a unique opportunity to engage with consumers authentically. By leveraging technologies, marketers can create familiarity, personalization, engagement, and consumer value.

Chapter 8
Can Social Media Be a Transformative Tool for Building a Better Society?
The Case of YouTube Videos on Consumer Sustainability Perception.............207
Neslihan Paker, Izmir Kavram Vocational School, Turkey

The study aims to evaluate consumers' perceptions of social marketing designed to enhance environmental awareness through social media platforms. The approach employed in this study is exploratory and interpretive. The data gathered from YouTube videos on the "Doğa İçin Çal" platform filmed during the 2019-2023 period were semiotically analyzed in terms of their content characteristics. Afterwards, the user comments were evaluated as well. During the analysis process, the consumer perception framework was used by utilizing the content analysis method through the Maxqda software program. The findings indicate that the videos effectively captured the target audience's attention and fostered social cohesion by promoting unity. However, the perception elements utilized in the videos indicate that the viewers pay greater attention to the aspects associated with musical performance, while the matter of environmental awareness remains in the background.

Chapter 9
How Would You Like Your (Sustainability) Influencer? A Cross-Cultural
Discrete Choice Experiment on Preferred Influencer Characteristics 235
    Moritz M. Botts, Turkish-German University, Turkey
    Ömer Hurmacı, Turkish-German University, Turkey

Despite influencer marketing being among the most popular digital marketing tools in practice, there are still many research gaps, especially when it comes to specific influencer types. Though technology is converging worldwide, the perception of social influencers may differ between cultures. In this study, a model of influencer characteristics is applied to cases of sustainable and regular products. The optimal influencer for German and Turkish consumers is investigated via a discrete choice experiment (DCE). Findings suggest that female influencers are preferred over male influencers, and trustworthiness is especially required for promoting sustainable products, regardless of the respondent's involvement for sustainability. For German consumers, attractiveness plays a larger role than for Turkish consumers, who prefer high levels of trustworthiness and expertise. The applicability of this methodology for larger studies with multi-country samples is discussed.

Chapter 10
Novel Forms of Consumption in the Postmodern Era 259
    Myriam Ertz, LaboNFC, University of Quebec in Montreal, Canada
    Walid Addar, LaboNFC, Université du Québec à Chicoutimi, Canada
    Asmaah Sultan, LaboNFC, Université du Québec à Chicoutimi, Canada

This chapter discusses collaborative and creative consumption. Collaborative consumption is the exchange of goods and services between individuals and challenges the fundamental concept of ownership. It is closely linked to the circular economy, promoting product lifetime extension and resource mutualization, which contribute to reducing environmental impact. Companies are working to adapt to this trend by rethinking their business models. In contrast, creative consumption refers to the (mostly digital) ecosystem in which consumers use digital tools and services to become active creators of original content primarily disseminated across various online platforms. Creative consumption is also tangential to consumers' design, creation, marketing, remarketing, and reutilization of products using traditional approaches (e.g., production and self-production) or technologies such as 3D printing. The chapter also deals with co-creation, which involves consumers partnering with organizations throughout the product or service life cycle from design to disposal.

Compilation of References 290

About the Contributors 336

Index 339

Preface

As the editors, we are pleased to introduce you to this collection of insights, analyses, and reflections on the intricate dance between consumers and the world of commerce. We aimed to create a cohesive narrative transcending traditional boundaries, weaving together diverse perspectives to form a rich tapestry that captured the essence of contemporary consumerism. The book *Navigating the Shifting Landscape of Consumer Behavior* is a thorough investigation that goes beyond the surface, unraveling all the details that define the modern consumer experience. It is a work that stands out in the expansive and complex realm of consumer behavior. This anthology, which was carefully assembled by a group of experienced authors, tries to provide not merely a surface-level understanding of the myriad of factors that influence how individuals interact with the market, but rather an in-depth comprehension of those factors.

Understanding consumer behavior is no longer an option but rather a strategic necessity in today's world, which is characterized by exceptional technological advancements, cultural shifts, and increased environmental awareness for the first time in human history. The book places itself at the forefront of this relevance by providing insights that are both timely and timeless at the same time. The purpose of the investigation that is contained within these pages is to provide academics, professionals working in the industry, and students alike with the strategies necessary to navigate the rapidly shifting landscape of consumer preferences and choices. The book is geared toward a wide range of readers, including academics, industry leaders, marketing professionals, researchers, and students who are interested in gaining a deeper comprehension of consumer behavior. To ensure that seasoned professionals find insightful depth, the content has been tailored to strike a balance between academic rigor and practical applicability. This ensures that newcomers to the field will find accessible entry points to the subject matter.

The book offers a compelling examination of modern consumer behavior, taking readers on an engaging intellectual journey. This anthology brings together profound insights from various perspectives to explain the dynamic forces that shape the modern consumer experience. Each chapter adds a distinct perspective to this vibrant canvas, covering everything from the modern consumer mindset and

Preface

minimalism to digital retailing and social media. Throughout the anthology, the complex interplay of psychology, culture, and technology is revealed, providing readers with strategic insights for navigating the ever-changing consumer landscape. Together, we will investigate the pulsating rhythm of social shifts and innovative approaches to consumerism. The dynamics of modern consumerism are thoroughly examined, navigating the complex terrain of changing consumer behaviors. Beginning with an in-depth examination of the modern consumer mindset and its underlying psychological factors, the investigation progresses to the polarization of consumer behavior and the rise of minimalism in a materialist society. Moving into the digital realm, the story delves into revolutionary retail trends, such as omnichannel and multichannel marketing strategies. Beyond current practices, the book predicts how technology will reshape consumer habits and emerging marketing strategies. The book's pages also thoughtfully address the impact of social media on consumers' perspectives on sustainability, as well as the valued characteristics of influencers across cultures. Finally, the anthology offers a new perspective on postmodern consumption, challenging long-held beliefs and encouraging businesses to embrace flexibility and innovation to stay ahead of the curve.

As we explore the modern consumer mindset in the first chapter, the journey unfolds by peeling back the layers of decision-making processes. We invite you to journey through the maze of psychological factors that influence consumer choices, gaining a nuanced understanding of the intricate factors that shape the tapestry of contemporary consumer behavior.

The first chapter endeavors to decode the desires that propel the modern consumer, exploring the psychological drivers that underpin the decisions made in the vibrant marketplace of the 21st century. Consumer behavior in today's market is the main factor influencing individual choices. Comprehending consumer decision-making is vital for traders and merchants, encompassing personal characteristics, environmental influences, and the decision-making process. Marketing strategies are crucial for the acquisition and retention of customers, and comprehending these factors is indispensable for marketers. Many factors, such as online reviews, social media platforms, and influencers, impact contemporary consumers. Online reviews on platforms like Amazon and Yelp influence customers' perceptions of brands and products, while influencers offer timely product updates. Comprehending these factors is crucial for establishing connections, exerting influence, and prospering in the current era of digital technology.

A recurring theme highlights the contrast between consumer preferences in a swiftly evolving world. The emergence of minimalism in a society driven by materialism is a compelling example highlighting the stark contrast in consumer preferences. The second chapter contemplates the dynamic nature of desire and the constantly evolving realm of consumer preferences.

The second chapter explores the dynamics of this polarization, providing insight into the emergence of minimalism as a contrasting response to the dominant materialistic values. The minimalist lifestyle, originating from the 1960s, has gained significant momentum as unsustainable consumption models become a global problem. This trend is seen as a niche market, particularly in the USA, Japan, and Europe. The 2008 global financial crisis and the COVID-19 pandemic have accelerated the rise of materialism, while the materialist consumption approach, which reflects ostentatious and exaggerated spending, has also risen. Consumers are driven by intrinsic and extrinsic motivations for luxury products, with the latter driven by extrinsic motives such as proving success or pleasure. Digital technologies and social media have catalyzed the spread of the minimalist lifestyle among consumers, with blogs, YouTube channels, and social networking sites promoting minimalism. This chapter examines the conceptual origins of minimalism, anti-consumption, and materialist consumption behavior, aiming to contribute to ongoing discussions and evaluate the conditions that lead consumers to materialistic consumption within the scope of Terror Management Theory.

Our journey continues into the heart of consumer culture, where the paradox of choice emerges. Consumers are faced with an abundance of options in an era marked by the emancipation of individual liberties, challenging businesses to decipher the subtle nuances of choice that influence their audiences.

The third chapter invites us to traverse the ambivalent terrain that emerges when individual freedoms find themselves emancipated within the vast marketplace of options. Contemporary consumer culture exhibits paradoxes, conflicts, and contradictions, which are characteristic of globalization trends and the rapid pace of life. This has resulted in an excessive growth of consumerist lifestyles and hedonistic values, which are reinforced by the marketing industry. Nevertheless, these advancements have also resulted in the deterioration of the environment, contamination, and alterations in the Earth's climate. The swift advancement of digitalization, automation, and robotization has heightened the process of individualization and the shaping of personal identity. Notwithstanding these alterations, the pattern of enhancing individual consumer liberties remains consistent. This chapter seeks to elucidate the shift in consumer mindset through a reinterpretation of Bauman's concepts and the introduction of a conceptual framework depicting the consumer as a consciously uncomplicated hunter/competitor, with a specific emphasis on ecological and environmental sustainability.

The digital age has ushered in a retail revolution, and our narrative reflects this tremendous shift. Multichannel and omnichannel marketing chapters delve into the complexities of digital retail trends, providing readers with a road map for navigating the ever-changing online marketplace.

Preface

In the fourth chapter of the author's investigation into the world of contemporary business, the author focuses on the influential trends of multichannel and omnichannel marketing, which are altering the landscape of online retail. The amalgamation of technology and consumer expectations has led to a dynamic transformation in how businesses interact with their audiences, surpassing conventional retail models to establish seamless and captivating brand experiences. This chapter discusses the systematic approach to digital marketing communications, focusing on the influence of digital technologies on direct marketing. It outlines the objectives of understanding the theory behind digital marketing communications, the impacts of digital technology on consumer behavior, and the difference between permission-based and permission-less marketing communications. The chapter also explores the role of mobile marketing in marketing innovation, its integration with social media, and the concept of mobile retailing. The systematic approach helps marketers revolutionize their marketing strategies by leveraging advanced media like smartphones and social media.

Technological advancements, which drove the digital revolution, are also at the core of modern marketing. This anthology investigates new marketing approaches that are in sync with technological advancements, providing a glimpse into the future of consumer engagement and the adaptive strategies that businesses must embrace.

In the fifth chapter, the authors explore the various marketing strategies that are in line with the rapid advancements in technology. These strategies have a significant impact on how brands engage with their target audience. Marketing is crucial in today's rapidly changing market conditions as consumers move between physical and digital channels, seeking personalized experiences and protecting personal data. With budgets falling, fast-growing brands are overhauling their strategies around customer data, particularly the customer experience. Three key themes are essential: inclusive marketing, building infrastructure around data, and designing dynamic customer experiences. Artificial intelligence can be integrated with human services to enhance customer service. Consumers' preferences now focus on price and quality, sensitivity to world problems, and trust, particularly in the banking and finance sectors.

In the sixth chapter, researchers undertake a thorough assessment of the development of digital retailing, analyzing its progression using advanced technologies. This chapter aims to explore the ways in which digitalization and technological advancements are reshaping the future of retail in the digital realm as the commerce landscape undergoes significant changes. The digitalization of retail has transformed essential business activities, including purchasing, selling, communicating, and inventory management. Consumers have taken on a more active role in the consumption process, engaging in online activities such as product selection, research, and purchasing. Traditional retailers have started adopting digital retail strategies through digital technology, enabling them to use new channels and shopper touch points. Traditional

xv

retailing is suitable for all types of shoppers, including social ones, while electronic retailing is popular with those who seek convenience and embrace technology. The pandemic has catalyzed the digitalization process, with 46% of consumers shopping online for the first time during the pandemic. Traditional retailers must adapt to the needs of digitally connected customers, offering seamless cross-channel shopping experiences and integrating physical and virtual presence through an omnichannel strategy. Advancements in digital retailing, such as artificial intelligence, virtual assistants, chatbots, robots, voice commerce, machine learning, augmented reality, and virtual reality, are critical in adapting to unforeseen risks and turning them into opportunities.

The adventure continues with an inspiring exploration of the déjà rêvé effect, an innovative concept that empowers customer realities. This chapter invites readers to consider marketing's transformative power in shaping not only desires but also the very essence of consumer realities in a virtual ambiance.

In the seventh chapter of the book, the author examines the captivating influence of marketing in creating the déjà rêvé effect—a phenomenon in which customers are transported into a dreamlike state of which they were previously unaware. This chapter explores the potential of marketing strategies to exceed the desires and aspirations of the modern consumer as businesses adapt to changing consumer expectations. The global population is growing, and disparities are decreasing. The digital era has led to hyperreality, with communication becoming a crucial social process. The digitalized global village refers to the shift from a conventional global village to a digitally interconnected one. The absence of a universally recognized reality has led to changes in human needs. Digital technologies have enabled individuals to construct their own interpretation of reality, blurring the boundaries between authenticity and fabrication. Marketers must provide valuable products or services that cater to consumers' self-actualization needs. Hyperreality plays a pivotal role in marketing, as technological advancements like Augmented Reality, Virtual Reality, and Mixed Reality create immersive experiences that induce a sense of déjà vu. Marketing managers should enable customers to actively mold their perception of reality, as both the consumer and the product influence market value.

As our investigation into social media continues, a critical question arises: can these platforms be transformative tools for building a better society? The analysis of social media content on consumer perceptions of sustainability provides a nuanced perspective, examining the potential for positive societal change through influential digital channels.

In the eighth chapter, the author explores the captivating convergence of social media, consumer sustainability, and societal improvement. This chapter digs into a detailed examination of whether social media, with its extensive scope and impact, can function as a transformative instrument for constructing a more sustainable and

Preface

conscientious society. Social marketing is a strategy that aims to influence human behavior, focusing on health and environmental sustainability. Its primary objective is to encourage the target audience to actively participate in shaping their lives. Perception plays a crucial role in shaping an individual's understanding of reality. In the modern era, digital marketing communications are increasingly used, with social media being a significant part of this landscape. Businesses use social media to promote shared awareness and create value. However, it is essential to follow up and evaluate the social marketing plan to determine the target market's responses, the extent of awareness, and the desired behavioral change. This study aims to assess consumer perceptions of social marketing promoting environmental awareness via social media platforms.

The anthology concludes with a cross-cultural examination of influencer traits, with a particular emphasis on sustainability. This chapter encourages readers to consider the critical role that influencers play in shaping consumer values and perceptions, providing a comprehensive view of the influencers who support the growing emphasis on sustainability.

In the nineth chapter, the authors explore the world of sustainability influencers, examining the factors that influence the decisions of environmentally aware consumers, such as their preferences and cultural influences. The authors conduct a cross-cultural discrete choice experiment to explore the complex nature of influencer characteristics. They aim to comprehend how different cultures approach sustainability by examining the role of digital influence. This chapter explores the preferred characteristics of social media influencers, particularly those focused on sustainability. It tests these characteristics in an online experimental setting, collecting data from Turkish and German subjects. The study aims to understand how cultural differences influence the preference of these characteristics. Social media influencers have gained attention in the media and research due to their less commercial and idealist focus. The study compares consumers in developed countries with prominent sustainability discourse, Germany, and a transition economy, Turkey, where sustainability and corporate social responsibility are less prominent.

The significant change in consumer behavior, influenced by non-traditional consumption patterns, plays a crucial role in shaping the consumer behavior landscape. This paradigm shift urges businesses to embrace innovation and adaptability, effectively addressing the ever-changing demands and preferences of consumers.

In the tenth chapter, the authors explore how collaborative and creative consumption are reshaping consumer behavior in the postmodern era. This transformation involves embracing flexibility, questioning hierarchies, and seeking authenticity. These practices promote active engagement from individuals in the creation and exchange of goods, services, and content, while also embracing diversity, pluralism, and fragmentation. The emergence of collaborative consumption signifies a pivotal moment in contemporary consumer behavior, propelled by a heightened consciousness of the environmental and social consequences of excessive consumption, and the aspiration to mitigate these repercussions. This shift revolutionizes our comprehension of consumption and carries significant ramifications for society and the economy. Adapting to this new environment and meeting the changing needs of consumers within consumer communities requires the use of innovative market research and business management approaches.

We encourage you to engage with the diverse perspectives presented by our esteemed contributors as you immerse yourself in the pages that follow. Whether you're a seasoned business professional, a marketing enthusiast, or a voracious reader looking to unravel the mysteries of modern consumer behavior, Navigating the Shifting Landscape of Consumer Behavior is your guide. May this anthology spark your interest, start a conversation, and provide a comprehensive understanding of the intricate patterns that define today's consumer landscape.

Your adventure begins here.

Fatih Şahin
Bandırma Onyedi Eylül University, Turkey

Cevat Söylemez
Kütahya Dumlupınar University, Turkey

Chapter 1

Understanding the Modern Consumer Mindset and the Psychological Elements Driving It

Astha Singh
https://orcid.org/0009-0008-8429-1314
PES University, India

Vedika Bhargaw
PES University, India

Zidan Kachhi
https://orcid.org/0000-0002-8317-6356
PES University, India

ABSTRACT

The chapter delves into the complex world of consumer behaviour, examining the profound impact of cognitive biases and social influences. In terms of cognitive bias, the issue unfolds through an examination of confirmation bias, anchoring bias, availability estimates, and endowment effects. These biases largely define decision-making, affecting how consumers perceive, interact with, and remain brand loyal. Methods for channeling and leveraging these biases have been clarified, enabling marketers to understand consumer behavior and adjust accordingly. Turning to social issues, the chapter reveals the dynamic interactions between peer influence, family traditions, word-of-mouth advocacy, social identity, and social norms and explores the role of social media in this development in the digital age. A thorough understanding of these social forces allows firms to develop strategies that align with customer values, preferences, and social expectations. The chapter emphasizes the importance of education in reducing cognitive biases and moderating social influences.

DOI: 10.4018/979-8-3693-1594-1.ch001

Copyright © 2024, IGI Global. Copying or distributing in print or electronic forms without written permission of IGI Global is prohibited.

INTRODUCTION

Consumer behaviour is the heartbeat of today's market, the very essence of every organisation's design, and the driving force behind individual choices every day. In this fast-paced and ever-evolving marketplace, understanding the mindset of today's consumers is useful and important for traders and merchants. In this chapter, we will explore the complex substructure of today's consumer decision-making.

Although consumer preferences keep changing from time to time, the psychology behind consumer behaviour and their decision-making skills has remained stable. Entrepreneurs and marketers need to be conscious of the emotions, cognitive biases, and social influences that all together shape the complex psychology of a consumer's mindset in today's world.

The American Marketing Association (AMA) defines consumer behaviour as "The study of how customers (individuals and organisations) satisfy their needs and wants by choosing, purchasing, using, and disposing of goods, ideas, and services" (*Consumer Behavior Archives*, n.d.). Various factors such as individual, environmental and decision-making influence consumer behaviour. The knowledge of these factors helps marketers frame effective marketing strategies. Marketing involves understanding the needs of the customer and driving them to purchase a specific product by generating certain desires in the minds of customers. To anticipate and understand the purchasing decisions of customers the study of consumer behaviour serves an important role. The study of consumer behaviour encompasses what consumers purchase, why they prefer to purchase it, how and when they purchase it, and how often they plan to purchase and use it. Individuals purchasing the same product may have varied motivations and pay different prices for it. They utilise the product in distinct ways and may attach diverse emotions to it. Marketing strategies are important for attracting and holding customers. The effectiveness of these strategies relies on understanding, serving, and influencing consumers. The purchasing behaviour of people is influenced either individually or within a group or organization. Nowadays, customers face a challenging situation with numerous choices in a highly advanced society. They have a wide range of products to choose from, various pricing options, convenient delivery methods, and an abundance of communication channels.

Consumer choice is not a passive response to advertising messages. They are well-informed decisions shaped by a multitude of influences. As we read ahead in the later sections, we will explore the impact of digital technology on consumer behaviour, the central role of emotions in decision-making, the impact of cognitive biases, and the important power of social roles and dynamics in guiding consumer choices. With this chapter, we have attempted to provide a comprehensive view of these factors as they combine to define the consciousness of the modern consumer.

Understanding the Modern Consumer Mindset

In a world where every online interaction, every product review, and every social media post is part of a massive consumer marketplace, understanding the multifaceted factors that drive consumer choice is not a luxury - it is a necessity. The insights and knowledge presented in this chapter are designed to give you a deeper understanding of the complex and dynamic nature of consumer preferences. By the end of this chapter, you will be better equipped to connect with, influence and thrive in an era of empowered and knowledgeable consumers in today's digital age.

THE MODERN CONSUMER MARKET

Impact of Online Reviews

In today's world with the increasing use of gadgets especially smartphones, customers are highly influenced by online reviews. Customers can now actively look for information and make well-informed decisions based on them. The customers are not solely dependent on marketing strategies and content to gather data. Online reviews available on platforms like Amazon and Yelp have a huge role in shaping the customer's view on different brands and their products. As the peer reviews have honest opinions, they are more likely to increase or decrease the rating and sales of a product or brand.

Social media has provided platforms for influencers. Influencers are experts who share valuable insights and honest reviews on products. Their "followers" are the general public looking for online reviews before making any purchasing decisions. They engage with these followers and provide timely updates on various products. They advise customers to make choices within the wide variety of goods available both online and offline. These shared experiences and peer reviews create a huge shift in customers' preferences.

The impact of these online reviews is highlighted through the success of platforms like Yelp. It provides a space for users to share their views and provides an overall rating for businesses combining them. With the presence of online shopping apps and countless choices available people often rely on these platforms to compare different products and ultimately decide what to buy. Online reviews by influencers and peers have a significant impact on creating customer's perceptions about various goods. (Ao et al., 2023)

Conscious Consumerism

The concept of Conscious Consumerism is trending with the increasing awareness of social and environmental issues. People look for products and companies that align with their values and principles. Now people not only consider the cost and quality of the product before purchasing but also consider factors like fair labour cost, recyclable materials, sustainability and environmental contribution (Bernard & Parker, 2021). For instance, companies like Patagonia have a mission of saving the planet. They mainly focus on sustaining the environment and following ethical production practices. They have attracted loyal customers and serve as an example by aligning with modern conscious values.

The new Gen Z and modern millennial customers tend to go beyond the brand name and their marketing claims. They are into the practice of reading labels. They also consider the environmental and social impact of the product before purchasing. Conscious consumers deal with two factors- consuming less and making sure whatever is consumed is sustainable. They back their values and ethics by choosing what to buy, even if it means paying more for certain products.

Another important factor to take into consideration is affordability. Consumers are faced with a tough choice to choose between sustainable products and affordable products. For instance, organic foods cost more to produce and certify. Although people want to buy them, they may go for cheaper, affordable foods. This incongruence highlights the importance of balancing sustainability and affordability. Hence, businesses targeting the market of conscious consumers need to have a balance between their products being sustainable and affordable.

Evolving Norms and Behaviours

With the modernisation of consumer markets, the dynamics of consumer behaviour are also experiencing a dramatic change. Technological improvements, societal revolutions, and the global economy's interconnectedness have all changed the limits within which customers navigate their options. Organisations feel the need to design their strategies according to the changing demands of customers. Traditional consumer behaviour models are no longer adequate for reflecting the intricate nature of the current consumer thinking. As a result of the introduction of digital platforms and the democratisation of information consumers are empowered, analytical, and cautious, seeking more personalised and meaningful experiences in their transactions.

Historical patterns of consumer behaviour are crucial to recognising the foundational paradigms that have shaped consumer habits over time. Early consumer behaviour was characterised by a localised and closeted economy that involved and depended solely on personal contacts and physical interaction. The increasing digitalisation has not only changed the consumer mindset and decision-making but has also brought changes in the norms and habits. It has empowered customers with access to vast knowledge and alternatives through social media, smartphone applications and e-commerce.

Understanding the Modern Consumer Mindset

One key element that remains similar in the comparison between early consumer behaviour and modern consumer behaviour is the role of trust and reputation. Especially after an introduction to the global market and digitalization, consumers still seek assurance and proper validation. This is eventually achieved in the form of online reviews or word-of-mouth recommendations, which indicates a persistent existence of interpersonal consumption beliefs. Organizations invest a lot in resources that build reputation and help promote familiarity. Companies need to provide a smooth, transparent experience to customers in order to stay competitive and relevant.

PayPal, Apple Pay and Google Pay provide safe online transactions for customers who desire seamless payment processes. In the fashion industry companies like ASOS and Gap provide virtual fitting rooms using virtual reality for customers to try on clothes online. This reduces the concern of buying clothes without trying them on and improves their online shopping experience. Warby Parker, an eyeglass company uses virtual try-ons to bridge the gap between online and offline stores. It provides customers with a more personalized and interactive shopping experience.

The Influence of Emotions on Consumer Decisions

Emotions heavily influence consumer decisions. It is a crucial aspect that businesses recognize easily and use it to exploit customers. Pleasure acts as a powerful emotion influencing consumer choices. Brands associated with pleasure appear more appealing to the customers. Customers are influenced by positive emotions while choosing products, perceiving them as a source of joy. (Asshidin et al., 2016) Brands like Coca-Cola advertise their products, associating them with feelings of happiness and celebration. They try to create a sense of togetherness in their advertisements.

Consumers feel emotions like anxiety which makes them hesitant or avoid a product while purchasing. Platforms like Amazon have come up with open-box delivery, easy return policies and open-access user feedback. It reduces their fear of making wrong choices and provides them with an option to return or exchange the product.

Anger is another main emotion aroused when customers receive damaged products or they face bad experiences. It is also caused by unethical business practices. It can also push customers to raise their concerns or even initiate a boycott of the brand if the issue is left unresolved. Companies must quickly respond to these complaints and try to resolve the issue as soon as possible. A single negative review or an irrational outburst on social media can reach a thousand or million users. Companies can use this as an opportunity to address their issues and turn them into their supporters successfully.

A lot of companies try to evoke desire and a sense of ownership in their marketing campaigns. Luxurious companies try to attract their audience by providing

Understanding the Modern Consumer Mindset

exclusivity in their products. They feature their products as a sense of prestige and accomplishment. This appeals to their target audience to purchase their products even if they are a lot more expensive.

When it comes to purchasing decisions, emotions are always mixed and complex. They can attract customers to a brand but still refrain from choosing their services. A customer may be concerned about the cost but still attracted to the beauty and usefulness of the product. Companies need to understand these complexities in order to make successful market strategies. They must address both the positive and negative aspects of these emotions in order to attract customers and increase their sales. It reduces their fear of making wrong choices and provides them with an option to return or exchange the product.

Empathy and Exceptional Customer Service

The ability to empathize with customers and provide outstanding customer service is crucial for organizations seeking to effectively handle heated circumstances in the complex realm of contemporary consumer behaviour (Wei et al., 2022). A key component of this tactic is showing real empathy for customers who have difficulties or have bad experiences, as this has a significant impact on how they see a company. In the consumer context, empathy is defined as the ability to comprehend and share the feelings of customers, respond to their worries, and show a genuine interest in their experiences. Businesses such as Zappos, which are well-known for their outstanding customer service, are prime examples of this compassionate attitude. Zappos goes above and beyond standard procedures, demonstrating empathy via proactive client engagement, comprehension of their requirements, and establishment of a rapport. Zappos leaves a lasting impact by changing potentially unpleasant emotional contacts into positive ones by responding to customer complaints in a timely and sincere manner.

The hallmark of exceptional customer service—which is an essential complement to empathy—is polite and proactive customer interactions. Brands need to respond to customers' queries, concerns and criticism. In today's digitalised world it has become even more important to address them in a timely and thoughtful manner. The giant multinational company Amazon provides the best customer support services. They address these issues across many channels including e-mail, live chat and social media. As a result of their dedication to providing the best customer services, Amazon has seen a high rise in its brand image and loyalty. It depicts the impact of good communication services on changing customers' opinions.

Providing effective solutions is another important aspect of empathy and customer service. Taking proactive measures to resolve these issues is as important as acknowledging them. When companies successfully resolve these issues, it generates positive emotions like relief and thankfulness in customers.

Active listening is another component of compassionate customer service. It involves paying close attention to the thoughts, worries and feelings of the customer. Salesforce serves as a great example of active listening. It uses channels like feedback forms, surveys, and social media interactions. Real-time engagement with the audience is an equally important step. Companies like Southwest Airlines are famous for their exclusive focus on customer service. It uses social media to actively engage with customers and build a strong emotional connection.

Customers' expectations are increasingly high in this generation of instant gratification. With the increasing demands for faster deliveries, quick responses and smooth customer experiences, online platforms have set really high standards. Amazon has set new bars by meeting these expectations with its one-click shopping, personalized recommendations, premium subscriptions and same-day delivery options. Businesses must consider these factors in order to stay competitive in the market and frame their strategies accordingly.

The decision-making of people is highly transformed and influenced by online and peer reviews. With the increasing use of Smartphones, people are constantly connected across the world through the internet. provides us with immediate access to information, availability of the products and reviews. Thus, changing us from passive receivers of marketing to active participants in the consumer market.

Brand Storytelling

Brand narratives are designed in such a way that they capture the essence of the company. It includes the history, missions and morals of the companies and goes beyond a simple sales presentation. Brands' compelling narratives have the power to appeal to customers and develop an emotional connection with the companies (Crespo et al., 2022). These narratives are used by companies like Coca-Cola to create joy and satisfaction. For example, the "Share a Coke" campaign by Coca-Cola encouraged people to develop an emotional connection with their personalized bottles. Brands may establish a strong emotional bond by ensuring that their narratives reflect the values and beliefs of their intended audience. A brand may establish strong emotional bonds with the customer when their stories reflect the values and beliefs of the target audience. Authenticity and consistency are essential elements of a successful brand narrative. A brand's narrative needs to align with its behaviour and principles. Any inconsistency between a brand's stated story and its real actions might lead to mistrust and hostile emotions.

Positive consumer perceptions of businesses that exhibit a dedication to sustainability and ethical activities are common. Taking part in environmentally beneficial projects or contributing to humanitarian issues may inspire pride and kindness. Knowing that the company they are supporting is using its products to have a more positive and constructive impact on the world may evoke warm sentiments and boost the overall sense of emotion. Building a sense of community is another strategy for fostering favourable connections between individuals. To promote a feeling of community, brands might donate to local organizations, events, or an NGO. Brands that actively take part in the community develop a strong emotional bond with their customers. Companies need to bring transparency in their policies as customers value more openness. Brands must try to be truthful and upfront about business practices, product origins, and supply chain ethics as it helps them build more positive relations.

User-Generated Content (UGC)

Businesses have started building a strong feeling of community and trust as a critical business strategy in the changing world of current customer behaviour. They encourage customers to share their experiences- either bad or good via social media, testimonials, and reviews. This is an effective way to build a sense of trust and family among themselves and their audience. Such User-Generated Content (UGC) has a significant impact on the feelings and choices of other potential customers. Reviews, testimonials, pictures, and social media postings present a real and approachable point of view, which influences how customers see and engage with businesses.

In an era dominated by social media, user-generated content (UGC) has emerged as a powerful tool for businesses trying to establish deeper emotional relationships with their audience. As it provides a genuine and unfiltered viewpoint on a brand, the authenticity found in user-generated content is especially valued. This honesty appeals to present-day customers, who value real, genuine narratives above slick marketing tactics. Brands that proactively promote and feature user-generated content (UGC) demonstrate their readiness to give their consumers centre stage, which strengthens the feeling of community and shared experiences (Smith, 2019).

The influence of user-generated material on customer decisions and emotions is further demonstrated by real-world instances. Consider Airbnb, where user-generated content—such as reviews and photos—plays a significant role in influencing prospective visitors' choices. By actively encouraging hosts and guests to share their stories, the platform builds a trustworthy community that extends beyond mere business dealings. Likewise, the massive cosmetics company Sephora uses user-generated content (UGC) to show off actual consumers using their goods, creating an authentic and communal feel that appeals to beauty enthusiasts everywhere. Furthermore, user-generated material possesses a unique capacity to arouse a variety of emotions. The emotional resonance of the brand is greatly enhanced when consumers use content creation to express their happiness, fulfilment, or enthusiasm. Heartfelt testimonials, unboxing videos, and pictures of delighted consumers with a product serve to create a deeper bond between the customer and the company.

In order to create a collective narrative that goes beyond the characteristics of the product and appeals to the emotional components of consumer decision-making, businesses ought to motivate customers to contribute their experiences and feelings (Smith, 2019). GoPro's marketing approach provides a clear illustration of this emotional connection. The manufacturer of action cameras proactively invites customers to share their thrilling GoPro-captured moments. By doing this, GoPro not only highlights the features of its gear but also appeals to feelings of excitement, adventure, and self-actualization. In addition to attesting to the product's excellence, this user-generated material builds a community composed of individuals who share a passion for travel and adventure.

Customer Feedback

Customer feedback is essential for organisations to help them explore their preferences and expectations based on the experiences of individuals. It is often derived through reviews, surveys or social media. Feedback not only serves as a purpose to better product quality but also gives insights into the consumer mindset helping organisations to develop products in accordance.

Consumer opinions and perceptions lie within a vital psychological framework. Consumers don't just provide feedback but also indicate and project their values, aspirations and self-concept regarding various products. Customers providing positive feedback not only indicate that they are satisfied with the product but also hint at their self-image and emotional desires (Dunning, 2007). Consumers also use certain products in an attempt to extend their own identity. Forming a broader social identity. The feedback they receive from society in turn plays a major role in their decisions to use products that align with this perceived self-image.

Positive customer feedback not only serves as validation of a product's quality but also creates a sense of satisfaction and builds loyalty towards a particular brand. Negative feedback, on the other hand, may cause frustration and create a lack of trust. It often leads consumers to never use any future product, which negatively affects the brand and organization. However, the company's continuous effort to strive for improvement helps generate a more positive outlook from customers.

Confirmation bias leads customers to selectively perceive existing feedback and alter it to fit their pre-existing beliefs about a brand or product. This bias affects the accuracy of feedback as individuals may unconsciously alter their existing opinions based on prevalent information.

COGNITIVE BIASES: A SHORTCUT TO DECISION-MAKING

People face many choices in today's world. Brands bombard customers with information overload and advertisements all the time. To speed up their decision-making process in this complex environment, people often resort to mental shortcuts and heuristics. However, this dependence on a high scale can lead to biases in people's thinking. It affects how people behave as consumers. This section looks at how different biases impact people's behaviours as customers and what it means for companies and businesses. Understanding these is the key to understanding how the mindset of a customer affects the modern market.

Cognitive biases are basic patterns in our thinking that manipulate us into making irrational decisions. This happens when people take shortcuts and make quick decisions before thinking them through. On the one hand, these shortcuts also help us live efficiently, but on the other hand, they can make us miss important details. This influences the choices we make as customers. A few of the biases talked about are confirmation bias, Anchoring bias, Availability Heuristic, and Endowment Effect.

Confirmation bias is one of the most common biases that alter consumer decisions (Jin, 2023). Confirmation bias is when people actively look for information that supports ideas that they already know and believe in. They also ignore anything that goes against those ideas. For example, a person loyal to a certain smartphone brand might focus only on the positive reviews or features that match their expectations and wants in a smartphone. At the same time, they might ignore any undesirable features or reviews and downplay any negative comments or flaws in them. It is like having a filter that makes you focus only on the desirable attributes of something.

This bias not only affects the information people choose to pay attention to but also shapes their view of a particular product or brand. This can develop brand loyalty as people stick to their existing opinions and create a cycle that makes them stick to that particular brand. This cycle is hard to break free from. Even if they are presented with much better options, people tend to stay loyal to their brand. Many businesses and companies can also be affected by this bias- both positively and negatively. They can adjust their business strategies and marketing styles to better align with the ideas and thoughts of their target audience. For example, a company looking to better its marketing strategy might highlight positive reviews from previous customers connecting with its target audience (Kahneman, 2011). This deepens the bond that consumers have with the brand and increases loyalty.

Both customers and businesses are challenged while navigating this bias. Customers can reduce the impact of confirmation bias by keeping an open mind to a variety of opinions, considering different ideas and evaluating all the information available critically before making a decision. Businesses, on the other hand, can promote openness among consumers, be transparent and provide fair information

Understanding the Modern Consumer Mindset

about products. This helps to create a more informed and educated customer base that can effectively work around the bias.

Anchoring Bias is a bias in which people rely on the first piece of information they receive, essentially turning them into "anchors". This initial information or "anchors", can highly influence their decisions later on. For example, a person who is looking for a laptop to buy and sees a high-end $2,000 laptop as his first choice can make that price an anchor. Later on, if they are offered a more affordable laptop, the initial anchor might make them view it as a better deal.

In real life, this bias can be seen in various scenarios. In the real estate market, the price listed initially on a property acts as a strong anchor. This influences the buyer's perception of the value of other houses they look at. When they see a ridiculously high first listing price, other houses with a lower price could seem more affordable, even if they are not. In the automobile industry, the first offer given by the dealer acts as a strong anchor. After negotiations and reducing the price by a small amount, the customers might believe that they are getting the vehicle at a lesser price when in reality there is no compromise and they are actually paying the amount that the dealer wanted.

Businesses and companies who understand the workings of this bias can influence how customers perceive their (and other's) products, thereby influencing their decisions. They can use strategies like tiered pricing, in which a high-priced option acts as the anchor. This can influence buyers to choose the mid-range priced options thinking that it's the more affordable and economical option.

Availability heuristic is another bias that affects the customer's attitudes towards businesses and their decision-making (Nazlan et al., 2018). It plays an important role in shaping how people perceive things and the decisions they make accordingly. People can estimate the likelihood of an event happening depending on how quickly they can recall similar cases from their memory. In their minds, certain pieces of information can have a tendency to stand out. This bias can lead them to overestimate risks and probabilities in consumer settings.

For example, a person is regularly exposed to news articles and advertisements about car crashes. These graphic and frequent depictions of the accidents may cause the person to overestimate their chance of being in a car crash, even though the actual risk is far lesser. This heuristic can also be seen in the healthcare industry. People can overestimate their chances of developing certain diseases. High media coverage focusing on uncommon diseases makes them more readily available in people's minds. When looking at certain symptoms, these diseases come to mind with ease and alter their perceptions of actual risks.

In the consumer market, it affects the purchasing decisions. Imagine a person who is repeatedly exposed to advertisements for a particular brand or line of skincare products. Because of the increased availability of information about those particular

Understanding the Modern Consumer Mindset

products, people might place more value on them than the other products which are less promoted even if statistics show otherwise.

In the trading industry, investment decisions are also affected by availability heuristics. Investors might overestimate the potential profits of an investment if there had been recent media attention given to a particular stock trend or a success story. The easy availability of these events can make people have a false impression of the trading market as a whole, which could result in biased or potentially harmful investing choices.

Businesses and marketers can have a much better understanding of customer behaviours if they can successfully understand the accessibility of the availability heuristic. They can improve marketing strategy by drafting messages that strategically use the information easily available in the consumer's minds and influence how they perceive things and what preferences they give them.

However, this heuristic poses challenges for both consumers and businesses alike. Consumers can seek different viewpoints, consider many ideas, and evaluate all information available critically before deciding to reduce the impact of the availability heuristic. Businesses, on the other hand, should promote openness and provide fair information to customers about all their products and services. This can help to create a more educated customer base that is less prone to be victims of this bias.

The last, but not the least bias is the endowment effect. It is a powerful cognitive bias in the decision-making process that has a huge impact on the attitudes of modern customers. This bias takes place when people place a higher value on certain products they own compared to similar or the same items that they do not own. While the effect of doing so could be subtle, it can have a huge impact on the final decision a customer makes while purchasing some product or service, particularly in terms of their loyalty to the brand and their resistance to change.

For example, a person who has used a particular brand of smartphone for a long period, according to the endowment effect may attribute a higher value to their phone simply because they own it. This can occur even if someone else has the same model but with a different ownership history. People tend to unconsciously overvalue and assign high prices to their possessions. This can make it challenging for them to switch brands or let go of their belongings.

In the real world, this effect can be seen in multiple places. In the ever-changing and developing world of technology, a person who has been loyal to a particular brand of laptop could develop strong attachments to that device. Even if other better options are available and presented to them, they assign high value to this particular brand only because of their ownership of the brand. This emotional bond based only on possession of this item acts as a powerful influence on people's minds while trying out other brands or upgrading to a better version of that item.

Understanding the Modern Consumer Mindset

This effect can extend to the apparel and textile industries as well. For example, a person who has owned a particular pair of jeans from a brand for a long may attach emotional value to it. They consider those brand jeans superior to other jeans in the market.

Brand loyalty in retail goods is also affected by the endowment effect. A customer who regularly purchases a brand of household cleaning supplies might assign high value to those products because they are regular users. Even if other brands provide them with better deals and products, they are reluctant to try them out because of this sense of ownership.

Businesses can foster brand loyalty by developing strategies that take into consideration the emotional attachment customers may have to their possessions. They can encourage customers to switch brands and emphasize the unique qualities of the goods to help overcome the endowment effect.

Consumers can reflect on the connection they have to their material belongings to understand this effect and take into consideration the impact of this bias on their decision-making. They can weigh other possibilities and analyse various brands which can help them to reduce the effects of this cognitive bias.

Awareness of these cognitive biases is crucial for both customers and businesses. Customers can make a more informed decision and businesses can alter their marketing strategies to better connect with their audience.

Implications of Cognitive Biases

Cognitive biases play a major role in consumer behaviours. They have major implications for businesses and marketers that are looking to connect with their audience. They must understand the workings of these biases to successfully influence customer decisions.

Brand loyalty

Cognitive biases, and confirmation bias, in particular, have a huge influence on brand loyalty. This bias acts as a reinforcing mechanism, creating a filter through which customers selectively process information that aligns with their existing perceptions of a brand. This selective processing reinforces emotional attachments to specific brands, making it challenging for competitors to alter these ingrained preferences. Marketers can intentionally leverage confirmation bias to strengthen existing customer connections and design loyalty programs that resonate with the preexisting attitudes and beliefs of their target audience. Nike's iconic motto, "Just Do It," is a great example of how intentional use of confirmation bias can solidify consumer connections.

Pricing Strategies

While making strategies for pricing, anchoring bias plays a major role. Companies strategically set their initial prices as anchors, shaping customers' perceptions of value and influencing subsequent purchase decisions. The establishment of a higher starting price may make future discounts more appealing while lowering the anchor price can impact customers' perceived value of goods and services. Businesses aiming to optimize their market positioning must grasp anchoring bias and employ pricing tactics that consider its effects. Luxury brands, using taglines like "Exclusive Indulgence," is a great example of promotional strategies capitalizing on anchoring bias to convey exclusivity and premium value.

Marketing Messages

Cognitive biases are pivotal in advertising as they shape how customers perceive and engage with businesses. The availability heuristic becomes an important weapon as companies expose customers to positive experiences and outcomes associated with their products or services. Crafting marketing messages that resonate with customers' cognitive biases can significantly impact attitudes and actions (Jovin, 2023). Businesses may see their products as having greater worth and appeal if they help consumers vividly remember positive experiences. Tailoring marketing strategies with cognitive biases in mind enhances their effectiveness in influencing customer behaviour.

Product Design

Cognitive biases like the endowment effect shape product design by influencing how customers perceive and use items. Businesses can intentionally design products to enhance the sense of ownership and connection, recognizing that consumers tend to overvalue what they already possess. Features and traits that foster a feeling of ownership become valuable tools in the competitive marketplace, impacting customer decisions and brand loyalty. Apple's design philosophy, embodied in the slogan "Designed by Apple in California," exemplifies this strategy by promoting a sense of ownership and craftsmanship.

The Role of Consumer Education

Navigating and mitigating the effects of cognitive biases depends heavily on consumer education. When people are aware of these biases and their impacts, they can make more informed decisions aligned with their genuine preferences and beliefs.

Understanding the Modern Consumer Mindset

Businesses play a critical role in this educational process by providing tools that empower customers to make decisions based on thorough information. For instance, a company selling organic goods may launch an educational campaign that offers a balanced assessment of the benefits and drawbacks of organic products, helping customers overcome confirmation bias and develop a more nuanced understanding of the product category.

Adding to that, businesses that understand how cognitive biases manifest in consumer behaviour can successfully anticipate and address potential challenges they may face. Recognizing that confirmation bias may lead consumers to focus on a few negative reviews while ignoring numerous positive ones, companies can develop strategies to provide fair information, rectify issues, and mitigate the impact of this bias on the decision-making process.

Hence, cognitive biases have a profound influence on various aspects of consumer behaviour, from brand loyalty to pricing strategies, marketing messages, and product design. Businesses that grasp these biases and tailor their approaches accordingly can forge stronger connections with their target audience and navigate the complex landscape of consumer decision-making more effectively. Consumer education emerges as a crucial tool in mitigating the impact of cognitive biases, empowering individuals to make choices aligned with their genuine preferences and beliefs.

SOCIAL INFLUENCES AND THE ROLE OF SOCIAL MEDIA

The social dynamics in today's world play a big role in how and what people decide to buy (Saura et al., 2020). This section looks into different social influences and how they affect what customers choose. It uncovers the connection that people have with their friends, family, and culture. Understanding how people interact with each other and the influence it has on purchasing decisions is extremely important for companies who are trying to connect with their audience.

This section also looks at the new digital age, primarily the rise of social media and how it has transformed consumer behaviours. It explores the working dynamics of online platforms, user-generated content (UGC), influencer marketing, and online social networks. Together, all these factors combine and shape the consumer experience.

Peer-to-Peer Influence

Peer-to-peer influence plays a significant role in consumer decision-making, reflecting our innate desire for acceptance and connection. Asch's influential social psychology experiments in 1955 demonstrated the influence of peer opinion on individual choices, highlighting the power of social proof (Schulman, 1967). Positive peer reviews and testimonials, which serve as social proof, enhance the persuasive impact of peer-to-peer interactions. Whether it's embracing fashion trends, making technological choices, or adopting lifestyle changes, social proof magnifies the influence of peer recommendations.

In the digital era, the impact of social proof is amplified through online platforms. Positive reviews and recommendations from peers serve as compelling signals for potential customers navigating the vast digital landscape. Recognizing and leveraging the influence of social proof in peer interactions becomes crucial for companies aiming to navigate the interconnected networks that shape modern consumer decisions.

Family Traditions

Deeply ingrained family traditions add layers of complexity to the social influences moulding consumer behaviour (Chandrasekar & RajR, 2013). These traditions function as cultural values passed down through generations, significantly influencing consumer preferences. The interplay of family traditions and social norms becomes apparent when certain choices align with broader societal expectations. Adapting to these dynamics enables companies to refine their strategies, aligning not only with familial heritage but also with overarching societal norms guiding consumer choices.

Understanding the cultural context within which family traditions operate empowers companies to navigate the delicate balance between tradition and innovation. By aligning products and marketing strategies with cultural expectations, companies position themselves not only as custodians of tradition but also as adaptive entities attuned to evolving societal norms.

Word-of-Mouth Recommendation

In the era of digital communication, word-of-mouth promotion continues to maintain its authenticity but has taken on new and dynamic forms (Aslam et al., 2011). Online reviews, testimonials, and discussions within digital communities now serve as the modern version of word of mouth, heavily influenced by social media's widespread reach and impact. The credibility associated with shared experiences and trustworthy opinions remains a powerful factor in shaping consumer decisions.

Social media platforms have become catalysts for spreading word-of-mouth recommendations, extending their reach and influence beyond traditional boundaries. The dynamics of user-generated content (UGC) and the effectiveness of influencer marketing further contribute to reshaping consumer preferences. To navigate this landscape successfully, companies must not only recognize the enduring influence

Understanding the Modern Consumer Mindset

of word of mouth but also actively engage with digital platforms that amplify its impact in a thoughtful and relevant manner.

Navigating Social Identity

Social identity is an individual's sense of self concerning the perceived membership of social groups. In the modern customer world, It plays a crucial role in consumer decision-making, as individuals tend to align their preferences with the groups they identify with. Effective corporate engagement with these social identities fosters a sense of belonging. In the digital age, the impact of social identity is amplified by online communities curated by individuals on social media.

Understanding the complexity of social identities empowers companies to customize their products and messaging to the values and preferences of their target audience. By identifying the various social identities within their customer base, companies can develop strategies that genuinely resonate with different segments, creating a profound sense of connection and belonging.

Social Norms

Social norms have a powerful impact on consumer behaviour, acting as invisible influencers that shape acceptable and expected conduct within societies. Whether it's following fashion trends, making lifestyle decisions, or determining purchasing habits, individuals often conform to these norms to align with societal expectations. Companies that grasp the importance of social norms can tailor their strategies accordingly, aligning with existing standards to gain recognition and resonance in their target markets.

Understanding the influence of social norms involves recognizing the unwritten rules that govern consumer behaviour. By offering products and messaging that align with these values, companies not only position themselves as fulfilling social expectations but also as contributors to the cultural context that shapes consumers' choices.

Navigating Interconnected Influences

Successfully navigating the complex web of social influences requires a holistic approach that acknowledges the interconnected dynamics at play. Crafting strategies that align with peer influence demands a deep understanding of the preferences of the target audience and strategic use of social proof.

Participating in and understanding family traditions requires a nuanced understanding of cultural contexts and the values embedded in these traditions.

17

Understanding the Modern Consumer Mindset

By incorporating elements that resonate with cultural heritage, companies can create connections that transcend mere behaviour, becoming integral components of cultural expressions that shape consumer choices (Cayla & Arnould, 2008). In the digital age, generating positive word-of-mouth involves active participation in online conversations, responding to customer reviews, and strategically positioning products to encourage a favourable digital reputation. Authenticity remains crucial, and businesses with a high-quality online presence that reflects a commitment to delivering valuable experiences thrive in this environment.

Understanding and incorporating social identity involves identifying the social identities within consumer groups. Tailoring content and messages to align with stakeholder values and aspirations allows businesses to foster a sense of belonging and connection. Embracing social norms and conforming to the unwritten rules governing consumer behaviour requires acceptance. By aligning products and messaging with these values, companies not only position themselves as fulfilling social expectations but also as contributors to the cultural content that shapes consumers' identities.

Strategically Navigating Complex Influences

Companies that excel at navigating complex social influences, encompassing social proof, social media, social identity, and social norms, position themselves not only as suppliers but also as contributors to the ever-evolving trends in consumers' lives. Recognizing the overlap of these influences enables companies to foster deeper relationships, build brand loyalty, and become integral parts of the cultural context that shapes the choices of today's consumers.

Hence, social norms are invisible guides that significantly influence consumer behaviour (Melnyk et al., 2021). Companies that acknowledge and adapt to these norms can strategically position themselves as contributors to cultural contexts, gaining resonance and loyalty in the dynamic marketplace. The interconnected forces of peer influence, cultural heritage, digital engagement, and social identity create a complex tapestry that businesses can skilfully navigate to become indispensable elements in the lives of contemporary consumers.

CONCLUSION

The study of consumer behaviours and the modern consumer market is useful and important for businesses and customers alike. In today's business world, conscious customers live a lifestyle that sees that individual consumption has larger consequences and that consumer power can transform society. The chapter talks about these conscious consumers and the evolving norms and behaviours related to the companies

Understanding the Modern Consumer Mindset

and their customers. Consumer decisions are also highly influenced by emotions. Marketers can develop successful campaigns that drive sales and enhance brand loyalty by creating emotional connections with customers, using social proof to influence decision-making, and tailoring marketing strategies to different cultures. Businesses are more likely to develop effective campaigns that resonate with their target audience by applying consumer psychology to their marketing strategies. Marketers need to be up-to-date with the latest trends and adapt their strategies to changing consumer trends and preferences. Empathy adds value as a strategic marketing skill. By providing unique, richly contextualised needs for a given target audience, we can get into the heads and hearts of consumers (Braig & Witt, 2023).

This chapter also reveals the complex interplay between cognitive biases and social influences in shaping consumer behaviour. Research on confirmation bias highlights its powerful role in strengthening brand loyalty and encourages marketers to use this bias positively to strengthen deals. Anchor bias, a key psychological force, reveals its impact on consumers' perceptions of value, emphasising the need for prudent management of pricing strategies. The impact of accessibility statistics on decision-making is profound, heightening the need for companies to tailor messages, taking into account the availability of information in the minds of consumers.

The chapter then shifts the focus to social influences, with peer recognition and social proof emerging as powerful forces. The digital age fuels these developments, with social media acting as a catalyst for word-of-mouth recommendations. Family traditions deeply embedded in culture add diversity to social influences, requiring firms to navigate the delicate balance of tradition and innovation.

Understanding and taking advantage of social identity is important as individuals align preferences with group identity. Social norms, the invisible guidelines that govern product choices, require companies to align their strategies with existing societal expectations. By tapping into these complex psychological biases and social influences, companies can build deeper relationships, build brand loyalty, and become key cultural expressions that shape consumer choice.

REFERENCES

Ao, L., Bansal, R., Pruthi, N., & Khaskheli, M. B. (2023, February 2). Impact of Social Media Influencers on Customer Engagement and Purchase Intention: A Meta-Analysis. *Sustainability (Basel)*, *15*(3), 2744. Advance online publication. doi:10.3390/su15032744

Aslam, S., Jadoon, E. K., Zaman, K., & Gondal, S. (2011, September 1). Effect of Word of Mouth on Consumer Buying Behavior. *Mediterranean Journal of Social Sciences*. Advance online publication. doi:10.5901/mjss.2011.v2n3p497

Asshidin, N. H. N., Abidin, N., & Borhan, H. B. (2016). Perceived Quality and Emotional Value that Influence Consumer's Purchase Intention towards American and Local Products. *Procedia Economics and Finance*, *35*, 639–643. doi:10.1016/S2212-5671(16)00078-2

Bernard, M., & Parker, L. (2021, May 24). *The effect of conscious consumerism on purchasing behaviours: the example of greenwashing in the cosmetics industry.* Academic Press.

Braig, B. M., & Witt, H. (2023, June 19). Developing empathy as a strategic and tactical skill in the context of innovating for transgender consumers. *Marketing Education Review*, 1–17. doi:10.1080/10528008.2023.2226124

Cayla, J., & Arnould, E. J. (2008, December). A Cultural Approach to Branding in the Global Marketplace. *Journal of International Marketing*, *16*(4), 86–112. doi:10.1509/jimk.16.4.86

Chandrasekar, K. S., & Raj, R. V. (2013, July 1). *Family and Consumer behaviour.* ResearchGate. https://www.researchgate.net/publication/331319721_Family_and_Consumer_behaviour

Consumer Behavior Archives. (n.d.). American Marketing Association. https://www.ama.org/topics/consumer-behavior/

Crespo, C. F., Ferreira, A. G., & Cardoso, R. M. (2022, January 23). *The influence of storytelling on the consumer–brand relationship experience.* Journal of Marketing Analytics. doi:10.1057/s41270-021-00149-0

Dunning, D. (2007, October). Self-Image Motives and Consumer Behavior: How Sacrosanct Self-Beliefs Sway Preferences in the Marketplace. *Journal of Consumer Psychology*, *17*(4), 237–249. doi:10.1016/S1057-7408(07)70033-5

Jin, P. (2023, September 13). *Research on Confirmation Bias and Its Influences on Purchase Decision-making.* Advances in Economics Management and Political Sciences. https://doi.org/ doi:10.54254/2754-1169/10/20230471

Jovin. (2023, June 6). The psychology of consumer behaviour: Understanding how customer make decision. *International Journal of Creative Research Thoughts, 11.*

Kahneman, D. (2011). *Thinking, Fast and Slow.* Farrar, Straus and Giroux.

Melnyk, V., Carrillat, F. A., & Melnyk, V. (2021, October 8). The Influence of Social Norms on Consumer Behavior: A Meta-Analysis. *Journal of Marketing*, *86*(3), 98–120. doi:10.1177/00222429211029199

Nazlan, N. H., Tanford, S., & Montgomery, R. J. V. (2018, July 13). The effect of availability heuristics in online consumer reviews. *Journal of Consumer Behaviour*, *17*(5), 449–460. Advance online publication. doi:10.1002/cb.1731

Saura, J., Reyes-Menendez, A., Matos, N., Correia, M., & Palos-Sanchez, P. (2020). Consumer Behavior in the Digital Age. *Journal of Spatial and Organizational Dynamics.*, *8*, 190–194.

Schulman, G. I. (1967, March). Asch Conformity Studies: Conformity to the Experimenter and/ or to the Group? *Sociometry*, *30*(1), 26. doi:10.2307/2786436 PMID:6037868

Smith, J. (2019). The Power of User-Generated Content: How UGC Impacts Consumer Behaviour. *Journal of Marketing Trends*, *6*(2), 45–56.

Wei, J., Wang, Z., Hou, Z., & Meng, Y. (2022, March 30). The Influence of Empathy and Consumer Forgiveness on the Service Recovery Effect of Online Shopping. *Frontiers in Psychology*, *13*, 842207. Advance online publication. doi:10.3389/fpsyg.2022.842207 PMID:35432063

ADDITIONAL READING

A. (2023, December 4). *What Does Consumer Behavior Mean for Marketing?* Appier. https://www.appier.com/en/blog/what-does-consumer-behavior-mean-for-marketing

Bhat, S. (2024, January 5). *The Psychology of Consumer Buying Behavior: Understanding How and Why People Buy*. SurveySparrow. https://surveysparrow.com/blog/consumer-buying-behavior/

Haugtvedt, C. P., Herr, P. M., & Kardes, F. R. (2018, December 7). *Handbook of Consumer Psychology*. Psychology Press. http://books.google.ie/books?id=lWEFYahmVk8C&printsec=frontcover&dq=handbook+of+consumer+psychology&hl=&cd=1&source=gbs_api

Lahunou, I. (2022, December 30). *Predicting Customer Behavior: Your Guide Complete Guide*. Verfacto. https://www.verfacto.com/blog/behavioral-data/predicting-customer-behavior/

Nan, L. X., Park, S. Y., & Yang, Y. (2023, April 20). Rejections Are More Contagious than Choices: How Another's Decisions Shape Our Own. *The Journal of Consumer Research*, *50*(2), 363–381. Advance online publication. doi:10.1093/jcr/ucad007

Understanding and shaping consumer behavior in the next normal. (2020, July 24). McKinsey & Company. https://www.mckinsey.com/capabilities/growth-marketing-and-sales/our-insights/understanding-and-shaping-consumer-behavior-in-the-next-normal

Understanding Consumer Behavior In Marketing. (2023, September 29). MoEngage. https://www.moengage.com/learn/consumer-behavior-in-marketing/#the-role-of-advertising-and-marketing-in-shaping-consumer-behavior

Vainikka. (2015, June). *Psychological factors influencing consumer behaviour.* Retrieved January 7, 2024, from https://core.ac.uk/download/pdf/38126112.pdf

Verplancke, J. (2022). *The effect of influencer marketing on the buying behavior of young consumers : A study of how the purchase intention of young consumers is affected by brands within the fashion and beauty industries.* DIVA. https://www.diva-portal.org/smash/record.jsf?pid=diva2%3A1668422&dswid=-8071

KEY TERMS AND DEFINITIONS

Anchoring Bias: Focusing mainly on the first piece of information or anchor and considering it as a baseline while making future judgments.

Availability Heuristics: Individuals rely heavily on the information easily accessible to them in order to make quick decisions.

Cognitive Biases: Cognitive biases are the irrational judgements that occur when people employ mental shortcuts by oversimplifying complicated data.

Confirmation Bias: People seek data supporting their pre-existing views while neglecting conflicting data.

Conscious Consumerism: Conscious consumerism is when a customer is educated and can make informed decisions regarding their purchases.

Endowment Effect: The tendency to put higher values on their own products.

Peer Influence: The choices and decisions made by individuals just to fit in or feel belong to their group.

Social Identity: The emotional attachment of the customers and sticking to a certain brand.

Chapter 2
Polarization in Consumer Behavior:
The Rise of Minimalism in a Materialist World

Meziyet Uyanik
Istanbul Topkapi University, Turkey

ABSTRACT

Polarizations in economic and social life caused by increasing income and wealth injustices worldwide also affect consumer behavior. In the polarization of consumers' lifestyles, at one end of the spectrum are the consumerist culture's representatives with ostentatious and exaggerated spending based on materialistic understanding. On the other hand, consumers who adopt an anti-consumption approach sensitive to social, environmental, or individual welfare, regardless of the necessity of economic difficulties or economic factors, are increasing rapidly. This study aims to conceptually evaluate the concepts of minimalist and materialist consumption, which represent two rising values regarding consumer behavior and are mutually exclusive, and to provide readers with a holistic perspective. In this context, in this study, the concepts of materialism, minimalist consumption, and anti-consumption were evaluated from environmental, social, and individual perspectives, and their effects on consumer welfare were discussed.

DOI: 10.4018/979-8-3693-1594-1.ch002

Copyright © 2024, IGI Global. Copying or distributing in print or electronic forms without written permission of IGI Global is prohibited.

INTRODUCTION

Although the origins of the concept of minimalism date back to the 1960s, it can be said that it has gained significant momentum in recent times as unsustainable consumption models have become a global problem (Pangarkar et al., 2021; Prothero et al., 2010). So much so that the minimalist lifestyle concept is seen not only as a small niche market but as a trend that is strongly adopted among consumers on a global basis, especially in the USA, Japan, and Europe (Duong et al., 2023; Gong et al., 2023; Martin-Woodhead, 2022).

Kotler et al. (2021) begin their book "Marketing 5.0: Technology for Humanity" by addressing three fundamental problems that marketing faces today: The generation gap, prosperity polarization, and the digital divide. The world's rapidly increasing income and welfare inequalities polarize society in all areas of life. While the ever-deepening gap between rich and poor people is expanding the ultra-luxury markets that will appeal to elite people, on the other hand, the demand for low-priced and valuable products of poor people who have difficulty meeting their basic needs to survive is rapidly increasing. This leads to the polarization of jobs, ideologies, lifestyles, and markets and affects consumer behavior. Thus, the evaluation of new paradigms in marketing requires bringing them to the agenda. Today, consumer behavior is polarized at two extremes. On one side of the spectrum, consumer culture representatives, with their striking and extravagant lives, strictly adhere to materialism. In contrast on the other hand, some minimalists reject excessive consumption and dependence on commodities and prefer to get rid of excess and clutter, thus focusing on fundamental values that add value to life (Kotler et al., 2021).

In the literature, minimalist consumers are conceptualized as consumers who consciously adopt voluntary simplicity as a lifestyle, avoiding materialistic addiction, as a state of well-being, regardless of economic conditions (McDonald et al., 2006; Seegebarth et al., 2016). However, the 2008 global financial crisis is thought to have accelerated the rise of a consumption approach that indirectly challenges the principles of economic productivity, consumption, and growth and advocates the ethics of minimalism (Meissner, 2019). In addition, it can be thought that the impact of the COVID-19 pandemic and the economic difficulties it brought with it on consumers' spending tendencies contributed to the spread of the minimalist approach (Kang et al., 2021; Kotler et al., 2021; Seegebarth et al., 2016).

In addition to the minimalist movement, which has become increasingly popular since the beginning of the 21st century, the materialist consumption approach, which reflects ostentatious and exaggerated spending, has also risen (Kotler et al., 2021). Despite the economic difficulties the world is experiencing, the luxury goods market revenue as of August 2023 is 355 billion US dollars. The market is expected to grow over the next five years (Statista, 2023).

Polarization in Consumer Behavior

Conspicuous consumption based on materialist understanding is one of the main driving forces in luxury product consumption (Verdugo & Ponce, 2023). It has long been known that people are motivated to have a certain social status and to prove it to others (Clingingsmith & Sheremeta, 2018). Luxury products are considered one of the main motivations of conspicuous consumption, with their features that give prestige or status to their owners and their functional benefits (Kastanakis & Balabanis, 2015). One of the basic classes regarding consumers' motivations for luxury and status goods is the distinction between intrinsic and extrinsic motivation. Accordingly, consumers consume luxury goods with extrinsic motives such as showing wealth, proving success to others, appearing to belong to a higher social class, or with intrinsic motives such as pleasure, satisfaction, and personal reward for luxury product consumption (Saruchera & Mthombeni, 2023).

In addition, conspicuous consumption, which is generally seen as undesirable and violating social norms by many researchers, is based by some researchers on the need to compensate for a series of psychological deficiencies that have their origins in childhood. While materialist consumption, which reflects the current social paradigm, is supported by certain circles because it encourages economic growth and benefits individuals with the identity it provides, it is frequently criticized by some circles due to its possible harmful effects on individual and social welfare.

It is seen that the conveniences provided to consumers by digital technologies and new consumption experiences increase current consumption trends (Tang, 2021). In addition, targeted advertisements and personalized messages provided by digital technologies seem to contribute to the spread of consumerism by encouraging consumption desire. In addition, seeing social media as a comparison tool among consumers (Kotler et al., 2021) and the fact that it has become essential for people to share what they own and buy with others increases consumption tendencies. In this respect, although digitalization is seen as an element of resistance to the spread of the minimalist movement, social media catalyzes the spread of the minimalist lifestyle among consumers. Many blogs, YouTube channels, and social networking sites such as Facebook and Instagram, which reveal the benefits of the minimalist lifestyle on social media, have enabled many minimalisms to be recognized and adopted by others (Kang et al., 2021; Wilson & Bellezza, 2022).

In light of this information, in this part of the book, minimalist and materialist consumption approaches, which represent two different extremes in consumer behavior, are examined in terms of their conceptual origins, and the effects of these consumption concepts on consumer welfare are evaluated. For this purpose, the concept of anti-consumption, the conceptual origin of the minimalist consumption movement, was explained. Then, different anti-consumption understandings were examined comparatively with the concept of minimalism. Thus, it is aimed to contribute to the ongoing discussions between these concepts in the literature. Then, materialist consumption behavior is explained in the light of current research, and the conditions that lead consumers to materialistic consumption are evaluated within the scope of Terror Management Theory.

BACKGROUND

Overview of Minimalism

The origins of minimalism, an increasingly widespread trend among consumers in the materialist world order, date back to ancient times. However, the minimalist lifestyle has gained significant popularity as people re-evaluate their consumption habits and the things they value in life after various crises and dangers to the economic, social, and physical environment the world faces.

Minimalism refers to voluntarily reducing consumption behavior by escaping materialistic addiction, regardless of economic factors, and choosing a simple and -sometimes- aesthetic lifestyle. Most minimalists have the resources and opportunities to consume, but their consumption behavior is limited to social, environmental, or individual welfare purposes (Blackburn et al., 2023). In other words, although minimalists have economic means, they seek the meaning and value of life outside of materialistic elements with a "less is more" approach (Dopierala, 2017; Hook et al., 2023). In this context, minimalism does not mean living in poverty or away from technology (Alexander, 2011).

Despite the growing interest in minimalism, research on minimalism is still at an early level and is not an adequately studied field, especially in quantitative and empirical terms (Duong et al., 2023; Martin-Woodhead, 2022). First, there are different views on the definition and scope of minimalism from a conceptual perspective. Minimalism has been conceptualized as a subset of anti-consumerism like other concepts, such as voluntary simplicity based on low consumption, sustainable consumption, and boycotts. Although many different definitions and typologies have been developed in the literature on minimalism, the structure and scope of minimalism remain unclear (Wilson & Bellezza, 2022).

One of the essential topics of debate in this field is the distinction between minimalism and the voluntary simplicity that surrounds it. At this point, while some studies do not distinguish between the two concepts (Hausen, 2019; Martin-Woodhead, 2022; Rodriguez, 2018), some researchers (Kang et al., 2021; Meissner, 2019; Wilson & Bellezza, 2022) argue that the two concepts have different motivations and purposes that indicates as the separate structures. The focus of these discussions is on the individual and collectivist antecedents of the minimalism and voluntary simplicity movements. Hook et al. (2023) state that voluntary simplicity mainly

Polarization in Consumer Behavior

focuses on environmental and social responsibility issues, but minimalism focuses more specifically on the individual's values. Similarly, Kang et al. (2021) state that there is a reasonable consensus in the literature that minimalism has an individualized personal development focus rather than a collectivist movement. In addition to these views, some state that minimalism has individual and collectivist tendencies, as in voluntary simplicity (Martin-Woodhead, 2022).

Another issue about the minimalist consumption approach that needs to be understood is whether this lifestyle supports sustainable consumption. In the literature, it is stated by various researchers that minimalists and simplifiers are ecologically and socially motivated and that they are sensitive to the impact on the environment and society by adopting the concept of sustainability and generally in their consumption behavior (Duong et al., 2023; Peyer et al., 2017). However, the diversity of different environmental and personal interest concerns in understanding anti-consumption reveals that the minimalist consumption approach does not always directly support sustainability principles (Black & Cherrier, 2010).

The Phenomena of Anti-Consumption

Zavestoski (2002, p. 121) defines anti-consumption as "a resistance to, distaste of, or even resentment of consumption." Conceptually, it includes many areas, from activist movements towards brands to anti-globalization, from voluntary simplicity to green consumption, sustainable consumption, and social marketing practices (Kozinets et al., 2010).

Anti-consumption literally means being against consumption. However, it is impossible to avoid altogether consumption, a part of human life. In general, it covers a series of deep anti-consumption attitudes such as dislike of consumption, resistance to consumption, rejection, and a series of phenomena that can be expressed more superficially, such as preferring one brand over another (Lee, 2022; Zavestoski, 2002). In this context, anti-consumption, which focuses on the facts against the acquisition and use of certain goods (Chatzidakis & Lee, 2013), is an umbrella term that includes a wide range of concepts such as consumer resistance, consumer activism, voluntary simplicity, minimalism, downshifting, and brand avoidance. The common point in these concepts, which express different dimensions of anti-consumerism, is that they aim to reject or reduce some aspects of the consumption process (Lee, 2022) and oppose consumer culture's power or influence (Cherrier, 2009).

The concepts of anti-consumption and non-consumption are not the same (Chatzidakis & Lee, 2013). Cherrier et al. (2011) classified the concept of non-consumption into three groups: intentional non-consumption, incidental non-consumption, and ineligible non-consumption. Intentional non-consumption refers to a consumer's deliberate refusal to consume a product as a decision not to consume something. Incidental non-consumption describes the state of non-consumption resulting from the choice of an alternative. Ineligible non-consumption is used to express situations where a consumer is unaware of the product or does not have suitable conditions (such as minors being unable to consume certain products). Accordingly, non-consumption due to prohibition or other contextual effects, or non-consumption of one alternative due to accidental consumption of another, does not express anti-consumption. Anti-consumption refers to the decision not to consume as a deliberate choice (Chatzidakis & Lee, 2013) and takes the view of actively boycotting consumption (Pangarkar et al., 2021).

Littler (2011) made a conceptual distinction between consumption and consumerism and explained the phenomenon of anti-consumption through this distinction. Accordingly, consumption refers to consuming products and services independently of the economic system and without an ideological context. Conversely, consumerism refers to consumption within a specific social and political system type.

In this context, anti-consumerism is a social and political phenomenon that opposes the capitalist consumer culture or "turbo consumerism" phenomenon created by neoliberalism. Anti-consumption refers to consuming less (since it is impossible to be entirely against consumption). Considering this distinction, voluntary simplicity and minimalism, which focus on reducing consumption, can be seen as anti-consumption movements (Zalewska & Cobel-Tokarska, 2016). Thus, minimalism, voluntary simplicity, sustainable consumption, boycotts, and activism as lifestyles based on low consumption can be defined as a subclass of anti-consumption. In summary, minimalism does not express anti-consumption in the literal sense because minimalists do not entirely reject consumption but try to keep consumption levels within balanced and reasonable limits in daily life. However, if consumerism is considered an excessive, impulsive, desire-based, and wasteful consumption model within an ecosystem based on continuous growth, which is the primary basis of the dominant social paradigm, minimalism can be considered anti-consumption since it takes a stance against all these (Dopierala, 2017).

Minimalism in Consumer Behavior

The minimalist approach, which expresses consciously avoiding consumption in a consumption-oriented world, has become an increasingly popular trend since the beginning of the 21st century. As a critical approach against the rising excessive consumption, especially in Western cultures, it has become widespread as a lifestyle that focuses on reducing excesses in individuals' lives so that they can concentrate on their values (Hook et al., 2023).

Minimalism is an anti-consumption lifestyle that seeks the meaning and value of life outside materialistic values and consumption-oriented attitudes and acts

Polarization in Consumer Behavior

with the "less is more" approach (Dopierala, 2017). It refers to the tendency of individuals to both quantitatively get rid of the excesses surrounding their lives and limit their wastefulness and qualitatively prevent excessive consumption by choosing more durable and multiple-use products instead of disposable products (Błoński & Witek, 2019). Minimalism does not mean completely giving up what one has or altogether rejecting consumption. It is the individual's advocacy of a minimal life by following the philosophy of "less is more," focusing only on objects that add value to his life, getting rid of cluttered and unnecessary possessions, and avoiding excessive consumption (Chen et al., 2023; Par, 2021)

As an etymological origin, minimalism emerged as an art form in architecture, furniture designs, and advertising in the 1960s and expanded into consumer culture in the following years (Martin-Woodhead, 2022; Wilson & Bellezza, 2022). Although minimalism is not an entirely new phenomenon, some authors believe it started to become popular with the crisis in the capitalist system in 2008 (Dopierala, 2017; Meissner, 2019). However, it is not a correct approach to evaluate the reasons for the popularity and spread of minimalism only in terms of the adverse effects of the global financial crisis on people's purchasing power. The global crisis has also caused people to confront the economic, social, and environmental problems created by a lifestyle based on materialistic values. Meisser (2019) stated that many popular minimalist lifestyle narratives were published in the decade following 2008. In addition, the COVID-19 epidemic and the health problems, financial crises, and social shocks it brought with it have affected many people's daily consumption habits and value perceptions of consumption (Gong et al., 2023).

Minimalism, like the voluntary simplicity approach that frames it, refers to a lifestyle based on voluntary choice, unlike poverty (Hausen, 2019; Leonard-Barton, 1981). Minimalism is explained as the implicit rejection of consumerism, focusing on improving the quality of life and increasing subjective well-being (Meissner, 2019). One explanation for the widespread interest in minimalism is that people who adopt this lifestyle believe they will have a happier and more meaningful life (Hook et al., 2023).

Although various definitions and typologies have been developed in the literature regarding the concept of minimalism, perhaps due to its many different forms, the structure of minimalism and the presence of which elements will be considered minimalist consumption are not well defined (Wilson & Bellezza, 2022).

Iyer and Munch (2009) considered the minimalist approach a subcategory of anti-consumption as a conceptual framework. Focusing on anti-consumerism, they identified four different typologies of anti-consumerism in a two-by-two matrix. Accordingly, consumers interested in reducing the general consumption level by considering general-social concerns and the benefit of society and the planet are defined as global impact consumers. In the second category, consumers who adopt

Polarization in Consumer Behavior

a more straightforward, less consumption-oriented lifestyle based on general-personal concerns and spiritual and ethical beliefs are defined as "simplifiers." In the third category, consumers who reject using brands and products that cause social problems due to specific social concerns are classified as "market activists." Finally, in the brand-personal category, the "anti-loyal customers" category, which refers to avoiding purchasing a brand/product due to a negative experience with a brand, has been defined. Accordingly, consumers in the "simplifiers" category, which describes minimalist consumers, are defined as consumers who adopt a simple lifestyle with an individual motivation, regardless of economic conditions. However, in many studies in the literature, the motivational factors that lead consumers to a minimalist lifestyle and, therefore, consume less have been discussed from a broader perspective than individual concerns. For example, McDonald (2006) defined voluntary simplifiers as those who prefer an anti-consumption life, taking into account environmental impacts. Accordingly, voluntary simplicity can include different values, such as environmental values, sustainability, and ethical principles.

Moreover, different types of minimalists express different values in the consumption process. For example, monochrome homeowners, small homeowners, those who advocate the capsule wardrobe approach, those who live in caravans, luxury minimalists, or those who evaluate minimalism in terms of aesthetics represent different values (Uggla, 2019; Wilson & Bellezza, 2022). For some, minimalism is a "decluttering" process that removes unnecessary items. In contrast, for others, it relates to meeting needs with second-hand products rather than buying new ones. For some, it means adopting a digital minimalist approach in which the Internet, social media, and smart devices are restricted or often rejected (Newport, 2019; Rodriguez, 2018).

Minimalism and Voluntary Simplicity

In the literature, minimalism has been chiefly discussed through the lens of anti-consumption and voluntary simplicity (Pangarkar et al., 2021). Although the origins of the search for simplicity and minimalism date back to the 1800s (Wilson & Bellezza, 2022), it is known that the term "voluntary simplicity" was first introduced to the literature by Richard Gregg in 1936 (Kang et al., 2021). Accordingly, voluntary simplicity refers to avoiding external clutter and many items unrelated to life's primary purpose (Leonard-Barton, 1981). Thus, it is expressed as a free will choice that expresses moving away from materialism in developing the sources of meaning and satisfaction in life (Matte et al., 2021). "Voluntary" indicates a deliberate choice based on critical awareness of overconsumption. The expression "simplicity" refers to reducing involuntary and unnecessary consumption and possession (Hausen, 2019, pp. 171–172). Thus, voluntary simplicity is seen as a way of life that rejects high

Polarization in Consumer Behavior

consumption and materialistic dependence by consciously reducing expenditures on consumer goods and services and approving the simple living and downshifting phenomena that focus on meeting needs as simply and directly as possible (Alexander, 2011).

Leonard-Balton (1981) defines voluntary simplicity as the degree to which an individual chooses a voluntary lifestyle that maximizes control over his daily life and reduces consumption and commitment. With this lifestyle, individuals seek to live a simple and uncomplicated life by giving up material activities that provide satisfaction, happiness, and fulfillment (Pangarkar et al., 2021). Although voluntary simplicity was initially shaped within the spiritual and religious values framework, it has expanded to ecological, social, and economic values over time (Kang et al., 2021).

Although there is a reasonable consensus in the literature that voluntary simplicity provides a basis for minimalism, their distinction and boundaries are unclear (Kang et al., 2021; Matte et al., 2021). Dopierela (2017) defines minimalism as a belief system embedded in the values of voluntary simplicity. Accordingly, minimalism is the second wave of voluntary simplicity, whose roots go back much further.

Woodhead (2022) similarly sees minimalism as a contemporary outcome of the voluntary simplicity movement. Accordingly, minimalism began to become widespread as the culture of simplicity became increasingly fashionable, along with concerns about the negative consequences of excessive consumption. For example, Hausen (2019) positions minimalism within voluntary simplicity by defining voluntary simplicity as an understanding that excludes materialism and rejects high consumption. Similarly, Uggla (2019) stated that the minimalist lifestyle shares common features with voluntary simplicity but underlined that although minimalism is evaluated within the umbrella of voluntary simplicity, the simplicity movement also focuses on social consequences from a broader perspective. Accordingly, voluntary simplicity includes lifestyle changes such as commodity simplicity, environmental concern, personal development, and establishing a work-life balance with reduced working hours (Blackburn et al., 2023). As a more specific concept, minimalism refers to an understanding in which individuals focus on their own values rather than environmental and social responsibilities (Hook et al., 2023). Accordingly, the voluntary simplicity approach can be seen as a social movement that evaluates the behavior of avoiding unnecessary consumption regarding the effects of consumption on the environment (Alexander & Ussher, 2012). Various researchers consider voluntary simplicity a type of political activism in which consumers are politically motivated by environmental concerns (Kang et al., 2021).

On the other hand, some authors define minimalism as "spirituality of inner peace," a search for inner balance (Dopierala, 2017, p. 79). However, it is difficult to separate the tendency to avoid flashy, conspicuous, and unconscious consumption (Dopierala, 2017), which constitutes the essence of the minimalist approach from the social and societal context and reduces it to individual motivations only. Some researchers state minimalism shows individual and collectivist tendencies, as in voluntary simplicity (Martin-Woodhead, 2022).

Rodriguez (2018) states that although minimalism does not always have an anti-capitalist orientation, it is an approach that looks critically at excessive consumption and tries to create new ways of life within capitalism. However, he points out that few minimalists are interested in social movements such as global resource equality and justice and underlines that this critical approach lacks collective political actions.

Some authors discuss the distinction between minimalism and voluntary simplicity in terms of aesthetic concerns. Wilson and Belezza (2022, p. 802) expressed the sparse aesthetic element, which reflects simple and uncomplicated designs, as a preference element that distinguishes minimalism from voluntary simplicity. Accordingly, the aesthetic concerns that highlight and characterize simple designs, which are the critical focus of minimalists, are not included in the concept of voluntary simplicity. Similarly, Jain et al. (2023) state minimalism reflects wealth, intelligence, and elitism. According to Loreau (2017), author of the book "Minimalist L'art de la Simplicité: How to Live More with Less," which is an important narrative in minimalism narratives, minimalism is not a way to maintain a less costly lifestyle but a method of increasing the aesthetic quality of what one has (Meissner, 2019).

Although the concepts of minimalism and downshifting are related to each other, their scopes are different. While downshifting requires lifestyle changes resulting from voluntary or involuntary decreases in income, a minimalist lifestyle is based on a conscious choice as a way to increase the quality of life (Uggla, 2019). For example, people who find themselves deeply in debt due to redundancy may be tempted to lower their living and spending standards as a way to continue their lives. A minimalist lifestyle is based on a person's voluntary choices, regardless of income, and is entirely different from the experiences of people living in poor conditions (Rodriguez, 2018). In fact, Huneke (2005, p. 530) states that lifestyles such as voluntary simplicity or minimalism can be a choice for consumers whose "basic needs are satisfied and who can be assured they will be met into the future."

Minimalism and Consumers' Well-Being

In modern Western societies, consumption is often associated with satisfaction and happiness for many people (Boujbel & D'Astous, 2012). However, it is supported by many studies that the effect of income level and related purchasing power and consumption behavior on well-being is limited. The impact of income on happiness is significant in meeting the primary biological needs of poor people. Still, the effect of additional income on the well-being of wealthy individuals is limited (Hook et al., 2023).

Polarization in Consumer Behavior

Early research indicates that a minimalist lifestyle contributes to individuals' emotional well-being in various aspects. Since minimalism refers to a life change in which the individual focuses on reducing materialistic addiction in his life, according to the Upward Spiral Theory, an individual's lifestyle change is considered an essential path to well-being, supported by positive emotions that will manage the change (Kang et al., 2021; Shafqat et al., 2023).

Hook et al. (2023) stated that social scientists focus on three primary factors that explain the effect of minimalism on consumers' well-being: Restriction of consumption desires, changing materialistic values, and satisfaction of psychological needs. First, minimalists focus on reducing consumption as a voluntary and conscious choice, thus managing materialistic desires. A desire that an individual wants to satisfy gives rise to a new desire as soon as the individual meets it. This situation reveals the desired cycle Campbell (1971) calls the "hedonic treadmill." Constantly desiring things and trying to satisfy them explains the difficulty of the individual in achieving and maintaining satisfaction and happiness (M. S. W. Lee & Ahn, 2016). Consumers, who have to make choices with limited resources such as money and time, experience various tensions of varying intensity, such as disappointment, stress, and anger when they cannot satisfy their consumption desires (Boujbel and Dastous, 2012). Adopting lifestyles such as voluntary simplicity and minimalism can increase a person's capacity to manage their consumption desires and enable them to desire less consumption, thus protecting them from internal tensions such as various disappointments, stress, and anger that arise when the consumption desire is not satisfied (Hook et al., 2023). Secondly, the positive effects of minimalism on consumers' well-being can be evaluated in terms of allowing one to replace materialistic values with other types of values (Hook et al., 2023). Materialism refers to the value an individual attaches to possessing material objects that carry value. Materialistic people try to increase their satisfaction and happiness by improving their material assets. However, there is a reasonable consensus in the literature that a materialistic lifestyle has long-term negative effects on the well-being of society at a general level and on the well-being of individuals specifically (Burroughs & Rindfleisch, 2002). Minimalist consumers aim to live a simple life by removing/reducing objects from their lives that distract them from their commitment to materialism and have nothing to do with the main purpose of life. Thus, they will attach more value to the relationships, activities, and hobbies that will provide them with satisfaction and happiness by spending more time on self-improvement. Thirdly, it is thought that minimalism and voluntary simplicity can improve people's welfare levels by satisfying their psychological needs (Hook et al., 2023). Minimalism makes people consciously distinguish between their wants and needs (Mary & Ming-Ming, 2022). Minimalists are interested in optimizing consumption patterns by focusing on self-awareness and personal development processes. For this reason, they focus on a life that will provide them with psychological satisfaction to minimize the overwork and stress that are the basis of the materialist life imposed by the current economic system. Having fewer things by removing the excess in a person's life, thus allows them to have more time and focus on their personal development and important moments in their lives (Mary & Ming-Ming, 2022; Shafqat et al., 2023). In addition, it is thought that donating unnecessary items for a minimalist lifestyle and developing a socially and environmentally responsible attitude will provide psychological satisfaction to the person (Shafqat et al., 2023).

Helm et al. (2019) reported that decreasing consumption behavior positively affects a person's general well-being. Self-determination Theory, which examines the processes and conditions that nourish people's potential and encourage the healthy development of individuals and societies, explains why individuals behave in a certain way with internal and external motivational factors (Ryan & Deci, 2000b). While intrinsic motivation explains individuals' behaviors with various internal rewards for the self, extrinsic motivation accepts that people behave in a certain way based on external incentives and different rewards (Oh & Syn, 2015).

Intrinsic motivational factors include pleasure and entertainment, internal satisfaction, altruism, competence and autonomy, and a natural satisfaction arising from the activity (Rode, 2016; Ryan & Deci, 2000a). Therefore, intrinsic motivation is important, especially in voluntary and prosocial behaviors (Welschen et al., 2012). Considering that minimalism is a lifestyle based on a voluntary choice, it can be thought that people act directly with their internal motivation and experience such psychological satisfaction.

In addition, Self-determination Theory suggests that when a person's psychological needs (competence, autonomy, relatedness) are satisfied, their self-motivation and well-being will increase (Ryan & Deci, 2000b). Competence or self-efficacy is the individual's belief that they're competent to perform a specific behavior (Bandura, 1977). Autonomy is the belief that a person feels free and autonomous and determines his behavior without thinking that he is under pressure or control by internal and external factors (Kasser, 2009). Relatedness refers to the tendency to establish connections/relationships with others and to be accepted by others (Ryan & Deci, 2000b). When the concepts of voluntary simplicity and minimalism are viewed through the lens of this theory, It can be thought that minimalists' rejection of the consumption culture that the current economic system and the dominant social paradigm impose on people, against their own free will, can provide satisfaction for the need for autonomy. Meeting their desires and needs with fewer items within a self-determined consumption optimization can satisfy people's self-efficacy motivation. In addition, behaviors such as sharing excess items with other people or using second-hand items to get rid of unnecessary items to create a simple lifestyle can provide psychological satisfaction to people by meeting their need

Polarization in Consumer Behavior

to establish relationships with others and be accepted by others. Moreover, when minimalists are considered a general social group as those who voluntarily adopt a particular lifestyle, they may feel like members of a large group of people with similar feelings, thoughts, and beliefs, even if they do not know others in this group. In their research conducted with this theoretical background, Rich et al. (2017) concluded that the satisfaction of three relevant psychological needs mediates the relationship between voluntary simplicity and life satisfaction. In addition, research in the literature shows that when a person's needs such as autonomy, competence, and relatedness cannot be met, they tend to continue an unsuccessful materialist cycle aimed at compensating for this with goods and providing satisfaction in this way (Lloyd & Pennington, 2020).

Minimalism and Sustainability

The negative effects of the widespread consumption culture based on excessive consumption on the economic, social, and physical environment and measures to reduce these effects have been on the agenda of the whole world for a long time (Lloyd & Pennington, 2020). During the COVID-19 pandemic and the quarantine that came with it, the period when people had to stay in their homes and retail and production operations decreased worldwide, which ironically provided a temporary recovery opportunity for nature (Gardiner, 2020). This situation has made some people realize humanity's destruction of the environment concretely. It has also made people question their consumption habits. Although minimalism emerged long before the pandemic, the problems brought by the pandemic and concerns about the future have caused this lifestyle to become widespread among consumers (Kang et al., 2021).

When considered superficially, minimalism reflects an understanding that values the principle of sustainability, which is regarded as a new paradigm in consumer behavior (Chen & Liu, 2023). Minimalism and voluntary simplicity are lifestyles with many different types that people engage in for various motivational reasons. Therefore, not every minimalist approach may have the mission of not directly harming the environment and nature. However, even if minimalists and voluntary simplifiers do not set out directly for this purpose, they contribute to a sustainable future by reducing the materials and possessions in their lives. Since minimalism is a lifestyle that reduces people's habit of acquiring and accumulating unnecessary goods, it emphasizes responsible consumption habits (Alexander & Ussher, 2012; Kang et al., 2021). Additionally, reducing individual consumption may ultimately provide an incentive to reduce the ecological footprint of the population (Lloyd & Pennington, 2020). Living in smaller homes, with fewer belongings, and consuming

Polarization in Consumer Behavior

less can lead to environmental benefits by reducing household emissions (Blackburn et al., 2023).

In various studies in the literature explaining the difference between voluntary simplicity and minimalist understanding, the main point of distinction is the individual or collectivist antecedents in reducing consumption behavior. Accordingly, voluntary simplicity focuses on social benefits and reduces consumption behavior to live a more meaningful life with a broader perspective. In the minimalist approach, it is stated that people aim to achieve subjective happiness and life satisfaction by focusing on their values and personal development processes with individual concerns. In this context, minimalism is seen as an individual approach far from a radical potential to challenge the capitalist system collectively (Palafox, 2020). On the other hand, some authors emphasize that the minimalist approach includes a solid motivation to protect the environment and personal well-being (Martin-Woodhead, 2022). Indeed, whether or not they directly focus on protecting the environment, both approaches can bring a potential solution to environmental problems as responsible consumption behavior, as they aim to reduce unnecessary and excessive consumption (Hüttel et al., 2020). In this context, although minimalism has an internal focus, individual activities on the environment can have a collective impact (Palafox, 2020).

Since minimalists aim to live with less and gain satisfaction by focusing on what is truly important in their lives, they may want to benefit from the freedom and flexibility of renting instead of purchasing the goods they need and sticking to them. The sharing economy is at the center of sustainable development and is about "sharing, exchanging, and renting resources without owning commodities" (Shukla et al., 2023, p. 2).

Pangarkar et al. (2021), in the minimalism typology developed based on two different structures: Consumption goal orientation and conditional sensitivity, consumers in the category they call inconspicuous minimalists are generally well-educated people belonging to the highest levels of society. For this reason, it is stated that these people are aware of social responsibility, adopt sustainability principles, and are more sensitive to environmental problems.

Nevertheless, people's efforts to reduce excess commodities and their consumption can occur without concern for the environment. In other words, minimalists may prefer a simple life to achieve satisfaction and happiness in their own lives without being a part of a collectivist movement. Some critics also raise concerns that the minimalist lifestyle may encourage new forms of consumption. Accordingly, consumers will develop new consumption approaches to adapt to a certain stereotype (e.g., capsule wardrobe, a smaller house) to adjust to a minimalist lifestyle. Indeed, consumers who have internalized the basic philosophy of minimalism can engage in re-evaluation/use or transformation of the items they own instead of purchasing the new commodities required by this lifestyle (Palafox, 2020). However, minimalism's effort to build the meaning and satisfaction of life through spiritual feelings and experiences instead of material values may result in environmentally harmful consumption behaviors such as traveling more frequently, thereby increasing carbon emissions (Blackburn et al., 2023).

In summary, although environmentally friendly practices and sustainability principles do not constitute the essential components of minimalism, they can lead to environmentally friendly behaviors and waste reduction, such as careful shopping, avoiding excessive consumption, and using what you have for a long time (Blackburn et al., 2023; Kang et al., 2021). However, environmentally harmful consumption models may also be created to construct the commodities and experiences required by the new lifestyle.

Materialism

Materialism is a value system in which the individual's wealth and the material objects he owns are the main focus of his life (Par, 2021). Individuals attempt to obtain the symbolic value they desire through products and services and establish their identities on this value (Shrum et al., 2014). Belk (1985, p. 265) defines materialism as "the importance a consumer attaches to worldly possessions" and characterizes materialism with several features such as possessiveness, nongenerosity, and envy (Kilbourne & LaForge, 2010; Richins & Dawson, 1992). Schiffman and Wisenblit (2019, p. 66) define materialism as a personality trait of purchasing and displaying non-essential and often conspicuous luxury items.

Materialist individuals put the things they own at the center of their lives and see them as a means of achieving happiness, life satisfaction, and prosperity (Richins, 1994). They attach more importance to their material possessions than other people or experiences (Fitzmaurice & Comegys, 2006). For these people, their assets are the criterion and evidence of success for themselves and others (Richins, 1994). Indeed, such a view system constantly confirms the individuals' need to compare themselves with others (Par, 2021). Materialists tend to judge themselves and others' success by the number and quality of possessions they own. For materialists, property is a means of reflecting the status and personal image they desire, and they see themselves as successful to the extent that they can own products that will create the image they want (Richins & Dawson, 1992).

Materialism has generally been discussed in terms of individual and social negative consequences (Kilbourne & LaForge, 2010; Lloyd & Pennington, 2020). Studies linking materialism to low well-being have mostly focused on long-term happiness, life satisfaction, and subjective well-being (Shrum et al., 2014). Accordingly, having materialistic values or desires has been evaluated as negatively related to a person's happiness, subjective well-being, satisfaction with life, sense of community, and environmental concerns (Segev et al., 2015). Although the potentially positive outcomes of materialism are rarely examined, some researchers also emphasize the positive individual and social outcomes of materialism (Kilbourne & LaForge, 2010; Shrum et al., 2014) (Kilbourne and LaForce, 2010; Shrum et al., 2014).

When materialism is considered a supporter of the current dominant social paradigm, it is possible to mention its positive social outcomes. As it is known, organizations focusing on economic growth and welfare, such as the OECD, associate social welfare with growth (Palafox, 2020). In capitalist societies, where economic growth is seen as the criterion of success, materialism is seen as both a result of the system and a driving force encouraging further growth of the system. In this respect, it has been evaluated as an element that benefits society in the long term by encouraging more growth (Kilbourne & LaForge, 2010). Indeed, the dominant social paradigm focuses on continuous growth to maintain the desired level of capital accumulation and profitability. The basis of personal satisfaction and happiness is the ever-increasing understanding of consumption (Belz & Peattie, 2013; Gollnhofer & Schouten, 2017).

However, the idea that materialism maintains the continuity of the system by encouraging growth and thus benefits society, in the long run has some arguments that refute it on the other side of the coin. A system based on a model of continuous growth, excessive consumption, and production on a planet with limited resources carries the risk of physical and social blockage and represents an unsustainable understanding (Kemper et al., 2019; Spry et al., 2021).

From an individual perspective, some researchers point out consumption's positive contributions to people's personal identity development, increasing the sense of belonging and achieving one's life goals (Holt, 1995; Kilbourne & LaForge, 2010). Accordingly, people's tendency towards materialistic consumption is defined as building their own identities with the products they own and conveying this identity to others, implicitly increasing their self-esteem and gaining the approval of others, thus strengthening the sense of belonging (Shrum et al., 2014). When products are considered in terms of their symbolic meanings, they play an essential role in forming the individual's identity and reflecting it to others (Koles et al., 2018). Additionally, compensatory consumption literature states that people turn to products and consumption behavior as compensation in response to motivations triggered by needs and desires that cannot be directly met. Thus, individuals can increase their self-worth based on materialistic consumption in response to a need they cannot satisfy or a threat to themselves(Koles et al., 2018; Shrum et al., 2014).

Polarization in Consumer Behavior

Terror Management Theory and Materialism

According to Terror Management Theory (TMT), in humans, who are the only living species aware of death, this awareness creates intense anxiety or terror that must be constantly managed. People develop various defense mechanisms to deal with this existential and typically unconscious death anxiety created by the certainty and inevitability of death (Arndt et al., 2004a; Becker, 1973; Greenberg et al., 1997).

TMT is related to a wide range of aspects of human behavior, including having children, parenting behavior, sexism, orientation towards religious and spiritual emotions, education, nationalism and racism, and consumption habits (Greenberg & Arndt, 2012).

TMT suggests that strengthening people's beliefs in their cultural worldview, self-esteem, and close relationships is effective in managing the potential anxiety brought on by death awareness and reducing this existential terror (Pyszczynski et al., 2021). The belief systems that form cultural worldviews give people literal or symbolic immortality. Literal immortality includes spiritual beliefs such as the afterlife and resurrection after death. Symbolic immortality is achieved through the symbolic reflections of one's existence by identifying with larger entities such as having children, nation, and race (Fransen et al., 2019; Greenberg et al., 1997). Thus, individuals will be able to feel that they are valuable in a meaningful world, in contrast to the feeling of transience and meaninglessness of the world (Pyszczynski et al., 2021). Cultural views guide the individual on what will be considered meaningful and valuable behaviors, and by maintaining these culturally coded behaviors, people feel good, and their self-esteem increases. The unconscious tension created by the awareness of death in people encourages people to increase their self-esteem, which will take the world and themselves to a more meaningful and valuable level of understanding (Arndt et al., 2004a).

Many studies in the literature indicate that self-esteem and fear of death are closely related (Arndt et al., 2004a, 2004b; Greenberg et al., 1997; Greenberg & Arndt, 2012). High self-esteem functions as an anxiety buffering (Arndt et al., 2004a). In other words, having high self-esteem reduces the internal tension created by death awareness (Walczak et al., 2018). Since death awareness increases people's efforts to improve their self-esteem, people are motivated to engage in various behaviors that will make them valuable. For example, a cultural worldview conveying that acquiring wealth and possessions will enable a happy and valuable life increases materialistic desires, considered a distinct indicator of self-worth (Arndt et al., 2004b, 2004a; Walczak et al., 2018).

TMT states that people's behavior of acquiring money and property and making these acquisitions central to life is partly due to their tendency to suppress the idea that they are mortal beings (Fransen et al., 2019). For example, Chopick and

Edelstein (2014) found that death anxiety increased the desire to purchase luxury products. Fransen et al. (2019) state that in capitalist societies, where a person's value is primarily determined by what they own, this can be interpreted as a way to achieve symbolic immortality. People increase their self-confidence by purchasing valuable and expensive products, thus suppressing their existential and unconscious death anxiety (Walczak et al., 2018).

FUTURE RESEARCH DIRECTIONS

The scope and conceptual framework of understanding minimalism remain unclear in the current literature. In particular, the ambiguities between the minimalist and voluntary simplicity approaches and the different views indicate the need for new studies in this field.

Defining different types of minimalism and developing different minimalist typologies will significantly contribute to the literature by future researchers, considering the diversity of individual and collectivist tendencies that motivate people in anti-consumption approaches. For example, Blackburn et al. (2023) stated that there can be two types of minimalists: aesthetic and eco-minimal.

Since this study aims to clarify the conceptual framework of the minimalism movement, which is becoming increasingly widespread among consumers in the dominant economic system based on materialism and consumption expenditures, the conditions that lead consumers to materialism are also discussed from the Terror Management Theory perspective. As explained in detail in the relevant section, many studies support a positive relationship between individuals' death anxiety and materialistic consumption expenditures. Terror Management Theory has generally been examined in the literature in terms of the negative consequences of people's efforts to manage their death anxiety for the individual and society. However, Vail et al. (2012) draw attention to the potential of death awareness to sometimes direct people positively. Future studies based on this perspective will contribute significantly to understanding paradigm shifts in consumer behavior. Although many studies examine materialistic consumer behavior through the lens of Terror Management Theory, there is no study yet on minimalist or sustainable consumption behavior. Determining the effects of conscious and unconscious death awareness on consumption behavior will contribute to understanding the conditions that lead consumers to materialism or anti-consumption and reduced consumption.

CONCLUSION

This study aims to give readers a holistic perspective on the minimalist lifestyle and consumption habits by evaluating minimalism, which is seen as a rising understanding of consumer behavior from a conceptual standpoint. For this purpose, the conceptual roots of the understanding of minimalism and the factors that lead consumers to a minimalist or materialist lifestyle were examined. Minimalism and voluntary simplicity approaches are examined comparatively and critically to contribute to the ongoing discussions in the literature regarding the differences or similarities between these two concepts.

Despite the increasing interest in minimalism, studies in this field are insufficient to draw the conceptual framework of relevant lifestyles. There are different opinions in the ongoing debates, especially in the individual-collectivist focus on minimalism and voluntary simplicity approaches. In this context, the most accepted view is that voluntary simplicity and minimalism are very close to each other and that voluntary simplicity forms a basis for the development of minimalism.

Sustainable development goals adopted by all UN member countries in 2015 point to new consumption habits for the planet's future. It has long been recognized that the current paradigm of continuous growth is not sustainable. Excessive consumption is seen as the biggest responsible for global environmental destruction. However, eliminating consumption, an integral part of human life, is out of the question. The aim is to create new and sustainable approaches to consumption. Another focus of these discussions about minimalism is whether this lifestyle supports sustainability.

Superficially, a minimalist lifestyle seems to support sustainable development with a responsible consumption approach, as it expresses the exact opposite of a commodity and consumption-oriented life. However, it is difficult to state that minimalism directly and under all circumstances supports sustainability. When minimalism requires a life change for the individual, fulfilling the requirements of this life form will give rise to new consumption styles and create new markets. Arguably, these emerging markets have always been compatible with sustainability principles. In addition, the "simple and aesthetic" perception of minimalists in their lives, furniture, and other home commodities may conflict with sustainability principles or foster wasteful consumption habits.

REFERENCES

Alexander, S. (2011). The voluntary simplicity movement: Reimagining the good life beyond consumer culture. *Int. J. Environ. Cult. Econ. Soc. Sustain., 7.*

Alexander, S., & Ussher, S. (2012). The voluntary simplicity movement: A multi-national survey analysis in theoretical context. *Journal of Consumer Culture, 1*(12), 66–86. doi:10.1177/1469540512444019

Arndt, J., Solomon, S., Kasser, T., & Sheldon, K. M. (2004a). The Urge to Splurge: A Terror Management Account of Materialism and Consumer Behavior. *Journal of Consumer Psychology, 14*(3), 198–212. doi:10.1207/s15327663jcp1403_2

Arndt, J., Solomon, S., Kasser, T., & Sheldon, K. M. (2004b). The Urge to Splurge Revisited: Further Reflections on Applying Terror Management Theory to Materialism and Consumer Behavior. *Journal of Consumer Psychology, 14*(3), 225–229. doi:10.1207/s15327663jcp1403_5

Bandura, A. (1977). Self-efficacy: Toward a Unifying Theory of Behavioral Change. *Psychological Review, 2*(84), 191–215. doi:10.1037/0033-295X.84.2.191 PMID:847061

Becker, E. (1973). *The denial of death*. Free Press.

Belk, R. W. (1985). Materialism: Trait aspects of living in the material world. *The Journal of Consumer Research, 12*(3), 265–280. doi:10.1086/208515

Belz, F., & Peattie, K. J. (2013). *Sustainability marketing: A global perspective* (2nd ed.). Wiley.

Black, I. R., & Cherrier, H. (2010). Anti-consumption as part of living a sustainable lifestyle: Daily practices, contextual motivations and subjective values. *Journal of Consumer Behaviour, 9*(6), 437–453. doi:10.1002/cb.337

Blackburn, R., Leviston, Z., Walker, I., & Schram, A. (2023). Could a minimalist lifestyle reduce carbon emissions and improve wellbeing? A review of minimalism and other low consumption lifestyles. *Wiley Interdisciplinary Reviews: Climate Change, 865*, e865. Advance online publication. doi:10.1002/wcc.865

Błoński, K., & Witek, J. (2019). Minimalism in consumption. *Annales Universitatis Mariae Curie-Skłodowska, Sectio H – Oeconomia, 53*(2), 7. doi:10.17951/h.2019.53.2.7-15

Boujbel, L., & D'Astous, A. (2012). Voluntary simplicity and life satisfaction: Exploring the mediating role of consumption desires. *Journal of Consumer Behaviour, 11*(6), 487–494. doi:10.1002/cb.1399

Burroughs, J. E., & Rindfleisch, A. (2002). Materialism and Well-Being: A Conflicting Values Perspective. *The Journal of Consumer Research, 29*(3), 348–370. doi:10.1086/344429

Chatzidakis, A., & Lee, M. S. W. (2013). Anti-Consumption as the Study of Reasons against. *Journal of Macromarketing, 33*(3), 190–203. doi:10.1177/0276146712462892

Chen, S., Kou, S., & Lv, L. (2023). Stand out or fit in: Understanding consumer minimalism from a social comparison perspective. *Journal of Business Research, 170*, 114307. doi:10.1016/j.jbusres.2023.114307

Chen, W., & Liu, J. (2023). When less is more: Understanding consumers' responses to minimalist appeals. *Psychology and Marketing, 40*(10), 2151–2162. doi:10.1002/mar.21869

Cherrier, H. (2009). Anti-consumption discourses and consumer-resistant identities. *Journal of Business Research, 62*(2), 181–190. doi:10.1016/j.jbusres.2008.01.025

Cherrier, H., Black, I. R., & Lee, M. (2011). Intentional non-consumption for sustainability: Consumer resistance and/or anti-consumption? *European Journal of Marketing, 45*(11/12), 1757–1767. doi:10.1108/03090561111167397

Chopik, W. J., & Edelstein, R. S. (2014). Death of a salesman: Webpage-based manipulations of mortality salience. *Computers in Human Behavior, 31*, 94–99. doi:10.1016/j.chb.2013.10.022

Clingingsmith, D., & Sheremeta, R. M. (2018). Status and the demand for visible goods: Experimental evidence on conspicuous consumption. *Experimental Economics, 21*(4), 877–904. doi:10.1007/s10683-017-9556-x

Dopierala, R. (2017). Minimalism – a new mode of consumption? *Przegląd Socjologiczny, 66*(4), 67–83. doi:10.26485/PS/2017/66.4/4

Duong, T. T.-T., Ngo, L. V., Surachartkumtonkun, J., Tran, M. D., & Northey, G. (2023). Less is more! A pathway to consumer's transcendence. *Journal of Retailing and Consumer Services, 72*, 103294. doi:10.1016/j.jretconser.2023.103294

Fitzmaurice, J., & Comegys, C. (2006). Materialism and Social Consumption. *Journal of Marketing Theory and Practice, 14*(4), 287–299. doi:10.2753/MTP1069-6679140403

Fransen, M. L., Arendsen, J., & Das, E. (2019). Consumer Culture as Worldview Defense. In *Handbook of Terror Management Theory* (pp. 485–512). Elsevier. doi:10.1016/B978-0-12-811844-3.00020-2

Gardiner, B. (2020, June 18). *Why COVID-19 will end up harming the environment.* Science. https://www.nationalgeographic.com/science/article/why-covid-19-will-end-up-harming-the-environment

Gollnhofer, J. F., & Schouten, J. W. (2017). Complementing the Dominant Social Paradigm with Sustainability. *Journal of Macromarketing*, *37*(2), 143–152. doi:10.1177/0276146717696892

Gong, S., Suo, D., & Peverelli, P. (2023). Maintaining the order: How social crowding promotes minimalistic consumption practice. *Journal of Business Research*, *160*, 113768. doi:10.1016/j.jbusres.2023.113768

Greenberg, J., & Arndt, J. (2012). Terror Management Theory. In P. A. M. Van Lange, A. W. Kruglanski, & E. T. Higgins (Eds.), *Handbook of Theories of Social Psychology* (Vol. 1, pp. 398–415). SAGE Publications Ltd. doi:10.4135/9781446249215.n20

Greenberg, J., Solomon, S., & Pyszczynski, T. (1997). Terror Management Theory of Self-Esteem and Cultural Worldviews: Empirical Assessments and Conceptual Refinements. In Advances in Experimental Social Psychology (Vol. 29, pp. 61–139).. Elsevier. doi:10.1016/S0065-2601(08)60016-7

Hausen, J. E. (2019). Minimalist life orientations as a dialogical tool for happiness. *British Journal of Guidance & Counselling*, *47*(2), 168–179. doi:10.1080/030698 85.2018.1523364

Helm, S., Serido, J., Ahn, S. Y., Ligon, V., & Shim, S. (2019). Materialist values, financial and pro-environmental behaviors, and well-being. *Young Consumers*, *20*(4), 264–284. doi:10.1108/YC-10-2018-0867

Holt, D. B. (1995). How Consumers Consume: A Typology of Consumption Practices. *The Journal of Consumer Research*, *22*(1), 1. doi:10.1086/209431

Hook, J. N., Hodge, A. S., Zhang, H., Van Tongeren, D. R., & Davis, D. E. (2023). Minimalism, voluntary simplicity, and well-being: A systematic review of the empirical literature. *The Journal of Positive Psychology*, *18*(1), 130–141. doi:10.1 080/17439760.2021.1991450

Huneke, M. E. (2005). The Face of the Un-Consumer: An Empirical Examination of the Practice of Voluntary Simplicity in the United States. *Psychology and Marketing*, *7*(22), 527–550. doi:10.1002/mar.20072

Hüttel, A., Balderjahn, I., & Hoffmann, S. (2020). Welfare Beyond Consumption: The Benefits of Having Less. *Ecological Economics*, *176*, 106719. doi:10.1016/j. ecolecon.2020.106719

Iyer, R., & Muncy, J. A. (2009). Purpose and object of anti-consumption. *Journal of Business Research*, *62*(2), 160–168. doi:10.1016/j.jbusres.2008.01.023

Jain, V. K., Gupta, A., & Verma, H. (2023). Goodbye materialism: Exploring antecedents of minimalism and its impact on millennials well-being. *Environment, Development and Sustainability*. Advance online publication. doi:10.1007/s10668-023-03437-0 PMID:37363025

Kang, J., Martinez, C. M. J., & Johnson, C. (2021). Minimalism as a sustainable lifestyle: Its behavioral representations and contributions to emotional well-being. *Sustainable Production and Consumption*, *27*, 802–813. doi:10.1016/j.spc.2021.02.001

Kasser, T. (2009). Psychological Need Satisfaction, Personal Well-Being, and Ecological Sustainability. *Ecopsychology*, *1*(4), 175–180. doi:10.1089/eco.2009.0025

Kastanakis, M. N., & Balabanis, G. (2015). Explaining Variation in Conspicuous Consumption: An Empirical Examination. In L. Robinson (Ed.), *Marketing Dynamism & Sustainability: Things Change, Things Stay the Same...* (pp. 248–248). Springer International Publishing. doi:10.1007/978-3-319-10912-1_81

Kemper, J. A., Hall, C., & Ballantine, P. (2019). Marketing and Sustainability: Business as Usual or Changing Worldviews? *Sustainability (Basel)*, *11*(3), 780. doi:10.3390/su11030780

Kilbourne, W. E., & LaForge, M. C. (2010). Materialism and its relationship to individual values. *Psychology and Marketing*, *27*(8), 780–798. doi:10.1002/mar.20357

Koles, B., Wells, V., & Tadajewski, M. (2018). Compensatory consumption and consumer compromises: A state-of-the-art review. *Journal of Marketing Management*, *34*(1–2), 96–133. doi:10.1080/0267257X.2017.1373693

Kotler, P., Kartajaya, H., & Setiawan, I. (2021). *Marketing 5.0: Technology For Humanity*. John Wiley & Sons.

Kozinets, R. V., Handelman, J. M., & Lee, M. S. W. (2010). Don't read this; or, who cares what the hell anti-consumption is, anyways? *Consumption Markets & Culture*, *13*(3), 225–233. doi:10.1080/10253861003786918

Lee, M. S. W. (2022a). Anti-consumption research: A foundational and contemporary overview. *Current Opinion in Psychology*, *45*, 101319. doi:10.1016/j.copsyc.2022.101319 PMID:35325808

Lee, M. S. W., & Ahn, C. S. Y. (2016). Anti-consumption, Materialism, and Consumer Well-being. *The Journal of Consumer Affairs*, *50*(1), 18–47. doi:10.1111/joca.12089

Leonard-Barton, D. (1981). Voluntary Simplicity Lifestyles and Energy Conservation. *The Journal of Consumer Research*, *8*(3), 243. doi:10.1086/208861

Littler, J. (2011). What's wrong with ethical consumption? In T. Lewis & E. Potter (Eds.), Ethical Consumption: A Critical Introduction (pp. 27–37). Routledge Taylor and Francis Group.

Lloyd, K., & Pennington, W. (2020). Towards a Theory of Minimalism and Wellbeing. *International Journal of Applied Positive Psychology*, *5*(3), 121–136. doi:10.1007/s41042-020-00030-y

Martin-Woodhead, A. (2022). Limited, considered and sustainable consumption: The (non)consumption practices of UK minimalists. *Journal of Consumer Culture*, *22*(4), 1012–1031. doi:10.1177/14695405211039608

Mary, P., & Ming-Ming, L. (2022). Minimalism Lifestyles Promote Well-Being: The New Paradigm. In A. Asmawi (Ed.), *Proceedings of the International Conference on Technology and Innovation Management (ICTIM 2022)* (*Vol. 228*, pp. 145–153). Atlantis Press International BV. 10.2991/978-94-6463-080-0_12

Matte, J., Fachinelli, A. C., De Toni, D., Milan, G. S., & Olea, P. M. (2021). Relationship between minimalism, happiness, life satisfaction, and experiential consumption. *SN Social Sciences*, *1*(7), 166. doi:10.1007/s43545-021-00191-w

McDonald, S., Oates, C. J., Young, C. W., & Hwang, K. (2006). Toward sustainable consumption: Researching voluntary simplifiers. *Psychology and Marketing*, *23*(6), 515–534. doi:10.1002/mar.20132

Meissner, M. (2019). Against accumulation: Lifestyle minimalism, de-growth and the present post-ecological condition. *Journal of Cultural Economics*, *12*(3), 185–200. doi:10.1080/17530350.2019.1570962

Newport, C. (2019). *Digital minimalism: On living better with less technology.* Portfolio/Penguin.

Oh, S., & Syn, S. Y. (2015). Motivations for sharing information and social support in social media: A comparative analysis of Facebook, Twitter, Delicious, YouTube, and Flickr. *Journal of the Association for Information Science and Technology*, *66*(10), 2045–2060. doi:10.1002/asi.23320

Palafox, C. L. (2020). When Less is More: Minimalism and the Environment. *Earth Jurisprudence & Envtl. Just, 10.*

Pangarkar, A., Shukla, P., & Taylor, C. R. (2021). Minimalism in consumption: A typology and brand engagement strategies. *Journal of Business Research*, *127*, 167–178. doi:10.1016/j.jbusres.2021.01.033

Par, T. (2021). Materialism to Minimalism. *Healt, Wellnes, and Life Sciences, BU WELL, 1*(6).

Peyer, M., Balderjahn, I., Seegebarth, B., & Klemm, A. (2017). The role of sustainability in profiling voluntary simplifiers. *Journal of Business Research, 70,* 37–43. doi:10.1016/j.jbusres.2016.07.008

Prothero, A., McDonagh, P., & Dobscha, S. (2010). Is Green the New Black? Reflections on a Green Commodity Discourse. *Journal of Macromarketing, 30*(2), 147–159. doi:10.1177/0276146710361922

Pyszczynski, T., Lockett, M., Greenberg, J., & Solomon, S. (2021). Terror Management Theory and the COVID-19 Pandemic. *Journal of Humanistic Psychology, 61*(2), 173–189. doi:10.1177/0022167820959488

Richins, M. L. (1994). Special Possessions and the Expression of Material Values. *The Journal of Consumer Research, 21*(3), 522. doi:10.1086/209415

Richins, M. L., & Dawson, S. (1992). A Consumer Values Orientation for Materialism and Its Measurement: Scale Development and Validation. *The Journal of Consumer Research, 19*(3), 303. doi:10.1086/209304

Rode, H. (2016). To Share or not to Share: The Effects of Extrinsic and Intrinsic Motivations on Knowledge-sharing in Enterprise Social Media Platforms. *Journal of Information Technology, 31*(2), 152–165. doi:10.1057/jit.2016.8

Rodriguez, J. (2018). The US Minimalist Movement: Radical Political Practice? *The Review of Radical Political Economics, 50*(2), 286–296. doi:10.1177/0486613416665832

Ryan, R. M., & Deci, E. L. (2000a). Intrinsic and Extrinsic Motivations: Classic Definitions and New Directions. *Contemporary Educational Psychology, 25*(1), 54–67. doi:10.1006/ceps.1999.1020 PMID:10620381

Ryan, R. M., & Deci, E. L. (2000b). Self-Determination Theory and the Facilitation of Intrinsic Motivation, Social Development, and Well-Being. *The American Psychologist, 1*(55), 68–78. doi:10.1037/0003-066X.55.1.68 PMID:11392867

Saruchera, F., & Mthombeni, L. (2023). Antecedents to the conspicuous consumption of luxury fashion brands by middle-income black South Africans. *Journal of Fashion Marketing and Management, 27*(6), 1–21. doi:10.1108/JFMM-06-2022-0126

Schiffman, L. G., & Wisenblit, J. (2019). *Consumer behavior* (12th ed.). Pearson.

Seegebarth, B., Peyer, M., Balderjahn, I., & Wiedmann, K. (2016). The Sustainability Roots of Anticonsumption Lifestyles and Initial Insights Regarding Their Effects on Consumers' Well-Being. *The Journal of Consumer Affairs*, *50*(1), 68–99. doi:10.1111/joca.12077

Segev, S., Shoham, A., & Gavish, Y. (2015). A closer look into the materialism construct: The antecedents and consequences of materialism and its three facets. *Journal of Consumer Marketing*, *32*(2), 85–98. doi:10.1108/JCM-07-2014-1082

Shafqat, T., Ishaq, M. I., & Ahmed, A. (2023). Fashion consumption using minimalism: Exploring the relationship of consumer well-being and social connectedness. *Journal of Retailing and Consumer Services*, *71*, 103215. doi:10.1016/j.jretconser.2022.103215

Shrum, L. J., Lowrey, T. M., Pandelaere, M., Ruvio, A. A., Gentina, E., Furchheim, P., Herbert, M., Hudders, L., Lens, I., Mandel, N., Nairn, A., Samper, A., Soscia, I., & Steinfield, L. (2014). Materialism: The good, the bad, and the ugly. *Journal of Marketing Management*, *30*(17–18), 1858–1881. doi:10.1080/0267257X.2014.959985

Shukla, Y., Mishra, S., Chatterjee, R., & Arora, V. (2023). Consumer minimalism for sustainability: Exploring the determinants of rental consumption intention. *Journal of Consumer Behaviour*, cb.2219. doi:10.1002/cb.2219

Spry, A., Figueiredo, B., Gurrieri, L., Kemper, J. A., & Vredenburg, J. (2021). Transformative Branding: A Dynamic Capability To Challenge The Dominant Social Paradigm. *Journal of Macromarketing*, *41*(4), 531–546. doi:10.1177/02761467211043074

Statista. (2023). *Luxury Goods—Worldwide | Statista Market Forecast*. Statista. https://www.statista.com/outlook/cmo/luxury-goods/worldwide

Tang, Q. (2021). Consumerism in the Digital Age. *2021 World Automation Congress (WAC)*, 97–99. 10.23919/WAC50355.2021.9559559

Uggla, Y. (2019). Taking back control: Minimalism as a reaction to high speed and overload in contemporary society. *Sociologisk Forskning*, *56*(3–4), 233–252. doi:10.37062/sf.56.18811

Verdugo, G. B., & Ponce, H. R. (2023). Gender Differences in Millennial Consumers of Latin America Associated with Conspicuous Consumption of New Luxury Goods. *Global Business Review*, *24*(2), 229–242. doi:10.1177/0972150920909002

Walczak, R. B., Gerymski, R., & Filipkowski, J. (2018). Would you fancy a premium five o'clock after the funeral? Application of Terror Management Theory in daily shopping decisions. *Acta Universitatis Lodziensis. Folia Psychologica, 22*(22), 5–15. doi:10.18778/1427-969X.22.01

Welschen, J., Todorova, N., & Mills, A. M. (2012). An Investigation of the Impact of Intrinsic Motivation on Organizational Knowledge Sharing. *International Journal of Knowledge Management, 8*(2), 23–42. doi:10.4018/jkm.2012040102

Wilson, A. V., & Bellezza, S. (2022). Consumer Minimalism. *The Journal of Consumer Research, 48*(5), 796–816. doi:10.1093/jcr/ucab038

Zalewska, J., & Cobel-Tokarska, M. (2016). Rationalization of Pleasure and Emotions: The Analysis of the Blogs of Polish Minimalists. *Polish Sociological Review, 196*(4).

Zavestoski, S. (2002). Guest editorial: Anticonsumption attitudes. *Psychology and Marketing, 19*(2), 121–126. doi:10.1002/mar.10005

ADDITIONAL READING

Becker, E. (1973). *The denial of death*. Free Press.

Becker, J. (2016). *The more of less: Finding the life you want under everything you own*. WaterBrook.

Crabbe, T. (2014). Busy: How to thrive in a world of too much. Hachette UK.

Kondo, M. (2014). *The Life-Changing Magic of Tidying Up: The Japanese Art of Decluttering and Organizing*. Ten Speed Press.

Kotler, P., Kartajaya, H., & Setiawan, I. (2021). *Marketing 5.0: Technology For Humanity*. John Wiley & Sons.

Loreau, D. (2017). *L'art de la Simplicité: How to Live More with Less*. St. Martin's Griffin.

Newport, C. (2019). *Digital minimalism: Choosing a focused life in a noisy world*. Penguin.

Sasaki, F. (2017). *Goodbye, things: The new japanese minimalism*. WW Norton & Company.

KEY TERMS AND DEFINITIONS

Anti-Consumption: Literally means being against consumption. Encompasses diverse spheres, ranging from activist movements directed against brands to sentiments aligned with anti-globalization. It also contains lifestyle choices such as voluntary simplicity, green consumption, sustainable consumption, and the implementation of social marketing practices (Kozinets et al., 2010).

Consumerism: The practice of consumption occurring within a particular social and political framework or system.

Downshifting: Simplified alterations in lifestyle that occur due to deliberate or involuntary reductions in income.

Materialism: A value system emphasizing material possessions as the primary focus and source of life satisfaction.

Minimalism: Minimalism involves the deliberate reduction of consumption habits, transcending materialistic tendencies, irrespective of economic considerations, in favor of embracing a straightforward and occasionally aesthetically oriented lifestyle.

Terror Management Theory: This theory posits that in humans, being uniquely aware of mortality engenders anxiety or terror, necessitating ongoing psychological management.

Voluntary Simplicity: Encompasses a broader scope than minimalism, representing a lifestyle that opposes excessive consumption and dependency on material possessions. It involves a conscious reduction in consumer goods and services spending, aligning with simple living and downshifting principles. The core philosophy emphasizes meeting one's needs in the most straightforward and uncomplicated manner possible.

Chapter 3

Consumer Culture and the Paradox of Choice in an Ambivalent Era of Emancipation of Individual Freedoms

Ondřej Roubal
University of Finance and Administration, Czech Republic

ABSTRACT

Consumer culture in modern societies is interpreted as a culture that maximizes the freedom of consumer choice. The emancipation of individual freedoms in the form of consumer choice is positively associated with the growth of material standards of living and the affluence of a society. At the same time, an ambivalent situation arises in the form of unintended consequences, whereby customers with increasing freedoms in the areas of consumer choice run into problems making decisions and the paradox of choice, all in a landscape that is becoming less clear and oversaturated with options and opportunities. The goal is to contribute to a deeper understanding of the ambivalent character of contemporary consumer culture in the context of intensified individualization and external options for consumer choice. The authors also seek to propose a theoretical model of consumer mentalities that is more resistant to the negative effects of the paradox of choice. This model is based on the Epicurean consumption pattern of voluntary simplicity, reducing aspirations, and delayed gratification.

DOI: 10.4018/979-8-3693-1594-1.ch003

Copyright © 2024, IGI Global. Copying or distributing in print or electronic forms without written permission of IGI Global is prohibited.

INTRODUCTION

Contemporary consumer culture is characterized by ambivalence in the form of a series of paradoxes, conflicts, and all manner of contradictions (Roubal, 2023).

Among the most serious problems facing the world are growing aspirations of societies (economically developed and otherwise) in terms of quantifying their material standard of living and the desire for more intensive and stable engagement in the sphere of ordinary consumption. This is linked to a hypertrophy of the consumerist lifestyle and a progression of hedonistic values, both of which are massively supported by the marketing industry. On the other hand, this has evidently led to a reckless plundering of natural resources, enormous pollution of the planet, and irreversible climate change, situations demanding an active approach of changing human behavior and thinking (Howarth et al., 2022). According to some researchers, the Earth is even becoming a place hazardous to life (Richardson et al., 2023).

The ambivalent nature of consumer culture is not an isolated phenomenon, but a reflection of broader and deeper changes in the social reality of late modern societies undergoing globalization trends in the form of structural changes in political and social life and the universalization and unification of many areas of the market environment of economic activities. At the same time, sociologists have reported findings on the accelerated pace of life and impulsive nature of consumer-oriented societies (Roberts, 2014), transformations of value orientations and the search for alternative (more economical and environmentally conscious) forms of lifestyles (Soper 2023), or intensifying individualization and problematic identity formation (Elliot et al., 2019). Last but not least, we cannot overlook the rapid development in the areas of digitalization, technologization, automation, and robotization, or the penetration of artificial intelligence into the routine activities of everyday life, along with the series of ethical and philosophical questions and uncertain prognoses of future directions from the perspective of humanity's values (Leonhard, 2016; Bridle, 2018).

Patterns of consumption behavior are also fundamentally changing, namely in the context of various events and developments such as the COVID-19 crisis in recent years (Ayman, 2023; Satish et al., 2021; Anastasiadou et al., 2020; Loxton et al., 2020). Patterns of consumption behavior have subsequently been undergoing another wave of social, political, and economic events and unexpected developments. In the context of the war in Ukraine, the energy crisis, and rising inflation, a thesis is emerging known as the cost-of-living crisis (Lapavitsas et al., 2023; Khan, 2022).

Despite all these social, political, and economic changes, which affect the different parameters of consumer culture with varying intensity, depth, and duration, what remains constant is the trend of strengthening individual consumer freedoms and the associated progression of options for consumer choice as a condition for the

Consumer Culture and the Paradox of Choice in an Ambivalent Era

emancipation of human freedom in consumerist types of societies (B. Schwartz, 2004; Iyengar, 2010; Sharma & Nair, 2017).

First, the goal of this chapter is to explain the transformation of the consumer mentality by reinterpreting the still applicable ideas of Bauman (Bauman, 2007; 2008; 2013). We point to the ambivalent nature of the emancipation of individual freedoms, decision space, and independence with its accompanying increases in uncertainty, doubt, and the fragility of consumer identity. The consumer mentality, most likely resembling that of a hunter or a competitor, is formed in constant interactions with the institutional structures of consumer culture, authentically reflecting its contemporary ambivalent nature. At the same time, we expand on Bauman's hypothesis of the crisis of consumer integrity in terms of the extension of freedom of choice.

Secondly, we propose our own conceptual model of the mentality of the consumer as a voluntarily simplistic hunter/competitor against the background of the theory of alternative hedonism. The voluntarily simplistic hunter/competitor, in contrast to the passionate hunter/competitor typified by predatory consumerism, is characterized by a change in life attitudes approximating the philosophical agenda of Epicurean hedonism of simplicity. We expand on our hypothesis of the mentality of a consumer potentially capable of minimizing not only psychological discomfort in an environment of extension and expansion of consumer opportunities, but also of making a lasting contribution to ecological and environmental sustainability. This model consumer mentality is a theoretical construct that offers possibilities for further empirical validation in the fields of sociology, psychology, and marketing.

BACKGROUND

Over the last 20 years or so, research on what is called the paradox of choice has been growing in academic discourse as an important significant phenomenon of contemporary consumer culture comprehensively described in the work of B. Schwartz (2004). The paradox of choice is a phenomenon of research interest, especially for sociologists, social psychologists, behavioral economists, and marketing specialists. It represents an interdisciplinary object of research that acquires completely new parameters of characteristics in the rapidly changing environment of markets and shopping.

The basic theory of paradox of choice is the assertion that too many choices reduce the motivation of consumers to buy and lead to overall paralysis to make a choice. In addition, for purchasing decisions the act of choice made by consumers is accompanied by psychological discomfort in the form of uncertainty, remorse, or disappointment.

According to some studies, the freedom of consumer choice and the paradox of choice are significantly amplified in the online virtual environment of digital formats of commercial transactions. In this context, Silverman (2019) highlights the accelerated proliferation of choice in online shopping environments. At the same time, he traces changes in patterns of shopping behavior strongly influenced by digital tools enabling shopping at any time and from anywhere. According to Silverman, consumers are overwhelmed by the escalating range of products on offer and often postpone the decision to make a choice.

According to Pandey and Desai (2020), online shopping preferences are now generally increasing, particularly in the case of clothing and electronics purchases. In so doing, e-shops offer an overwhelming number of similar items and choices. At the same time, each of the products on offer is accompanied by detailed descriptions and detailed information, potentially complicating further decision-making particularly for those types of consumers looking for the best possible choice (Mittal, 2016, p. 362; Roubal, 2018, pp. 48-50).

Thus, consumers experience intense feelings of uncertainty and indecision in the online shopping environment, and they often leave e-shop sites without buying anything. Recently, consumers during the COVID-19 crisis underwent a relatively fast and fluid conversion of market activities into the cyberspace of a growing number of e-shops and online supermarkets, unconstrained by the physical space of shelves and counters. This fact is reflected in a number of recent studies focusing on changes in consumption behavior during the COVID-19 pandemic (Roggeveen & Sethuraman, 2020).

The paradox of choice has been repeatedly empirically analyzed on the practical level of the relationship between the quantity of items offered and the psychological triggering of consumer choice paralysis. Researchers search for optimal numbers of products on offer for which the paradox of choice may not yet manifest. Oulasvirta et al. (2009) experimentally manipulated the number of choices offered and observed the decision-making behavior of a total of 24 respondents in different choice situations limited to a period of 30 seconds. The authors concluded that the optimal number of possible choices was 6 items, for which respondents felt some level of satisfaction and confidence.

Kinjo and Ebina (2015) propose a proprietary mathematical model to calculate the optimal quantity of products offered by retailers in order to maximize sales, depending on the size of customers' invested costs in product selection. These authors confirm the thesis that markets in the real world and in cyberspace should adapt to a moderately sized product offering, which would lead not only to higher sales but also to much more favorable psychological effects on customer behavior.

The hypothesis that a high number of available items decreases consumer activity to make a decision and increases the likelihood of passive behavior and procrastination

Consumer Culture and the Paradox of Choice in an Ambivalent Era

to make a choice has also been confirmed by other authors (Manolică et al., 2021; Cunow et al., 2021; Adriatico et al., 2022).

Czech (2016) also reached conclusions supporting this hypothesis while studying the functioning of Swedish pension funds in recent decades. While 70 financial companies in Sweden had offered a total of 465 pension funds in 2000, this increased to 800 in 2006; by 2015, 102 companies were involved in the administration of a total of 843 pension funds in Sweden. The consequence of the increasing supply of types of pension savings was a delay in potential buyers pursuing such savings and an overall decline in pension savings contracts. For example, Google, following the recommendation of the results of one of its marketing studies, decided to increase the number of links listed on a single page when a specific password was entered. This move was oriented toward accommodating Google's customers, who had repeatedly expressed in surveys a desire to increase the amount of input when searching for information. When Google tripled the number of links per page, search and information tracking through Google began to plummet (Graves, 2013, p. 228).

And yet other, namely behavioral economics studies consider this type of paralysis and resignation from making decisions due to being overwhelmed with large volumes of choices to be rather rare (Scheibehenne et al., 2010).

The more significant problem, as they see it, is the implementation of decisions that are not only disadvantageous, but often fatally damaging to the interests of the actors themselves. This is attributed to people's limited attention spans, their easy manipulability, and the underestimation or unintentional disregard of important product parameters, referencing their price or quality. In general, the behavioral economics perspective accepts the thesis that freedom of choice is not a guarantee of an efficient decision-making process, but only the potential to achieve individual interests and goals. The effectiveness of the decision-making process is significantly impaired by the limits of people's cognitive capacities and limited attention. When cognitive resources are depleted and attention is declining, the decision-making process turns into a shallow, intuitive affair, generating many missteps. This is especially true when dealing with information, where increasing volumes of information often do not lead to more efficient solutions and decisions, but rather to suboptimal outcomes and higher overall transaction costs. However, an overload of options may not only lead to objectively worse decision outcomes, but also to negative psychological effects. Dar-Nimrod et al. (2009) empirically demonstrate that upon an increase in motivation to maximize the best possible choice and an increase in willingness to invest resources in the form of time or cognitive attention in the actual decision-making process, less satisfaction is experienced and greater disappointment accompanies each similar decision.

Kida et al. (2010) take issue with the typically psychologizing research on the paradox of choice and point out its limitations in examining the decision-making

Consumer Culture and the Paradox of Choice in an Ambivalent Era

processes of individuals regardless of their prior experience with similar decision-making situations. The authors focus on understanding the relationship between the investment decisions of individuals and the volume of investment choices in the context of whether the effect of the paradox of choice is mitigated or otherwise altered by prior investment decision experience. Kida et al. (2010) conclude that the paradox of choice, determined by an increasing volume of choices, clearly affects respondents without prior investment decision experience more. In contrast, individuals possessing investment decision-making experience were strongly resistant to the paradox of choice. In these cases, the likelihood of investing even decreased as the selection of investment options decreased. As such, their findings relativize the paradox of choice phenomenon in new contexts of knowledge.

Nikolaev and Bennett (2016) use data from the World Values Surveys (WVS) and the Economic Freedom of the World (EFW) index to provide a more detailed understanding of the relationship between people's individual perceptions of control and institutional adherence to principles of economic freedom in different countries. In so doing, they place the paradox of choice in a broader social, economic, and political context. "Higher levels of economic freedom may, however, lead to more restlessness, higher material aspirations, and decision paralysis as more responsibility is placed on the individual to make the right choice in a world with more options and uncertainty. The so called 'paradox of choice'...." (Nikolaev & Bennett, 2016, p. 40).

MAIN FOCUS OF THE CHAPTER

In affluent societies of a consumer orientation, the values of material well-being and rising living standards are closely intertwined with the notion of simultaneously maximizing people's individual freedoms. Existential security and its further strengthening and affirmation in a spiral of increasing abundance should be echoed in parallel at a similarly accelerated and progressive existential level in terms of the emancipation of human freedoms. An integral part of such freedoms is the fulfillment of the premise of a proliferation of choices and decisions in a variety of life situations. It is therefore true that the greater the plurality of choice in each individual decision-making situation, the more intense the personal freedoms people achieve. It should be added that the more freedoms there are, the greater the well-being.

One of the indicators of the emancipation of individual freedoms in the environment of consumer culture is the simultaneous maximization of choice or the variability of choice in the range of products on offer. The larger and more diverse the space of consumer choice, the more intense the feelings of personal freedom, dependent on variations in the options for making choices and exercising them independently.

Consumer Culture and the Paradox of Choice in an Ambivalent Era

It is in this logic, however, that a problem is entrenched, in the form of the paradox of choice (B. Schwartz, 2015).

The paradox of choice is precisely one of the possible manifestations of the highly ambivalent character of consumer culture, setting the scene for a confrontation of certain incompatible values and contradictory tendencies. These contradictions risk eroding consumer integrity and disrupting consumer identity. This requires adaptations in consumer behavior and deeper changes in consumer attitudes, values, lifestyles, and mentalities.

This chapter focuses on a deeper understanding of the ambivalent character of contemporary consumer culture in the context of intensified individualization and external options for consumer choice. Using Bauman's (2013) theory of liquid modernity, we detail the hypertrophied trend of individualization and identify its ambivalent features in the context of consumer behavior. Using our own metaphors, we interpret the mentality of the contemporary consumer and propose a theoretical model for an alternative consumer mentality based on adopting the principles of voluntary simplicity, reduction of consumption aspirations, and delayed gratification. We assume that changes in consumption behavior oriented towards voluntary simplicity will reduce the problem of choice and the associated negative psychological effects on the one hand and on the other hand contribute to the overall reduction of environmental and ecological burdens determined by the increasing level of consumption in consumer societies.

This chapter presents a theoretical study based on the method of critical literature review and evaluation of selected review and empirical studies focusing on the dynamics of the consumer culture of "many opportunities" and the problem of decision-making of modern consumers. The chapter is supplemented with its own theoretical model of the mentality of a contemporary consumer potentially more resilient to the conditions of overconsumption in a chaotic environment of extension of choice. This chapter is accompanied by a number of critical remarks, suggestions, and recommendations.

THE MENTALITY OF THE CONSUMER AS A PASSIONATE HUNTER/COMPETITOR

The empirical evidence on the phenomenon of the paradox of choice is very broad and inspires further research interest focused on the area of purchasing decisions. This typically takes place in the context of consumer culture, defined by the principles of the constant growth of choice as an expression of the preferred and affirmed values of individual freedoms in democratic consumerist societies. The paradox of choice on the one hand refers to a strong trend towards individualization, the desire to expand personal freedom and achieve ever higher levels of well-being and life comfort. On the other hand, the paradox of choice is an unintended consequence of the emancipation of individual freedoms and of living in conditions of material abundance, accompanied by the potential for negative economic, social, or psychological effects. Retailers and marketing departments are faced with the dilemma of adequacy of the form and volume of the range of products on offer relative to the procrastination and passivity of consumers, who often decline to take action. Psychologists have been addressing the psychological discomfort of overstretched consumers suffering from insecurity and remorse over their purchases. Sociologists examine changes in shopping patterns in the context of broader social and economic events and try to define different consumer typologies, searching for regularities and commonalities in their consumption behavior (often, unfortunately, in vain). Sociological data shows that modern consumers, despite the many negative effects proceeding from their ability to make free and independent choices, still prefer a model based on maximizing choice and independence of decision-making. The results of the Eurobarometer 508 (2021, p. 13), a sociological survey conducted in 27 EU countries, clearly indicate a preference for independence and individual freedom. The ability to make free choices about the circumstances of one's own life (i.e. including consumer choices) is important to a total of 95% of respondents.

Ideas exploring the ambiguity of the individualization process and the model of a life project imbued with an intense desire to expand personal freedoms have been brilliantly elaborated by Bauman (2001) in his sociological work. In particular, Bauman notes the hidden and rarely contemplated risks and threats of accelerated individualization and the desire for independence of the people in consumerist types of societies. His ideas are still relevant and applicable to the search for answers to some questions of consumer behavior and consumer mentality (Blackshaw, 2016).

Individualization in Liquid Times of Uncertainty

The unprecedented intensity and scale of individuation processes, which are more clearly amplified in the context of the emergence of societies of material abundance, has been the subject of sociological debates on the nature of late modernity (Roubal, 2012, pp. 9-11).

In these discussions, the approaches of Bauman (2008) dominate in particular, who is sufficiently convincing in his philosophical-sociological essays at revealing and clarifying the processes that constitute the society of late modernity and the mentality of people formed ever more profoundly by their activities within the sphere of consumerism. Bauman has come up with the term liquid modernity as an original designation of the era which contemporary late modern society is currently entering (Bauman, 2013).

Consumer Culture and the Paradox of Choice in an Ambivalent Era

Life in liquid modernity is characterized not only by the rise of radical individualism, deregulation, and privatization, and the ensuing greater degree of personal freedom, but particularly by pervasive uncertainty and unpredictability and the higher level of risk arising from this freedom.

Life increasingly resembles a work of art or a design or structure, the specific and distinctive form and expression we must achieve individually, each of us on our own. Life as a work of art is therefore increasingly in the power of individuals, who are at once the architects, builders, and investors in a single person. From this perspective, we take responsibility for the seeming project of the life scenario, its design and originality, and for providing the necessary resources for carrying it out. However, the project of the life scenario of a human in the era of late modernity is not overseen (and certainly not designed) by any higher arbiter, super-personal force, or other authority, who decides or at least judges its meaning and purpose and pointing to its further possibilities, as well as the risks of its realization. In the spirit of the theory of liquid modernity, the realization of such a project is up to us alone, and for all practical purposes there is no one else to assign to it. All the hopes and dreams in planning life scenarios, as well as fulfilling them, fall to us – individuals with ever greater freedom to choose the directions of life trajectories, and at the same time with ever greater responsibility for the consequences of possible turbulence disrupting the fluidity of the direction of these trajectories. A significant problem for us, artists and creators of our lives as a work of art, is that while we formerly used to deflect any setbacks, failures, or disappointments affecting our life trajectories towards God or fate, i.e. to higher impersonal and often abstract instances, today these "slings and arrows" are interpreted quite inexorably as the result of individual failure, insufficient effort, minimal personal preparedness, i.e. our own bankruptcy. Previously failures, disappointments, or suffering were socialized, i.e. individually judged and accepted in the context of the activities and actions of "others"/"another"; in the situation of late modernity, all this is strictly privatized, the context of "others"/"another" has disappeared in an impenetrable fog and the consequences are simply borne by each individual.

The notion of a life scenario as the smooth and seamless fulfillment and achievement of goals, hopes, and dreams is an illusion; an unforeseen situation, a "black swan" (e.g. COVID-19, the war in Ukraine, Israel's conflict with Hamas) can always emerge, forcing us to make cuts or rewrites in the carefully prepared and guarded project of the life scenario. In this case, life in the era of liquid modernity is particularly tricky. Our life trajectories, in an individualized society and an atmosphere of privatism, are at greater risk of turbulence than at any time in the past. This is namely because we are forced to confront entirely new forms of uncertainty and risk that are far more intrusive, aggressive, and insistent in our lives.

Consumer Culture and the Paradox of Choice in an Ambivalent Era

Bauman (2013) takes a generally skeptical view of the phenomenon of uncertainty in the era of late modernity. Spreading with unprecedented speed from new resource hotspots in an uncontrolled and untamed global space, it represents the pervasive danger of a quite fundamental existential threat.

It is possible to polemicize about this view. Feelings of insecurity to a certain extent can prepare you for all manner of better or lesser-known dangers and life risks (Taleb, 2014). The aforementioned "slings and arrows" then need not be perceived as lightning bolts out the blue, as something exceptional that happens only and solely to us, but as a natural part of our lives that can be counted upon to appear with some probability at some point in the future and could catch us completely unprepared. Living with uncertainty can stimulate and develop to some extent the capacity for anticipation: that is, the ability to grasp events and situations in life as they come while at the same time to some extent anticipating those events and situations. Like a chess player who must learn to think multiple moves ahead, to choose a strategy so as not to end up "in check" right at the beginning of the game. It activates efforts to guess at future states and teaches you to think ahead and consider various alternatives. We learn to live and work with the uncertainty and randomness of the conditions of existence and to identify the set of possible outcomes of our actions. In the form of risk awareness, we learn the possibilities for quantifying the probability of different alternatives from the sets of uncertainties in our environment. Awareness of uncertainty, risk, and unexpected life pitfalls can teach us to think and act strategically. Such action is always active action, where we do not leave the achievement of our set life goals to chance and fate, but strive for their own purposeful fulfillment. In this way, we also learn to take some responsibility for our actions and can effectively build self-confidence. Likewise, the ability to stay flexible is likely to develop in an environment of uncertainty, namely as a useful quality of being able to adapt, respond to new challenges, and navigate the changing world of late modernity. At the same time, however, one cannot help but agree with Bauman that flexibility cannot be accepted as a miracle panacea as accessible and effective for all as a state-of-the-art psychopharmaceutical that reduces the intensity of experiencing unbearable states of uncertainty. Nor do we agree with the ideology that flexibility in the sense of individual abilities and skills, wherein the quality of being solitary is elevated to the highest value worth aspiring to, should become a permanent and revered life strategy.

Gamekeeper, Gardener, and Hunter

Bauman provides an original metaphorical account of the transformations of a person's relationship to the world in the era of traditional, modern, and late modern societies (2007, pp. 94-104).

Consumer Culture and the Paradox of Choice in an Ambivalent Era

Man's relation to the world in the era of traditional society was in many ways different from man's relation to the world in the era of industrial modernity. The life of pre-modern man was largely governed by tradition, taking place typically in a faithfully familiar social environment of a communal nature. The world was a divinely determined network woven from individual existences, each assigned a precise position within this network, subordinate to divine purposes. Changing these positions was not easy; one was born into them, and usually died in them.

Man of the modern type believed that he could weave this God-given and ordered web himself; even better, he hoped. He sensed a chance to break free from divine predetermination of human existence and longed for the net he wove to be loose enough to allow the full emancipation of human freedom. In other words, there was no absence of the belief that the world could be changed under human guidance and, to some extent, controlled. It was faith in progress and human reason, faith in giving the world a concrete shape and filling it with clear content.

Bauman (2007) compares the relationship to the world of pre-modern man to the position of a gamekeeper. The main mission of the gamekeeper is to guard the territory entrusted to him, to protect it from any human interference, and to allow no outsiders to enter. The task of the gamekeeper is mainly to maintain the established order, the natural balance based on the very nature of nature or by order of the divine. It is indeed any interference by the human hand within the territory entrusted to it that threatens to upset this natural balance, an unwanted intervention in the natural state of harmony and peace. The gamekeeper is thus firmly convinced that the territory he guards can only function well if it is not interfered with. The gamekeeper only guards what has always existed as the unquestionable order of the natural and therefore perfect state of affairs. No human spirit simply has the right to alter the wisdom and harmony of divine purposes within such a belief.

This conviction of the gamekeeper is not, however, shared by the gardener, metaphorically symbolic of humanity in the modern world. The gardener displays a not insignificant amount of distrust of the natural and once-and-for-all determined order of the world and resolutely rejects man's passive role in that order. On the contrary, he is distinguished by his firm belief that an order to the world can only exist through his active intervention. The gardener tends his garden, deciding what will and will not grow in his garden. He carefully chooses and breeds different kinds of plants, thinks about which ones to water and fertilize, systematically searches for weeds, which he eliminates as something unwanted (that is, unwanted and unplanned by the gardener) because they are contrary to the order and harmony of the gardener's garden project. The gardener simply believes that the garden can be cultivated in a meaningful way, seeking ever more perfect forms, promoting what should flourish with his own efforts and bearing the expected fruit in the garden, as well as purposefully and systematically preventing from flourishing everything

Consumer Culture and the Paradox of Choice in an Ambivalent Era

that, according to the gardener, should not belong in his garden. The gardener feels responsible for what grows in the garden. He is in no way indifferent to whether he has enough water for watering and the necessary tools for weeding. Of course, it is always up to the gardener to decide what should and should not be in the garden.

According to Bauman (2007), in the era of contemporary consumer culture, the gardener mentality is giving way to a hunter mentality. The latter is not concerned with maintaining, the natural order as is the task of the gamekeeper, nor with maintaining the artificial order as created by the gardener. His only task is to hunt and find prey. Typical of the contemporary hunter is the fact that once he has taken the prey, he does not stop hunting and immediately concentrates on the next quarry. He does not take much interest in the hunting ground itself, does not worry about whether there is enough game in his hunting ground, does not keep track of the numbers of animals hunted, is indifferent to whether the numbers of game are replenished. The hunter moves freely through nature; he knows that it is possible to hunt in other forests, that fish can be caught in other waters. If it should ever occur to the hunter that the forests may one day be without game and the water without fish, surely these thoughts will not be a source of distress for him. Such forward-looking worries about future abundance of prey do not concern hunters, for they do not threaten today's or tomorrow's hunt. The hunter does not feel a responsibility to the hunting ground where he is currently operating, nor does he show sufficient devotion and loyalty to that ground. According to Bauman (2007, p. 96), in an era of uncertainty, we are forced to behave like hunters and the hunter mentality is literally instilled in us. To remain a hunter and not become the object of a hunting trophy means to be constantly on the move, to be alert, to alternate between the strategies of the lone hunter and the group hunter operating in a pack as needed and quite purposefully. The hunter must excel in flexibility if he is to be successful and equal to other hunters. In any case, the hunter is always as if on the run; his efforts are without end, nothing ends with the hunted prey, the purpose of his actions is the hunt itself, the aim is to remain a hunter, to keep moving and not end up as a target for the hunter's arrows. The hunter knows that the hunted prey will not relieve him of his insecurity or give him a lasting sense of happiness. He believes that the agonizing uncertainty he experiences as a hunter will only be relieved if he runs after his prey and tries to hunt it. And once he has achieved his goal, he will seek happiness in more and more similar hunts. The trouble is that once one starts hunting, hunting becomes a compulsion, an addiction, an obsession (Bauman, 2007, p. 101). Successful hunts often bring hunters only disappointment, and the idea of another hunt is their next hope. Most seductive are probably just the expectations and desires that are placed in the hunt. Once the quarry has been taken, all hopes come to an end; for the hunter, this act is not the end, but the beginning, as new hopes and new desires emerge. He can now look forward to the next hunt. The idea that this hunt should ever be ended or for some reason refused evokes terror in a hunter. To end the hunt is not to achieve satisfaction and happiness once and for all, but to be free from the uncertainties and risks of other possible hunts. On the contrary, it is a sign of personal failure for the hunter, evidence of an inability to keep up the pace and good form in the fierce competition of other hunters. The dream that the hunt will ever end is the hunter's "pavor nocturnus".

The logic of the marketing industry and the complex consumer culture is based around supporting hunters in their endless hunt by replenishing the forests with game and planting the most attractive trophy fish in rivers and streams. At the same time, none of this is the concern of hunters. Making the hunt as fun as possible, making it worthwhile to hunt tomorrow, ensuring that there is enough varied prey, that this prey is not easily accessible to all hunters equally and yet can be hit, all this and more is professionally handled by solidly paid teams of experts in communication marketing strategies. Their job is to figure out what these hunting grounds should look like. They advise and persuade hunters on how to equip themselves for the hunt, which hunting grounds are worth visiting, and what prey is worth fighting for. The hunters then need concern themselves with nothing but the hunt itself. Being on the hunt means spending a lot of time and energy chasing prey, and by hunting as a kind of entertainment, hunters may be voluntarily distracting themselves from unpleasant and unwanted thoughts such as "What if one day there is nothing to hunt?" "How many more quarries will I be able to take?" "Will I not become prey myself someday?" The hunter can thus successfully escape from thoughts of his unhappy conditions of existence, escape from uncertainty, and thus prefer the hunt to the catch itself. Keeping the hunter in action, stimulating the hunter's appetite with a variety of targets, options, and possibilities, not making the hunter wait too long before committing to the hunt, all of this is the task of communication marketing strategies whose effects in social space contribute to what can be described as the hunter mentality.

Referee, Coach, and Competitor (An Alternative to Bauman's Metaphors)

We can now try to replace Bauman's metaphors of the gamekeeper, the gardener, and the hunter with the alternative metaphors of the referee, the coach, and the competitor. The referee, like the gamekeeper, guards a certain order; in this case, the referee oversees the rules that the competitors must unconditionally follow in order to continue the game. The authority of the referee as enforcer of the rules of the game is unquestionable. Upon the breaking of the rules of the game by any of the participants, the referee has the right to punish or even expel the competitor from the game according to these rules. Each competitor has a strictly defined space within

Consumer Culture and the Paradox of Choice in an Ambivalent Era

which he can move; the coach does not discuss with the referee the correctness of his verdicts. They believe in the sanctity of the rules, a predetermined order that both coaches and competitors follow. It is the referee's job to not allow coaches or competitors to interfere with these rules or change them during the course of the game.

The coach (gardener) believes he can influence much during the game. He discusses innovations in the game rules with a committee of referees, suggests changes, and hopes to construct the racecourse himself next time. Above all, however, he is concerned about the fitness of his charges, trying to encourage the able and promising specimens and prescribing double training allotments for the weaker ones. He believes that the performance of his charges is entirely in his control and the final outcome of the match depends on how he can prepare his team. The rules increasingly adapt to the needs of the competitors, catering to the demands of the spectators, pursuing an increase in the attractiveness of the matches.

However, the mentality of the coaches, the leaders and creators of team spirit whose goal is to achieve the final victory, is giving way to the mentality of the competitors (the hunters). The latter are emancipating themselves from their coaches, and are increasingly setting their own training allotments. Their loyalty to the team is minimal, and they only reluctantly participate in building team spirit. They have no problem transferring from club to club; they simply go wherever they can get a better contract. To compete in one team and defend its colors for an entire sporting career is utopian. They try to play in such a way as to remain active for as long as possible; they enjoy the game, any wins are just a challenge to take on more games. They don't play and compete to achieve some final and definitive victory. Their desire to compete never ends, just as their endless toil and drive to win never end. Nothing ends with victory for a competitor; they desire above all to continue playing, competing, and contending, to move in the peloton of the rest, to stay in their lane, not to go off the track prematurely or end up on the bench. Once they slow down, they risk becoming spectators, those who stand passively behind the fence, merely frantically shouting.... but never to enjoy the thrill of a race right from the track.

According to Bauman (2008, p. 121), the mentality of the hunter or the competitor corresponds to the contemporary unprecedented expansion of individual opportunities for choice and the hope of achieving ever greater quantities, varieties, and types of consumption targets and commercial pleasure. Hunter/competitors crave the entertainment they seek in the hunt/competition itself, they seek thrills and all sorts of emotional stimuli, and therefore prefer to be in unexplored areas full of game, or where they can expect the most attractive sporting experiences. The world of the hunter is the colorful world of the hunting ground. The world of the competitor is the adventurous field of competition. Needless to say, the managers of hunting grounds as well as those of sporting arenas are the marketing industry actors pursuing the economic interests of companies. Consumer culture and consumer lifestyle thus act as a force shaping types of hunter/competitor mentalities.

A CRISIS OF CONSUMER INTEGRITY

Where should we look for the social sources of liquid life scenarios that on the one hand bring more choices based on individual life strategies and on the other bring greater uncertainty and anxiety that cannot be resolved otherwise than by again using individual, and therefore necessarily limited, resources?

The nature of consumer culture increasingly demands of its members a more flexible ability to maneuver not only in an environment of expanding choices, but also to navigate between a range of incompatible values and conflicting stimuli. On the one hand, consumers are exposed to a myriad of temptations and desires for experiences, with marketing and advertising campaigns becoming ever more sophisticated at convincing them of the attractiveness of various products, while on the other hand the same products are burdened with a number of risks in the form of unwanted (and unintended) side effects. The pursuit of new joys and pleasures in life brings with it a bitter aftertaste, namely the fear and uncertainty of the possible risks that these joys and pleasures may entail. It is as if every pleasure that the hunter/competitor can indulge in has at heart a kind of signum diabolicum. A crisis of consumer integrity can arise precisely in a situation where repulsiveness is an integral part of any attraction. In other words, when a balance has been gained between attraction and repulsion as opposing stimuli.

This ambivalence of hunters/competitors as professional consumers is perhaps most marked nowadays in the food and gastronomy sector. Television programs, magazines, and books on the culinary arts proliferate and ever more sophisticated recipes and guides to enjoying dishes to the fullest and delighting in their aromas and more refined flavors continue to appear. Professionals and laymen alike race through the media with recipes that reveal their culinary skills and awaken the gourmet potential of their audiences through the television screen. And yet diet books are also being produced at a similarly rapid pace, whereas television stations are broadcasting popular reports warning viewers about the dangers of food and the side effects of various chemicals and food ingredients. Doctors, nutritionists, and other advisors raise the warning finger against dangerous fats, sugars, and extra calories under the slogan "you are digging your own grave with a fork". Paradoxically, however, these very different messages accentuate a common denominator – le souci de soi (take care of yourself) – and use identical marketing slogans such as "you owe it to yourself"; "you deserve it"; "do it for yourself"; "go your own way"; "go for the goal", etc.

Consumer Culture and the Paradox of Choice in an Ambivalent Era

Just as the erosion of consumer integrity can be seen in the food and gastronomy sectors due to conflicting calls to action, similarly schizophrenic consumer tendencies can be observed to some extent in the sex industry. While in the former case consumers metaphorically choose between anorexia and bulimia, in the latter case they choose between promiscuity and celibacy. Books with instructions for a better and richer sex life and new sexual adventures compete in the same stores and on the bookstore shelves with publications devoted to the possible health risks of sex and, last but not least, with moral appeals to maintain lasting partnerships, fidelity, and love. The advice of experts on how to achieve more intense sexual experiences and greater sexual performance coexists with the advice of other (and in some cases even the same) experts pointing out the possible undesirable risks of such activities (e.g. health, social, psychological). Some recommend action, others abstinence. Viagra from one side, contraception from the other.

The crisis of consumer integrity is to some extent exacerbated by another phenomenon. Advertising campaigns and the marketing industry as a whole do not limit messaging to potential consumers to the functionality and objective parameters of products, but rather endeavor to focus on intangible values. They disseminate visions, emotionality, and metaphoricity, i.e. symbolic systems that are in no way related to the functional and practical reality of products (Lipovetsky, 2007, p. 52).

They seek to offer a lifestyle through their products, one often identified with a better, more successful, more attractive, more active, and overall happier life. The problem, of course, is that these marketing-produced incentives for a happier and better quality of life for consumers are fleeting, disappearing as quickly as they appear, subject to constant innovation and change. Just as quickly as marketing communications inscribe new visions in their commercial messages and play with consumers' imaginations, the desires of these consumers and their ideas of happiness can change accordingly. What guaranteed a happier and more contented life yesterday may not be true today. It is as if the creativity of the creators of advertising campaigns is designed to keep consumers, the hunters/competitors, in suspense and uncertainty as to where or on what they will direct their future desires and ideas for a better life. Recall that the point of this is to keep the hunter hunting and the competitor in the game, i.e., hope that the hunt and the game are not over and have many more acts to go. Indeed, markets are subtly shifting the dream of happiness from the notion of a fulfilled and wholly satisfying life to the pursuit of the means deemed necessary to achieve such a life, taking care that the pursuit never ends.

The consumer thus becomes a long-distance runner, never knowing what route he or she will take or whether he or she will even reach the finish line. The important thing is to stay on track. Hunters/competitors, in fact, do not run along the clearly marked lane of a stadium running track or a well-trodden hunting trail, where the distance of the route is clearly predetermined and where you can see the finish

Consumer Culture and the Paradox of Choice in an Ambivalent Era

line or the quarry to be hunted. At the same time, competitors can only dream of a bell signaling the last lap of the run. Their run is an orienteering run, where they diligently search for individual checkpoints and once they reach these points, they run to the next one. The route of the orienteering run is drawn up by sophisticated professionals, experienced course commissioners who, with a creativity all their own, think through the positions of the checkpoints and twist the route in every possible way for the consumers. As they do so, the course must not become too difficult to allow as many competitors as possible to run, nor too easy and accessible to all to make it worth racing. It must also be attractive enough to make it worthwhile to stay on the course. The maps they run on are very imperfect, become outdated during the race, and the runner often has to figure it out on their own. And if they don't know what to do, where or to whom should a confused and uncertain orienteer turn? Are there still any places on the maps that can be trusted? Consumers with a hunter/competitor mentality have no choice but to rely on their own skills and flexibly adapt to a life of uncertainty.

The Extension of Freedom of Choice

In contemporary consumer culture, the values of material wealth are linked to the notion of simultaneously maximizing people's individual freedoms and independence (B. Schwartz, 2004, p. 304).

Rising living standards and opportunities for more frequent and intensive participation in various forms of shopping and product consumption correspond to growing demands for the emancipation of consumers' individual freedoms. The defining characteristic of individual consumer freedoms is not only the universalized possibility to participate actively in shopping processes as often as possible and without restrictions, but in particular the proliferation of shopping platforms with an extensive range of product choices. It is therefore true that the greater the plurality of choice in each individual decision-making situation, the more intense the personal freedoms people achieve. The more individual freedoms consumers have, the greater their prosperity and the higher their living standards.

The extension of product choice is characterized by its ambivalent nature. It liberates and emancipates a consumer with a hunter/competitor mentality within his or her possibilities for free and authentic decision-making, becoming a standard feature of the consumerist type of life under conditions of affluence. At the same time, this extension of choice is a source of doubt and uncertainty, crippling decision-making and generally undermining the integrity of consumers often confused by the complexity of the offering and mutually competing products (Mayol & Staropoli, 2021).

Consumer Culture and the Paradox of Choice in an Ambivalent Era

In the spirit of rational choice theory, this is an uncomplicated situation, as each individual decision, and each specific choice, responds to a relatively stable hierarchy of priorities and preferences of the social actor (Scott, 2000).

Consumers then rationally apply such a system in every similar situation requiring an act of choice, regardless of the number of options that need to be compared and evaluated against each other in the exercise of choice. In such a perspective, the hunter/competitor is a type of consumer maximizing their own utility in each choice situation, and each decision is the result of rational deliberation, optimizing the outcome of their choice (Hedström & Stern, 2017).

In addition to economic theories of rational consumer decision making, there is another alternative perspective, among others, that explains consumer decision-making in an environment with a proliferation of choice as less problematic (Soper, 2023, p. 65). The diversity of product offerings in different types, variants, or modifications is a stable imperative for business success and a guarantee of profit, but the emphasis on this variability ultimately leads to the mutual differentiation of products and their marketing presentations end up being much less clear, their functions and practical parameters become more similar, and customers are essentially unable to distinguish the specific benefits of products of different types and brands in similar price ranges.

Accepting such a hypothesis would, however, presuppose that customers are aware of this fact and subjectively perceive the choice outcomes as optimal in a real or imaginary comparison to other alternative product choices and their potential effects. They will continue to adapt their decision-making across a broad spectrum of offerings, reduce time and cognitive investment in the process of making a buying decision, stop making complex product comparisons, simplify the overall process of choice, and avoid psychological discomfort as a result of that choice. This hypothesis is most often tested using models of consumption types referred to as "maximizers" and "satisficers" (Barta, Gurrea & Flavián, 2023; Khare, Chowdhury & Morgan, 2021; Coba, Rook, Zanker & Symeonidis, 2018; Kim & Miller, 2017; Cheek & Schwartz, 2016).

Contemporary consumer culture is not characterized solely by accelerated quantification of types, variants, and models of consumption goals. Product variation runs in parallel with the proliferation of impersonal digital shopping platforms (Lury, 2011, p. 245).

A robust conversion is taking place, whereby conventional product offerings, traditionally determined by physical store parameters and personal interactions between sellers and shoppers, are being moved into the virtual environment of digitized shopping. The online environment of consumer activities is not limited by the space or physical capacity of points of sale and shelves. It does not require the physical presence of shoppers, is not restricted to business hours, and eliminates

Consumer Culture and the Paradox of Choice in an Ambivalent Era

customer transaction costs associated with transportation, waiting in line, or parking. The virtual shopping environment is an attractive alternative not only because of the reduction of customer transaction costs associated with personal presence in stores, but also because of the volume of the assortment of goods on offer. Shelves, display windows, and sales floors in digitized shopping formats are undergoing a fundamental transformation and acquiring completely new features of virtual sales and design of product offerings. The digitalization of shopping formats clearly accelerated in the COVID-19 crisis of 2020-2021, when the forced conversion of conventional shopping to a virtual environment took place due to broad-based lockdowns. The confrontation of customers with an abundance of supply has been intensified in the context of online shopping, with virtually no alternative in the form of physical shopping, which is often hampered by a limited range of products compared to e-shops. During the COVID-19 pandemic, it was expected according to some studies based on public opinion survey data tracking changes in consumption behavior that a progression would be evident of the paradox of choice in the form of increased levels of shopper procrastination (Smith & Machova, 2021).

Virtual shopping conditions are not only potentially more creative, fun, interactive, varied, and comfortable, but also much more psychologically complicated, not infrequently inducing negative psychological experiences. In digital shopping formats that accelerate the variability of choices also increase the opportunity cost of sacrificing. This is a situation where, as the number of options increases, the satisfaction of each individual decision decreases. For each individual choice at the same time means the rejection of other opportunities and options that remain unrecognized, unused, and untried.

In this context, Masatlioglu and Suleymanova (2021) search for adequate consumer decision-making strategies in the shopping process that could practically optimize the results of the choice made, saving time and other investments by overloaded customers in an environment of extensive supply of different types of products. They propose an extension of the constrained search model, where the customer does not have to browse and compare all available choices and terminate this search prematurely.

While psychologists and sociologists offer various sophisticated models and theoretical constructs of customer decision-making processes, these find application more within scientific discourse, academic levels of thought, or marketing applications and business strategies. They do not yet penetrate so much into the practical realm of customer behavior changes, routine shopping patterns, and everyday consumer decision-making. Nor do such models address the practical problems of maintaining the integrity of satisfied customers who are faced with uncertainty, cognitive dissonance, psychological turmoil, inner tension, or feelings of disappointment, remorse, or regret over decisions made.

THE MENTALITY OF THE VOLUNTARILY SIMPLISTIC HUNTER/COMPETITOR

The consumer mentality, metaphorically identified with the mentality of the passionate hunter/competitor, corresponds to the value orientation of unbridled individualism, based on the search for hedonistic pleasure and enjoyment (S. H. Schwartz, 1994).

This type of consumer is oriented towards the present and a preference for fulfillment of sensual pleasures. This mentality is characterized by activity, restlessness, impulsiveness, and willingness to spend. It is moderated by the imperative "enough is never enough" and the principle "more is better". The consumer culture of many opportunities and the accelerated emancipation of individual freedoms confirm and deepen this mentality. However, the unintended negative effects of the extensive environment of freedom of choice in the form of increasing uncertainty, doubt, dissatisfaction, oversaturation, disorientation, disillusionment, disappointment, and other possible feelings of psychological discomfort also come to bear in full force on the passionate hunter/competitor. There are interesting attempts in some philosophical and sociological theories to call attention to the potential for changing consumer lifestyles and mentalities, leading to a more enjoyable, high-quality, and meaningful life, filled with joy and more respectful of self, family, society, and nature. In this context, the theory of alternative hedonism (Soper, 2023), an authentically inspiring model of the mentality of the voluntarily simplistic consumer, is promoted in particular.

Alternative Hedonism captures the many contradictions and risks within the very practices of predatory consumerism, moderated by the mentality of passionate hunter/competitors. It questions the mechanisms of its social support as well as its specific effects on the social, ethical, environmental, and psychological levels of human existence. Like Epicureanism before it, alternative hedonism emphasizes the principles of moderate, temperate, prudent, and considerate living, without, however, resigning to a life theme of "enjoyment". Alternative Hedonism, like Epicureanism, does not consist of ascetic programs of renunciation and radical self-limitation. On the contrary, their theme is fulfilling the potential of life's pleasures where the paths to those pleasures are more accessible and generally more conscientious of self and the environment. Alternative hedonism presupposes creativity and courage, being Epicureanly indifferent to the volatile goals of consumption promoted by marketing. This can liberate and free one's capacities towards activities that lead to a higher level of personal satisfaction and enjoyment in life. It moves away from the ideal of the "perfect consumer", ready at any time to shop and accumulate sensory pleasures in the episodic series of the experience economy. It does not accumulate things or superficial experiences. It seeks a slower pace of life, realizes the value of interpersonal relationships, silence, stillness, and nature, and appreciates the sensations of physical exertion or a job well done. It limits activities in the online world, replacing these with more physical proximity and personal contact. It replaces the luxury of consumer goods with restrained consumption and delayed gratification. Alternative Hedonism, like Epicureanism, thus does not lack calm alongside moderation.

Here the theory of alternative hedonism is the starting point for a possible solution to the problems of consumer integrity under the conditions of the extension of freedom of choice and the culture of "overchoice". It is against the background of alternative hedonism and its value-oriented type of lifestyle that we propose a concept for the mentality of the voluntarily simplistic hunter/competitor, drawing on several interrelated principles. The mentality of the voluntarily simplistic consumer is value-oriented towards attitudes of non-ascetic restraint, willingness to reduce consumption aspirations, and a motivation toward delayed gratification.

Voluntary Simplicity

The first and also the dominant principle is voluntary simplicity as one of the fundamental lifestyle concepts (Librova, 2016, p. 47).

The voluntarily simplistic consumer prefers the principle "less is more" and changes an orientation towards the present into an orientation towards the future. However, this is not a type of "negative consumer" who actively boycotts consumption and protests consumerism. Voluntary simplicity does not lack the drive of asceticism. It is based on a non-ascetic approach to life, preferring the principle of "enjoyment", albeit within a rationally limited range of physical and mental pleasures, following the ancient tradition of the philosophical agenda of the hedonistic school of the Epicureans, or the cynics and the skeptics. The voluntarily simplistic consumer turns away from material values towards the immaterial sphere of existence and finds a place in the sphere of social relations, aesthetics, and spiritual values. A life motivation of frugality and restraint and of being undemanding in terms of material goods and considerate of others, represents an appealing and pleasurable alternative to the hurried style of consumerism and brings joy and inner satisfaction. The typical orientation here is towards aesthetic values, religious currents, and individual fulfillment of spiritual needs. It lacks the more pronounced manifestations of subcultural life, the collective dimension of civil engagement movements, publicly criticizing the unethical practices of companies and boycotting their products. Instead, it is based on variously adapted individual strategies of consumer behavior and non-conflict initiatives of direct support for ethical purchasing. The principle of voluntary simplicity is "living richly by frugal means" (Roubal, 2022, p. 119). Voluntary simplicity can, under certain conditions in a situation of hypertrophy of freedom of choice, reduce the risks of erosion of consumer integrity and dampen

Consumer Culture and the Paradox of Choice in an Ambivalent Era

negative feelings about the choices made. While the voluntarily simplistic consumer often remains involuntarily exposed to an extension of product choices, the choice itself is only made in the case of those products that generally meet the criteria of ethical purchasing and thrift. This means that voluntary simplicity does not lead to frequent and impulsive shopping or to active searching and comparison of different offers in a chaotic environment of shopping opportunities. Rather, consumption patterns of voluntary simplicity are moderated by indifference and mild passivity towards routine shopping and consumption attitudes. While the passionate consumer decides what type of product to buy and searches hard for the most interesting and attractive option, the voluntarily simplistic consumer decides whether to buy anything at all. Voluntarily simplistic shopping is much more motivated by practical needs and rational considerations of frugality, ethical, and environmental principles than by egoistic desires to achieve subjective wants, unrestrained whims, and fleeting experiences. In such a perspective, excessive volumes of product types may not be such a burdensome circumstance for the voluntarily simplistic consumer. His or her attention is usually oriented beyond the confines of store sales platforms, replete with customer reviews and marketing product descriptions, to the more intangible values of a life of frugality, conscientiousness toward nature, and social relationships.

Reducing Aspirations

Consumer aspirations are rising in parallel with conditions of material affluence, rising living standards, and the expansion of opportunities for consumer choice (B. Schwarz 2004). In essence, rising consumer aspirations respond to what consumers would like to achieve in terms of consumption. The aspirations of shoppers are powerfully influenced by a marketing communication complex, particularly for advertising communications, that is increasingly sophisticated, pervasive, original, and ubiquitous. The media productions of the advertising industry intensively promote a value orientation of consumerist hedonism that initiates purchasing and awakens the ethos of "a life of unlimited possibilities", "a world without limits", "a life of endless opportunities", or "life as a show that never ends". The atmosphere of material abundance and advertisements convincing the need for the most intense consumer participation in the shopping carousel create the impression that the intensity of consumption activities determines not only the individual dimensions of meaningfulness of life and identity, but also the related social parameters of life in the form of recognition and respect for one's environment. The problem is that the imaginary worlds of advertising create considerable expectations of what we should achieve, while the reality of everyday life reveals only what we actually achieve. The deeper the gap between expectations and reality, the more the integrity of the consumer is compromised. The passionate hunter/competitor consumer is obsessed

Consumer Culture and the Paradox of Choice in an Ambivalent Era

with the atmosphere of consumer hedonism and interprets aspirations in the field of consumption as a challenge to achieve them. The voluntarily simplistic consumer is generally lax in responding to such advertising appeals, unwilling to aspire to the never-ending hedonistic pleasures of the shopping carousel. Reducing consumer aspirations is also an important step towards reducing the risk of disappointment and disillusionment arising from the gap between the expected level of material life and reality. This is also true in decision-making situations: the lower the expectation of the outcome of the choice, the less potential disappointment, doubt, and regret from the opportunity cost of the sacrificed opportunities.

Delayed Gratification

Under the developed ethos of predatory hedonism, the cult of instant gratification, and the marketing-supported mentality of consumers as avid hunters/competitors living in the episodic present, we often search in vain for more pronounced and frequent manifestations of what many economists refer to as "anticipated utility". Some empirical studies by behavioral economists analyze this phenomenon and point to its preference in various life situations. For example, people would ideally wait 3 days for a kiss or a week for dinner at a French restaurant (Loewenstein & Prelec, 1993, p. 95). Thus, these are situations in which immediate consumption of a good gives way to delayed, later consumption. It turns out that some consumption goals evoke such strong feelings of enjoyment that the preference for deferred consumption over immediate consumption proves to be subjectively preferable from a psychological point of view. Thus, subjective feelings of delight, enjoyment, and pleasure may not only be brought about by excessive and immediate consumption, but also by delayed gratification. This can consist of a long-term planned purchase, with a responsible approach to the household budget and the concentration of sufficiently large savings. Delayed gratification, in the form of a specific purchase, is typically future-oriented, based on self-control, the ability to resist instant gratification, and a willingness to forgo the possibility of immediate gratification. According to Bauman, delayed gratification is a real sacrifice for people in the rapidly changing environment of consumer society and under the pressure to immediately satisfy subjective needs and fulfill desires (Bauman, 2008, p. 23). A willingness to make such sacrifices is heavily integrated into the mentality of voluntarily simplistic consumers. Increased self-control and self-regulation of consumption behavior, preventing succumbing to the tempting impulses of instant gratification, brings several benefits. The voluntarily simplistic consumer can look forward to delayed gratification, develop fantasies and imaginations of their own, and live in the pleasant expectation that something positive, new, and interesting is yet to come. This is not the passivity or procrastination typical of the paradox of choice, but thoughtful, responsible, and deliberate planning for the future, what to buy and when. The strategy of delayed gratification is not only psychologically pleasurable but also effective in an environment of hypertrophy of choice. Delayed gratification, realized in the future in the form of a planned purchase, is also a postponement of choice and thus a postponement of the often unproductive and exhausting search and comparison of the most appropriate purchase alternative. When reducing the aspiration for the outcome of the choice, it may be a functional combination of consumption behavior that will not be under such frequent decision-making pressure in a chaotic environment of different product types and variants.

SOLUTIONS AND RECOMMENDATIONS

The theoretical model of the mentality of the voluntarily simplistic consumer represents a defensive strategy of adaptive behavior in an environment of extension of freedom of choice and consumerist ethos. It is characterized by the potential for some resistance to the paradox of choice and the associated elimination or at least mitigation of negative psychological experiences associated with the exercise of choice in an oversaturated purchasing environment. The sources of such a mentality can be sought firstly in the ancient tradition of the philosophical agenda of Epicureanism, which focused on individual values of life, promoting the ideas of frugality, restraint, rationality, and prudence. In the spirit of Epicureanism, the achievement of a happy life is alleged to be threatened by growing life aspirations: the desire for possessions, experiences, and entertainment, which correspond to the contemporary atmosphere of consumer-oriented societies. Secondly, there is the inspiration of the theory of alternative hedonism (Soper, 2023), which indirectly reflects some of the principles of Epicureanism. Similarly, far from being an ascetic program, alternative hedonism merely seeks and recommends other ways of achieving life's joys and pleasures in a more creative, accessible, economical, and conscientious way. Alternative hedonism presupposes not only an expansion of one's own creativity, but also a certain degree of indifference to the fleeting goals of commercial consumption initiated by marketing. The consumer should reduce shopping opportunities, not waste time and energy on detailed product selection, and devote much more attention and effort to the care of one's own health, family, and interpersonal relationships. Both Epicureanism and alternative hedonism directly promote life orientations that conform to the axiom "less is more". A third source of possible inspiration for the mentality of the voluntarily simplistic consumer are the contemporary theoretical-empirical models such as liquid consumption (Beretta, Miniero & Ricotta, 2021; Bardhi & Eckhardt, 2017; Ritzer & Rey, 2016). Liquid consumers are a modern type of consumer whose consumption patterns correspond to the principles of the sharing economy, rationalized purchasing, frugality, and saving behavior. These are

Consumer Culture and the Paradox of Choice in an Ambivalent Era

consumers who are oriented on the future and sustainability, not insisting on owning things and accumulating them. Their consumption patterns are based on an approach of ephemeral and dematerialized consumption and flexibility and elastic adaptability to a rapidly changing market environment. A fourth possible underpinning of the voluntarily simplistic consumer can be found in the profile of consumers referred to as "satisficers" in various sociological and social psychology studies (Jain, Bearden & Filipowicz, 2013; Weaver, Daniloski, Schwarz & Cottone, 2015; Khare, Chowdhury & Morgan, 2021; Barta, Gurrea & Flavián, 2023). Consumers of the satisficer type are typically confronted with a type of consumer labeled maximizers and these are examined as mutually opposed customer models. In their mutual confrontation, various circumstances of the consumer decision-making process, choice, and the social and psychological context of shopping are examined. Satisficers are interpreted as less demanding and more frugal consumers who, unlike maximizers, do not invest as much time in selecting products and comparing them with each other. Their criterion of choice is what can be subjectively perceived and experienced as "good enough". Satisficers, according to available empirical studies, are less sensitive to feelings of disappointment and remorse and, on the contrary, achieve higher levels of satisfaction with the outcome of their choice than maximizers (Polman, 2010; Oishi, Tsutsui, Eggleston & Galinha, 2014; Barta, Gurrea & Flavián 2023).

The combination of the interconnections between the concepts of Epicureanism, alternative hedonism, liquid consumption, and the satisficers consumer type can authentically complete and constitute the profile of the voluntarily simplistic consumer defined by frugality, willingness to reduce consumption aspirations and delayed gratification, and greater resistance to disappointment and regret over choices made. This type of consumer ought to be much more resistant to disintegrating forces of the market, including the paradox of choice. But even this model has its limitations.

First, it is a theoretical model of an "ideal type" of consumer mentality, requiring further empirical verification. A voluntarily simplistic consumer may adapt consumption patterns differently in the context of specific purchasing situations, apply combinations of different consumption strategies depending on the type of products, and simultaneously change consumption postures at different stages of life and external events. Some attributes defining voluntary simplicity may dominate, while others may recede or disappear altogether due to changes in consumers' life circumstances.

Secondly, the model is dependent on individual and intrinsically motivated decisions to change consumption attitudes and reasons for putting such attitudes into practice in everyday life and continuing to maintain them. Adopting a more frugal and economical mode of material life may be experienced as a voluntary abdication of certain types of pleasures, life joys, and experiences, an unnecessary and impractical self-limitation, and a reduction of prestige in the eyes of others. At the same time, the voluntary suppression of consumer aspirations is difficult and is only marginally attractive in the face of the massive influence of marketing and advertising in the areas of lifestyle and values. Moreover, in a situation where, in consumer societies, the level of consumption is the source of constructing human identity, the reduction of consumption aspirations can act as a complicating factor in its formation, often depending on the forms and intensity of consumption (Sassatelli, 2019). Even the motif of delayed gratification may not be appealing in an ethos of predatory hedonism of immediate gratification of needs and wants. Promoting the principles of delayed gratification is not in the commercial interests of the impersonal institutionalized structures that shape the consumer spirit, directing all efforts towards quick economic gains. Nor need it be in the interests of the consumers themselves, who would need to slow down the merry-go-round, ease the pace of spasmodic scampering from experience to experience, and forgo opportunities that may not reappear in the future.

FUTURE RESEARCH DIRECTION

In the field of sociological and marketing research, there should be much more intensive empirical monitoring of changes in consumer mentality under the conditions of the consumer culture of "many opportunities" and the search for alternative consumption patterns. Specifically, empirical studies should focus on identifying and analyzing motives for voluntary simplicity in the context of broader changes in lifestyles and consumer attitudes as individually beneficial and meaningful strategies that at the same time emphasize notions of ecological and environmental sustainability. There is a need to look for closer connections and relationships between voluntary simplicity of the Epicurean type and the related and similar attitudes of alternative hedonism and liquid consumers and satisficers. The phenomenon of delayed gratification, which has been studied only minimally in marketing yet could become a sought-after shopping pattern by a significant proportion of customers, requires special empirical attention based on a combination of quantitative and qualitative sociological methods. Research attention could, for example, focus on customer attitudes towards waiting lists for luxury goods or ordinary online shopping where certain time zones are created between ordering and delivery. How do these time zones affect customers? Alternative hedonism, as well as the development of ethical consumption and life minimalism, for example, or the rise and popularity of projects such as Slow Cities, Slow Living, Slow Travelling, or Slow Food and popular civic initiatives such as Zero Waste Life or Buy Nothing Day indicate a more significant change in the mentality of consumers and a willingness not to accept the principles of hypertrophied consumerism underlying societies of material wealth. At the same time, there is a need to analyze in greater detail the population of marketing managers and specialists whose activities, developed through various strategies of integrated marketing communication, certainly contribute to changes in the consumer mentality and partially form its appearance.

CONCLUSION

Consumers represent active actors of markets, entering into mutual interactions with producers and sellers, as well as with an impersonal system of the institutionalized effects of integrated marketing communication. Many complex processes take place in these interactions, on the one hand influencing consumption patterns and consumer behavior, attitudes, preferences, and last but not least purchasing decision-making strategies, on the other hand actively adapting event the formats of communication campaigns, marketing, and advertising to changes in the social environment of customers, as well as production and distribution strategies. These dynamic and changing interactions also model different types of consumer behavior and reinforce different formats of consumer mentalities, defined by life values, lifestyles, and identity. Despite this ambiguity and diversity, we can identify a common feature of the consumer culture of late modern societies. This is the expansion of consumption opportunities and the flourishing of consumer choices in the purchasing environment as a direct response to a longer and deeper trend of individualization and the promotion of a world of value fulfilled by authenticity and independence. In this situation, an ambivalent situation arises, which has been documented by many sociological and social psychological studies. The rising material standard of living, defined significantly by the quantity of consumer choices, is not only an attractive and desirable circumstance of consumer life and an expression of well-being, but also conforms to more general notions about the need to expand and strengthen individual freedoms. At the same time, the expansion of consumer choice places increased demands on consumers' cognitive abilities, requires considerable investment of time and attention, and produces negative psychological effects in the form of reduced levels of satisfaction or regret or disappointment with the choice made. The paradox of choice appears to be one of the possible factors contributing to the erosion of the integrity of the overwhelmed and disoriented customer.

According to Bauman (2007), the human mentality in the era of liquid modernity can be compared to that of a hunter. This consists essentially of a type of thinking and acting that corresponds to the mentality of a predatory hedonist, a consumer of the consumerist type who seeks excitement, sensual pleasures, accumulating things and experiences, immodest, determined to pursue every next experience, willing to spend, oriented towards the present. Here we interpret the hunter type mentality in our own way and find an alternative in the metaphor of the competitor. The hunter/competitor consumer mentality corresponds to an offensive "more is better" shopping strategy. In the context of the risks of erosion of consumer integrity due to the ambivalent nature of consumer culture, we propose our own theoretical model of the mentality of the voluntarily simplistic hunter/competitor, a more resilient, considerate, creative, and above all, more satisfied consumer who is at the same time better able to cope with an environment of accelerated volumes of choices. The voluntarily simplistic consumer implements a defensive strategy and adheres to the principle of "less is more". In addition to frugality, this type of consumer is characterized by a willingness to voluntarily reduce consumption aspirations and a preference for delayed gratification as an aspect of future orientation. The inspiration here comes from the ancient tradition of the philosophical agenda of Epicureanism, the theory of alternative hedonism, liquid consumption, and the type of consumers known as satisfiers.

ACKNOWLEDGMENT

The result was created with the use of institutional support for long-term conceptual development of research of the University of Finance and Administration.

REFERENCES

Adriatico, J. M., Cruz, A., Tiong, R. C., & Racho-Sabugo, C. R. (2022). An analysis on the impact of choice overload to consumer decision paralysis. *Journal of Economics, Finance and Accounting Studies*, *4*(1), 55–75. doi:10.32996/jefas.2022.4.1.4

Anastasiadou, E., Chrissos Anestis, M., Karantza, I., & Vlachakis, S. (2020). The coronavirus' effects on consumer behavior and supermarket activities: Insights from Greece and Sweden. *The International Journal of Sociology and Social Policy*, *40*(9/10), 893–907. doi:10.1108/IJSSP-07-2020-0275

Ayman, U. (2023). *A New Era of Consumer Behavior-In and Beyond the Pandemic*. IntechOpen. doi:10.5772/intechopen.100829

Bardhi, F., & Eckhardt, G. M. (2017). Liquid consumption. *The Journal of Consumer Research*, *44*(3), 582–597. doi:10.1093/jcr/ucx050

Barta, S., Gurrea, R., & Flavián, C. (2023). The double side of flow in regret and product returns: Maximizers versus satisficers. *International Journal of Information Management*, *71*(4), 102648. doi:10.1016/j.ijinfomgt.2023.102648

Bauman, Z. (2001). *The Individualized Society*. Polity Press.

Bauman, Z. (2007). *Liquid times: Living in an Age of Uncertainty*. Polity Press.

Bauman, Z. (2008). *The art of life*. Polity Press.

Bauman, Z. (2013). *Liquid modernity*. John Wiley & Sons.

Beretta, E., Miniero, G., & Ricotta, F. (2021). Consumers' journey between liquid and solid consumption. *Sustainability (Basel)*, *13*(24), 13730. doi:10.3390/su132413730

Blackshaw, T. (2016). Bauman on consumerism–living the market-mediated life. In *The Sociology of Zygmunt Bauman* (2nd ed., pp. 117–136). Routledge.

Bridle, J. (2018). *New Dark Age: Technology and the End of the Future*. Verso Books.

Cheek, N. N., & Schwartz, B. (2016). On the meaning and measurement of maximization. *Judgment and Decision Making*, *11*(2), 126–146. doi:10.1017/S1930297500007257

Coba, L., Zanker, M., Rook, L., & Symeonidis, P. (2018). Decision making of maximizers and satisficers based on collaborative explanations. *arXiv preprint arXiv*:1805.11537.

Cunow, S., Desposato, S., Janusz, A., & Sells, C. (2021). Less is more: The paradox of choice in voting behavior. *Electoral Studies*, *69*(1), 102230. doi:10.1016/j.electstud.2020.102230

Czech, S. (2016). Choice overload paradox and public policy design. The case of swedish pension. *Equilibrium*, *11*(3), 559–584. doi:10.12775/EQUIL.2016.025

Dar-Nimrod, I., Rawn, C. D., Lehman, D. R., & Schwartz, B. (2009). The maximization paradox: The costs of seeking alternatives. *Personality and Individual Differences*, *46*(5-6), 631–635. doi:10.1016/j.paid.2009.01.007

Elliott, A. (Ed.). (2019). *Routledge Handbook of Identity Studies* (2nd ed.). Taylor & Francis. doi:10.4324/9781315626024

European Commission. (2021). *Special Eurobarometer 508 on Values and Identities of EU citizens* (508 – Wave EB94.1). Publications Office of the European Union.

Graves, P. (2013). *Consumer.ology. The Truth about Consumers and the Psychology of Shopping* (2nd ed.). Nicholas Brealey Publishing.

Hedström, P., & Stern, Ch. (2017). Rational Choice Theory. In B. S. Turner, Ch. Kyung-Sup, C. F. Epstein, P. Kivisto, J. M. Ryan, & W. Outhwaite (Eds.), *The Wiley-Blackwell Encyclopedia of Social Theory* (pp. 1925–1931). Wiley-Blackwell. doi:10.1002/9781118430873.est0305

Howarth, C., Lane, M., & Slevin, A. (2022). *Addressing the Climate Crisis: Local Action in Theory and Practice*. Springer Nature. doi:10.1007/978-3-030-79739-3

Iyengar, S. (2010). *The Art of Choosing*. Little Brown.

Jain, K., Bearden, J. N., & Filipowicz, A. (2013). Do maximizers predict better than satisficers? *Journal of Behavioral Decision Making*, *26*(1), 41–50. doi:10.1002/bdm.763

Keita, K., & Ebina, T. (2015). Paradox of choice and consumer nonpurchase behavior. *AI & Society*, *30*(2), 291–297. doi:10.1007/s00146-014-0546-7

Khan, N. (2022). The cost of living crisis: How can we tackle fuel poverty and food insecurity in practice? *The British Journal of General Practice*, *72*(720), 330–331. doi:10.3399/bjgp22X719921 PMID:35773000

Khare, A., Chowdhury, T. G., & Morgan, J. (2021). Maximizers and satisficers: Can't choose and can't reject. *Journal of Business Research*, *135*(5), 731–748. doi:10.1016/j.jbusres.2021.07.008

Kida, T., Moreno, K. K., & Smith, J. F. (2010). Investment decision making: Do experienced decision makers fall prey to the paradox of choice? *Journal of Behavioral Finance*, *11*(1), 21–30. doi:10.1080/15427561003590001

Kim, K., & Miller, E. G. (2017). Vulnerable maximizers: The role of decision difficulty. *Judgment and Decision Making*, *12*(5), 516–526. doi:10.1017/S1930297500006537

Lapavitsas, C., Meadway, J., & Nicholls, D. (2023). *The Cost of Living Crisis: (and how to get out of it)*. Verso Books.

Leonhard, G. (2016). *Technology vs. Humanity: The Coming Clash Between Man and Machine*. FutureScapes.

Librová, H., Pelikán, V., Galčanová, L., & Kala, L. (2016). *Věrní a rozumní. Kapitoly o ekologické zpozdilosti* [The Faithful and the Reasonable: Chapters on Ecological Foolishness]. Masarykova univerzita.

Lipovetsky, G. (2007). Paradoxní štěstí [Paradoxal Happiness]. *Prostor*.

Loewenstein, G. F., & Prelec, D. (1993). Preferences for sequences of outcomes. *Psychological Review*, *100*(1), 91–108. doi:10.1037/0033-295X.100.1.91

Loxton, M., Truskett, R., Scarf, B., Sindone, L., Baldry, G., & Zhao, Y. (2020). Consumer behaviour during crises: Preliminary research on how coronavirus has manifested consumer panic buying, herd mentality, changing discretionary spending and the role of the media in influencing behaviour. *Journal of Risk and Financial Management, 13*(8), 166. doi:10.3390/jrfm13080166

Lury, C. (2011). *Consumer Culture* (2nd ed.). Polity Press.

Manolică, A., Guță, A. S., Roman, T., & Dragăn, L. M. (2021). Is consumer overchoice a reason for decision paralysis? *Sustainability (Basel), 13*(11), 5920. doi:10.3390/su13115920

Masatlioglu, Y., & Suleymanov, E. (2021). Decision Making within a Product Network. *Economic Theory, 71*(1), 185–209. doi:10.1007/s00199-019-01238-z

Mayol, A., & Staropoli, C. (2021). Giving consumers too many choices: A false good idea? A lab experiment on water and electricity tariffs. *European Journal of Law and Economics, 51*(2), 383–410. doi:10.1007/s10657-021-09694-6

Mittal, B. (2016). The maximizing consumer wants even more choices: How consumers cope with the marketplace of overchoice. *Journal of Retailing and Consumer Services, 31*(6), 361–370. doi:10.1016/j.jretconser.2016.05.003

Nikolaev, B., & Bennett, D. L. (2016). Give me liberty and give me control: Economic freedom, control perceptions and the paradox of choice. *European Journal of Political Economy, 45*, 39–52. doi:10.1016/j.ejpoleco.2015.12.002

Oishi, S., Tsutsui, Y., Eggleston, C., & Galinha, I. C. (2014). Are maximizers unhappier than satisficers? A comparison between Japan and the USA. *Journal of Research in Personality, 49*, 14–20. doi:10.1016/j.jrp.2013.12.001

Oulasvirta, A., Hukkinen, J. P., & Schwartz, B. (2009). When More is Less: The Paradox of Choice in Search Engine Use. In *Proceedings of the 32nd international ACM SIGIR conference on Research and development in information retrieval.* Association for Computing Machinery. 10.1145/1571941.1572030

Pandey, A. K., & Desai, J. (2020). Analysing the paralysis: Inquiry into the paradox of choices in online apparel shopping. *Our Heritage, 68*(22), 101–123.

Polman, E. (2010). Why are maximizers less happy than satisficers? Because they maximize positive and negative outcomes. *Journal of Behavioral Decision Making, 23*(2), 179–190. doi:10.1002/bdm.647

Richardson, K., Steffen, W., Lucht, W., Bendtsen, J., Cornell, S. E., Donges, J. F., Drüke, M., Fetzer, I., Bala, G., von Bloh, W., Feulner, G., Fiedler, S., Gerten, D., Gleeson, T., Hofmann, M., Huiskamp, W., Kummu, M., Mohan, C., Nogués-Bravo, D., ... Rockström, J. (2023). Earth beyond six of nine planetary boundaries. *Science Advances*, *9*(37), 1–16. doi:10.1126/sciadv.adh2458 PMID:37703365

Ritzer, G., & Rey, P. J. (2016). From 'Solid' Producers and Consumers to 'Liquid 'Prosumers. In M. Davis (Ed.), Liquid Sociology. Metaphor in Zygmunt Bauman's Analysis of Modernity (pp. 157-176). Routledge.

Roberts, P. (2014). *The Impulse Society: America in the Age of Instant Gratification*. Bloomsbury Publishing USA.

Roggeveen, A. L., & Sethuraman, R. (2020). How the COVID-19 pandemic may change the world of retailing. *Journal of Retailing*, *96*(2), 169–171. doi:10.1016/j.jretai.2020.04.002

Roubal, O. (2012). Éra nejistoty a nástup „lovecko-hráčské" společnosti [Era of Uncertainty and Accession into the Age of „Hunter-gamer"Society]. *Communication Today*, *3*(1), 6–20.

Roubal, O. (2018). Maximizers and satisficers in consumer culture changes. *Communication Today*, *9*(2), 38–54.

Roubal, O. (2022). The ethical consumer and the religious nature of environmental thinking. *European Journal of Science and Theology*, *18*(1), 113–124.

Roubal, O. (2023). Consumer Culture and Abundance of Choices: Having More, Feeling Blue. In U. Ayman (Ed.), *A New Era of Consumer Behavior - In and Beyond the Pandemic* (pp. 3–21). IntechOpen. doi:10.5772/intechopen.105607

Sassatelli, R. (2019). Consumer Identities. In A. Elliott (Ed.), *Routledge Handbook of Identity Studies* (pp. 237–255). Routledge. doi:10.4324/9781315626024-14

Satish, K., Venkatesh, A., & Manivannan, A. S. R. (2021). Covid-19 is driving fear and greed in consumer behaviour and purchase pattern. *South Asian Journal of Marketing*, *2*(2), 113–129. doi:10.1108/SAJM-03-2021-0028

Scheibehenne, B., Greifeneder, R., & Todd, P. M. (2010). Can there ever be too many options? A meta-analytic review of choice overload. *The Journal of Consumer Research*, *37*(3), 409–425. doi:10.1086/651235

Schwartz, B. (2004). *The Paradox of Choice: Why More is Less*. Harper Perennial.

Schwartz, B. (2015). The Paradox of Choice. In S. Joseph (Ed.), *Positive Psychology in Practice: Promoting Human Flourishing in Work, Health, Education, and Everyday Life* (pp. 121–138). Wiley. doi:10.1002/9781118996874.ch8

Schwartz, S. H. (1994). Beyond Individualism-Collectivism: New Cultural Dimensions of Values. In U. Kim, H. C. Triandis, C. Kagitcibasi, S-C. Choi & G. Yoon (Eds.), Individualism and Collectivism: Theory, Method, and Applications (pp. 85-119). Sage Publications.

Scott, J. (2000). Rational Choice Theory. In G. Browning, A. Halcli A. & F. Webster (Eds.) Understanding Contemporary Society: Theories of the Present (pp. 126-138). Sage Publications Ltd. doi:10.4135/9781446218310.n9

Sharma, A., & Nair, S. K. (2017). Switching behaviour as a function of number of options: How much is too much for consumer choice decisions? *Journal of Consumer Behaviour*, *16*(6), 153–160. doi:10.1002/cb.1670

Silverman, A. (2019). Breaking the paralysis of choice. *Twice*, *34*(13), 9–9.

Smith, A., & Machová, V. (2021). Consumer tastes, sentiments, attitudes, and behaviors related to COVID-19. *Analysis and Metaphysics*, *20*(0), 145–158. doi:10.22381/AM20202110

Soper, K. (2023). *Post-growth living: For an alternative hedonism*. Verso Books.

Taleb, N. N. (2014). *Antifragile: Things that gain from disorder* (3rd ed.). Random House Trade Paperbacks.

Weaver, K., Daniloski, K., Schwarz, N., & Cottone, K. (2015). The role of social comparison for maximizers and satisficers: Wanting the best or wanting to be the best? *Journal of Consumer Psychology*, *25*(3), 372–388. doi:10.1016/j.jcps.2014.10.003

ADDITIONAL READING

Akhtar, N., Akhtar, M. N., Usman, M., Moazzam, A., & Siddiqi, U. I. (2020). COVID-19 restrictions and consumers' psychological reactance toward offline shopping freedom restoration. *Service Industries Journal*, *40*(13-14), 891–913. doi:10.1080/02642069.2020.1790535

Argouslidis, P. C., Skarmeas, D., Kühn, A., & Mavrommatis, A. (2018). Consumers' reactions to variety reduction in grocery stores: A freedom of choice perspective. *European Journal of Marketing*, *52*(9-10), 1931–1955. doi:10.1108/EJM-12-2016-0844

Cross, S. N. N., Ruvalcaba, C., Venkatesh, A., & Belk, R. W. (2018). *Consumer Culture Theory*. Emerald Publishing Limited. doi:10.1108/S0885-2111201819

Gupta, S. (2021). *How People Buy Online. The Psychology Behind Consumer Behaviour*. SAGE Publications India Pvt, Ltd. doi:10.4135/9789354793066

Inbar, Y., Botti, S., & Hanko, K. (2011). Decision speed and choice regret: When taste feels like waste. *Journal of Experimental Social Psychology*, *47*(3), 533–540. doi:10.1016/j.jesp.2011.01.011

Kimmel, A. J. (2018). *Psychological Foundations of Marketing: The Keys to Consumer Behavior*. Taylor & Francis Group. doi:10.4324/9781315436098

Pettinico, G., & Milne, G. R. (2020). *The Coming Age of Robots: Implications for Consumer Behavior and Marketing Strategy*. Business Expert Press.

Rajagopal, R. (2018). *Consumer Behavior Theories: Convergence of Divergent Perspectives with Applications to Marketing and Management*. Business Expert Press.

Rinallo, D., Scott, L., & Maclaran, P. (2012). *Consumption and Spirituality*. Taylor & Francis Group. doi:10.4324/9780203106235

Salecl, R. (2011). *The Tyranny of Choice*. Profile Books.

Santo, P. E., & Marques, A. M. A. (2022). Determinants of the online purchase intention: Hedonic motivations, prices, information and trust. *Baltic Journal of Management*, *17*(1), 56–71. doi:10.1108/BJM-04-2021-0140

Smith, A. (2019). *Consumer Behaviour and Analytics*. Taylor & Francis Group. doi:10.4324/9780429489921

Vardi, M. Y. (2021). The paradox of choice in computing-research conferences. *Communications of the ACM*, *64*(11), 5. doi:10.1145/3488554

Wisetsri, W., Vijai, C., Agrawal, R., & Jirayus, P. (2021). Consumer behaviour during pandemic of covid-19. *Journal of Management Information and Decision Sciences*, *24*(6S), 1–10.

Yin, B., Yu, Y., & Xu, X. (2021). Recent advances in consumer behavior theory: Shocks from the COVID-19 Pandemic. *Behavioral Sciences (Basel, Switzerland)*, *11*(12), 171. doi:10.3390/bs11120171 PMID:34940106

KEY TERMS AND DEFINITIONS

Ambivalence: Represents ambiguity of thought and randomness of action, fundamentally complicating situations of decision making and future planning. It evokes uncertainty, feelings of ambivalence, internal conflict, and tension, anchored in the simultaneous experience of attraction and repulsion, interest and fear, hope and disappointment.

Consumer Culture: Part of the material dimension of human life, but also the non-material dimension of human existence comprised of symbolic meanings and signs that develop and direct intimate, individual, and social directions in life, including identity and worlds of value.

Maximizer: A type of discerning consumer who seeks the best outcome in the process of making a choice.

Paradox of Choice: A situation in which too many choices reduce the motivation of consumers to buy and lead to overall paralysis to make a choice. In addition, for purchasing decisions the act of choice made by consumers is accompanied by psychological discomfort in the form of uncertainty, remorse, or disappointment.

Predatory Hedonism: A value orientation focused on immediate gratification of needs and attainment of sensual pleasures. It is typified by a focus on the present, enjoyment of life, unrestrained consumption, and consumerist attitudes toward life.

Satisficer: A type of more frugal consumer who in the process of making a choice is satisfied with an outcome defined as "good enough" .

Voluntary Simplicity: A specific non-ascetic lifestyle and attitude incorporating practices for minimizing the complexity of life. It is usually a response to a materialistic, consumerist, and environmentally and ecologically unsustainable type of consumer life. Voluntary simplicity consists of living richly by frugal means.

Chapter 4
Multichannel and Omnichannel Marketing:
The New Trends in Digital Retail

Monaliz Amirkhanpour
https://orcid.org/0000-0002-2092-2710
University of Gloucestershire, UK

ABSTRACT

The purpose of this chapter is to investigate the role and importance of using advanced digital marketing communication channels in retail and to analyze how adaptive the marketers are towards smartphone-based mobile technologies. This will be achieved through the synthesis of the findings in digital marketing literature, especially mobile marketing in addition to exploring the significance of adopting a multichannel or omnichannel marketing approach and investigating the role of social media and modern mobile devices such as smartphones in selecting the appropriate marketing strategy. The theoretical considerations from the literature are further conceptually developed to construct a provisional framework for empirical validation. The identified research gaps and inconsistencies are presented within the chapter as a result of systematic review of qualified literature sources.

INTRODUCTION

This chapter starts with a discussion on the literature review methodology which is based on Paul and Barari (2022) systematic review methodology that explains why a systematic approach is preferred over a narrative approach. A review protocol is therefore defined, and the steps outlined in the protocol are carefully followed.

DOI: 10.4018/979-8-3693-1594-1.ch004

Copyright © 2024, IGI Global. Copying or distributing in print or electronic forms without written permission of IGI Global is prohibited.

Multichannel and Omnichannel Marketing

The thematic analysis of literature focuses on the influence of digital technologies on the promotional mix specifically direct marketing. Then, digital marketing is discussed in more depth with special emphasis on the digital direct marketing channels particularly social media and mobile marketing. The specific objectives covered in this chapter are listed below:

- To understand the theory behind digital marketing communications
- To understand the impacts of digital technology on consumer behavior
- To identify the difference between permission-based and permission-less marketing communications
- To understand the theory behind mobile marketing communications via advanced media, i.e. smartphones
- To distinguish the difference among mobile marketing campaigns, the key performance indicators, and the mobile analytics
- To understand the concept of mobile retailing in more depth

Mobile marketing communication techniques provide the opportunity to revolutionize marketing by supporting digital marketers in dealing with their major challenges today: getting time, attention and trust from customers. For many years, marketers and advertisers have created communication strategies based on print, radio, TV, and Internet to broadcast their marketing messages. With rapid developments in technology, the effectiveness of these traditional media has significantly decreased and newer channels such as social media and mobile marketing have emerged. The purpose of this chapter is to investigate the role and importance of mobile marketing as a new communication channel for innovation management. This will be achieved by theoretically defining mobile marketing; exploring the effect of mobile on marketing innovation; investigating its role in integrating with social media; and proposing a conceptual framework towards its utilization in the wider context of innovation management in digital marketing communications.

BACKGROUND

The aim of the literature review is to investigate and analyze how adaptive the marketers are towards smartphone-based mobile technologies. This will be achieved through the synthesis of the findings in digital marketing literature, especially mobile marketing. To accomplish this aim, the author adopts a systematic approach for the literature review. Systematic reviews adhere to a strict scientific structure based on specific, well-organized and reproducible methods which make them reliable in demonstrating knowledge gaps in the specific research area and highlighting potential areas for future research. The use of systematic and explicit methods distinguishes the systematic literature reviews from the traditional narrative reviews and commentaries (Paul and Barari, 2022). On the other hand, the traditional narrative reviews are mainly descriptive and potentially biased because they do not specify the types of databases and methodological approaches used to conduct the review nor the literature inclusion/exclusion criteria for the retrieved articles during database search process. Due to the lack of strict methodological approaches, the retrieved data from a narrative literature review cannot be reproduced and the research questions cannot be answered specifically. The systematic reviews; however, are specifically structured, use transparent search approaches, and facilitate evaluation and reproduction of the retrieved data.

There are four reasons behind reviewing the literature systematically: (1) it demonstrates the fundamental ideas behind the research questions, (2) the preliminary search assists the author to generate and refine the general research questions, (3) it shows that the author is well-informed about the related research topic and the surrounding theories that support the study, and (4) the critical review of the available literature indicates that the author has identified potential knowledge gaps in previous studies and the proposed research will enhance knowledge about the specific research area and assist in clarifying the research questions in more depth. Hence, the author follows the methodological approach proposed by Tranfield et al. (2003) and Paul and Barari (2022) for the systematic review of related literature sources. To justify the need for a systematic review on digital marketing communications especially smartphone-based mobile marketing, the author adopts a preliminary plan. The preliminary plan searches the relevant databases comprehensively to check whether there are existing or ongoing reviews on the field of interest, and whether a new review is justified. The most relevant databases that include a wide range of peer-reviewed journal articles in the field of business and management are the ABI/INFORM, EBSCO Host, Emerald Insight, Science Direct, and Inderscience Publishers. Furthermore, these databases are frequently used by many scholars in the field of marketing communications and more specifically digital marketing communications. Figure 1 illustrates the investigation process on the selected electronic databases.

The search process subsumes initial search efforts using general search terms/keywords in the relevant business and management electronic databases regardless of the journal impact factor to avoid research bias. Cross-referencing between various research studies is performed to minimize the possibility of excluding relevant articles. The initial search does not apply any filters such as the publication date, author(s), language and geographical location on the subject terms/keywords used. The basic search strings 'mobile marketing' OR 'm-marketing' are applied in the initial search to screen articles based on title, subject terms/keywords, and abstract. However, the

Multichannel and Omnichannel Marketing

search process is restricted to published peer-reviewed academic journal articles because they are valid and credible knowledge sources with high impacts on the mobile marketing discipline. Grey literature sources such as booklets, brochures, case studies, catalogues, conference proceedings, dissertations, e-books, fact sheets, handbooks, infographics, newsletters, reports, web pages, white papers and other non-refereed publications are eliminated from the review process because they do not go through a strict and reliable peer-review process.

Figure 1. Investigation process for systematic reviews on mobile marketing

Electronic Database	Initial Search (No filters applied)	Scope	Scope Search	Total Relevant
ABI/INFORM	154	Title, Keywords, Abstract	27	1
EBSCO Host	137	Title, Subject Terms, Abstract	25	2
Emerald Insight	118	Title, Keywords, Abstract	20	1
Science Direct	106	Title, Keywords, Abstract	17	1
Inderscience Publishers	85	Title, Keywords, Abstract	12	1

Included Search String
mobile AND marketing AND review

To ensure that the boundaries of the research objectives are clearly defined, the literature inclusion/exclusion criteria should be carefully set in the review protocol. The inclusion criteria should capture all studies of interest within a specific timeframe. If the inclusion criteria are narrowly defined, there is a risk of missing relevant studies and the generalizability of the search results may be reduced. On the other hand, if the inclusion criteria are too broad, then the review process and data synthesis will be more complicated. The author defined the inclusion/exclusion criteria to be moderate and applicable on the selected research studies and the abstracts were examined based on their approach to theory and methodology. The studies written in languages other than English were excluded after examining and documenting all the relevant citations regardless of the language they were written. Furthermore, the study was restricted to peer-reviewed academic journal articles to ensure the validity and reliability of the derived information. Duplicate studies were identified and removed in parallel to the application of inclusion/exclusion criteria. A considerable number of articles were excluded mainly because their approach to theory and methodology was not properly justified and their study time was not within the defined timeframe.

The world becomes heavily "mobile-first" in all aspects of everyday life; hence research in the areas of digital marketing communications particularly social media and mobile marketing can lose relevance rapidly and become obsolete. Upon the application of inclusion/exclusion criteria on the selected research studies, those articles that were published in the early 2000s (2000-2008) were not considered for complete review and quality assessment because they equaled mobile marketing to Short Message Service (SMS) marketing only. With the widespread propagation of advanced mobile devices such as smartphones, tablet computers (commonly shortened to tablets), phablets (a portmanteau of the words phone and tablet), smart-watches and other wearable devices from 2012 onwards, mobile marketing communication is no longer limited to SMS marketing. Some of the most outstanding smartphone-based communication channels are mobile websites, mobile applications (commonly shortened to apps) and advanced media (such as Quick Response (QR) codes, Location-Based Services (LBS), Near-Field Communications (NFC), etc.). Figure 2 2 illustrates the inclusion/exclusion criteria for the selected articles in addition to the reasons of inclusion/exclusion.

Colicev et al. (2018) and Paul and Barari (2022) state that thematic analysis is an important part of systematic literature reviews as it involves identifying, examining and recording themes or perspectives within data which assist in the analysis of the extracted theoretical content. The author studied all the qualified articles carefully and has identified seven distinct perspectives within the findings: (1) understanding digital marketing communications, (2) digital technology and consumer behavior, (3) permission-based communications, (4) understanding mobile marketing communications, (5) mobile marketing campaigns: multichannel, omnichannel and So-Lo-Mo, (6) mobile KPIs and analytics and (7) mobile retailing and technology readiness of the retail sector. These perspectives are further discussed within the chapter.

Multichannel and Omnichannel Marketing

Figure 2. Literature inclusion/exclusion criteria

Inclusion Criteria	Reason for Inclusion	Exclusion Criteria	Reason for Exclusion
Content Type Conceptual and empirical research papers (published peer-reviewed academic journal articles)	Examine the theories, concepts and methodologies related to smartphone-based mobile marketing communications (both qualitative and quantitative papers) published in all journals to avoid bias and missing important content	Content Type Grey literature sources and non-peer-reviewed academic journal articles	They cannot be examined like journal articles.
Publication Date Studies published from 2009 onwards	Capture the studies related to the propagation of smartphones and their impact on revolutionizing mobile marketing practices	Publication Date Studies published before 2009	Studies published before the widespread adoption of smartphones focus only on mobile marketing via SMS. There is no evidence of smartphone-based mobile marketing communications.
Language Content written in English only	The researcher is not multi-lingual.		

UNDERSTANDING DIGITAL MARKETING COMMUNICATIONS

The world of digital marketing is changing remarkably fast. This is mainly due to the constantly evolving technologies and the way customers are using them which transform not just how information is accessed, but how marketers interact and communicate with customers on a global scale (Oancea and Mihaela, 2015; Jackson and Ahuja, 2016; Brown, 2017). The author raises the question that most businesses particularly the SMEs may not have a proper understanding of the phenomenal change in marketing communications brought about by digital technologies because they do not feasibly use the digital channels for their marketing communication activities and apparently, they do not benefit from the vast opportunities that these channels provide. Digital technologies are seamlessly integrated into the everyday life of ordinary people as customers adopt digital technologies to communicate with each other in ways that would have been unthinkable few years ago. The print media, TV, radio, telephone, and the Internet are all examples of major milestones in technology that ultimately adjusted and changed the marketer-consumer relationships;

however, technology is only interesting from a marketing perspective when it connects marketers with customers more effectively. In simpler terms, technology has the power to open completely new markets and to influence the existing ones. The adoption of digital technologies such as the Internet, the software applications that run on it, and the devices that allow customers to connect and communicate with each other such as laptops, tablets, mobile devices particularly smartphones dominate all the developments in the history of marketing. Colicev et al. (2018), Narang and Shankar (2019) highlight in their findings the influence of digital technologies on the division of direct marketing communication channels into two distinct categories: (1) traditional and (2) digital or online channels. The traditional direct marketing channels are characterized as broadcast, outbound, and one-way form of communication media. The marketing activities are message-driven based on brand features or benefits which makes them didactic. In simpler terms, the marketing message tells, explains, elaborates or instructs, and it may not include a direct Call-to-Action (CTA) for customers. Examples of traditional direct marketing channels are direct selling, direct mail, telemarketing, TV/radio marketing, print media and billboard advertising. Heinze et al. (2017) state that the traditional channels such as print media, TV/radio, or telephone constrain the marketing content to fit in with print schedules and geographic boundaries in addition to being calendar-bound with a fixed start date and a fixed end date which makes them inflexible from a customer's viewpoint. Moreover, the power and influence with traditional channels is retained by the media owner and the advertiser.

On the other hand, Hogberg (2017) and Akter et al. (2021) state that digital direct marketing channels are characterized as interactive two-way form of communication media. The digital marketing activities are consumer and content-driven through personalization of content that is in tune with customer interests and expectations. Examples of digital direct marketing channels are Search Engine Marketing (SEM), Digital Display Advertising (DDA), E-mail marketing, Social Media Marketing (SMM), and mobile marketing. The digital channels such as search engines, digital displays, email, social media, and mobile-specific channels liberate from publishing schedules, budgetary and calendar schedules, and geographic limitations. Furthermore, the power and influence with digital channels is transferred to the consumer (Jackson and Ahuja, 2016; Gok, 2020). The evolution of the promotional mix elements particularly direct marketing and how mobile marketing is related to the Integrated Marketing Communications (IMC) mix is illustrated in Figure 3.

Figure 3. The promotional mix evolution with emphasis on direct marketing (Amirkhanpour and Vrontis, 2017)

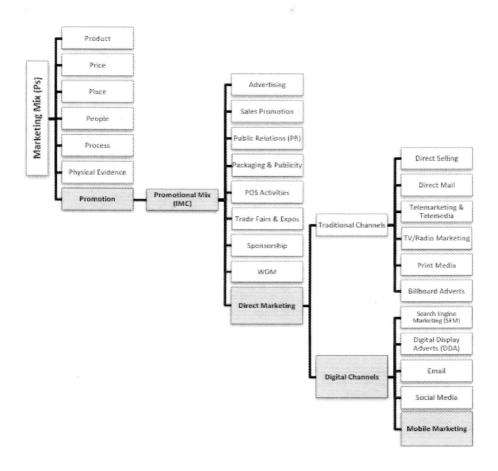

DIGITAL TECHNOLOGY AND CONSUMER BEHAVIOR

Okazaki (2012) and Kotler et al. (2017) state that consumers are informed and connected better than before because with digital channels they have increased ability to access and sift an abundance of information anytime and anywhere in addition to instantly communicate with others across time zones. Furthermore, the research findings of Labrecque et al. (2013), Brown (2017), Roy et al. (2017), and Smith (2018) revealed five key factors in which the widespread adoption of digital technologies is influencing consumer behavior and at the same time it presents a plethora of new challenges for marketers to consider. These key factors are interconnectivity, shift in balance of power, relevance filtering, rise of postmodern consumers, and on-demand nature.

Multichannel and Omnichannel Marketing

- Interconnectivity: With networked digital technologies such as search engines, email, instant messaging, social networks, and mobile applications consumers communicate and interact with people around the world without concerns like time zones or geographical boundaries. This form of peer-to-peer interaction reinforces the importance of incorporating digital technologies into marketing communication activities.

- Shift in Balance of Power: Digital technologies enable marketers to create and publish content quicker and easier than using traditional channels like print, TV or radio. As a result, the scope of information available to consumers is broader and deeper than before. Consumers can research, access, and compare products and services before they make a purchase. This implies that digital technologies thoroughly shift the balance of power from marketers to consumers.

- Relevance Filtering: Digital consumers learn to filter items relevant to them and ignore anything they recognize as irrelevant due to the overabundance of information available to them. They use personalization techniques such as permission-based communication to sift irrelevant content and block unsolicited marketing messages. Permission-based marketing is discussed later in the chapter.

- Rise of Postmodern Consumers: Online consumers are greatly involved in the creation and customization of the products and services they purchase due to the shift in balance of power to consumers. This makes the level of interaction and communication between producers and consumers unprecedented. Cova et al. (2013), Hamouda and Gharbi (2013), Oancea and Mihaela (2015), and Roy et al. (2017) in their articles indicate that various consumption patterns and experiences can be noticed especially by digital consumers because they reveal who they are by searching for specific products or services, clicking on specific links or advertisements, registering for updates on products or services that interest them, and purchasing products or services that they need.

- On-Demand Nature: The ubiquitous digital technologies allow consumers to satisfy their needs and wants easily and with fewer barriers such as time, location, and physical store space.

PERMISSION-BASED COMMUNICATIONS

Permission-based marketing, or permission marketing is a type of marketing which seeks permission in advance from consumers before they are sent marketing communication messages where such communications may be distributed through

Multichannel and Omnichannel Marketing

emails, social media, and mobile-specific channels (Kumar et al., 2014; Kotler et al., 2017).

Moreover, Brassington and Pettitt (2013), Kotler et al. (2017), and Smith (2018) indicate that permission marketing is a broad term covering all kinds of permission seeking; consumers provide marketers with information about the types of communication they would like to receive, and this information enables marketers to target interested customers. The emergence of advanced mobile devices such as smartphones has enabled marketers to upgrade the level of permission-based marketing to include the mobile-specific features. Armstrong et al. (2015), Chaffey and Ellis-Chadwick (2015), and Roy et al. (2017) define permission-based mobile marketing as *the practice of gaining consent from consumers in advance of a continuing marketing dialogue taking place on mobile devices.* This form of value exchange is accomplished by consumers who give their consent and sometimes personal demographic and preference information in exchange for a product, service, or offer that they deem of interest, of relevance, or of worth to them.

Consequently, the author emphasizes the fact that permission-based marketing communications turn strangers into friends and friends into loyal customers because they simply change the advertising paradigm from interruption to communication which enables the brands to move from a broadcast monologue to a dialogue that offers to continue a deep engagement with the loyal customers.

UNDERSTANDING MOBILE MARKETING COMMUNICATIONS

Mobile marketing as stated by Okazaki (2012) and Jobber and Ellis-Chadwick (2016) emerged in the late 1990s with the sending of simple messages through Short Message Service (SMS), but the strategies have changed since the introduction of better technologies and the propagation of smartphones, tablets/phablets, and wearable devices where many other mobile communication channels have emerged. Similarly, Hopkins and Turner (2012), Cova et al. (2013), Brown (2017), and Akter et al. (2021) believe that mobile devices such as smartphones are an essential part of the daily life of people and they will be the primary tool for connection to the Internet for most people in the world by the year 2025. Mobile marketing has rapidly become one of the most attractive digital marketing channels for retail businesses, both small and large, as it is an innovative way to market a specific product or service to new and potential customers (Gok, 2020; Neslin, 2022).

Being more connected has altered the ways consumers use their mobile devices. The fact that mobile phones can only make calls is less relevant mainly because the mobile consumers now perform other tasks like social networking, sharing, browsing and shopping via their advanced mobile devices. Moreover, since 2012 smartphones and tablets are the predominant mobile devices because they support mobile websites, mobile apps, and other mobile functionalities that lead to increased interactivity; however, the existing mobile marketing models do not cover the post-smartphone era because their focus is on SMS marketing only. Obviously, a high-level and updated plan for smartphone-based mobile marketing is needed to highlight and demonstrate the correlation between:

- Mobile marketing objectives
- Mobile marketing campaigns
- Types of mobile marketing
- Mobile performance monitoring
- Customer segmentation criteria
- Adaptive mobile retailing

Asmare and Zewdie (2021) and Neslin (2022) believe that the world of digital marketing is getting more complicated with the increased number of digital communication channels available in addition to the vast number of online customers distributed across different channels which make the job of digital marketers more challenging because they focus mainly on the channels and the new trends among customers rather than having clearly specified marketing objectives. This clearly indicates that for an effective smartphone-based marketing campaign, marketers should define specific objectives before choosing the campaign type and the proper communication channels to reach the target market. Iglesias-Pradas and Acquila-Natale (2023) highlight the most significant digital marketing objectives that assist marketers in planning effective campaigns. Some of these objectives are:

- Brand Awareness
- Lead Generation (new customer acquisition)
- Lead Conversion Rate (turn visitors to loyal customers)
- Online Sales
- Page Views
- Download Rate
- Quality of Online Content
- Return-on-Investment (ROI)
- Bounce Rate (store traffic)

Gok (2020) and Hayes and Kelliher (2022) state that a digital marketing campaign can have one or more objectives where each objective is linked to a specific campaign type and appropriate marketing communication channels to reach the target customers and mobile marketing is no exception.

MOBILE MARKETING CAMPAIGNS: MULTICHANNEL, OMNICHANNEL AND SO-LO-MO

Mobile strategy is the framework that defines how the different mobile marketing communication types (MMCTs) are used to satisfy the customers' needs and achieve the marketing objectives. Marketers are always searching for innovative, cost-effective, and highly influential methods to increase revenue and customer response rates by designing targeted and content-driven marketing campaigns. The traditional marketing campaigns are becoming obsolete after the widespread propagation of digital marketing technologies which transform passive brand consumption to active brand engagement and passive consumers to active digital consumers. Mobile marketing is an appropriate medium to achieve these objectives especially when it is integrated with other digital marketing communication channels such as social media (Amirkhanpour and Vrontis, 2017; Smith, 2018). Lamberton and Stephen (2016), and Neslin (2022) believe that mobile marketing fails as an isolated channel; it works best within a multichannel marketing strategy. In multichannel marketing, marketers directly invest in several channels such as social media, email, mobile apps, and a physical and/or online store to target customers. Smith (2017) states that the goal of multichannel marketing is to build a strong and unique marketing strategy for each channel to target customers based on their specific preferences (Figure 4).

Figure 4. Illustration of multichannel and omnichannel marketing (Smith, 2017)

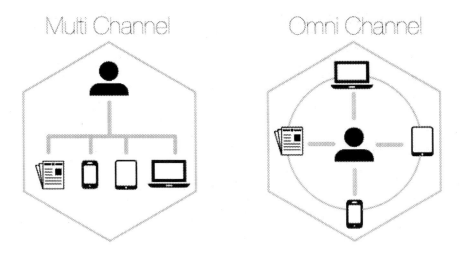

Omnichannel marketing is an advanced form of multichannel marketing with a balanced approach. This form of marketing views the entire business experience from the customers' perspective because it keeps the customer at the center of its business model by seamlessly coordinating positive customer experience across multiple channels.

Marketers are increasingly combining mobile marketing with social media to deepen their interactions with customers because it is estimated that by 2025, more than a billion people will access their favorite social networks using smartphones and other advanced mobile devices. Therefore, marketing campaigns should pay extra attention to this fundamental transition by first understanding the preferences of their digital customers (Cheah et al., 2022).

The term So-Lo-Mo refers to one of the latest digital marketing trends which is essentially based on multichannel or omnichannel marketing strategies for integrating social media, location-based services, and the mobile channel. So-Lo-Mo marketing is a novel concept of providing digital customers access to locally-focused promotions and store offerings through mobile searches based on their current location. For instance, suppose that a customer is looking for a Greek restaurant while walking in town. So-Lo-Mo-based mobile applications can provide instant search results and locations of restaurants with Greek cuisine in the customer's vicinity in addition to showing if the specific restaurant has special offers or if friends are available at the same location. This is a very innovative method of targeting customers in a personalized and location-centric manner. Moreover, it enables businesses to promote their offers easily mainly because customers can receive highly relevant search results specific to their current location.

Depending on the marketing objectives, marketers select the most relevant digital marketing strategy in addition to the campaign type. Kotler et al. (2017) and Smith (2018) define a mobile campaign as a digital marketing campaign that can have marketing, advertising, or promotional nature. There are different types of digital marketing campaigns, but the most common ones are:

- On/Off-Page SEO campaign
- Content marketing campaign
- Email campaign
- Social media campaign

The Search Engine Optimization (SEO) campaigns have two forms: on-page which deals with the local content, i.e. everything presented on the website and off-page which deals with making the content appear in the right places and builds goodwill with big search engines such as Google, Yahoo!, and Bing (Nguyen et al., 2022). The content marketing campaigns deal with distributing consistent and

Multichannel and Omnichannel Marketing

relevant online material such as videos, blogs, and social media posts to attract and retain profitable and loyal customer action. They do not explicitly promote a brand, but they leverage customers' desire to learn and stimulate interest in the specific products and services (Smith, 2018; Hayes and Kelliher, 2022). The email campaigns are based on sending permission-based emails to communicate with current and potential customers. Brown (2017) and Neslin (2022) believe that email campaigns should be strategic and planned before they are implemented. The most common forms of email campaigns are newsletters (digital magazines), event invitations, transaction confirmations, welcome messages, lead nurturing emails, sales follow-ups, and review requests. The social media campaigns as their name indicates are coordinated marketing efforts to reinforce the specific marketing objectives using one or more social media platforms particularly social networks, microblogging services, photo and video sharing services.

Consequently, the author believes that combining one or more campaign types together and forming an omnichannel marketing strategy lead to seamless and unified customer experience.

MOBILE KPIs AND ANALYTICS

Chaffey and Ellis-Chadwick (2016), Vaishnav and Ray (2023) define mobile Key Performance Indicators (KPIs) as quantifiable measures used to evaluate the effectiveness of mobile marketing campaigns. The pre-defined objectives, campaign types, and MMCTs influence the selection of mobile KPIs and how they can be measured using different analytics methods.

Mobile analytics are reporting tools that include key statistical data about the performance of a mobile marketing campaign. They simply create the story behind the retrieved data that give marketers valuable insights to improve and optimize business performance, enhance customer engagement and accurately measure their experience, and prioritize resources that lead to better conversion rates (Narang and Shankar, 2019; Gok, 2020). The analytics tools can be divided into four categories: (1) mobile web analytics, (2) social media analytics, (3) SEO analytics, and (4) user experience (UX) analytics. The mobile web analytics collect and report on the key data related to website performance. The social media analytics refer to the tools that monitor the effectiveness of social media strategy. The search engine optimization (SEO) analytics track the overall organic (unpaid) search performance of the website and finally the user experience (UX) analytics encompass the metrics related to the experience of users in the website. Figure 5 lists some of the standard mobile KPIs in each analytics category. It should be noted that these examples are

Multichannel and Omnichannel Marketing

not exhaustive; marketers need to research and find the best solution for their specific mobile marketing campaigns.

Figure 5. Standard mobile KPIs
(Research-Developed)

Category	Standard KPIs
Mobile Web Analytics	- Page Views
	- Bounce Rate and Conversion Rate
	- New/Returning Visitors
	- Average Time on Page
	- Device Type
	- Traffic Source
	- Keyword Analysis
Social Media Analytics	- Reach
	- Engagement
	- Conversions
	- Customer Loyalty
SEO Analytics	- Position
	- Traffic
	- Conversions
User Experience (UX)	- Task Completion Rate and Time
	- Qualitative Metrics

MOBILE RETAILING AND TECHNOLOGY READINESS OF THE RETAIL SECTOR

Ngo and O'Cass (2013) and Quintana et al. (2016) show in their findings that digital technology within traditional business models allows retailers to provide advanced consumer experience, increased profitability, and improved performance if they are well-informed about the new technologies. Hogberg (2017) underlines the need for new organizational capabilities and practices, consequent to the innovativeness of the new technologies. Furthermore, Iglesias-Pradas and Acquila-Natale (2023) believe that online retailing is expectedly changing consumer behavior throughout the search, purchase, consumption and after-sales process. Retailers are currently in the investment and adoption phase of digital technologies, a plateau on which

Multichannel and Omnichannel Marketing

consumer behavior and marketing practices have yet to catch up and get synchronized with technology.

Despite the ubiquitous usage of smartphones, tablets/phablets and wearable devices, their utilization for mobile retailing activities is inherently low mainly because the literature related to smartphone-based mobile retailing and its sub-categories has drawn little attention and is under-researched; hence the adoption rate of mobile retailing by consumers is relatively low. Wan Hussain and Aziz (2022) specify the three sub-categories of smartphone-based mobile retailing as:

- Mobile Banking (m-banking): the use of mobile devices for finance management activities
- Mobile Payments (m-payments): the use of mobile devices to pay for products/services in-store

Mobile Shopping (m-shopping): the use of mobile devices to search, browse, compare and purchase products/services online

Mobile retailing is the latest form of online retailing where consumers make a purchase through advanced mobile devices (i.e. smartphones, tablets/phablets, wearable devices) and collect the purchased item(s) either at home or at store (Nguyen et al., 2022). Smartphone-based mobile retailing has become a crucial milestone in consumer buying habits from simply browsing to completing the entire shopping process on the mobile devices which is faster and more convenient. Traditional retail businesses find it challenging to operate as an adaptive retailer to satisfy customer expectations because they need to establish themselves as flexible and agile retailers, but in many cases, they fail to create engaging and personalized content due to the lack of knowledge and familiarity with the pervasive mobile technologies and the tendency to ignore customers' privacy (Vaishnav and Ray, 2023).

The research findings of Roy et al. (2017) and Neslin (2022) indicate that adaptive retail is essentially built upon three stages of online retail: (1) seamless (omnichannel) retail, (2) customer-centric retail, and (3) scientific retail. The seamless or omnichannel retail is when the customers are convenient to take control of their shopping experience across various digital channels. The customer-centric retail is when different customer segmentation criteria are applied to understand the needs and preferences of customers and satisfy their expectations. Scientific retail is basically the analytics methods used to optimize the overall customer experience (Figure 6).

The research findings of Wan Hussain and Aziz (2022) emphasize that only Agile, Flexible and Adaptive (AFA) retailers are efficient users of smartphone-based mobile marketing campaigns and turning them into effective mobile retailing experiences. This clearly indicates that retail businesses need to adapt themselves with digital technologies and integrate them with their traditional business models to better understand the needs and expectations of their online customers.

Figure 6. Adaptive retail infrastructure
(Research-Developed)

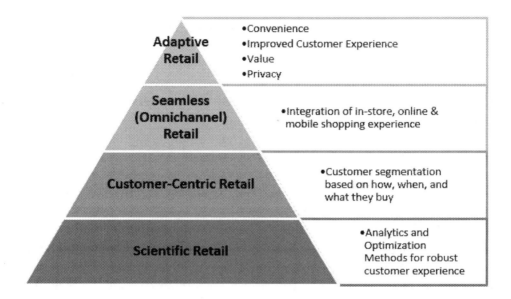

ISSUES, CONTROVERSIES, PROBLEMS

Mobile marketing and mobile advertising are the most challenging topics in the digital marketing domain. This is mainly because of the latest technological advancements which brought about a totally new era in marketing communications. Asmare and Zewdie (2021) and Neslin (2022) highlight some of the most significant benefits of mobile marketing communications:

- Affordability: Mobile marketing offers a better value because the postage and printing costs of using traditional marketing channels are eliminated and therefore prices are very reasonable.
- Distribution: Marketers can reach people all over the world using various mobile marketing techniques because the delivery of marketing messages is almost always guaranteed, unlike the use of other forms of unsolicited direct marketing channels.

Multichannel and Omnichannel Marketing

- Immediacy: Mobile marketing campaigns are simplified, flexible, and easy to execute because they are delivered to the potential recipients within seconds.
- Interactivity: Mobile marketing enables the marketers to reach potential customers on-the-go by creating an interactive and highly effective two-way communication.
- Marketing Campaign Integration: Due to the flexibility of mobile marketing, it is very easy to integrate new and innovative forms of promotional tools with existing ones to boost their effectiveness and interactivity.
- Measurability: The outcomes of mobile marketing campaigns are measurable because they can be monitored through mobile analytics tools and KPIs.
- Mobility: Marketing through the mobile channel has high reachability because most people have their mobile phones 90% of the time within their personal reach.
- Targeted: The mobile marketing content is personal and tailored based on the preferences of those customers who have opted-in to receive them. In simpler terms, the customers who have explicitly announced their consent to receive marketing messages will get targeted forms of marketing content directly on their mobile phones.
- Viral Potentials: The mobile marketing messages can be easily shared by the customers who have already received them with other people. This obviously increases the potential of reaching new customers at no cost.

Even though mobile marketing has many advantages, it has some drawbacks too. Marriott and Williams (2018) identify the two main drawbacks of mobile marketing:

- Diverse mobile platforms: unlike the desktop computers and laptops, mobile devices do not have a standard as they come in many shapes and screen sizes in addition to having different operating systems (Android, iOS, etc.) and different browsers. Therefore, mobile marketing campaigns should be created in a way to support at least the most important mobile platforms. For example, most of the mobile marketing campaigns support both Google Android and Apple iOS platforms.
- Privacy issues: mobile marketers need to understand and respect the fact that users would like to maintain their privacy online. They should only indulge in promotional activity if they have the customers' permission for it. In simpler terms, permission-based mobile marketing communications are mandatory for customer satisfaction and retention.

Jackson and Ahuja (2016), Brown (2017), and Cheah et al. (2022) found out that advanced mobile devices such as smartphones have surpassed both desktop computers and laptops as the main gateway to the Internet for most users. Over one-half of all searches on Google are now performed on smartphones and tablets/phablets, but there is still a gap between the time spent on mobile and the use of mobile for marketing communications. Despite the rapid growth of mobile marketing and its increased impact on consumers' shopping behavior, there is poor evidence of planning and implementing highly effective mobile marketing campaigns. Many business leaders who use mobile marketing in their firms have difficulties in determining the correct marketing strategy especially smartphone-based marketing strategies. Similarly, many consumers have inconsistent experiences with different mobile applications and advanced mobile media. This inconsistency in consumer experience has emerged after the introduction of advanced mobile devices because before the propagation of smartphones, mobile marketing communications were based on the homogeneous communication channel of SMS marketing. Considering today's digital marketing trends and the presence of multichannel/omnichannel marketing communications, there is limited evidence of the key factors related specifically to smartphone-based mobile marketing campaigns such as campaigns based on So-Lo-Mo marketing and other advanced mobile media (i.e. QR codes, VR/AR, AI, etc.). Therefore, developing an effective mobile marketing campaign in today's environment requires more complex system design and usability criteria in addition to high-level user satisfaction which is more difficult to achieve than before.

Roy et al. (2017) and Smith (2018) state that any marketing strategy without a consumer-centric perspective is destined to fail because the most important prerequisite for any marketing effort is to place the consumer at the center of planning, developing, and executing the marketing campaign and mobile marketing is no exception. As stated by Varnali et al. (2011, p. 68), prior academic research on mobile marketing has identified an extended set of factors that may have an influence on the acceptance and adoption of mobile marketing practices by consumers. However, they believe that the available academic knowledge is split across various journals and books which makes it difficult and impractical for both academic researchers and practitioners to keep track of the rapid technological advancements. This clearly implies that there is a large gap between consumer behavior and how businesses are choosing to spend their budget on mobile marketing communications. Furthermore, Colicev et al. (2018), and Gok (2020), and Hayes and Kelliher (2022) state that the topic of mobile marketing via smartphones has attracted little attention even though it is important to both marketing executives and marketing researchers, but marketers are simply basing their decisions on anecdotal case studies and random reports published in the popular press. They emphasize the need for further research evidence on this area.

Multichannel and Omnichannel Marketing

Labrecque et al. (2013), Kumar et al. (2014), Oancea and Mihaela (2015), Lamberton and Stephen (2016), Brown (2017), and Nguyen et al. (2022) found out that most organizations tend to ignore the drawbacks of permission-less mobile marketing communication with their customers and they listed unsolicited marketing communications as a potential gap in most of the executed mobile marketing campaigns that eventually failed. In fact, obtaining consumers' consent and sending them relevant messages guarantee efficient mobile marketing campaigns because consumers who do not give permission to get marketing messages on their mobile devices, perceive unsolicited marketing communications as an invasion to their privacy.

Moreover, Akter et al. (2021) revealed in their studies that there is no commonly accepted framework for mobile marketing because a proper conceptualization of mobile marketing is still missing. They state that there is no agreement on an explicit definition of mobile marketing that captures the true nature of the concept. Therefore, the scope of mobile marketing is still vague.

Neslin (2022) add to the findings of Smith (2017) by shedding light on the fact that the domains of mobile marketing strategy and tactics require continual researcher attention due to the rapidly changing nature of the technology infrastructure and the business environments. This is further supported by Vaishnav and Ray (2023) who believe that existing strategies and business models can quickly become obsolete due to the emergence of new technologies and consumer trends. Additionally, they state that cross-cultural studies in the domain of mobile marketing are rare. Although there is substantial progress in the field of mobile marketing, academic research is still in its infancy and can offer fruitful research avenues.

Consequently, planning a marketing strategy for the mobile channel is different from mass marketing strategies in that mobile marketing has the capability to target consumers directly with personalized marketing messages which could have advertising or promotional nature. Therefore, businesses should be aware of "where they are" and "where they want to be" when planning any marketing strategy including mobile and social features. Marketers are increasingly combining mobile marketing with social media in order to deepen their interactions with consumers. The author proposes a conceptual framework that better illustrates and subsumes the attributes and strategic role of mobile marketing activities, offering a more flexible and more comprehensive understanding of its nature (Figure 7).

It should be noted that the findings of this research and the proposed framework are neither definitive nor absolute. They are simply an alternative perspective to the ones provided by authors over the last two decades; a less conventional aspiration to detach the concept of mobile marketing from its practical aspects and to place it within a wider consumer-oriented context. The aim is not to offer a different point of view, but to propose a value-added implementation that better fits contemporary strategic marketing theory and practice. In essence, mobile marketing has transcended its nature as a functional tool to become a means of both creating and implementing marketing strategy.

Figure 7. Proposed conceptual framework for mobile marketing communications in retail

SOLUTIONS AND RECOMMENDATIONS

The systematic literature review has established a new structure on the previous body of literature and uncovered several gaps and limitations which provided the basis for narrative synthesis of the qualified literature sources and the development of an initial comprehensive framework. Endeavoring to interrelate the theoretical outcomes of the research towards a comprehensive understanding of digital marketing communications was noticeably more complex than originally expected. The difficulty was not related to the expected complexity of the subject, but to three specific aspects of it. First, it is evident that scientific marketing research, owing to the long realization-publication processes involved, generally cannot keep up with the pace of change of digital marketing technology particularly social media and mobile marketing. Second, the pace of change of consumer behavior is significantly fast due to the technological advancements in digital marketing. The third aspect originates from the second and deals with the evident focus of literature on the functional attributes of digital marketing neglecting partially its contextual attributes.

In other words, while research exhibits the practical benefits and determinants of smartphone-based mobile marketing such as mobility, cost, usability and ubiquity, it is not equally successful in linking it with the emerging consumer behavior. For a business to connect with its target market successfully, innovative forms of marketing and advertising should be deployed in conjunction with traditional marketing methods.

The main purpose of mobile marketing is to increase the awareness level of the businesses by assisting them in gathering relevant information about the needs and preferences of their target customers in a timely and profitable manner. Moreover, smartphone-based mobile marketing plays a significant role in enhancing the interaction between the customers and their favorite brands. This is particularly due to the specific characteristics that marketing through the mobile channel has: intimacy, immediacy, intelligence, and innovation.

Considering today's competitive business world and the global economic crisis, business owners and more specifically marketing managers should choose the most efficient, cost-effective strategies to be efficient and profitable. Customers are somehow attached to mobile phones and use them for online shopping, social networking, reading books, and several other things in addition to making phone calls. Mobile marketing opens new horizons for businesses and marketing managers which ultimately result in increasing sales and leads, driving offline sales up by incorporating location-based search strategies, and building customer loyalty and trust by asking for their permission prior to initiating a marketing dialogue with them. Connecting with mobile customers helps businesses keep them informed and updated about various issues such as launching new products or services, special offers, sales periods, special promotions and several other issues in addition to gaining more credibility in comparison with their competitors.

REFERENCES

Akter, S., Taufique Hussain, T. M., & Strong, C. (2021). What omnichannel really means? *Journal of Strategic Marketing*, *29*(7), 567–573. doi:10.1080/096525 4X.2021.1937284

Amirkhanpour, M., & Vrontis, D. (2017). Mobile Marketing: A Contemporary Strategic Perspective. *International Journal of Technology Marketing*, *9*(3), 252–269.

Armstrong, G., Kotler, P., Harker, M., & Brennan, R. (2015). *Marketing: An Introduction* (3rd ed.). Pearson.

Asmare, A., & Zewdie, S. (2021). Omnichannel retailing strategy: A systematic review. *International Review of Retail, Distribution and Consumer Research*, *32*(1), 59–79. doi:10.1080/09593969.2021.2024447

Brassington, F., & Pettitt, S. (2003). *Principles of Marketing* (3rd ed.). Financial Times.

Brown, R. (2017). Location-based marketing: the pitfalls and promise of retail campaigns. *Mobile Marketer*. Available from: https://www.mobilemarketer.com/news/location-based-marketing-the-pitfalls-and-promise-of-retail-campaigns/440927/

Chaffey, D., & Ellis-Chadwick, F. (2015). *Digital Marketing* (6th ed.). Pearson.

Cheah, J. H., Lim, X. J., Ting, H., Liu, Y., & Quach, S. (2022). Are privacy concerns still relevant? Revisiting consumer behavior in omnichannel retailing. *Journal of Retailing and Consumer Services*, 65, 102242. Advance online publication. doi:10.1016/j.jretconser.2020.102242

Colicev, A., Malshe, A., Pauwels, K., & O'Connor, P. (2018). Improving consumer mindset metrics and shareholder value through social media: The different roles of owned and earned media. *Journal of Marketing*, 82(1), 37–56. doi:10.1509/jm.16.0055

Cova, B., Maclaran, P., & Bradshaw, A. (2013). *Rethinking consumer culture theory from the postmodern to the communist horizon. In Marketing Theory*. SAGE Publishing. doi:10.1177/1470593113477890

Gök, Ö. A. (2020). How does omnichannel transform consumer behavior? In Managing Customer Experiences in an Omnichannel World: Melody of Online and Offline Environments in the Customer Journey. Emerald Publishing Limited. doi:10.1108/978-1-80043-388-520201005

Hamouda, M., & Gharbi, A. (2013). The Postmodern Consumer: An Identity Constructor? *International Journal of Marketing Studies*, 5(2), 41–47. doi:10.5539/ijms.v5n2p41

Hayes, O., & Kelliher, F. (2022). The emergence of B2B omnichannel marketing in the digital era: A systematic literature review. *Journal of Business and Industrial Marketing*, 37(11), 2156–2168. doi:10.1108/JBIM-02-2021-0127

Heinze, A., Fletcher, G., Rashid, T., & Cruz, A. (2017). *Digital and Social Media Marketing: A Results-Driven Approach*. Routledge Taylor and Francis Group.

Hogberg, K. (2017). Challenges of Social Media Marketing – An Explorative International Study of Hotels. *International Journal of Technology Marketing*, 12(2), 127–141. doi:10.1504/IJTMKT.2017.083372

Hopkins, J., & Turner, J. (2012). Go Mobile. John Wiley and Sons, Inc.

Iglesias-Pradas, S., & Acquila-Natale, E. (2023). The future of E-commerce: Overview and prospects of multichannel and omnichannel retail. *Journal of Theoretical and Applied Electronic Commerce Research*, 18(1), 656–667. doi:10.3390/jtaer18010033

Jackson, G., & Ahuja, V. (2016). Dawn of the digital age and the evolution of the marketing mix. *Journal of Direct, Data and Digital Marketing Practice*, *17*(3), 170–186. doi:10.1057/dddmp.2016.3

Jobber, D., & Ellis-Chadwick, F. (2016). *Principles and Practice of Marketing* (8th ed.). McGraw Hill Higher Education.

Kotler, P., & Keller, K. (2017). *Marketing Management* (15th Global Edition). Pearson Education Limited.

Kumar, V., Zhang, X., & Luo, A. (2014). Modeling customer opt-in and opt-out in a permission-based marketing context. *JMR, Journal of Marketing Research*, *51*(4), 403–419. doi:10.1509/jmr.13.0169

Labrecque, L. I., vor dem Esche, J., Mathwick, C., Novak, T., & Hofacker, C. F. (2013). Consumer power: Evolution in the digital age. *Journal of Interactive Marketing*, *27*(4), 257–269. doi:10.1016/j.intmar.2013.09.002

Lamberton, C. & Stephen, A. T. (2016). A thematic exploration of digital, social media, and mobile marketing: research evolution from 2000 to 2015 and an agenda for future inquiry. *Journal of Marketing, 80,* 146-172. doi:10.1509/jm.15.0415

Narang, U. & Shankar, V. (2019). Mobile marketing 2.0: state of the art and research agenda. *Marketing in a Digital World, 16*, 97-119. doi:10.1108/S1548-643520190000016008

Neslin, S. A. (2022). The omnichannel continuum: Integrating online and offline channels along the customer journey. *Journal of Retailing*, *98*(1), 111–132. doi:10.1016/j.jretai.2022.02.003

Ngo, L. V., & O'Cass, A. (2013). Innovation and business success: The mediating role of customer participation. *Journal of Business Research*, *66*(8), 1134–1142. doi:10.1016/j.jbusres.2012.03.009

Nguyen, A., McClelland, R., Thuan, N. H., & Hoang, T. G. (2022). Omnichannel Marketing: Structured Review, Synthesis, and Future Directions. *International Review of Retail, Distribution and Consumer Research*, *32*(3), 221–265. doi:10.1080/09593969.2022.2034125

Oancea, O., & Mihaela, E. (2015). The Influence of the Integrated Marketing Communication on the Consumer Buying Behavior. *Procedia Economics and Finance, 2nd Global Conference on Business, Economics, Management and Tourism*, 23, 1446-1450.

Okazaki, S. (2012). *Fundamentals of Mobile Marketing Theories and Practices.* Peter Lang Publishing, Inc.

Paul, J., & Barari, M. (2022). Meta-analysis and traditional systematic literature reviews – What, why, when, where and how? *Psychology and Marketing*, *39*(6), 1099–1115. Advance online publication. doi:10.1002/mar.21657

Quintana, M., Menendez, J. M., Alvarez, F., & Lopez, J. P. (2016). *Improving retail efficiency through sensing technologies.* Pattern Recognition Letters, Elsevier B. V. doi:10.1016/j.patrec.2016.05.027

Roy, S. K., Balaji, M. S., Sadeque, S., Nguyen, B., & Melewar, T. C. (2017). Constituents and consequences of smart customer experience in retailing. *Technological Forecasting and Social Change*, *124*, 257–270. doi:10.1016/j. techfore.2016.09.022

Smith, P. R. (2018). SOSTAC Guide to your Perfect Digital Marketing Plan 2018. PR Smith Marketing Success.

Smith, S. (2017). A brief look at multichannel vs omnichannel marketing. *Customer Think.* Available from: https://customerthink.com/a-brief-look-at-multichannel-vs-omnichannel-marketing/

Vaishnav, B., & Ray, S. (2023). A thematic exploration of the evolution of research in multichannel marketing. *Journal of Business Research*, *157*, 113564. Advance online publication. doi:10.1016/j.jbusres.2022.113564

Varnali, K., Toker, A., & Yilmaz, C. (2011). *Mobile Marketing Fundamentals and Strategy* (1st ed.). McGraw Hill.

Wan Hussain, W. M. H., & Aziz, N. (2022). Mobile marketing in business sustainability: A bibliometric analysis. *TEM Journal*, *11*(1), 111–119. doi:10.18421/ TEM111-13

ADDITIONAL READING

Akter, S., Taufique Hussain, T. M., & Strong, C. (2021). What omnichannel really means? *Journal of Strategic Marketing*, *29*(7), 567–573. doi:10.1080/096525 4X.2021.1937284

Asmare, A., & Zewdie, S. (2021). Omnichannel retailing strategy: A systematic review. *International Review of Retail, Distribution and Consumer Research*, *32*(1), 59–79. doi:10.1080/09593969.2021.2024447

Multichannel and Omnichannel Marketing

Cheah, J. H., Lim, X. J., Ting, H., Liu, Y., & Quach, S. (2022). Are privacy concerns still relevant? Revisiting consumer behavior in omnichannel retailing. *Journal of Retailing and Consumer Services*, *65*, 102242. Advance online publication. doi:10.1016/j.jretconser.2020.102242

Hayes, O., & Kelliher, F. (2022). The emergence of B2B omnichannel marketing in the digital era: A systematic literature review. *Journal of Business and Industrial Marketing*, *37*(11), 2156–2168. doi:10.1108/JBIM-02-2021-0127

Iglesias-Pradas, S., & Acquila-Natale, E. (2023). The future of E-commerce: Overview and prospects of multichannel and omnichannel retail. *Journal of Theoretical and Applied Electronic Commerce Research*, *18*(1), 656–667. doi:10.3390/jtaer18010033

Jackson, G., & Ahuja, V. (2016). Dawn of the digital age and the evolution of the marketing mix. *Journal of Direct, Data and Digital Marketing Practice*, *17*(3), 170–186. doi:10.1057/dddmp.2016.3

Labrecque, L. I., vor dem Esche, J., Mathwick, C., Novak, T., & Hofacker, C. F. (2013). Consumer power: Evolution in the digital age. *Journal of Interactive Marketing*, *27*(4), 257–269. doi:10.1016/j.intmar.2013.09.002

KEY TERMS AND DEFINITIONS

2D Barcodes: Mobile barcodes such as the commonly known Quick Response (QR) codes that are encoded with information. QR codes are small square graphical images that can be captured by the camera of a smartphone or tablet/phablet and then decoded by software on the phone known as QR code reader to execute specific tasks. These tasks could be links to any website address, geographical coordinates, scan-to-call, sending a text message or email, viewing an online video, downloadable coupons or special offers, or social networking activities such as "Like", "Follow" or "Subscribe".

Augmented Reality (AR): A live, direct, or indirect view of a physical, real-world environment whose elements are augmented by computer-generated sensory input such as sound, video, graphics or GPS data. Augmented reality applications can be incorporated in education, digital games, medical apps, and retail. For example, IKEA (the world's largest furniture retailer based in Sweden) developed an app that allows its products to be seen in augmented reality to give customers a better idea of how a specific product will fit into their home/office and to see how everything might look once assembled.

Multichannel and Omnichannel Marketing

Beacon Technology: A new form of marketing communication that mainly consists of advertisements sent through small data packets in one-way only which means the retailers can contact customers, but those receiving beacon messages on their smartphones or tablets/phablets cannot reply.

Location-Based Services (LBS): Digital systems that broadcast marketing messages to advanced mobile devices within specific vicinity by using Bluetooth, NFC or Wi-Fi. This form of marketing communication is known as proximity marketing via beacon technology that is mainly used to disseminate advertising and promotional content to nearby customers. Proximity marketing has the power to transform the customer experience to be more personalized and seamless, increase brand affinity and loyalty, enhance mobile app usage and boost sales, and enable the retailers to gain more detailed insight about their target customers.

Near-Field Communications (NFC): A set of standards for advanced mobile devices such as smartphones and tablets/phablets to initiate radio communication with each other in very close proximity to transfer data in a more secure way compared to similar technologies such as the Bluetooth. NFC-enabled mobile devices can also be used for contactless mobile payments instead of using cash, cheques or physical credit cards. Mobile payments encompass mobile wallets and mobile money transfer activities which are regulated transactions initiated through advanced mobile devices. NFC-based mobile payments are extremely secure, convenient, and the fastest payment method available to digital customers.

QR Code Marketing: One of the simplest forms of mobile marketing to connect businesses with customers mainly because marketers can send a plethora of information stored online which are related specifically to a business. QR code marketing is a good place to start with mobile marketing as many companies still use print media for their marketing activities. It is of great significance to educate both the businesses and the customers to know what a QR code is, how to interact with it, and what the customer expectations are once it has been scanned.

Virtual Reality (VR): Rapidly evolving technologies used in both physical and online retailing to boost the shopping experience of customers and to improve the selling environment. VR is an artificial environment that is created with software and presented to the user in such a way that the user believes and accepts it as a real environment. Virtual reality applications can be incorporated in education and training, video games, and retail.

Chapter 5
New Marketing Approaches and Consumer Trends in Line With Technological Developments

Aylin Atasoy

https://orcid.org/0000-0003-3996-2752
İstanbul Gelişim University, Turkey

Murat Basal
İstanbul Gelişim University, Turkey

ABSTRACT

Today, it is clear that brands that want to provide consumers with useful and helpful experiences must use information and technology to positively influence the future process. In the digital age, masses of data about consumers, products and services are coming from many channels. This big data is now being used for customers who expect to be special, through personalization-based marketing approaches such as phygital, data-based and content marketing. Also, data-driven, predictive, contextual, augmented and agile marketing approaches as components of Marketing 5.0 are new marketing trends that increase the performance of brands and their competitiveness in the market. These new technology-enabled marketing trends include augmented reality (AR) and virtual reality (VR), chatbots and digital assistants, influencer marketing, video marketing, location-based marketing, machine learning and artificial intelligence, and content marketing.

DOI: 10.4018/979-8-3693-1594-1.ch005

Copyright © 2024, IGI Global. Copying or distributing in print or electronic forms without written permission of IGI Global is prohibited.

INTRODUCTION

The change in production relations with the Industrial Revolution led to many changes and transformations in the world, not only economically, but also socially, culturally and politically. In the age we live in, we are experiencing revolutionary changes thanks to the Internet. In simple terms, there has been an acceleration of everything in our lives because of the Internet. We live, produce, communicate, make choices and decisions faster, and inevitably consume faster.

In today's fast-changing, dynamic marketplace, brands and companies must work harder to stay relevant. Marketing, as one of the main functions of companies, needs to innovate in line with technological developments. In order to maintain their market share, companies must carefully address the changing profiles of consumers and their needs and expectations. Today's consumers no longer make choices along a linear path. They are more likely to move between physical and digital channels. They also want to access products and services through more differentiated, personalized and tailored experiences. However, protecting their personal information and preventing it from being compromised are also among their priorities. The fact that every step they take in the digital environment is recorded as data by brands and companies is perhaps the most negative aspect of digitization for customers.

Today, customers are also aware of their power over brands. They feel that they are the driving and influencing force in their relationship. In the Edelman Trust Barometer Special Report 2021, 63% of customers say they believe they have the power to force brands to change (Edelman, 2021, p. 15). On the other hand, the increasing and diversifying number of channels is at a critical juncture in terms of customer trust in brands (Edelman, 2021, p. 7). Especially brands that try to position themselves as love brands should implement marketing strategies that strengthen the feeling of trust before love in their customer relationships.

Marketing budgets have fallen to record lows at a time when consumer expectations are at an all-time high. That's why fast-growing brands are moving beyond point solutions by rethinking their entire strategy around customer data and, in particular, the customer experience, taking a comprehensive view of everything (Deloitte Insights, 2022, p. 5).

Deloitte's report (Deloitte Insights, 2022), based on interviews with 1099 senior executives in five countries, highlights that marketing trends should have three key themes at their core. The first of these three themes is a uniquely inclusive marketing approach that focuses on *people*, not *profit*. The second is building infrastructure around data from a myriad of data sources and designing human-first data experiences to better understand the balance between people who find the use of their data useful or actually frightening. The third is the importance of designing dynamic customer experiences. Specifically, how brands can use key principles of human-centered

New Marketing Approaches and Consumer Trends

design to create dynamic and cohesive experiences in both digital and in-person environments. By augmenting customer service with artificial intelligence, one of the most prominent digital technologies of recent times, timely recommendations and knowledgeable customer service will better assist customers in their purchase decisions. It is therefore necessary to see in practice how artificial intelligence can be integrated with human service and how best to bring the two together in the overall customer journey.

Price and quality have always been the primary determinants of consumer brand preference. Today, however, consumers are looking beyond what brands promise them, to how sensitive they are to the world's problems, or whether they are willing to take action to solve them, and their approach to sustainability. On the other hand, trust comes to the fore in how consumers want to engage with brands. In particular, the trust-based relationship that consumers establish with a brand is based on their sensitivity to the data they receive about their customers. Banking and finance stand out as areas where they need to pay attention to data security (Deloitte Insights, 2022, p. 12).

BACKGROUND

Research shows that consumer values and sensibilities are influenced by the changing and accelerating dynamics of the digital world. As a result, marketers and companies need to replace traditional marketing strategies with new technology-enabled approaches, or at least carefully blend traditional and digital. Recent marketing approaches that have led to a paradigm shift in marketing offer companies the opportunity to both create new activities for consumers and gain competitive advantage. In the following, we will look at digital marketing, content and data-driven marketing, agile marketing, contextual marketing, predictive marketing, and augmented marketing as components of Marketing 5.0.

MAIN FOCUS OF THE CHAPTER

Phygital Marketing

The consumption possibilities offered by new digital technologies are now referred to as "phygital" consumption. Phygital marketing is a marketing approach that offers consumers a new consumption experience design by integrating experiences in physical and digital environments. Brands that want to incorporate this approach into their marketing activities can create these experiences, especially through the use of new technologies (Johnson & Barlow, 2021, pp. 2365). The term "phygital" was first created and trademarked by the Australian agency Momentum in 2013. The concept is part of the new World Wide Web era, where everything is not just offline or online, but both at the same time (Mustajbasic, 2018, pp. 3). Digital approaches have strategic applications in many sectors, from education to tourism, banking to retail. Examples include contactless payment systems, interactive touchscreens, seamless digital payment systems, and the integration of augmented reality into the customer experience (Johnson & Barlow, 2021, pp. 2365). One of the earliest examples of phygital marketing is Amazon's Amazon GO, a store application that offers both digital and physical experiences in the form of customers paying for their own card payments and packing their purchases without the use of staff. Although still new as a research topic, early studies suggest that phygital marketing can be effective in the omnichannel world, which relies on touching customers at every point in both digital and physical environments. Phygital is often used in the customer experience literature to refer to different types of channels, such as multichannel, cross-channel, or omnichannel, but according to Batat (2023, p. 3), this is an operational approach that limits the application of phygital marketing. From a customer experience perspective, phygital marketing should be defined as a holistic ecosystem that creates a continuum of value and should be embraced as a comprehensive and integrative approach that goes beyond a channel perspective. Thus, phygital encompasses the customer experience delivered both online and offline across multiple channels with different components (Batat, 2023, p.3). Research shows that consumers gather information about brands by conducting research on online channels before making a purchase. In particular, when it comes to luxury brands, customers who are considering purchasing high interest products tend to conduct online research beforehand, even if they prefer to shop offline (Arora & Sahney, 2017). On the other hand, studies show that brands can positively influence customers' perceptions of the brand if they design experiences for their customers in new and seamless ways that users enjoy through physical and digital channels. (Purcarea, 2019, pp. 8). Recognizing the growing impact of phygital marketing, luxury brands have increasingly expanded the scope of their marketing efforts. They have begun to emphasize the integration of online and offline in their stores. For example, they apply augmented or virtual reality in offline stores to provide parallel product visualization and attribute description (Batat, 2021, pp. 4; Talukdar & Yu, 2021, pp. 12). The customer experience created by phygital marketing is becoming increasingly important to people who are now looking for experiences rather than just buying products. Batat (2022, p.11-18) defines the phygital customer experience as the interactions between different entities in the physical ecosystem with three variables. Batat identifies the key components of the phygital customer experience as *drivers, connectors*, and *pillars. Drivers* consist of extrinsic and intrinsic values.

New Marketing Approaches and Consumer Trends

Economic and social are subcomponents of extrinsic values, while hedonism and altruism are subcomponents of intrinsic values. The *connectors* of the framework are media, digital, physical, and human; the *pillars* are practicality, sociability, immersiveness, technicality, sensuality, and affect. Together, these components can influence the design of phygital customer experiences. Van Tichelen emphasizes that for phyigital marketing to take place, it must meet 4 conditions. First, the phygital experience must take place in a physical environment such as a venue, street, or public transportation; second, it must capture the customer's interest; third, it must use one or a combination of technologies such as touch technology, mobile technology, augmented and virtual reality, etc.; and finally, it must personalize the customer/visitor experience (Van Tichelen, 2019, pp. 37). A deeper connection can also be developed through personalization, one of the new approaches that digital brings to marketing from a consumer perspective. Many retailers are experimenting with phygital tactics for deeper personalization. For example, Walgreens is piloting "smart coolers" in its Manhattan stores. When consumers approach these coolers, they are instantly "scanned" by facial recognition technology based on their age, gender or other demographics. The coolers then offer personalized beverage options to those scanned. Similarly, The Container Store's flagship stores have developed a digital interface that allows consumers to browse hundreds of possible material combinations and create and purchase these custom models on site. Similar interactive tools have been used in Levi's stores dedicated to customized jeans (Johnson & Barlow, 2021, pp. 2371).

Content marketing

In this information-driven age, content marketing enables businesses to share important and valuable information with their customers. Content marketing can be defined as a management process by which a firm identifies, analyzes and satisfies customer demand to generate profit through the use of digital content distributed through electronic channels. Information has always been an integral part of marketing. However, today, with content marketing in the digital environment, useful and real information that customers need in their decision-making processes can be presented more easily. Because customers now know that they have the right to access information, to choose information, to choose the format of the information, and to choose whether or not to believe the content (Wong An Kee & Yazdanifard, 2015, pp. 1055-1056). Content marketing, which is a different form of communication than advertising, is closer to storytelling. In content marketing, the message must be culturally localized. It must be in a language and format that the target audience understands. Digital channels, in particular, allow marketers to create content that is rich and engaging. Today's consumers spend a great deal of time on the Internet and on social media. This is important for companies using content marketing because it is easier to capture the audience's attention and influence their thoughts, decisions, and behaviors than traditional communication channels. As the marketplace evolves, customers recognize that they are unique individuals with different needs, and a standardized, inflexible brand message can no longer influence them. A personalized message allows a company to stand out from many competitors in the market because the content is relevant to the target audience (Wong An Kee & Yazdanifard, 2015, pp. 105-107). To sum up, customers expect brands to come up with customized and personalized offers that suit their consuming journey and preferences. Most brands prefer to create special websites to share content that supports their brand image and values, separate from the corporate website but still bearing the brand name. As it is a new generation of marketing to attract the attention of the target audience, they use content prepared with text, audio, photos, videos, graphics and inographics through online platforms of brands and companies. To be successful in content marketing, brands need to identify their target audience, as they do in any other marketing activity. On the other hand, it is important to keep the content provided simple. It is very beneficial for brands to do promotion, advertising and marketing without tiring the target audience. In the next stage, brands need to analyze their competitors. In this way, they will know how to differentiate themselves from the competitors. With thousands of content examples all around, brands should try their best to be "unique", because original content production, is the key to content marketing. Google's Think With Google site (https://www.thinkwithgoogle.com/) is a successful example of using unique content marketing to differentiate itself from competitors. Google's content creation for this site is primarily in support of the work of marketing professionals. The site is designed to be easy to understand and interesting, with tons of original research and case studies. One of the strategies used by content marketers is social media. Today, it has become a facilitator of content marketing and an effective channel for two-way communication with customers. Customers visit social media sites and platforms to access up-to-date content on topics of interest, such as videos, blogs, and articles (Wong An Kee & Yazdanifard, 2015, pp. 105-107). The fact that the content they access during these visits provides personalized, engaging experiences is effective in creating a bond with the brand.

Marketing 5.0

The marketing professor Philip Kotler evaluates the change and development process of marketing until today in 3 basic stages. These stages are product-centric marketing 1.0, consumer-centric marketing 2.0 and people-centric marketing 3.0. Marketing 4.0, which follows, refers to the digital evolution of human-centered marketing

New Marketing Approaches and Consumer Trends

3.0 (Kotler et al., 2010). Marketing 1.0, which corresponds to the period of mass and large-scale production of companies, begins with the Industrial Revolution. Production and the product produced are prioritized in the early 20th century. There is standardization in production, and Henry Ford's statement "Every customer can have an automobile painted in any color he wants, as long as it is black" is the best example of this (Fucui & Dumitrescu, 2018, pp. 43-48).

The importance of the consumer has been recognized in the next phase, Marketing 2.0. It is also a period in which technological developments and information come to the fore. Therefore, it is the marketing period of transition to the information society. Not only companies but also consumers can easily access information and make comparisons between brands (Kotler et al., 2010).

In Marketing 2.0, the evolution of people's needs for a product has shifted marketing activities to a customer-centric field. As customers' needs have increased, the variety of product offerings has also increased. During this period, customers made their purchase decisions from a wide range of options and benefited from obtaining higher product value. In this context, Marketing 2.0 has shifted from "transactional marketing" to a new approach characterized as "marketing facilitation" (Andhyka, 2020, pp. 49-52). Marketing 2.0 has been shaped as a combination of Web 2.0, Web marketing and social media, especially as the use of the Internet has become widespread and has influenced and changed the way of communication. The merging of Web 2.0 technology and marketing practice resulted in adapting the era known as Marketing 2.0 (Erragcha & Romdhane, 2014, pp. 137-142).

The third stage in the evolution of the marketing concept is Marketing 3.0, which can also be described as the "value-driven era" (Fucui & Dumitrescu, 2018, pp. 46). In this era, efforts were made to maintain mutually beneficial and sustainable relationships with customers by providing them with personalized offers. During this period, the customer was also the focus. However, companies implementing Marketing 3.0 aim to provide solutions to address problems in society with the impact of having a greater mission, vision and values to contribute to the world as well as their customers. As Kotler stated, "Marketing 3.0 brings marketing into the arena of human aspirations, values, and spirit, and believes that consumers are whole" (Kotler et al, 2010, p. 4).

The field of marketing has always been sensitive to the changing dynamics and technological developments in the world. Marketing 4.0 has been shaped by the impact of these changing dynamics. Marketing 4.0 is "an approach to marketing that combines online and offline interactions between companies and consumers. It blends machine or artificial intelligence with other technologies to increase productivity, while at the same time strengthening the human-to-human connection to enhance the customer interaction process (Kotler et al. 2017, pp. 46). In other words, Marketing 4.0 is an expanded and deepened version of communication and interaction between the company and the customer. A wide range of internet resources such as advanced technological devices, computers, mobile phones, and social media platforms are used to enable and maintain this communication and interaction. In the Marketing 4.0 era, customers are not only consumers but also part of the production process. In the digital sharing economy, players such as Airbnb, Uber, Zipcar and Lending Club are transforming the traditional service approach of the hotel, taxi, car rental and banking industries. Customers have easier access to products and services provided by other customers (Kotler et al., 2017, pp. 51).

Digitalization has spread so effectively and rapidly in the business world that it cannot be ignored. Digital technologies have penetrated every aspect of our lives, especially due to the forced closures during the pandemic. In marketing, this rapid digitalization process has made the transition from Marketing 4.0 to Marketing 5.0 inevitable. Companies that failed to incorporate digital technologies into their business models were weakened and left behind to compete.

Marketing 5.0, which refers to the integrated form of people-oriented Marketing 3.0 and technology-oriented Marketing 4.0, has emerged when companies consider Society 5.0 in order to use advanced technologies in their marketing strategies and business processes (Ok & Kağıtcı, 2023, pp. 66). Society 5.0 is a society that is able to solve various challenges and social problems by using various innovations that have emerged in the era of the Industrial Revolution 4.0, such as the Internet of Things, artificial intelligence, big data, and robotics, to improve the quality of human life. (Sajidan et. al.2020, pp. 2). It is obvious that Society 5.0, which emphasizes human-robot cooperation, is expressed as a transition to super smart societies and is an enhanced connection between virtual space and physical space, enabling people to delegate or support the work and adjustments they have been doing. This frees people from tedious daily work. In short, at the center of this society is the "human being" (Çalış Duman, 2022, p. 88).

In the current period, the Marketing 5.0 approach includes the use of virtual reality, augmented reality, Internet of Things (IoT), natural language processing, infinite data, sensor technologies, robotics, blockchain technologies and artificial intelligence systems in marketing activities. In this context, Marketing 5.0 is seen as the creation, delivery and enhancement of value through the customer experience created by using these technologies and systems. Thus, Marketing 5.0 starts with creating, delivering and enhancing value in the customer experience by imitating humans with these technologies and systems in order to improve performance in this process (Ok & Kağıtcı, 2023, pp. 67).

At the point we have reached today, marketing can be data-driven, predictive, contextual, augmented and agile with the impact of technology, and these are the five basic components of Marketing 5.0. In addition, these components also name data-driven marketing, predictive marketing, contextual marketing, augmented marketing, and agile marketing practices that are formed in relation to each other, which are the new era's marketing approaches.These approaches are interrelated and also built on two organizational disciplines: data-driven marketing and agile marketing (Kotler et al., 2021, p. 12).

Data-Driven Marketing

Data-driven marketing is the process of collecting and analyzing complex data from online and offline channels to understand consumer sentiment and buying behavior, helping the marketing function develop personalized strategies to connect with target consumers. The role of technology in building predictive models is growing as companies begin to use data to predict customer needs and expectations and develop strategies to meet them. With these models, companies can create customer-centric processes that engage customers. In addition, the data obtained can be used to identify the factors that influence consumers' needs and expectations at each stage of their buying and decision-making processes (Grandhi et al., 2021, p. 384).

With the effective use of digital media, it has become important for the marketing function to carefully analyze and understand how targeted consumers interact on digital platforms. If the rich data left by consumers in digital media can be well utilized, it will be possible to access information that will ensure the right data is delivered to the target audience at the right time. At this stage, data analysis through data-driven marketing will provide companies with valuable information that will help them better read the behavior of their consumers (Bhandari et al., 2014).

Data-driven marketing emphasizes the analysis of data and the integration of the insights gained from this analysis into the development of products and services. As a result, it is effective in attracting new customers and retaining existing ones, while providing efficient connections for consumers. It can also help reduce costs and increase productivity and efficiency (Grandhi et al., 2021, p. 384).

Understanding consumer wants and needs is key to the success of the marketing function. Big data, collected both online and offline, provides organizations with significant advantages in understanding consumer preferences and ensuring that marketing efforts are effective and efficient. These benefits include increasing customer satisfaction, identifying new market opportunities and assessing market growth, and developing new goods and services that meet consumer needs and expectations (Grandhi et al., 2021, p. 391).

The innovations that are emerging in today's evolving and renewed technological world have brought with them different needs. The need to store the data generated by smart factories, smart robots and smart machines is important in the process of making management decisions. In this regard, the storage of the data generated or created is of the same importance. In this context, it is also used in terms of keeping, storing, managing, accessing and analyzing the data (Akben & Avşar, 2018, pp. 26-37). The ability of companies to see the future and make decisions in a short period of time will increase in direct proportion, thanks to big data. (Akben & Ös, 2019, pp. 28-30).

Data-driven marketing is not just about collecting and analyzing data from a variety of internal and external sources. It is also about building a data ecosystem that can be used to guide and optimize marketing decisions. Data-driven marketing is the first discipline of Marketing 5.0, where every decision is based on sufficient data (Kotler et al., 2021, p. 12).

Through an analytics engine, brands can look at their prospects' past purchases to predict the likelihood of future purchases. This allows them to make personalized offers and create special campaigns. Today's technologies and digital infrastructures make it possible to stop segmenting consumers and work on individual customers (Kotler et al., 2021, p. 130).

Predictive Marketing

Companies use predictive marketing to take advantage of technology to enter new markets, effectively manage their customer portfolio and customer relationships, and increase customer satisfaction and loyalty. This new approach to marketing allows companies to conduct and use analytical modeling studies to predict the possible results of their marketing activities before the activities are even launched. By uploading descriptive statistics about past work, market and business data to a machine learning engine, companies can use artificial intelligence to perform analytics. This allows them to predict the profiles of their potential customers, what products these customer profiles may prefer, and what campaign content may be effective (Artun & Levin, 2015).

Predictive modeling is not a new concept for marketers who analyze and work with data to understand consumer behavior and market dynamics. However, with today's advanced technologies and machine learning, computers no longer need pre-determined algorithms and are now able to uncover patterns much faster and beyond the human brain and reasoning power (Kotler et al., 2021, p.144).

Today, there are many different Advanced Predictive Analytics Models. Companies can apply these analytical models according to their business areas and the needs and expectations of their target consumers. Some of these advanced predictive analytics models are as follows (Artun & Levin, 2015):

The engagement propensity model predicts the likelihood that a customer will engage and remain engaged with a brand. This model can be used to keep customers from drifting away by sending customized messages and offers based on their propensity.

The total wallet size model can estimate the maximum possible spend for each customer. While this model is often used to describe the total annual spend of an individual customer, it can also be used to estimate spend for a specific product category. In this way, customers who have the potential to be higher spenders for the brand can be identified.

The pricing optimization model can provide very useful insights for increasing a company's profitability. It helps the company forecast the price most likely to increase revenue, volume, or profitability. With this type of model, a company's transformation can be structured to maximize revenue or margin. This model makes it easier to send the right offers to the right people at the right time.

The keyword-to-contact recommendation model can be used to predict consumer interest in a newsletter, email, or similar content based on data such as consumer behavior in digital environments or past online purchases. This predictive model is particularly useful for effective content marketing planning and execution.

A predictive clustering model can help predict which customer cluster a consumer will belong to in the future. Marketers can use these predictions to begin differentiated and personalized applications for new customers, especially immediately after they are acquired.

Organizations' marketing practices are mostly product- and channel-focused. However, predictive marketing helps companies adopt customer-centric marketing practices. This allows companies to prioritize developing and managing customer relationships beyond product and channel development. Predictive marketing builds long-term customer relationships and provides customer data and insights directly to marketers, customer-facing staff, and applications that deliver personalized experiences to individual customers (Ok & Kağitci, 2023, pp. 73).

In this context, predictive marketing increases customer loyalty and revenue by providing businesses with the following benefits (Artun & Levin, 2015):

- Discovering what products customers will demand in the future, rather than identifying customers who will demand the company's products.
- Focusing on optimizing customer lifetime value to increase the profitability of the business.
- Using big data and predictive analytics to structure processes and organizations to customize interactions with customers.
- Targeting communications to increase relevance and meaningfulness rather than reach.

Predictive marketing also offers significant benefits in product management. For example, the use of predictive analytics in the design and development of product ideas can provide companies with a competitive advantage and effectively increase customer satisfaction. For example, the analysis of historical data is used to perform activities such as developing new products or improving existing products, combining them, determining what features the new product should have to be successful, customizing the product, and creating a broad product portfolio (Kotler et al., 2021, p. 148).

Another application is predictive brand management. Predictive brand management can be applied at all stages, from the design of the product or service to the creation of its identity and image. It also includes applications such as planning communication processes around the brand, determining campaign messages, communication channels, and marketing content appropriate for different customer groups. In all these applications, methods such as machine learning and artificial intelligence are used thanks to predictive marketing (Kotler et al., 2021, p.149).

Contextual Marketing

Contextual marketing is not a new field, but today it is part of Marketing 5.0 applications as it is handled with the help of the Internet of Things and artificial intelligence and is performed automatically in wider environments thanks to new technologies (Ok & Kağıtcı, 2023, pp. 75).

Contextual marketing is an opportunity for real-time, one-to-one interaction with customers through the use of sensors and digital interfaces in physical spaces. It is also a form of customer identification and profiling (Kotler et al., 2021, p. 14). With the help of this marketing application, personalized messages can be sent and marketing campaigns conducted according to the customer's context. In a sense, contextual marketing is an online mobile marketing method that provides customized ad impressions by tracking consumers' online behavior and using customer information (Çalışkan & Erdoğan, 2023, pp. 87-102).

Contextual marketing works through big data. With customer insights from big data, marketers can design contextual marketing activities and targeted advertising campaigns so that each customer receives the best offer and message based on their dynamic past behavior. Many customers ignore ads on digital media channels - banners, videos, sponsored search - if they are not relevant to their needs or preferences. To overcome this barrier, marketers should look for ways to create contextual ads and campaigns. Today, contextual marketing is widespread because customers' online behavior can often be tracked. The web browser and mobile device profiles each of us uses can know what we are looking for, what site we have visited, or where we have been. This contextual marketing information is critical for marketers. With this information, they can target customers more accurately because contextual marketing is a way to improve the customer experience by tailoring marketing to real-time behavior (Vanessa & Japutra, 2021, p. 56).

Contextual marketing creates opportunities for companies that, for a variety of reasons, have not been able to build successful and lasting digital relationships online and on Web sites. These include consumer packaged goods manufacturers, single-product companies, and sporadic service providers. On the other hand, advances in Internet technology no longer limit contextual marketing opportunities to places like the home. The increased use of the latest mobile devices and the ease of wireless Internet access in large and public places allow contextual marketing practices to link real-life situations with information and offers in the virtual environment (Kenny & Marshall, 2020).

Augmented Marketing

With digital technologies, we are now able to realize things we have only seen in utopian movies. Soon, we will be living in a completely digital world, in a smart home, where actions will be automated or controlled by voice. We will have robotic assistants to help us with household chores. For example, refrigerators will recognize what's missing and order it, and drones will deliver food. We will be able to print anything we need in our daily lives thanks to 3D printers. The autonomous electric vehicle in our garage will be ready to take us where we want to go. The digital world we're connected to won't be limited to our phones. The interface will extend to smaller devices that can be worn and implanted in the human body. This will create an augmented life (Kotler et al., 2021, p. 58).

Elon Musk's Neuralink is an example of augmented technology. With the chip implant technology they are trying to develop, Musk aims to create a brain-computer interface that will allow people to control computers with their minds. As of September 2023, Neuralink has opened an application link on the project's website for those who wish to volunteer for clinical trials related to the project (https://neuralink.com/).

Marketing practices must be at the forefront of any development that impacts the lives of consumers. Augmented marketing is an approach to marketing that aims to increase the efficiency of consumer-facing marketing activities through the use of digital technologies that mimic humans, such as chatbots and virtual assistants. Through this approach, marketers effectively enable human-machine collaboration by combining the speed and convenience of the digital interface with the warmth and empathy of human touchpoints (Kotler et al., 2021, p. 14).

On the other hand, according to Kotler (2021, p. 170), it seems more logical to use artificial intelligence, the revolutionary digital technology application of the last period, to support marketing in areas where humans are still effective and dominant. In this context, it would be more appropriate to use augmented marketing in marketing activities that primarily use human-human interfaces, such as sales and customer service.

Augmented Reality, which is constantly evolving, can create a privilege in communicating with customers in different sectors such as tourism, architecture, construction, education, health and personal care. For example, many real estate agencies are incorporating the technology into their daily practices, enabling interaction with clients both on-site and over the phone. In place of often hard-to-understand descriptive text and photos, the technology used effectively shows customers many details at the touch of a button. This gives buyers the opportunity to explore the home they are interested in without having to go to a real estate agent.

Agile Marketing

By definition, marketing agility is a concept related to how quickly a company moves between understanding the market and implementing marketing decisions (Kalaignanam et al., 2021, p. 36). Based on this definition, it would be appropriate to say that agile development, the change of agility, including new capabilities is a necessity in the digital age. The most important factor is that the new name of the marketing game is "agility", and "agile marketing" offers a suitable way to the current transformation in the opportunities they face. Agile marketing structure is used in situations where events occur and are likely to occur with the purchased parts. The main difference between structure and crisis management is the scope of planning change, instead of foreseeing a possible crisis and planning step by step what to do in case of division (Zengin, 2022, p. 100).

Agile marketing also affects organizational structure. In this new approach to marketing, cross-functional teams are used to rapidly conceptualize, design, develop, and validate marketing campaigns or products and services. This is because an agile organization is needed to cope with constantly and rapidly changing market dynamics. The second discipline that Marketing 5.0 companies need to master in order to be successful relative to their competitors is agile marketing (Kotler et al., 2021, p. 13).

In industries dominated by advanced technologies, product life cycles are short. Companies developing new technologies compete to be first to market and to dominate the market. The speed to market for new products is also high, and the time to profit from them is short. It is important to monitor changing customer behavior in line with this speed. For this reason, high-tech companies need to be agile in their marketing activities. Other industries that use digital technology in their production and business processes, such as apparel, packaged fast-moving consumer goods, consumer electronics, and automotive, are also inevitably affected by this speed and their product lifecycles are shortening. Satisfying customers and designing and delivering an effective and lasting experience is becoming increasingly difficult. An experience that is appealing today can quickly become outdated by the time it reaches a large audience (Kotler et al., 2021, p. 183).

New Marketing Approaches and Consumer Trends

In an era of uncertainty, complexity, and ambiguity, companies are struggling to execute their long-term plans. This is because most need to adjust their long-term plans along the way to keep up with the pace of market and customer change. This requires agility. To ensure the operational stability that is essential for growth, companies need to run their business processes with agile teams. Agile marketing is a key enabler for companies to implement the components of Marketing 5.0 in a fast-paced and uncertain business environment (Kotler et al., 2021, p.183).

Although an agile marketing transformation will appear and the common goal of the organization, which may feel different for each marketing, is to create a successful framework to address complex issues and break them down into smaller, more manageable pieces. In PWC's report on agile transformation, this framework generally follows four basic steps (Agile transformation, 2014, pp. 8-9):

Step 1: **Assess the current situation:** Story is a way to organize teams around specific tasks to deliver a quality experience to the customer. To help describe the current situation, companies should ask some questions to understand customer insights, customer experiences, how their employees and business functions work, and how they use resources.

Step 2: **Get organized for success:** A key element of agile is the use of cross-functional teams. This will make it easier to plan, execute and deliver defined tasks. To do this, it is important to start with a core group of departments performing adjacent functions such as sales, operations and finance who can understand the process and act as advocates for the broader team. Executive sponsorship is critical to getting the rest of the team on board.

Step 3: **Design and test:** The biggest challenge for marketing teams may be adapting to fast, repetitive project cycles in an agile manner. Each phase is designed to deliver specific results within a set time frame, typically two to four weeks.

Step 4: **Refine and scale:** Each phase should inform the next as the team gathers project insighs from the build and test phases. Gaps that may be encountered in the next phase are identified by gathering feedback from various stakeholders. As agility spreads throughout the organization, this process of continuous improvement should continue. The important thing is to be able to modify the arrangements the organization needs according to feedback and changing objectives. This is where agility comes into play.

Developing Technologies in Marketing

We see many trends emerging with technology in the field of marketing. These new trains, which have won the admiration of consumers, have not become more popular with the development of businesses (Belk, 2020, pp. 168-171).

Among these; it is a video marketing model that is on its way to becoming the most effective sales channel of the future. The video content here attracts the attention of consumers and allows brands to tell their own stories. For example, regarding the rechargeable vacuum cleaner produced, the device can introduce through a video that its brush can also be used for this purpose for the hair shedding of pets. These channels, where information about products and services are obtained, attract the attention of the target consumer segment in digital areas such as social media and websites (Faulkner & Runde, 2011, pp. 4-8).

Machine learning and artificial intelligence technology, which is a more advanced process in digital marketing, is seen as having great potential in its own right. Examples include Apple's Siri and Google's DeepMind, where natural language processing (NLP) is used to understand and respond to voice commands, such as those given by Apple's Siri. This opens up new dimensions in personal marketing. It is also used in various applications such as automated advertising, voice assistants or chatbots. This method can change many dimensions of marketing in the future (Deighton, et al., 2021, p. 1-6).

Optimization for search engines or voice assistants is increasingly being used to provide consumers with information about a product or service. It would be more beneficial for businesses to produce content for this area on their own platforms. Businesses that are optimized in this way can become more visible in voice badges. To this end, the use of colloquial keywords is one of the more useful activities (Thinkwithgoogle, 2023).

With the rise of mobile devices, digital marketing has become more effective. Companies that design websites that are suitable for this area will help them reach mobile shoppers. In addition, SMS marketing, mobile advertising, and location-based marketing methods in this area are among the areas that should be addressed in the marketing strategy to be created (Donthu, et al., 2021, pp. 834-865).

The location of the mobile phones used can be determined thanks to some operators used, and thanks to the application installed on the customer's phone, it informs about the campaign by sending a special notification to a customer within 250 meters. The most important digital marketing channels are social media marketing opportunities. Here, too, the system is constantly changing, so it is necessary to constantly change to determine the appropriate area and the right content for the product. Some of the most effective here are influencer marketing, video content, and livestream marketing (Grewal, et al., 2020, pp. 1-8).

Companies will spend more time on mobile advertising. They will need to prioritize the data available here. Third-party cookies will be stopped once they reach the target audience. Identity will disappear. Anonymous information will lose value. It will be more effective to conduct subscription-based studies. This should be done

New Marketing Approaches and Consumer Trends

in sync with others. Interaction design will ensure that meaningful communication with the consumer is not lost to a close competitor (Pazarlama30, 2023).

Active, liquid customers will be the most valuable type of customer for the company in the future. It must provide these customers with the necessary technological infrastructure to enrich them with various digital signals to protect them effectively, timely and accurately across all channels. This system will allow the client to stop the advertising in the event of a problem and to optimize its expenditure. On the other hand, the sales unit can determine the customer's interactions and prepare a special offer for him. In such fluid and actionable activities, data chains can be recovered and appropriate personalization and optimization can be achieved (Aramamotoru, 2023).

The transformation seen in marketing, the persona expression, which is called the characteristic situation consisting of the information obtained from different sources and the attitudes of the individual in daily life in accordance with them, turns into a way of determining and separating the typologies of consumers. We divide them into segments. In this way, it will be able to deliver the right message to the right customer at the right time. Digital commerce in the form of e- (electronic), s- (social), m- (mobile), and v- (voice) will provide companies with extraordinary opportunities to reach consumers (Hassouneh & Brengman, 2015). There is also a change in the skills available in marketing and advertising processes within marketing departments. Marketing employees, who will add value to the profitability of the company, see the need for regeneration, that is, renewal, through the development of new generation strategies (Hunt, 2020, pp. 8-17).

Spending on marketing research has begun to decline in recent years. The roles of chief marketing officers (CMOs) and marketing directors, responsible for both marketing and sales, are also being redefined and changed. Here, the customer will be the voice of the company and will be able to journey into the customer experience with technology that embraces them. A data-driven marketing organization can be created within the company as a result of empowering marketing professionals, measuring marketing activities, and combining and singularizing all online and offline studies. If the consumer is approached with the right elements in terms of time and message, the process of staying in communication will be successful (Bolton, 2020, pp. 172-178).

In the process, real experiences must be brought into the consumer's life, where he or she can change the brand through natural, easy and beneficial physical experiences. The consumer needs to trust the brand, and the value of trust is clear. All of this is evidence that the creation of a digital world between the consumer and the brand is important. It will progress in an extraordinary period of time as a result of many changes and transformations from marketing personnel to organizations together with technology (Järvinen, et al., 2015, pp. 117-127).

As the hybrid shopping experience takes place in marketing, companies will begin to see e-commerce as a new playing field for social commerce. In addition to the production of content from online advertising, the advancement of the production of quality content without the use of cookies in advertising will open new doors of opportunity for companies. Marketing, which is seen as the new future, will now take place in the virtual environment. New sales universes will emerge, built on the meta-database for this topic (Chohan & Paschen, 2021, pp. 43-50). Companies will start to use audio advertising, in-game advertising and virtual influencers. As a result of post-cast advertising and the creation of content on the new generation of digital platforms, audio advertising applications will be more preferred for the gaming segment (Balis, 2022, pp. 1-6).

Brands are beginning to understand the value of influencers. Influencers who interact only with their own customers instead of many people will gain value, and companies that use micro-influencers will integrate with an order that creates advertising and content in this direction (Siradisidigital, 2023).

The goal for companies that will invest in the future is to establish social interaction with their target audience, offer personalization opportunities and move forward in a sustainable way. In this direction, the value of the voice of the company's brand will be determined by the creation of gene influencers and nano influencers from influencers, which will bring originality to the brand. Brand storytelling will become popular for consumers who want to see the story of the brand (Tueanrat, et al., 2021).

As many different applications such as marketplaces, messaging and payment services are offered to consumers, super-application concepts created by prioritizing the customer will become more attractive. This can be seen as a growing area for retail media.

In the future, sustainability will become more active. Campaigns and advertising to measure carbon footprints will be an increasingly effective area for companies. Companies that recognize the environmental sensitivity of Generation Z will be strengthened in this regard.

In addition to e-commerce and mobile applications, which include technological and innovative techniques to develop trends in marketing, the development of artificial intelligence and metaverse concepts also put advertising processes on the agenda. The products in the NFT collection will attract the attention of Generation Z. Providing a qualified e-commerce experience will also increase brand loyalty. Reaching large audiences and increasing loyalty through trust will always be a competitive differentiator (Nan, et al., 2004, pp. 7-30).

Through the use of Flywheel, where employees are trained to be customer-focused in the handling of inquiries and issues, reach can be expanded as a result of customer satisfaction.

New Marketing Approaches and Consumer Trends

This method, which is a form of sponsored advertising designed to introduce the brand to a new audience of consumers, is more effective than banner ads thanks to the local advertising that is created using native ads. Real-life stories in this area are studies in the form of click-to-watch video ads that contain embedded messages and calls to action (Pazarlama, 2023).

Blockchain

Blockchain has come a long way in the last decade, becoming popular with cryptocurrencies (Harvey, 2018). The blockchain associated with these issues is the most suitable design for the process. With this system, the problem of spending is solved without third parties. Payments become more cost-effective in this process. It offers consumer-to-consumer activation by providing additional income in the form of content rights.

Metaverse and Marketing

The metaverse commercial world is an entirely new and unprecedented consumption space. Today's tech-savvy young people are beginning to spend their time in many areas, from social media to virtual reality games. They are using their multiple identities by spending more and more time in these areas. The metaverse, which is thought to be effective in gaming today, will increase its effectiveness in many areas in the future. There are avatars in the metaverse that represent the job or person appropriately. The fact that luxury stores also attract attention by selling items such as costume items is perceived as a new channel in sales and marketing. As a result of the intense interest in this area of the virtual world, tokens, digital assets and new areas for them are created. It becomes a target position, since it gains the trust and loyalty of consumers thanks to its transparency and traceability.

Consumer Rights and Ethics in Digitalization

The great transformation that computer technology has brought to economic life also raises many legal problems. The development of information technology has made it possible to transform information, once considered a temporary phenomenon, into something that can be traded as if it were a commodity with a physical existence. This area is of great interest because it affects both businesses and consumers in terms of marketing ethics. The reason why marketing is so prominent is because the main function of marketing is to serve as a connecting point or bridge between business and consumers. It is clear that consumer ethics must be created by taking into account general moral principles and norms to guide the behavior and consequences of consumption actions.

Consumer protection is one of the most important issues of legal policy, as a result of society becoming more and more a consumer society. When it comes to consumer protection; It is also understood that consumers come together, become a social force and eventually the activities of various organizations related to this issue. In fact, the concept of consumer protection includes not only protecting the consumer but also helping the consumer. As a result of the advances in the digital field, digital consumer protection processes in areas such as banking, GSM, e-commerce and freight transportation are becoming more and more important. A person who shops on an e-commerce site and pays by credit card is simultaneously a party to a distance contract, a credit card user, and a buyer expecting service from the freight company.

FUTURE RESEARCH DIRECTIONS

As digitization and related technologies rapidly take their place in consumers' personal and business lives, marketers will need to integrate digital technologies more and more into their business processes. For this reason, each of the new marketing approaches and areas of digital technology development mentioned in this section should be discussed separately and in detail in terms of consumer behavior and decision-making processes. In particular, the role and impact of digitization on consumers' relationship with brands should be considered as a separate area of research. In addition, future research will inevitably need to take into account demographic and cultural variables when considering consumers' relationships with digital channels, platforms, and processes.

CONCLUSION

Today, the widespread use of the Internet, technological developments, globalization, changing consumer profiles, lifestyles and consumption habits have led target audiences to form new expectations. Marketing has inevitably had to develop new approaches to respond to these new expectations, as it is one of the functions that most closely follows technological developments in companies. With the introduction of digital technologies into our lives, traditional marketing practices have been largely replaced by digital marketing. This is because, in order to continue their activities, companies must inevitably benefit from digitalization.

Traditional marketing includes all marketing activities that take place outside the Internet. Digital marketing, on the other hand, is based on technology. Digitalized businesses benefit from artificial intelligence, recommendation systems, personalization, inventory management, customer relations, sales and after-sales operations, logistics, and in-store task creation. With artificial intelligence, companies can offer customized services and different products by answering customers' questions. Augmented reality offers the opportunity to virtually experience a product or service before actually buying it. Accurate prediction increases customer satisfaction and benefits retailers. Robot technology enables companies to provide fast, efficient and standardized service. By storing the digital footprints left by consumers as they walk around digital platforms as data, data-driven marketing activities are conducted, and with analytical predictive models, they can make predictions on many issues from pre-sale price to product design and minimize risks. On the other hand, the agile marketing approach provides a sustainable competitive advantage in a rapidly changing and dynamic market environment.

Companies need to constantly innovate to keep up with changing market dynamics and differentiate themselves from the competition, and they need to be able to lead and evolve, rather than follow, to avoid losing market share. To this end, they should work to keep their finger on the pulse of consumers, effectively use digital platforms to interact with them, and reflect technological developments in their marketing activities.

REFERENCES

Agile Transformation. (2014). *Marketing at the speed of agile A CMO's guide to applying agile methodologies to transform marketing*. PWC. https://www.pwc.com/us/en/advisory/business-strategy-consulting/assets/agile-marketing.pdf

Akben, İ., & Avşar, İ. İ. (2018). Endüstri 4.0 ve Karanlık Üretim: Genel Bir Bakış. *Türk Sosyal Bilimler Araştırmaları Dergisi*, 3(1), 26–37.

Akben, İ., & Ös, M. (2019). Akıllı ve Veriye Dayalı Tedarik Zincirleri. 3rd International EMI Entrepreneurship & Social Sciences Congress, 28-30.

Andhyka, B. (2020). Marketing 4.0 a Literature Review. *Journal of Business and Management*, 22(4), 49–52.

Aramamotoru. (2023). https://www.aramamotoru.com/icerik-pazarlamasi-ve-2023-yili-trendleri/

Arora, S., & Sahney, S. (2017). Webrooming behaviour: A conceptual framework. *International Journal of Retail & Distribution Management, 45*(7/8), 762–781. Advance online publication. doi:10.1108/IJRDM-09-2016-0158

Artun, O., & Levin, D. (2015). *Predictive marketing: Easy ways every marketer can use customer analytics and big data*. John Wiley & Sons. doi:10.1002/9781119175803

Balis, J. (2022). How brands can enter the metaverse. *HBR Online*, 1-6.

Batat, W. (2021). How augmented reality (AR) is transforming the restaurant sector: Investigating the impact of "Le Petit Chef" on customers' dining experiences. *Technological Forecasting and Social Change, 172*(C), 3–10. doi:10.1016/j. techfore.2021.121013

Batat, W. (2022). What does phygital really mean? A conceptual introduction to the phygital customer experience (PH-CX) framework. *Journal of Strategic Marketing*, 10–18. doi:10.1080/0965254X.2022.2059775

Belk, R. (2020). Resurrecting marketing. *AMS Review, 10*(3), 168–171. doi:10.1007/s13162-020-00182-9

Bhandari, R., Singer, M., & van der Scheer, H. (2014). Using Marketing Analytics to Drive Superior Growth. *The McKinsey Quarterly*.

Bolton, R. N. (2020). First steps to creating high impact theory in marketing. *AMS Review, 10*(3), 172–178. doi:10.1007/s13162-020-00181-w

Çalış Duman, M. (2022). Toplum 5.0: İnsan odaklı dijital dönüşüm. *Sosyal Siyaset Konferansları Dergisi, 82*, 309–336. doi:10.26650/jspc.2022.82.1008072

Çalışkan, G., & Erdoğan, Y. (2023). Marketing 5.0. In The Essentials of Today's Marketing (pp. 87-102). Efe Akademi.

Chohan, R., & Paschen, J. (2021). What marketers need to know about non-fungible tokens (NFTs). *Business Horizons, 66*(1), 43–50. doi:10.1016/j.bushor.2021.12.004

Deighton, J. A., Mela, C. F., & Moorman, C. (2021). Marketing thinking and doing. *Journal of Marketing, 85*(1), 1–6. doi:10.1177/0022242920977093

Deloitte Insights. (2022). *2022 Global Marketing Trends, Thriving through customer centricity*. https://www2.deloitte.com/content/dam/insights/articles/us164911_gmt_2022_master/DI_2022-Global-Marketing-Trends.pdf

Donthu, N., Kumar, S., Pattnaik, D., & Lim, W. M. (2021). A bibliometric retrospection of marketing from the lens of psychology: Insights from Psychology & Marketing. *Psychology and Marketing, 38*(5), 834–865. doi:10.1002/mar.21472

Edelman. (2021). Edelman Trust Barometer Special Report 2021. *Trust the New Brand Equity*, 7-15. https://www.edelman.com/sites/g/files/aatuss191/files/2021-06/2021%20Edelman%20Trust%20Barometer%20Specl%20Report%20Trust%20The%20New%20Brand%20Equity.pdf

Erragcha, N., & Romdhane, V. (2014). New Faces of Marketing In The Era of The Web: From Marketing 1.0 To Marketing 3.0. *Journal of Research in Marketing*, 2(2), 137–142. doi:10.17722/jorm.v2i2.46

Faulkner, P., & Runde, J. (2011, July). The social, the material, and the ontology of non-material technological objects. In European Group for Organizational Studies (EGOS) Colloquium, Gothenburg (Vol. 985, pp. 4-8). Academic Press.

Fucui, M., & Dumitrescu, L. (2018). From Marketing 1.0 To Marketing 4.0 – The Evolution Of The Marketing Concept In The Context Of The 21st Century. *International Conference Knowledge-Based Organization, 24*(2), 43-48.

Grandhi, B., Patwa, N., & Saleem, K. (2021). Data-driven marketing for growth and profitability. *EuroMed Journal of Business*, 16(4), 381–398. doi:10.1108/EMJB-09-2018-0054

Grewal, D., Hulland, J., Kopalle, P., & Karahanna, E. (2020). The future of technology and marketing: A multidisciplinary perspective. *Journal of the Academy of Marketing Science*, 48(1), 1–8. doi:10.1007/s11747-019-00711-4

Hassouneh, D., & Brengman, M. (2015). *Retailing in social virtual worlds: developing a typology of virtual store atmospherics*. Academic Press.

Hunt, S. D. (2020). Indigenous theory development in marketing: The foundational premises approach. *AMS Review*, 10(1), 8–17. doi:10.1007/s13162-020-00165-w

Järvinen, J., & Karjaluoto, H. (2015). The use of Web analytics for digital marketing performance measurement. *Industrial Marketing Management*, 50, 117–127. doi:10.1016/j.indmarman.2015.04.009

Johnson, M., & Barlow, R. (2021). Defining the Phygital Marketing Advantage. *Journal of Theoretical and Applied Electronic Commerce Research, 16*(6), 2365–2385. doi:10.3390/jtaer16060130

Kenny, D., & Marshall, J. (2020). Contextual Marketing: The Real Business of the Internet. *Harvard Business Review*. https://hbr.org/2000/11/contextual-marketing-the-real-business-of-the-internet

Kotler, P., Kartajaya, H., & Setiawan, I. (2010). *Marketing 3.0*. John Wiley & Sons, Inc. doi:10.1002/9781118257883

Kotler, P., Kartajaya, H., & Setiawan, I. (2017). *Marketing 4.0*. John Wiley & Sons, Inc.

Kotler, P., Kartajaya, H., & Setiawan, I. (2021). *Marketing 5.0*. John Wiley & Sons, Inc.

Mustajbasic, A. (2018). *Introducing an E-Marketplace and Phygital Store to the Swiss Market: The Key Success Factors for the Fashion Industry in Switzerland*. Haute Ecole de Gestion de Genève, Bachelor Project.

Nan, X., & Faber, R. J. (2004). Advertising theory: Reconceptualizing the building blocks. *Marketing Theory*, *4*(1-2), 7–30. doi:10.1177/1470593104044085

Ok, Ş., & Kağıtçı Candan, S. (2023). Endüstri 5.0'a Doğru Pazarlama 5.0. In İnsan ve Teknoloji, Sanayi Yönetiminde Gelecek yaklaşımları Dijitalleşme ve Yetenekler (pp. 59-82). Nobel Yayınevi.

Pazarlama30. (2023). https://www.pazarlama30.com/2023-yili-icerik-pazarlama-trendleri/

Pazarlama. (2023). https://pazarlamailetisimi.com/2023-pazarlama-trendleri-ve-pazarlama-dunyasini-bekleyen-riskler/

Purcarea, T. (2019). Modern Marketing, CX, CRM, Customer Trust and Identity. *Holistic Marketing Management Journal*, *9*(1), 8.

Sajidan, S. Saputro, R. Perdana, I. R., Atmojo W. & Nugraha D.A. (2020). Development of science learning model towards Society 5.0: A conceptual model. *Journal of Physics: Conference Series, 1511*, 2. . doi:10.1088/1742-6596/1511/1/012124

Siradisidigital. (2023). https://siradisidigital.com/blog/2023-dijital-pazarlama-trendleri

Talukdar, N., & Yu, S. (2021). Breaking the psychological distance: The effect of immersive virtual reality on perceived novelty and user satisfaction. *Journal of Strategic Marketing*, *12*, 1–25. Advance online publication. doi:10.1080/096525 4X.2021.1967428

Thinkwithgoogle. (2023). https://www.thinkwithgoogle.com/intl/tr-tr/icgoruler/tuketici-trendleri/2023-dijital-pazarlama-trendleri/

Tueanrat, Y., Papagiannidis, S., & Alamanos, E. (2021). A conceptual framework of the antecedents of customer journey satisfaction in omnichannel retailing. *Journal of Retailing*.

New Marketing Approaches and Consumer Trends

Van Tichelen, B. (2019). *The Role and Opportunities of Phygital in the Digital Omni-Channel Strategy*. Louvain School of Management, Université Catholique de Louvain. http://hdl.handle.net/2078.1/thesis:21074

Vanessa, N., & Japutra, A. (2021). Contextual Marketing Based on Customer Buying Pattern in Grocery E-Commerce: The Case of Bigbasket.com (India). *ASEAN Marketing Journal, 9*(1). Advance online publication. doi:10.21002/amj.v9i1.9286

Wong An Kee, A., & Yazdanifard, R. (2015). The Review of Content Marketing as a New Trend in Marketing Practices. *International Journal of Management. Accounting and Economics, 2*(9), 1055–1064.

Zengin, S. (2022). Çevik Pazarlama Yapısının İşletmelerde Uygulanmasına İlişkin Öneriler. *Beykent Üniversitesi Sosyal Bilimler Dergisi, 15*(2), 98–111. doi:10.18221/bujss.1140640

ADDITIONAL READING

Akour, I. A., Al-Maroof, R. S., Alfaisal, R., & Salloum, S. A. (2022). A conceptual framework for determining metaverse adoption in higher institutions of gulf area: An empirical study using hybridSEM-ANN approach. *Computers and Education: ArtificialIntelligence, 3*(100052), 1–14. doi:10.1016/j.caeai.2022.100052

Artun, O., & Levin, D. (2015). *Predictive marketing: Easy ways every marketer can use customer analytics and big data*. John Wiley & Sons. doi:10.1002/9781119175803

Balis, J. (2022). How brands can enter the metaverse. *HBR Online*, 1-6.

Batat, W. (2022). What does phygital really mean? A conceptual introduction to the phygital customer experience (PH-CX) framework. *Journal of Strategic Marketing*, 1–24. Advance online publication. doi:10.1080/0965254X.2022.2059775

Bezovski, Z., Apasieva, T. J., & Temjanovski, R. (2021). The Impact and the Potential Disruption of the Blockchain Technology on Marketing. *Journal of Economics, 6*(1), 13–22. doi:10.46763/JOE216.10013b

Johnson, M., & Barlow, R. (2021). Defining the Phygital Marketing Advantage. *Journal of Theoretical and Applied Electronic Commerce Research, 16*(6), 2365–2385. doi:10.3390/jtaer16060130

Kim, J. (2021). Advertising in the Metaverse: Research Agenda. *Journal of Interactive Advertising, 21*(3), 141–144. doi:10.1080/15252019.2021.2001273

Kotler, P., Kartajaya, H., & Setiawan, I. (2021). *Marketing 5.0*. John Wiley & Sons, Inc.

KEY TERMS AND DEFINITIONS

Artificial Intelligence: It is the ability of a computer or computer-controlled robot to perform tasks generally associated with intelligent beings, changing with the development of technology.

Content Marketing: Content marketing can be defined as a management process by which a firm identifies, analyzes and satisfies customer demand to generate profit through the use of digital content distributed through electronic channels.

Influencer Marketing: It refers to the use of influencer marketing by businesses, brands and companies to market their products, services and promotional content through social media channels through social media influencers on the internet.

Machine Learning: It is a field that enables a computer system to learn using data. It helps algorithms automatically learn from data in order to perform a specific task and provides these algorithms with analysis, prediction and decision-making capabilities.

Marketing 5.0: Marketing 5.0 is considered as creating, delivering and enhancing value through the customer experience that is created by using these technologies and systems. The components of Marketing 5.0 are data driven, predictive, contextual, augmented and agile marketing approaches.

Metaverse: It is called a universe or environment created by the combination of many digital platforms and tools. These platforms and tools include social media, augmented reality, virtual reality, cryptocurrencies, and similar elements.

Mobile Advertising: It is a multi-channel marketing strategy that helps marketers reach audiences via smartphones, tablets and other mobile devices. More consumers are using mobile devices. The use of mobile devices for activities other than communication is increasing.

Phygital Marketing: Phygital marketing is a marketing approach that offers consumers a new consumption experience design by integrating experiences in physical and digital environments.

Chapter 6

Where Is Digital Retailing Evolving?
An Evaluation From the Perspective of Digital Retailing Technologies

Cansu Gökmen Köksal

(iD) https://orcid.org/0000-0001-9139-0451
Istanbul Topkapi University, Turkey

ABSTRACT

This study delves into the intricacies of digitalization in the retail industry and how it has evolved with the onset of the industrial revolution. It explores the dynamics of this process and proposes several frameworks for categorizing digital retailing technologies. Additionally, the study highlights the core technologies that are integral to this transformation. Moreover, it examines the shift from conventional retail practices to metaverse retailing, showcasing the distinctive attributes of this model. Lastly, the research delves into the factors that are set to shape the future of retailing and offers recommendations for further exploration in this area.

INTRODUCTION

The introduction of technology has brought about a new era of digitalization, making communication possible through telephones, computer networks, the Internet, and mobile phones. One of the most significant outcomes of this shift has been the emergence of e-commerce in the mid-1990s, which transformed essential business activities like purchasing, selling, communicating, and inventory management

DOI: 10.4018/979-8-3693-1594-1.ch006

Copyright © 2024, IGI Global. Copying or distributing in print or electronic forms without written permission of IGI Global is prohibited.

(Bourlakis et al., 2009; Grewal et al., 2004). As a result, shopping has undergone a paradigm shift, transforming the retail environment, the actors involved in retailing, and the critical issues surrounding it (Hagberg et al., 2016). Moreover, consumers have taken on a more active role in the consumption process, with the power to engage in online activities such as product selection, research, and purchasing (Labrecque et al., 2013). However, retailers have also faced these developments, including changing economic conditions, globalization, and evolving business practices (Dawson, 2000). In this competitive and ever-changing market, retailers must quickly adapt to digitalization to stay competitive and minimize losses. Responding to these challenges, traditional retailers have started adopting digital retail strategies through digital technology, enabling them to use new channels and shopper touch points (Hagberg, et al., 2016; Hokkanen et al., 2020).

In retail, physical stores let customers try products, while digital stores offer ease of use, customization (Baker et al., 1992; Bitner,1992). Srinivasan et al., 2002), website design(Grewal et al., 2004; Wolfinbarger & Gilly, 2003; Yoo & Donthu, 2001), security (Wolfinbarger & Gilly, 2003; Yoo & Donthu, 2001), and speed(Dabholkar, 1996; Yoo & Donthu, 2001). Traditional retailing is suitable for all types of shoppers, including social ones. Electronic retailing is popular with those who seek convenience and embrace technology (Bourlakis et al., 2009). However, this situation has changed with the pandemic process (OECD, 2020). While research shows that 46% of consumers shopped online for the first time during the pandemic period and 71% will continue to shop due to the uncertain course of the epidemic (Retail customer experience, 2020), they predict that sales will reach 6.5 trillion (Blake, 2020; Kazancoglu and Demir, 2021).

Undoubtedly, the compulsory and troublesome pandemic process has catalyzed the digitalization process. Especially during this period, the problems faced by retailers who had to slow down or even stop their sales in stores and even their production processes due to the virus ranged from focusing on the management of fixed assets to concerns about planning regarding traditional logistics and store locations to the management of information technologies, the creation of information infrastructure and the storage of consumer data and its practical use. It has given way to concerns about its proper use and management (Pantano et al., 2020). Traditional retailers compete to offer their services in the right store design, store location, and ideal location while dealing with issues related to stock, communication, and interaction with consumers and the problems arising from these processes (Nanda et al., 2021). On the other hand, electronic retailers focus on security and privacy issues, which are one of the most important handicaps of developing communication technologies, on the realization of timely delivery, and most importantly, on accelerating the focus on the adaptation process by catching the latest technological trends and constantly developing new ideas (OECD, 2020; Shankar et al., 2021). To succeed in today's

Where Is Digital Retailing Evolving?

retail landscape, traditional retailers must adapt to the needs of digitally connected customers (Kotler et al., 2021). Seamless cross-channel shopping experiences and integration of physical and virtual presence through an omnichannel strategy are essential for retailers (Verhoef, 2021). The transformational impact of digital retail technologies for businesses and consumers cannot be overstated, as these technologies provide a range of tools and options to streamline operations, enhance shopping experiences, and boost sales (Har et al., 2022). To understand the future of retailing, it is critical to examine the evolution of technology. This section first will discuss the technologies driving the development of digital retailing and provide insight into future projections of the major players in this field: Artificial intelligence (e.g., Kishen et al., 2021), virtual assistants, chatbots and robots (e.g., Kamoonpuri & Sengar, 2023), voice commerce (e.g., De Regt & Barnes, 2019), machine learning, augmented reality (AR) and virtual reality (VR) (e.g., Caboni & Hagberg, 2019; Zhang, 2020).

According to a recent classification by McKinsey, the term "zero consumers" reflects a consumer group that operates without traditional constraints or loyalty, actively seeks value in terms of both cost and quality and places a high premium on convenience and sustainability in their purchasing decisions. Nowadays, consumers prioritize ethical and environmental considerations in their purchasing decisions and spend significant time on social media. Furthermore, they are less loyal and dissatisfied with traditional shopping experiences, placing convenience as their top priority (Begley et al., 2023). As new consumers become more prevalent, the successful retailers of the future will be those with large and highly loyal consumer bases. To achieve this, retailers must establish long-term relationships with their customers by becoming indispensable in as many areas of their lives as possible and offering unique experiences. This requires providing a seamless experience integrating physical and online activities while considering evolving technologies and changing sensitivities. By adopting these innovations, retailers can add value to their processes and consumers (Begley et al., 2023; Das et al.,2023). The retail industry is experiencing a technological revolution with advancements such as micro-cloud computing, virtual and augmented reality, mixed reality, 5G networks, robotics, the Internet of Things (IoT), and drones. These innovations reshape retail and are critical in adapting to unforeseen risks and turning them into opportunities. This dynamic environment presents the potential for metaverse retailing to offer a unique experience to both consumers and retailers (Narin et al., 2022). Metaverse applications offer the chance to leverage the advantages of digitalization simultaneously. They are expected to introduce innovative financial solutions that address privacy and security concerns that still need to be resolved (Bacher, 2022; Bourlakis et al., 2009). Moreover, metaverse retailing is described as the missing piece of the e-retailing puzzle that will go beyond the limitation of online channels and allow consumers to immerse themselves in the experience offered (Papagiannidis et al, 2010). In this context, this study aims to explain the trend in digital retailing in the context of prominent technologies in digital retailing. Based on this, the first part, the study's theoretical background, discusses digital transformation in retailing and classifications of digital technologies. In the second part of the study, digital retail technologies and technologies that accelerate digital transformation are defined, and the purposes for which these technologies are used are explained. The last part of the research discusses the development process of metaverse retailing to explain its role in the future of digital retailing.

THEORETICAL BACKGROUND

Digitalization Process in Retailing

The impact of digitalization on modern society has been significant, leading to new industry standards and technological advancements in various sectors, including retail. Over the past few decades, the retail industry has undergone a significant transformation driven by technological developments (Hagberg et al., 2016). The Internet has enabled retailers to expand their business opportunities to global markets, leading to changes in business models, types of commerce, and purchasing processes (Sorescu et al., 2011). Although digitization, digitalization, and digital transformation sometimes have similar meanings, they represent different development processes and characteristics regarding their definitions and scopes. Digitization, which is at the first stage according to the digital transformation hierarchy, is defined as "the process of changing from analog to digital form" (O'Leary, 2023, p. 3). Accordingly, it is about transforming something that is not digital into a digital representation, an artificial structure. Examples include scanning barcodes or using RFID tags to create digital records of products. On the other hand, digitalization is about using digital technologies to develop new business models and obtain new opportunities. This process has enabled consumers to make all kinds of information about products and purchase transactions online, with the new business model that emerged with electronic retailing. Thus, the purchasing process has gone beyond physical visits to stores (Bloomberg, 2018; Gupta, 2020; O'Leary, 2023). Hagberg et al. (2016) define digitalization as the integration of internet-connected digital technologies primarily between retailers and customers, encompassing the digitization of all aspects of the consumption process. This includes converting physical products into digital services, consumer recommendations on social media, and the use of digital devices throughout the purchasing process. According to the authors, digitalization offers more than just an online presence and has the potential to shape the future of

Where Is Digital Retailing Evolving?

retailers, consumers, employees, and society. On the other hand, Digital (Business) Transformation is "the process of exploiting digital technologies and supporting capabilities to create a robust new digital business model" (O'Leary, 2023, p.3). Accordingly, it covers the uninterrupted experience created by integrating online and offline channels. Data analytics in each strategy developed at this point reflects a customer-focused, advanced business model by utilizing technologies such as augmented reality to enrich consumers' experiences. Digital retail technologies have transformed how consumers and organizations conduct business. They provide various tools and options to improve the shopping experience, streamline processes, and increase sales (Har et al., 2022). Retailers can use technology-enabled resources such as instruments, devices, bots, tools, teams, protocols, processes, networks, and methodologies to provide employees and customers access to vast content. This includes expert and social reviews, data, information, reports, analysis, and games, enabling users to make more informed decisions, leading to increased revenue and margin, improved service levels, and reduced costs (Deloitte, 2017). However, it is essential to evaluate the transformation process that began with the Industrial Revolution in the context of retailing to make future projections about digital retailing. The Industrial Revolution was a period that profoundly impacted how societies conducted business and how they lived, worked, and socialized. As a result of the transformative effect of these technologies, the retail industry has gone through four stages of evolution. These innovations have played a pivotal role in improving business operations, enhancing customer experiences, and driving revenue growth. Therefore, exploring the classification and explanation of digital retailing technologies within the context of the current evolutionary retailing process is crucial as the industry continues to embrace digitalization with unwavering determination.

Development and Classification of Digital Retail Technologies

The advancements since the first industrial revolution in the 18th century have completely transformed the production and consumption process. The invention of steam engines increased production efficiency, reducing the need for human labor. The implementation of mass production assembly lines during the Second Industrial Revolution made high-quality products accessible to consumers at lower prices, and enabled manufacturers to produce at lower costs (Hollinshead, 1996; Noble et al., 2022). Subsequently, the third industrial revolution brought about changes in information and communication technologies, leading to the emergence of the information society and the electronicization and globalization of commercial transactions (Hollinshead, 1996). Finally, Industry 4.0 has introduced the Internet of Things, paving the way for unmanned technology by connecting devices and systems over the internet to facilitate data exchange. Despite not being initially designed

143

for the retail industry, many technological advancements, especially during the late 19th and early 20th centuries, were embraced by retailers and became catalysts for significant changes (Varadarajan et al., 2010). The industrial revolution, powered by digital technologies, has revolutionized industrial processes and brought about a significant transformation to the retail industry (Grewal et al., 2021; Noble et al., 2022).

The rise of digital technologies and platforms such as computers, the internet, smartphones, and social media has significantly transformed the way companies present their products/services to their clients. These technologies have also transformed the way companies interact with customers. In this vein, the retail industry's transformation appears in Figure 1.

Figure 1. The transformation of the retailing industry
(Adapted from Har et al., 2022)

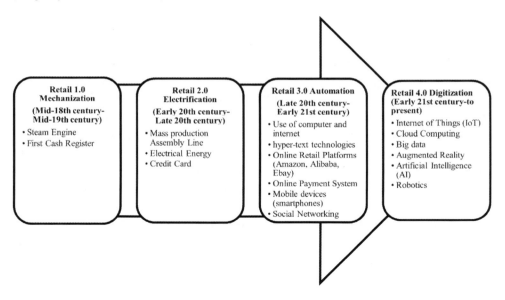

Retail is transforming with the help of emerging technologies that have helped consumers interact with firms and shop in new ways. This evolution is ongoing and dynamic, with each step bringing new platforms and technologies, such as the metaverse, that enrich the consumer experience. By combining developed technologies with new daily features, retailers promise to enhance the retail experience. However, as technology continues to rapidly evolve, researchers in the retail field are working to gain a deeper understanding of the impact of digital retailing technologies on various industry stakeholders (Bourlakis et al., 2009; Grewal et al., 2004). They are analyzing

Where Is Digital Retailing Evolving?

the effects of these technologies on different aspects of retailing, such as consumer behavior, supply chain management, and marketing strategies. This systematic approach provides valuable insights to help retailers adapt and stay competitive in an increasingly digital world. To categorize digital retailing technologies, researchers have developed typologies based on their impacts on consumers and retailers. Some researchers have also explored the capabilities gained by combining these typologies with consumers' decision-making and purchasing processes (Grewal et al., 2019; Sethuraman & Parasuraman, 2005; Varadarajan et al.,2010, etc.)

For instance, according to Sethuraman and Parasuraman's (2005) classification, retail technologies are cost-saving and service-enhancing. Cost-saving technologies may have a positive, negative, or no impact on customer service while service-enhancing technologies can similarly affect product costs or prices. The researchers assert that investing in technology can significantly enhance retail offerings, providing better service and lower prices, especially for retailers targeting most consumers. By investing in technology, these retailers can improve their offerings and provide a superior experience for their customers.

Varadarajan et al. (2010) examined how technologies have influenced retail strategies and operations. The researchers classified existing technologies based on their historical development to predict the potential effects of new interactive technologies. They identified three categories: infrastructure technologies, communication technologies and interactive technologies. This classification allowed them to analyze the impact of each technology type on retailing practices. Researchers synopsis an overview of the effects of interactive technologies on consumers' shopping experiences in different retail types and how they affect retailers' capabilities and business models.

Willems et al. (2016) have created a comprehensive inventory of retail technologies through a systematic review of studies conducted between 2008 and 2016. This inventory is based on the type of shopping value provided by the technologies in the context of point-of-sale retailing and the stages involved in consumers' purchasing process. Table 1 defines the classification of retail technologies according to their ability to offer utilitarian and hedonic values and their positioning of consumers' purchasing processes. The results suggest that while most technologies provide cost savings, convenience, and utility value, few offer hedonic or symbolic benefits.

Grewal et al. (2019, p. 98) classified technologies into 4 categories "according to their level of convenience (low/high) and social presence(low/high)" for consumers. It is important to note that when it comes to the effects of technology on shopping experiences, some technologies benefit companies' operations more than the customers' comfort and social presence. However, this does not mean these technologies are not valuable to the retail firm. For example, an embodied inventory robot like Schnuck's may provide customers with little convenience or social presence.

145

However, it can improve the retailer's operational efficiency by monitoring shelves and taking stock of inventory (Cong et al., 2021). On the other hand, according to this typology, certain technologies can enhance customer convenience and social presence. For example, scanning QR codes into a mobile phone to access detailed product information can be very helpful. Additionally, Siri, Microsoft Cortana or Alexa may not look like humans, but they can engage in two-way conversations, improving social presence (Rafailidis & Manolopoulos, 2019).

Roggeveen and Sethuraman (2020, pp. 300-305) have categorized "retailing technologies developed since 2000 based on the three stages of a consumer's purchasing journey: pre-purchase, purchase, and post-purchase". The technologies were grouped under six subheadings based on the functions they offer to consumers in each stage. This classification has provided a clear framework for analyzing the impact of these technologies on the consumer behavior. During the pre-purchase stage, technology can be incredibly useful for consumers by helping them define their needs and find suitable options before making a purchase. For instance, chatbots and virtual shopping assistants are designed to assist customers in finding answers to their questions (Rese et al., 2020). Retailers like Amazon have also incorporated recommendation agents to suggest comparable and alternative products, which can attract the attention of potential customers (Blut et al., 2023).

Shankar et al. (2021) have developed their technology inventories by combining consumer-focused and retail-focused approaches, considering elements related to shoppers' perceptions and retailers' business models. This research delves into the motivations behind technology integration among shoppers, retailers, employees, and suppliers and its impact. The authors posit that technology is a versatile framework that can revolutionize the retail industry and facilitate its ability to adjust to unforeseen circumstances. Consequently, inventive tactics devised to cater to evolving consumer preferences across various store models, including compact stores, exhibition spaces for novel product debuts, temporary stores, rental outlets, repair and return centers, expansive, immersive retail spaces, community-based retailers, and convenience stores, are projected to become increasingly indispensable in the coming years.

This research makes a valuable contribution to the existing literature on retail technology. For example, Grewal (2019) proposed a framework to categorize consumer-only in-store technologies based on convenience and social presence, while Sethurmana and Parasuraman's research focused on cost-saving and service-enhancing technologies. However, as the retail environment continues to evolve with the emergence of omnichannel experiences and new technologies, it is clear that this classification needs to be expanded to include additional elements beyond cost and services. As summarized in the classification studies of the researchers, the number of technologies utilized in digital retailing is relatively high (Grewal et al., 2019; Roggeveen & Sethuraman, 2020; Shankar et al., 2021). This number

Where Is Digital Retailing Evolving?

is increasing daily with the integration of various methods. Now, considering all technologies and tools together has become increasingly challenging than before. On the other hand, in the Covid-19 period, when sales made with web and mobile tools have become obliged, the fact that consumers are involved in the faster digitalization process and feel more comfortable using digital channels has caused future retail opportunities in the context of the metaverse to become more apparent (GFK, 2023). Considering its recent popularity and development potential, this study focuses on metaverse retailing in the context of digital retailing trends. In this sense, the study deals with Machine Learning (ML), Augmented Reality (AR), Virtual Reality (VR), and Artificial Intelligence (AI) technologies, defined as the emerging technologies on which the metaverse is based (Bacher, 2022) and emphasized as the focus of retailers' technological investments in the GFK report (GFK, 2023). The section explains technologies with a classification that describes the fundamental technology behind each one.

Table 1. Summary of selected research focusing on the classification of technologies in retailing

Study	Classification Focus	Classification
Sethuraman and Parasuraman (2005)	customer-interfacing retail technologies	i. Cost-saving technology that does not affect service level *"- Cross-docking intended to reduce inventory costs"* ii. Cost-saving technology that reduces service level *-Automatic self-checkout lanes* iii. Cost-saving technology that enhances service level Information technology *"-IT and collaborative planning, forecasting, and replenishment (CPFR); RFID; and computerized shopping carts."* iv. Service-enhancing technology that does not affect costs to consumers *"- Biometric technology such as thumbprint identification instead of signature"* v. Service-enhancing technology that may increase costs to consumers *"-Navigation or payment system attached to grocery cart)"* vi. Service-enhancing technology that can result in potential cost savings for customers *"-E-commerce"*
Varadarajan et al. (2010)	A retrospective look at technological developments	i. Infrastructure Technologies *-Electricity, elevators, escalators, automobiles, railroads* ii. Communication Technologies *"Telephone, radio, television, catalogs, newspapers and billboards"* iii. Interactive Technologies *-"E-mail, hyper-text technologies, web browsers, instant messaging, access technologies, cellular phones with web browsing capability, GPS technologies, social networking, search technologies, bookmarking/ information organization technologies"*

continues on following page

Where Is Digital Retailing Evolving?

Table 1. Continued

Study	Classification Focus	Classification
Willems et al., (2016)	customer-interfacing retail technologies at the point of sale -Integrated path-to-purchase stages	i. Need Recognition *"Beacon technology (utilitarian)"* *"Digital Signage (hedonic)"* ii. Information Search *"Mobile shopping assistant (utilitarian)"* *"Virtual Shopping Assistant (hedonic)"* iii. Evaluating alternatives "RFID (utilitarian)" *"Augmented Reality Makeup Mirror(hedonic)"* iv. Purchase *"Window QR & Augmented Reality Codes (utilitarian)"* *"RFID-Based Smart Shopping Assistant(utilitarian)"* v. Post-purchase *"RFID-Based Smart Shopping Assistant (hedonic)"*
Grewal et al.,2019	customer-interfacing in-store retail technologies	i. Low convenience/low social presence *"Digital price tags"* *"Scent machines"* *"Smart shelves"* ii. Low convenience/high social presence, *"Embodied Inventory Robots"* *"Scatter Wall"* *"Ceiling Projection"* *"Augmented Reality"* *Virtual Reality* iii. High convenience/low social presence *"Self-Checkout"* *"3-D Printers"* *"Augmented Reality"* *"In-Store Kiosks"* *"Digital Comm. Recycling Bins"* *"Narrowcasting"* iv. High convenience/high social presence *"Augmented Reality"* *"Virtual Reality"* *"Embodied Robots"* *"Disembodied Robots"* *"Click-and-Flick Smart Windows"* *"Avatars"* *"Smart Displays"* *"Hero (Omnichannel platform connector)"*

continues on following page

Where Is Digital Retailing Evolving?

Table 1. Continued

Study	Classification Focus	Classification
Roggeveen and Sethuraman, 2020	customer-interfacing retail technologies -*since 2000* -Integrated customer journey stage	i. Pre-purchase stage a. Needs management technology 　*"Artificial intelligence and machine learning technology, chatbots, chatlines, cookies, recommendation agents, social listening, web morphing".* b. Search engagement technology 　"Beacon technology, digital catalog/kiosk/touchwalls, electronic shelf edge, gamification, livestream channel, robotic shopping assistant-static / mobile, store apps-product info/geo targeting, virtual glasses/trial room/ showroom, visual eyescan/image tech, voice activated computer/command device, wearable technology". ii. Purchase stage a. Purchase transaction technology 　*Cloud computing, e-wallet, one-click, smart cart* b. Physical acquisition technology 　*"Automated curbside pickup, digitally connected store, drone delivery, shoppable platform, touchless transfer"* iii. Post-purchase stage a. Follow-up service 　*"Auto-notification App, Product-based IoT"* b. Loyalty management technology 　*"App-based Rewards Program, Blockchain technology"*
Shankar et al.,2021	integration of customer-interfacing technologies and back-end technologies	i. "Stakeholder: shopper-facing, employee facing, supplier-facing" *eg. Mobile devices, wearables, smart speakers, AR, VR, and MR systems, IoT, chatbots, payment, and blockchain technologies.* ii. "IT Relatedness" iii. "Source of origin: internal vs. external, outside-in vs. inside out span *e.g., mobile payment, magic "* iv. "Newness: incremental vs. radical *eg.5G telecommunications wireless battery"* v. "Nature of change: facilitating vs. disruptive *eg., Apple Pay, Blockchain"* vi. "Outcome: commoditizing vs. value adding *eg., price comparison mobile app, adding a VR system to an existing offering"*

Digital Retail Technologies

a.　Artificial Intelligence (AI)

Artificial Intelligence (AI) is "a system's ability to interpret external data correctly, to learn from such data, and to use those learnings to achieve specific goals and tasks through flexible adaptation" (Haenlein & Kaplan, 2019, p.17). In the retail industry, retailers have access to vast amounts of customer data, and AI can be used to enhance customer interactions and decision-making processes. AI is essential to managing the data because it offers a reliable, real-time solution that lets retailers make well-informed decisions quickly. Table 2 shows that effective management provides retailers with significant opportunities and advantages. AI technology offers numerous benefits to the retail industry. By analyzing customer data, it can provide personalized shopping experiences and tailored recommendations to boost profits in Omnichannel and mobile shopping. Artificial intelligence (AI) algorithms can revolutionize inventory management and demand forecasting processes. These algorithms can predict future demand accurately, helping businesses optimize inventory levels and avoid stockouts. It saves costs and increases supply chain efficiency, increasing customer satisfaction. Retailers can also provide instant, personalized support through AI-powered chatbots and virtual voice assistants, thus enhancing customer service (Kishen et al., 2021). AI can also help in optimizing prices, enabling retailers to set competitive prices and maximize profits. Additionally, visual search technology powered by AI allows customers to search for products using images or descriptions, improving product discovery. According to recent studies (Guha et al., 2021; Pillai et al., 2020; Shankar et al., 2018), Amazon is a leading retailer that has embraced cutting-edge AI technology to gather, organize, and evaluate vast amounts of data to inform critical business decisions. This information feeds into customer interactions, creating a cycle of continuous data collection, analysis, and decision-making that grows exponentially with the increasing volume of data (Wang et al., 2021). Consequently, AI is a powerful system that operates in real-time, enabling retailers to make informed decisions quickly and efficiently (Shankar et al., 2018).

On the other hand, AI, ML, and Deep Learning are often used interchangeably, but they have distinct meanings and applications. Machine learning and deep learning are the subdomains of AI. AI encompasses early automated systems and ML systems that improve over time. ML can make predictions with minimal human intervention, while Deep Learning uses neural networks to mimic the human mind's decision-making processes (Morgan et al., 2020). See Figure 2 for the hierarchy. Recently, AI-based technologies such as robots, chatbots, augmented reality, virtual reality, machine learning, deep learning, computer vision, and cognitive speech commerce are becoming increasingly common in retail settings (Pillai et al., 2020) Within the scope of this study, explanations about the widespread effects of these artificial intelligence-based algorithms and technologies in retailing will be positioned under the umbrella of artificial intelligence and conveyed under subheadings.

Figure 2. Taxonomy of artificial intelligence technologies
(Morgan et al., 2020)

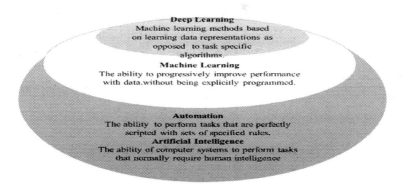

i.   Virtual Assistants, Chatbots and Robots

Artificial intelligence (AI) is the driving force behind various automated systems, such as *virtual assistants*, chatbots, and robots. The introduction of virtual assistants has revolutionized the online shopping industry, providing unmatched convenience and ease. These advanced computer programs, such as Siri, Cortana, and Alexa, can understand and fulfill user requests, ensuring a seamless shopping experience for customers (Hoyer et al., 2020). Additionally, virtual shopping assistants act as personalized advisors, providing customers with comprehensive product information, tailored recommendations based on their preferences, and assistance with payment and order tracking. These retail bots are designed to help customers find the products they need while also addressing any concerns they may have. With virtual assistants, online shopping becomes more enriching, personalized, and enjoyable (Hoyer et al., 2020; Rane, 2023).

Chatbots are "software programs that interact with users in natural language, either through audio or written communication" (Shawar & Atwell, 2007, p. 29). These virtual assistants use sophisticated natural language processing (NLP) algorithms to interpret user input and respond accordingly. Chatbots can handle multiple customer queries and requests simultaneously without requiring human intervention (Hoyer et al., 2020). For instance, the pioneering chatbot ELIZA, created by Joseph Weizenbaum, uses predetermined keywords for prompt replies to user questions. If it cannot generate a solution, it will use other methods to extract additional information from the user (Singh et al., 2018). The impressive side of chatbots is their ability to mimic human interactions authentically (Chong et al., 2021). Retailers use them as shopping assistants to answer questions, make recommendations, understand complex dialogues, offer discounts, and suggest products. These retail chatbots use advanced artificial intelligence and can be accessed online or through mobile applications (Kaczorowska-Spychalska, 2019; Singh et al., 2018). Chatbots have the potential to serve as customer service representatives at every stage of the customer journey. By providing written responses to customer inquiries 24/7, they offer a cost-effective and automated form of first-level support (Backhaus & Awan, 2019; Rese et al., 2020). Whether handling simple or complex inquiries, retail chatbots can help customers find products, navigate the purchasing process, and inform them of loyalty programs. They can even offer personalized recommendations based on shopping behavior and user data. When it comes to conversational commerce, chatbots are incredibly beneficial for retail. By allowing customers to engage in natural language conversations, they can create more meaningful interactions with brands, leading to increased customer satisfaction and sales. (Leung & Yan Chan, 2020). As per future projections, chatbots are expected to become the primary customer support channel for all companies. The transactions carried out through chatbots are expected to reach a whopping $112 billion by 2023 and save businesses almost 2.5 billion hours of work. Therefore, investing in and enhancing chatbots as an artificial intelligence tool is crucial, especially in today's highly competitive environment (Ritter, 2023). By leveraging AI-powered chatbots, businesses and organizations can provide round-the-clock customer service, improve operational efficiency, and enhance the overall customer experience (Backhaus & Awan, 2019; Hoyer et al, 2020; Rese et al., 2020).

The market for service *robots* is rapidly expanding. It is estimated that by 2026, the industry will generate a revenue of over USD 103 billion (Markets and Markets, 2020). Xiao and Kumar (2021) defined *"service robots as physical machines embedded with AI technologies that can interact with one another and contribute to the dynamics of consumers' service experience"*. Retail robots can be used for tasks such as inventory management, restocking of shelves, assisting customers, and even providing checkout services. Retail robots can help store owners improve customer experience and reduce labor costs (Kumar et al., 2014; Bertacchini et al., 2017). Advancements in artificial intelligence are expected to enhance the operational capabilities of service robotics, leading to improved productivity and data-driven performance in the long term. AI-based robots can perform tasks faster and with greater precision than humans, increasing efficiency and productivity across various industries. They can use sensors and other technologies to measure and analyze data accurately, resulting in more precise outcomes and better decision-making abilities (Markets & Markets, 2020).

Where Is Digital Retailing Evolving?

ii.   Voice Commerce

Voice commerce is a groundbreaking service that allows people to shop with ease using voice assistants developed by retail giants. Voice assistants like Amazon Alexa, Samsung Bixby, Apple Siri, Microsoft Cortana, and Google Assistant have become an essential part of our daily lives, making it simpler for us to interact with them through speech (Mittal & Manocha, 2023). Rzepka et al. (2020) defines "voice commerce as retailor shopping-related activities through voice assistants." Voice assistants are integrated into various devices such as smartphones, cars, TVs, and smart speakers, and can assist us in finding things, comparing products, and making purchases.This cutting-edge software employs advanced artificial intelligence techniques such as automatic speech recognition (ASR), text-to-speech synthesis (TTS), and natural language understanding (NLU) to facilitate seamless interaction (Mari, 2019; Nguyen et al., 2021) This technology is predominantly featured in intelligent devices. Voice shopping is the process of placing orders online via voice assistants. Voice commerce, thus, provides customers with the added advantage of personalized recommendations, thereby augmenting their shopping experience. Additionally, AI-powered chatbots are capable of enhancing customer engagement, while voice search mechanisms streamline product catalogs, enabling easy access to top-rated products. The integration of such technological advancements proffers a promising future for the retail industry, as customers are empowered to shop more efficiently and conveniently (Böhm et al., 2022; Mittal & Manocha,2023; Villegas et al., 2023). In the coming years, the global voice recognition market is expected to exceed $26 billion, indicating a growing number of people adopting voice commerce and discovering new opportunities (Ruby, 2023). While an increasing number of people are utilizing smart speakers to make purchases, the proportion of people using voice assistants varies depending on the product type. For this reason, It is crucial to examine the factors that impact consumers' use of voice assistants to promote widespread adoption of the technology.

iii.   Machine Learning

Machine learning is a powerful tool that allows systems to learn patterns from data, continuously improve performance, and make predictions based on those patterns (LeCun, 2015; Wang et al., 2021). Many industries, especially retail, are increasingly using machine learning to provide better experiences for both consumers and retailers with techniques including web searches, social media filtering, e-commerce recommendations, image recognition, speech-to-text and more. Machine Learning (ML) has proven to be a powerful tool for businesses. For example, Walmart uses ML to sort similar products from different sellers by analyzing their features and descriptions. This model has an error rate of less than 0.01% after analyzing over 35 million products. Another example is IKEA, which has managed to reduce wastage rates by using ML (Wang et al., 2021).

ML can help businesses improve their marketing campaigns by providing insights into consumer behavior. Market structures can be better understood by analyzing consumer preferences with ML. User-generated content like comments and tags can be analyzed using ML, making it possible to extract valuable insights for market analysis. Additionally, businesses can provide personalized product recommendations and discounts based on a consumer's shopping history using ML. Loyalty programs can also be enhanced using supervised ML algorithms. Finally, analyzing consumer posts can give businesses a deeper understanding of their customers' needs and preferences (Mathur & Mathur, 2019; Wang et al., 2021).

Augmented Reality (AR) and Virtual Reality (VR)

Augmented Reality (AR) is a powerful technique that seamlessly blends natural and computer-generated digital information into the user's view of the physical world, making it appear as a single environment (Olsson et al., 2013). By offering "context-specific information" at or near the point of purchase, AR has the potential to transform the retail industry (Hilken et al., 2020; Jessen et al., 2020; Scholz & Smith, 2016). It has successfully united the worlds of offline and online experiences. It can significantly enhance customer satisfaction and loyalty by creating an immersive experience of a real-world environment through computer-generated displays. Through the use of AR, customers can seamlessly overlay digital data onto physical products, explore various product variations, and confidently make informed purchasing decisions. By promoting customer engagement and reducing the likelihood of product returns, AR technology empowers retailers to differentiate themselves from competitors by showcasing their dedication to innovation and delivering customer-centric experiences (Hoyet et al., 2020; Jessen et al., 2020) This results in more interactive, vivid, and richer experiences for consumers (Caboni & Hagberg, 2019; Scholz & Smith, 2016). This is often done on handheld or smartphone devices where additional information, in textual, visual, or other sensory form, may be displayed (e.g., Instagram filters, Pokemon Go app) (Har et al., 2022)

A simulated environment that blocks out the real world is created by virtual reality (VR). Typically, a wearable headset is used in VR to immerse users in virtual 3-D worlds, such as virtual video games, and block out the sensory experiences of the real world. While using a VR device, users can physically interact and move within the virtual world, primarily through head movements, but also through limb motion tracking. Devices such as 3-D glasses, headsets, and gloves are utilized in VR to create an experience that simulates real-life, while AR is achievable through everyday devices like computers and smartphones (Sharma et al., 2023).

Where Is Digital Retailing Evolving?

Table 2. Summary of digital retail technologies with purposes and examples

Technology Type	Purpose	Examples
Artificial Intelligence	• measurement of the sales response to price changes • Personalization and Recommendation Systems • Understanding/Anticipating Omnichannel and Mobile Shopping Behavior • Sales/Customer Relationship Management • In-store Customer Experience Management • Media Optimization • Customer Service and Payment Management • Inventory Optimization • Logistics, Transportation, and Delivery • Store Cleaning and Layout Management	**Personalized shopping experience** Amazon uses AI-powered recommendation systems Amazon's chatbot, Alex Sephora's chatbot, Sephora Virtual Art **AI for inventory management** **Walmart:** Walmart uses an AI-powered system called Eden **Fraud Detection and Prevention** Amazon uses an AI-powered system called Fraud Detec PayPal uses an AI-powered system called Deep Learning Fraud Detection **Supply Chain Management** Zara Alibaba **Enhancing Customer Service** Virtual assistants, like Alexa (Amazon), Siri (Apple), and Google Assistant, use AI algorithm
Chatbots	• uninterrupted service • east access and communication • complain management • immensive customer experience • establish a close relationship • continuous responsiveness	Eliza Siri Amazon Lex
Voice commerce	• reduce consumer effort • faster sales • personalized shopping experiences • simplify the product catalog	Amazon Alexa, Samsung Bixby, Apple Siri, Microsoft Cortana, and Google Assistant
Machine learning	• more attractive campaigns • market structure analysis. • market analysis • suggest products or discounts • in loyalty programs • gain insight about consumers	**market structure analysis** -Walmart, Amazon to reduce wastages- IKEA
Augmented Reality Virtual Reality	• immersive experience • customer satisfaction • loyalty	Ikea Place YouCam Samsung Gear VR

Journey from Traditional Retailing to Metaverse Retailing

In recent years, the retail industry has undergone a significant transformation due to the rise of e-commerce, advancements in technology, and evolving consumer behavior. The retail landscape is being revolutionized by modern technologies that enhance traditional channels and introduce new possibilities (Roggeveen & Sethuraman, 2020; Quinones et al., 2023). The retail industry has experienced significant transformations over the course of history due to advancements in technology and society. These changes have impacted the industry's technological infrastructure, economic conditions, and social environment, resulting in the emergence of novel retailing paradigms with each technological wave. Figure 3 represents the shift in customer focus and the evolution. Digitalization is transforming the way that retail companies engage with customers and suppliers, communicate, transact, distribute products, design retail spaces, and offer services (Hagberg et al., 2016). Today's consumer, newly referred to as the 'zero consumers,' is constantly connected, less loyal, and dissatisfied with traditional shopping experiences, seeks value in terms of both cost and quality, prioritizes convenience and personalized experiences, and possesses greater expectations, control, and options than in than ever before (Begley et al., 2023).

The role of product and store ambiance is crucial in traditional retailing since it allows customers to try the products before buying them (Baker et al.,1992; Bitner,1992). In digital retail, these atmospheric elements can be substituted by different aspects such as ease of use/understanding (Dabholkar, 1996; Loiacono et al., 2002; Wolfinbarger & Gilly, 2003; Yoo & Donthu, 2001), website design (Grewal et al., 2004; Wolfinbarger & Gilly, 2003; Yoo & Donthu, 2001), customization (Srinivasan et al., 2002), security (Wolfinbarger & Gilly, 2003; Yoo & Donthu,2001), and website speed (Dabholkar, 1996; Yoo & Donthu, 2001). Various studies indicate that electronic retailing and traditional retailing offer different advantages and disadvantages (Grewal et al., 2004; Lee & Tan, 2003). Although traditional retailing options are suitable for all types of shoppers, including social shoppers, electronic retailing is more appealing to users who prefer convenience and embrace technological innovations (Bourlakis et al., 2009). Thriving in the retail industry demands that brick-and-mortar retailers possess the right location, store design, and optimal placement, all while efficiently managing inventory, communication, and customer interactions (Nanda et al., 2021). Conversely, online retailers prioritize security and privacy matters, which pose major challenges in the development of communication technologies. They also concentrate on prompt delivery and keeping up with the latest technological trends to enhance their adaptability (OECD, 2020; Shankar et

Where Is Digital Retailing Evolving?

al., 2021). In today's retail landscape, it is essential for traditional retailers to cater to digitally connected customers by offering a seamless cross-channel shopping experience and merging their physical and virtual presence through an omnichannel approach (Kotler et al., 2021; Verhoef, 2021). Digital retail technologies have transformed the way consumers and organizations do business, providing a plethora of tools and options to enhance the shopping experience, streamline processes, and increase sales (Har et al., 2022).

While traditional retailers focus on optimizing store design, location, and consumer interaction, they face various challenges such as inventory management, communication, and consumer satisfaction (Nanda et al., 2021). Online retailers, on the other hand, prioritize security and privacy concerns, as they operate in the ever-evolving communication technology landscape. They also focus on timely delivery and stay up-to-date with the latest technological trends by continuously developing innovative ideas (OECD, 2020; Shankar et al., 2021). To remain competitive in today's retail market, traditional retailers must adapt to the expectations of tech-savvy customers (Kotler et al., 2021). This requires seamless cross-channel shopping experiences and integrating their physical and virtual presence through an omnichannel strategy (Verhoef, 2021). Digital retail technologies have revolutionized how businesses and consumers interact, offering a range of tools and options to enhance the shopping experience, simplify processes, and increase sales. Until this shift, retailers focused on creating products that simply met customer needs. However, they have significantly shifted their approach to become more customer-centric over time, thanks to the growth of technology and e-commerce. Retailers are now adopting an experience-focused strategy called 'retail theatre.' This strategy involves creating exciting and immersive environments beyond just selling products. Retailers aim to create unique experiences that foster customer interaction and participation, building a stronger connection between the customers and the brand (Gupta & Ramachandran, 2021; Jaiswal & Singh, 2015; Fırat & Dholakia, 2006).

With the emergence of the metaverse, retailers now have an exceptional platform to deliver the experiences that customers are seeking. The retail theatre trend within metaverses is changing how consumers shop by providing a space to connect with other avatars and actively participate in the experience rather than simply browsing passively on the internet. The metaverse lets retailers create virtual environments for customers to explore and interact. By leveraging the metaverse, retailers can enrich their brand image and make unique experiences that leave an endless impression on their customers (Papagiannidis et al., 2010). Facebook (now Meta), Microsoft, and Nvidia are financing millions to create a digital universe aligned with the metaverse concept. This will revolutionize virtual interaction and have far-reaching implications for industries like gaming, entertainment, and education (Barrera & Shah, 2023).

Figure 3. Development of retailing from past to present
(Adapted from Bourlakis et al., 2009)

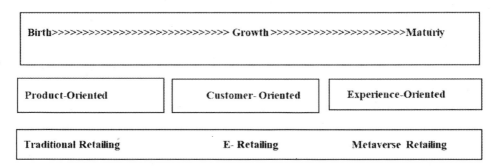

In the world of e-retailing, virtual stores emulate the physical shopping experience, enabling customers to browse via the virtual store, create a shopping basket, peruse the aisles, select items from shelves and racks, and interact with other shoppers just as they would in real life (Jin et al., 2021; Lee & Leonas, 2018; Papagiannidis et al., 2017). The metaverse widens the scope for creating and living out one's fantasies without any physical limitations. According to Papagiannidis (2008), merely replicating real-world shopping experiences won't suffice since avatars in the metaverse can take flight, and pushing a trolley on the ground may not be the most efficient way to shop. Therefore, the metaverse offers retailers exciting opportunities to enhance shopping experiences in distinctive and cooperative ways.

In the realm of metaverse retailing, the creation of avatars is a crucial aspect as they serve to promote immersion and real-time social interaction (Kyrlitsias & Michael-Grigoriou, 2022). This digital representation is unique to each user and can be customized to interact with other digital personas within a specific metaverse. Users can create or provide personal information as part of a platform's terms of service to form their digital persona. In metaverses, digital personas allow users to express their creativity, emphasizing individuality and digital ownership. Users interact with other customers, shopping assistants, and objects within the virtual environment via these. They often support social strolling and chatting, which enable users to share advice, write reviews, and offer recommendations.

Automated avatars act as shopping assistants and provide customers with vital information and support. Such social interactions enhance the experience of other consumers and can significantly contribute to the success of a firm (Papagiannidis, 2008). In addition, metaverse retailing adopts a user-oriented approach, motivating users to participate in creating the product, service, or experience. Virtual environments offer users the freedom to unleash their creativity and create anything they desire. Users, also called co-producers in the value-creation process, can customize their products or generate new content, sell them, and earn money. According to Papagiannidis et al. (2013), engagement positively affects user satisfaction and purchase intention. Furthermore, incorporating digital personas enhances the immersive experience of metaverses and promotes diversity within online communities. Digital personas offer users enhanced privacy protection, addressing concerns about personal data.

CONCLUSION

The emergence of digital technologies and platforms, including computers, the internet, smartphones, and social media, has drastically altered how businesses showcase their offerings to consumers. To grasp the full scope of this impact, the study delves into the digitalization process within the retail industry, drawing parallels to the transformation experienced during the Industrial Revolution. The second part of the study elucidates the paramount technologies that are propelling this transformation. The last part of the section provides an in-depth explanation of the transformation process that occurs when traditional retailing evolves into metaverse retailing. It also delves into the characteristics of the meta world and explores the requirements necessary to manage this world effectively.

While digital transformation allows retailers to offer more customer-focused options with operational efficiency, developing and renewed technologies also significantly affect consumers. Digital technologies affect the consumer, whose decision journey is no longer linear, throughout the shopping journey (Thaichon et al., 2023). Technologies such as AI, AR, and VR have provided the opportunity to interact with customers at multiple touchpoints, strengthen their ties with consumers, and offer them a unique, personalized experience. At this point, the goal of retailers who want to be successful in the long term is to complement and reinforce each other with experiences offered through omnichannel experience and to present personalized content. In this sense, artificial intelligence with personal recommendations for consumers and the personalized content it creates, as well as AR and VR applications, which reduce the difference between physical experience and virtual experience, are the digital technologies most adopted by retailers. Gartner's research portal (2023), which provides data on the future trend of retailing, also states that these digital technologies will remain valid for 2024 and the following years. On the other hand, according to Gartner, improved or newly released examples of these technologies (e.g. generative AI, causal AI, and neuro-symbolic AI) will produce new versions of existing strategies and designs, thus improving customer experiences. In addition, it is anticipated that Metaverse, which uses augmented reality, virtual reality, and interaction-based technologies, will enrich consumers' experiences and make them more immersive.

The building blocks of the metaverse have been in existence for some time, with the integration of AR/VR technologies, online multiplayer games, digital virtual twins, and blockchain applications. Recent technological advances have also enabled the buying and selling of NFT-based artworks, souvenirs, and lands, which have garnered a surge in popularity, bringing us one step closer to the promised metaverse. However, to fully realize this fictional universe, the implementation of 5G technology, widespread availability of AR/VR hardware and content, and an increase in peer-to-peer technologies must be achieved (Narin, 2021).

To leverage the metaverse concept, businesses must understand their unique selling proposition, customers, and capabilities. They should create a transformation strategy, identify use cases, and consider customer needs, challenges, and market trends. Robust foundations in data, architecture, organization, and processes are essential. Retailers must experiment with various use cases on multiple platforms and receive continuous feedback. Agile project management should be implemented to respond promptly to changes and issues. The iterative and incremental approach is critical in meeting customer expectations and providing an optimized end solution (Barrera & Shah, 2023).

For brands, it's essential to assess their approach and implement tangible actions. One effective method for retailers to gain an edge is to venture into the virtual world early and evolve alongside the technology, shaping the direction of the metaverse. As the metaverse advances, they can establish themselves as dominant industry players and experts. Since customers are projected to use the virtual platform for co-creating, personalizing, viewing, and engaging with products, brands should strive to provide unique experiences during the customer journey stages. While the metaverse has been regarded as an additional channel to the online channel, it presents fresh prospects for brands. Because digitizing physical experiences, such as trying on products, may require more time, retailers should consider that customers will most likely make their final purchases online or in brick-and-mortar stores. Consequently, virtual sales via metaverse retailing may generate low profits in the initial stages.

To thrive in the metaverse, brands must identify alternate revenue streams and/ or set up a virtual channel that complements their physical and online stores. The metaverse should expand the range of experiences for customers rather than limit them and should not replace traditional sales channels but instead complement them. Therefore, it's highly recommended to establish an integrated omnichannel sales system that enables customers to transition seamlessly between offline, online, and virtual channels at every stage of their shopping experience. Linking sales channels can help businesses gain a comprehensive view of their customers, cater to their needs more effectively, and improve their overall shopping experience across all channels (Barrera & Shah, 2023; Ramadan, 2023; Yoo et al.,2023).

Where Is Digital Retailing Evolving?

On the other hand, the physical experience, which is impossible to create in digitalized retailing, is established through touch and its haptic perception with touchscreen interfaces (Del Chiappa et al., 2019; Liu, 2022). This experience enhances consumers' sense of ownership of the product, resulting in psychological ownership, and psychological ownership results in higher purchase intentions (Luangrath et al., 2022) and willingness to pay (Atasoy & Morewedge, 2018; Brasel & Gips, 2014). In addition, recent studies reveal the importance of psychological ownership in strong bonds established with customers in digital retailing (Kirk & Swain, 2018; Nguyen et al., 2023). In addition to the positive effects of psychological ownership (i.e., trust, satisfaction, perceived benefits, and risks) on consumers' perceptions, psychological ownership is enhanced by developing feelings of ownership in various digital environments such as websites or the virtual world, especially with the opportunities offered by digital technologies (Nguyen et al., 2023). For this reason, omnichannel retailers should offer a user-friendly shopping environment with an attractive, practical website that will enrich customers' experience in digital environments. Furthermore, digital simulation with augmented reality (AR) technology and metaverse applications can create a more engaging experience and positively affect consumers' willingness to purchase.

Metaverse, on the other hand, offers businesses the opportunity to establish their brand identity and build stronger relationships with customers. The immersive experiences of the Metaverse can help increase brand awareness, generate interest, and encourage engagement with the brand and its products. To attract and retain tech-savvy customers, retailers must ensure that their Metaverse presence is secure, trustworthy, and professional, which includes user privacy and protection, ethical principles, and real-time assistance throughout the customer journey (Dos Remedios, 2023). Retailers can also sell digital or virtual assets, which can be lucrative if they spark customer interest. One strategy is to offer digital products alongside physical ones. Moreover, businesses can use the Metaverse as a marketing platform by containing in-game advertisements and product placements. Retailers can also use virtual stores to test new products, designs, styles, or colors to determine consumer interest before committing to physical production.

For any business to thrive, it is essential to prioritize customer satisfaction and building strong relationships. Beyond providing goods and services, fostering positive experiences and connections is crucial. These aspects are necessary to maintain customer loyalty and, ultimately, revenue. Therefore, adopting a customer-centric approach is critical to achieving lasting success and growth. In summary, as Stéphane Bérubé said, the real problem in future projections will not be the development of technology but the finding of the final goal (Wang, 2021). Interlocking technologies, determining the practical part of countless data from different platforms, and producing new content and areas for the consumer will be the keys to success in future retailing. However, the public must monitor major Metaverse projects to ensure that all companies work together to create a unified Metaverse instead of focusing solely on their own goals. Unlike websites, Metaverse's different platforms are like three-dimensional virtual worlds that should be managed and decentralized by companies, organizations, institutions, or private individuals. To create a fairer Metaverse that follows the principles of the Internet, the Metaverse might use blockchain technology. If this happens, the Metaverse could be considered the next generation of the Internet. If not, it may not qualify as a new generation of the Internet (Liu, et al., 2022).

Within the scope of future research, it would be helpful to test the versatile opportunities offered by the metaverse and determine the perceived obstacles for consumers and retailers to adopt the applications. On the other hand, this study makes limited predictions regarding the emerging digital retail technologies it focuses on. Adding other technologies to the discussion may enrich these. On the other hand, expanding the current conceptualization attempts in the literature and creating a broad map of digital retail technologies will guide both practitioners and researchers.

REFERENCES

Atasoy, O., & Morewedge, C. K. (2018). Digital goods are valued less than physical goods. *The Journal of Consumer Research*, *44*(6), 1343–1357. doi:10.1093/jcr/ucx102

Bacher, N. (2022). *Metaverse Retailing* [Unpublished master thesis]. Universita Di Pavia.

Backhaus, K., & Awan, A. (2019). *The Paradigm Shift in Customer Analysis: Marketing or IT-Driven? The Art of Structuring.* doi:10.1007/978-3-030-06234-7_32

Baker, J., Levy, M., & Grewal, D. (1992). An experimental approach to making retail store environmental decisions. *Journal of Retailing*, *68*(4), 445.

Barrera, K. G., & Shah, D. (2023). Marketing in the Metaverse: Conceptual understanding, framework, and research agenda. *Journal of Business Research*, *155*, 113420. doi:10.1016/j.jbusres.2022.113420

Begley, S., Coggins, B., Green, C., Hamdan, J., Kuijpers, D., & Laizet, F. (2023). Retail reset: A new playbook for retail leaders. *The McKinsey Quarterly*.

Bertacchini, F., Bilotta, E., & Pantano, P. (2017). Shopping with a robotic companion. *Computers in Human Behavior*, *77*, 382–395. doi:10.1016/j.chb.2017.02.064

Bitner, M. J. (1992). Servicescapes: The impact of physical surroundings on customers and employees. *Journal of Marketing, 56*(2), 57–71. doi:10.1177/002224299205600205

Blake, D. (2020). *Covid-19 has almost doubled e-commerce sales.* Available. https://insideretail.co.nz/2020/04/22/covid-19-has-almost-doubled-e-commerce-sales/

Bloomberg. J. (2018). Digitization, digitalization, and digital transformation: confuse them at your peril. *Forbes.* https://moniquebabin.com/wp content/uploads/articulate_uploads/Going Digital4/story_content/external_files/Digitization%20Digitalization%20and%20Digital%20Transformation%20Confusion.pdf

Böhm, E., Eggert, A., Garnefeld, I., Holzmüller, H. H., Schaefers, T., Steinhoff, L., & Woisetschläger, D. M. (2022). Exploring the Customer Journey of Voice Commerce: A Research Agenda. *SMR-Journal of Service Management Research, 6*(4), 216–231. doi:10.5771/2511-8676-2022-4-216

Bourlakis, M., Papagiannidis, S., & Li, F. (2009). Retail spatial evolution: Paving the way from traditional to metaverse retailing. *Electronic Commerce Research, 9*(1-2), 135–148. doi:10.1007/s10660-009-9030-8

Brasel, S. A., & Gips, J. (2014). Tablets, touchscreens, and touchpads: How varying touch interfaces trigger psychological ownership and endowment. *Journal of Consumer Psychology, 24*(2), 226–233. doi:10.1016/j.jcps.2013.10.003

Caboni, F., & Hagberg, J. (2019). Augmented reality in retailing: A review of features, applications and value. *International Journal of Retail & Distribution Management, 47*(11), 1125–1140. doi:10.1108/IJRDM-12-2018-0263

Chakrabarti, A., & Chaudhuri, A. K. (2017). Blockchain and its scope in retail. *International Research Journal of Engineering and Technology, 4*(7), 3053–3056.

Chaveesuk, S., Khalid, B., & Chaiyasoonthorn, W. (2021). Digital payment system innovations: A marketing perspective on intention and actual use in the retail sector. *Innovative Marketing, 17*(3), 109–123. doi:10.21511/im.17(3).2021.09

Cheng, C., Eagan, J. T., & Yurko, A. (2022). ChicagoLand Popcorn®—Examining Online Retailer Nexus Following Wayfair Using Data Visualization and Robotics Process Automation. *Journal of Emerging Technologies in Accounting, 19*(1), 133–164. doi:10.2308/JETA-2020-044

Chong, T., Yu, T., Keeling, D. I., & de Ruyter, K. (2021). AI-chatbots on the services frontline addressing the challenges and opportunities of agency. *Journal of Retailing and Consumer Services, 63*, 102735. doi:10.1016/j.jretconser.2021.102735

Cong, L. W., Li, B., & Zhang, Q. T. (2021). Internet of Things: Business Economics and Applications. *Review of Business, 41*(1).

Dabholkar, P. A. (1996). Consumer evaluations of new technology-based self-service options: An investigation of alternative models of service quality. *International Journal of Research in Marketing, 13*(1), 29–51. doi:10.1016/0167-8116(95)00027-5

Das, R., Kalia, S., & Kuijpers, D. (2023). Zero consumers': What they want and why it matters. *McKinsey.* https://www.mckinsey.com/industries/retail/our-insights/zero-consumers-what-they-want-and-why-it-matters#/

Dawson, J. (2000). Retailing at century end: Some challenges for management and research. *International Review of Retail, Distribution and Consumer Research, 10*(2), 119–148. doi:10.1080/095939600342325

De Regt, A., & Barnes, S. J. (2019). V-commerce in retail: nature and potential impact. *Augmented reality and virtual reality: The power of AR and VR for business,* 17-25. doi:10.1007/978-3-030-06246-0_2

Del Chiappa, G., Serravalle, F., & Viassone, M. (2019). Perceiving a haptic experience: how augmented reality could increase willingness to buy without physically touching products. In Atti del XVI Convegno annuale della Società Italiana di Marketing. Marketing 4.0: le sfide della multicanalità (pp. 1-6). Academic Press.

Deloitte. (2017). *Disruptions in Retail through Digital Transformation Reimagining the Store of the Future.* https://www2.deloitte.com /content/dam/Deloitte/in/Documents/CIP/in-cip-disruptions-in-retail-noexp. pdf

Dennis, C., Brakus, J., & Alamanos, E. (2013). The wallpaper matters: Digital signage as customer-experience provider at the Harrods (London, UK) department store. *Journal of Marketing Management, 29*(3-4), 338–355. doi:10.1080/026725 7X.2013.766628

Dos Remedios, L. (2023). The influence of the Metaverse on Brand Management: A study. *Communities, 2*(2), 5.

Đurđević, N., Labus, A., Barać, D., Radenković, M., & Despotović-Zrakić, M. (2022). An approach to assessing shopper acceptance of beacon triggered promotions in smart retail. *Sustainability (Basel), 14*(6), 3256. doi:10.3390/su14063256

Fırat, A. F., & Dholakia, N. (2006). Theoretical and philosophical implications of postmodern debates: Some challenges to modern marketing. *Marketing Theory, 6*(2), 123–162. doi:10.1177/1470593106063981

GFK. (2023). *Global retailer report 2023 executive summary*. https://www.gfk.com/state-of-tech-and-durables/global-retailer-report-2023-executive-summary

Grewal, D., Gauri, D. K., Das, G., Agarwal, J., & Spence, M. T. (2021). Retailing and emergent technologies. *Journal of Business Research, 134*, 198–202. doi:10.1016/j.jbusres.2021.05.004

Grewal, D., Iyer, G. R., & Levy, M. (2004). Internet retailing: Enablers, limiters and market consequences. *Journal of Business Research, 57*(7), 703–713. doi:10.1016/S0148-2963(02)00348-X

Grewal, D., Lindsey-Mullikin, J., & Munger, J. (2004). Loyalty in e-tailing: A conceptual framework. *Journal of Relationship Marketing, 2*(3-4), 31–49. doi:10.1300/J366v02n03_03

Guha, A., Grewal, D., Kopalle, P. K., Haenlein, M., Schneider, M. J., Jung, H., Moustafa, R., Hegde, D. R., & Hawkins, G. (2021). How artificial intelligence will affect the future of retailing. *Journal of Retailing, 97*(1), 28–41. doi:10.1016/j.jretai.2021.01.005

Gupta, M. S. (2020). What is Digitization, Digitalization, and Digital Transformation? *ARC Advisory Group*. https://www.arcweb.com/blog/what-digitization-digitalization-digital-transformation

Gupta, S., & Ramachandran, D. (2021). Emerging market retail: transitioning from a product-centric to a customer-centric approach. *Journal of Retailing, 97*(4), 597-620. https://doi.org/.2021.01.008 doi:10.1016/j.jretai

Hagberg, J., Sundstrom, M., & Egels-Zandén, N. (2016). The digitalization of retailing: An exploratory framework. *International Journal of Retail & Distribution Management, 44*(7), 694–712. doi:10.1108/IJRDM-09-2015-0140

Har, L. L., Rashid, U. K., Te Chuan, L., Sen, S. C., & Xia, L. Y. (2022). Revolution of retail industry: From perspective of retail 1.0 to 4.0. *Procedia Computer Science, 200*, 1615–1625. doi:10.1016/j.procs.2022.01.362

Hoehle, H., Aloysius, J. A., Chan, F., & Venkatesh, V. (2018). Customers' tolerance for validation in omnichannel retail stores: Enabling logistics and supply chain analytics. *International Journal of Logistics Management, 29*(2), 704–722. doi:10.1108/IJLM-08-2017-0219

Hokkanen, H., Walker, C., & Donnelly, A. (2020). Business model opportunities in brick and mortar retailing through digitalization. *Journal of Business Models, 8*(3), 33–61.

Hollinshead, M. (1996). Retailing: Historical patterns and Future Trends. *Plan Canada*, 12-18.

Hoyer, W. D., Kroschke, M., Schmitt, B., Kraume, K., & Shankar, V. (2020). Transforming the customer experience through new technologies. *Journal of Interactive Marketing, 51*(1), 57–71. doi:10.1016/j.intmar.2020.04.001

Jaiswal, S., & Singh, A. (2015). Customer Experience Management: A Paradigm Shift in e-Retailing. *VIMARSH - A Bi-Annual Peer-Reviewed Refereed Journal, 9*(2).

Jessen, A., Hilken, T., Chylinski, M., Mahr, D., Heller, J., Keeling, D. I., & de Ruyter, K. (2020). The playground effect: How augmented reality drives creative customer engagement. *Journal of Business Research, 116*, 85–98. doi:10.1016/j.jbusres.2020.05.002

Jin, B., Kim, G., Moore, M., & Rothenberg, L. (2021). Consumer store experience through virtual reality: Its effect on emotional states and perceived store attractiveness. *Fashion and Textiles, 8*(1), 1–21. doi:10.1186/s40691-021-00256-7

Kaczorowska-Spychalska, D. (2019). How chatbots influence marketing. *Management, 23*(1), 251–270. doi:10.2478/manment-2019-0015

Kamoonpuri, S. Z., & Sengar, A. (2023). Hi, May AI help you? An analysis of the barriers impeding the implementation and use of artificial intelligence-enabled virtual assistants in retail. *Journal of Retailing and Consumer Services, 72*, 103258. doi:10.1016/j.jretconser.2023.103258

Kazancoglu, I., & Demir, B. (2021). Analysing flow experience on repurchase intention in e-retailing during COVID-19. *International Journal of Retail & Distribution Management, 49*(11), 1571–1593. doi:10.1108/IJRDM-10-2020-0429

Kirk, C. P., & Swain, S. D. (2018). Consumer psychological ownership of digital technology. *Psychological ownership and consumer behavior*, 69-90. doi:10.1007/978-3-319-77158-8_16

Kishen, R., Upadhyay, S., Jaimon, F., Suresh, S., Kozlova, N., Bozhuk, S., ... Matchinov, V. A. (2021). Prospects for artificial intelligence implementation to design personalized customer engagement strategies. *Journal of Legal, Ethical and Regulatory Issues, 24*(1).

Kotler, P. A. G. O. M., Armstrong, G., & Opresnik, M. O. (2021). Principles of Marketing (18e Global). Harlow: Pearson Education Limited.

Kumar, S., Sharma, G., Kejriwal, N., Jain, S., Kamra, M., Singh, B., & Chauhan, V. K. (2014, April). *Remote retail monitoring and stock assessment using mobile robots. In 2014 IEEE international conference on technologies for practical robot applications (TePRA).* IEEE.

Kyrlitsias, C., & Michael-Grigoriou, D. (2022). Social interaction with agents and avatars in immersive virtual environments: A survey. *Frontiers in Virtual Reality, 2*, 786665. doi:10.3389/frvir.2021.786665

Labrecque, L. I., vor dem Esche, J., Mathwick, C., Novak, T. P., & Hofacker, C. F. (2013). Consumer Power: Evolution in the Digital Age. *Journal of Interactive Marketing, 27*(4), 257–269. doi:10.1016/j.intmar.2013.09.002

LeCun, Y., Bengio, Y., & Hinton, G. (2015). Deep learning. *Nature, 521*(7553), 436-444. doi:10.1038/nature14539

Lee, H., & Leonas, K. (2018). Consumer experiences, the key to survive in an omni-channel environment: Use of virtual technology. *Journal of Textile and Apparel, Technology and Management, 10*(3).

Lee, K. S., & Tan, S. J. (2003). E-retailing versus physical retailing: A theoretical model and empirical test of consumer choice. *Journal of Business Research, 56*(11), 877–885. doi:10.1016/S0148-2963(01)00274-0

Leung, C. H., & Yan Chan, W. T. (2020). Retail chatbots: The challenges and opportunities of conversational commerce. *Journal of Digital & Social Media Marketing, 8*(1), 68–84.

Li, X., Zhao, X., & Pu, W. (2020). Measuring ease of use of mobile applications in e-commerce retailing from the perspective of consumer online shopping behaviour patterns. *Journal of Retailing and Consumer Services, 55*, 102093. doi:10.1016/j.jretconser.2020.102093

Liu, Y. (2023). How and why a touchscreen interface impacts psychological ownership and its downstream consequences. *Journal of Retailing and Consumer Services, 70*, 103182. doi:10.1016/j.jretconser.2022.103182

Liu, Y. J., Du, H., Niyato, D., Feng, G., Kang, J., & Xiong, Z. (2022). Slicing4Meta: An intelligent integration framework with multi-dimensional network resources for Metaverse-as-a-service in Web 3.0. *arXiv preprint arXiv:2208.06081.*

Loiacono, E. T., Watson, R. T., & Goodhue, D. L. (2002). WebQual: A measure of website quality. American Marketing Association. *Conference Proceedings, Suppl.2002 AMA Winter Educators' Conference, 13*, 432. https://www.proquest.com/scholarly-journals/webqual-measure-website-quality/docview/199486360/se-2

Luangrath, A. W., Peck, J., Hedgcock, W., & Xu, Y. (2022). Observing product touch: The vicarious haptic effect in digital marketing and virtual reality. *JMR, Journal of Marketing Research, 59*(2), 306–326. doi:10.1177/00222437211059540

MariA. (2019). Voice Commerce:Understanding Shopping-Related Voice Assistants and their Effect on Brands. In *IMMAA Annual Conference*. Northwestern University in Qatar. doi:10.5167/uzh-197725

Markets and Markets. (2020). *Service robotics market*. Available at: https://www.marketsandmarkets.com/Market-Reports/service-robotics-market-681.html

Mathur, P. (2019). Overview of Machine Learning in Retail. In *Machine Learning Applications Using Python*. Apress. doi:10.1007/978-1-4842-3787-8_7

Mittal, M., & Manocha, S. (2023). Alexa! What is Voice Commerce?" Examining Consumer Behavior towards Voice Assistants. *International Management Review, 19*(2).

Mondol, E. P. (2021). The impact of block chain and smart inventory system on supply chain performance at retail industry. *International Journal of Computations, Information and Manufacturing, 1*(1). Advance online publication. doi:10.54489/ijcim.v1i1.30

Nanda, A., Xu, Y., & Zhang, F. (2021). How would the COVID-19 pandemic reshape retail real estate and high streets through acceleration of E-commerce and digitalization? *Journal of Urban Management, 10*(2), 110–124. doi:10.1016/j.jum.2021.04.001

Narin, N. G. (2021). A content analysis of the metaverse articles. *Journal of Metaverse, 1*(1), 17–24.

Nguyen, D. T., Pham, M., Chovancová, M., & Duc hoang, S. (2023). How service operations, perceived benefit, and psychological ownership enhance customer retention in retail-evidence in Vietnam supermarkets. *Cogent Business & Management, 10*(2), 2200519. doi:10.1080/23311975.2023.2200519

Nguyen, H., Mladenow, A., Strauss, C., & Auer-Srnka, K. (2021, November). Voice commerce: Anthropomorphism using voice assistants. In *The 23rd International Conference on Information Integration and Web Intelligence* (pp. 434-442). Academic Press.

Noble, S. M., Mende, M., Grewal, D., & Parasuraman, A. (2022). The Fifth Industrial Revolution: How harmonious human–machine collaboration is triggering a retail and service [r] evolution. *Journal of Retailing*, *98*(2), 199–208. doi:10.1016/j.jretai.2022.04.003

O'Leary, D. E. (2023). Digitization, digitalization, and digital transformation in accounting, electronic commerce, and supply chains. *International Journal of Intelligent Systems in Accounting Finance & Management*, *30*(2), 101–110. doi:10.1002/isaf.1524

OECD. (2020). *OECD Policy Responses to Coronavirus (COVID-19) E-commerce in the time of COVID-19.* Available at: https://www.oecd.org/coronavirus/policy-responses/e-commerce-in-the-time-of-covid-19-3a2b78e8/#section-d1e102

Olsson, T., Lagerstam, E., Kärkkäinen, T., & Väänänen-Vainio-Mattila, K. (2013). Expected user experience of mobile augmented reality services: A user study in the context of shopping centres. *Personal and Ubiquitous Computing*, *17*(2), 287–304. doi:10.1007/s00779-011-0494-x

Pantano, E., Pizzi, G., Scarpi, D., & Dennis, C. (2020). Competing during a pandemic? Retailers' ups and downs during the COVID-19 outbreak. *Journal of Business Research*, *116*, 209–213. doi:10.1016/j.jbusres.2020.05.036 PMID:32501307

Papagiannidis, S., & Bourlakis, M. A. (2010). Staging the New Retail Drama: At a Metaverse Near You! *Journal of Virtual Worlds Research*, *2*(5), 425-446.

Papagiannidis, S., Pantano, E., See-To, E. W., Dennis, C., & Bourlakis, M. (2017). To immerse or not? Experimenting with two virtual retail environments. *Information Technology & People*, *30*(1), 163–188. doi:10.1108/ITP-03-2015-0069

Pillai, R., Sivathanu, B., & Dwivedi, Y. K. (2020). Shopping intention at AI-powered automated retail stores (AIPARS). *Journal of Retailing and Consumer Services*, *57*, 102207. doi:10.1016/j.jretconser.2020.102207

Quinones, M., Gomez-Suarez, M., Cruz-Roche, I., & Díaz-Martín, A. M. (2023). Technology: A strategic imperative for successful retailers. *International Journal of Retail & Distribution Management*, *51*(4), 546–566. doi:10.1108/IJRDM-03-2022-0088

Rafailidis, D., & Manolopoulos, Y. (2019, June). Can virtual assistants produce recommendations? In *Proceedings of the 9th International Conference on Web Intelligence, Mining and Semantics* (pp. 1-6). 10.1145/3326467.3326468

Ramadan, Z. (2023). Marketing in the metaverse era: Toward an integrative channel approach. *Virtual Reality (Waltham Cross)*, *27*(3), 1–14. doi:10.1007/s10055-023-00783-2 PMID:37360809

RaneN. L. (2023, October 17). Multidisciplinary collaboration: key players in successful implementation of ChatGPT and similar generative artificial intelligence in manufacturing, finance, retail, transportation, and construction industry. doi:10.31219/osf.io/npm3d

Rese, A., Ganster, L., & Baier, D. (2020). Chatbots in retailers' customer communication: How to measure their acceptance? *Journal of Retailing and Consumer Services*, *56*, 102176. doi:10.1016/j.jretconser.2020.102176

Retail Customer Experience. (2020). *COVID-19 spurring impulse spending, reveals survey.* Available at: https://www.retailcustomerexperience.com/news/covid-19-spurring-impulse-spending-reveals-survey/

Ritter, D. (2023). *The 36 key chatbot statistics: how chatbots help businesses grow in 2023*. https://www.dashly.io/blog/chatbot-statistics/

Roggeveen, A. L., & Sethuraman, R. (2020). Customer-interfacing retail technologies in 2020 & beyond: An integrative framework and research directions. *Journal of Retailing*, *96*(3), 299–309. doi:10.1016/j.jretai.2020.08.001

Ruby, D. (2023, April 6). *65 Voice Search Statistics For 2023 (Updated Data)*. https://www.demandsage.com/voice-search-statistics/

Rzepka, C., Berger, B., & Hess, T. (2020). Why another customer channel? Consumers' perceived benefits and costs of voice commerce. *Proceedings of the 53rd Hawaii International Conferenceon System Sciences*, 4079-4088.

Scholz, J., & Smith, A. N. (2016). Augmented reality: Designing immersive experiences that maximize consumer engagement. *Business Horizons*, *59*(2), 149–161. doi:10.1016/j.bushor.2015.10.003

Shankar, V., Inman, J. J., Mantrala, M., Kelley, E., & Rizley, R. (2011). Innovations in shopper marketing: Current insights and future research issues. *Journal of Retailing*, *87*(No. S1), 29–42. doi:10.1016/j.jretai.2011.04.007

Shankar, V., Kalyanam, K., Setia, P., Golmohammadi, A., Tirunillai, S., Douglass, T., Hennessey, J., Bull, J. S., & Waddoups, R. (2021). How technology is changing retail. *Journal of Retailing, 97*(1), 13–27. doi:10.1016/j.jretai.2020.10.006

Sharma, P., Ueno, A., Dennis, C., & Turan, C. P. (2023). Emerging digital technologies and consumer decision-making in retail sector: Towards an integrative conceptual framework. *Computers in Human Behavior, 148*, 107913. doi:10.1016/j.chb.2023.107913

Shawar, B. A., & Atwell, E. (2007). Chatbots: are they really useful? *LDV-Forum, 22*(1), 29–49. https://jlcl.org/content/2-allissues/20-Heft1-2007/Bayan_Abu-Shawar_and_ Eric_Atwell.pdf

Sherry, J. F., & Storm, D. (2001). Being in the zone: Staging retail theater at ESPN Zone Chicago. *Journal of Contemporary Ethnography, 30*(4), 465–510. doi:10.1177/089124101030004005

Singh, R., Paste, M., Shinde, N., Patel, H., & Mishra, N. (2018). Chatbot using TensorFlow for small Businesses. *Proceedings of the 2018 Second International Conference on Inventive Communication and Computational Technologies (ICICCT),* 1614–1619.

Sorescu, A., Frambach, R. T., Singh, J., Rangaswamy, A., & Bridges, C. (2011). Innovations in retail business models. *Journal of Retailing, 87*, S3–S16. doi:10.1016/j.jretai.2011.04.005

Srinivasan, S. S., Anderson, R., & Ponnavolu, K. (2002). Customer loyalty in e-commerce: An exploration of its antecedents and consequences. *Journal of Retailing, 78*(1), 41–50. doi:10.1016/S0022-4359(01)00065-3

Thaichon, P., Quach, S., Barari, M., & Nguyen, M. (2023). Exploring the Role of Omnichannel Retailing Technologies: Future Research Directions. *Australasian Marketing Journal.* Advance online publication. doi:10.1177/14413582231167664

Varadarajan, R., Srinivasan, R., Vadakkepatt, G. G., Yadav, M. S., Pavlou, P. A., Krishnamurthy, S., & Krause, T. (2010). Interactive technologies and retailing strategy: A review, conceptual framework and future research directions. *Journal of Interactive Marketing, 24*(2), 96-110. doi:10.1016/j.intmar.2010.02.004

Villegas-Ch, W., Amores-Falconi, R., & Coronel-Silva, E. (2023). Design Proposal for a Virtual Shopping Assistant for People with Vision Problems Applying Artificial Intelligence Techniques. *Big Data and Cognitive Computing, 7*(2), 96. doi:10.3390/bdcc7020096

Wang, X. S., Ryoo, J. H. J., Bendle, N., & Kopalle, P. K. (2021). The role of machine learning analytics and metrics in retailing research. *Journal of Retailing*, *97*(4), 658–675. doi:10.1016/j.jretai.2020.12.001

Web. (2023). *Gartner Trends 2023: How a Retailer Can Turn Them Into Growth.* Available at: https://blog.contactpigeon.com/gartner-trends-2023/

Wolfinbarger, M., & Gilly, M. C. (2003). eTailQ: Dimensionalizing, measuring and predicting etail quality. *Journal of Retailing*, *79*(3), 183–198. doi:10.1016/S0022-4359(03)00034-4

Yoo, K., Welden, R., Hewett, K., & Haenlein, M. (2023). The merchants of meta: A research agenda to understand the future of retailing in the metaverse. *Journal of Retailing*, *99*(2), 173–192. Advance online publication. doi:10.1016/j.jretai.2023.02.002

Zhang, J. (2020). *A systematic review of the use of augmented reality (AR) and virtual reality (VR) in online retailing.* https://hdl.handle.net/10292/13339 doi:10.1057/s41270-022-00161-y

ADDITIONAL READING

Doherty, N. F., & Ellis-Chadwick, F. (2010). Internet retailing: The past, the present and the future. *International Journal of Retail & Distribution Management*, *38*(11/12), 943–965. doi:10.1108/09590551011086000

Grönroos, C. (2011). Value co-creation in service logic: A critical analysis. *Marketing Theory*, *11*(3), 279–301. doi:10.1177/1470593111408177

Hagberg, J., Jonsson, A., & Egels-Zandén, N. (2017). Retail digitalization: Implications for physical stores. *Journal of Retailing and Consumer Services*, *39*, 264–269. doi:10.1016/j.jretconser.2017.08.005

Kaplan, R. S., Kaplan, R. E., Norton, D. P., Davenport, T. H., & Norton, D. P. (2004). *Strategy maps: Converting intangible assets into tangible outcomes.* Harvard Business Press.

Kyrlitsias, C., & Michael-Grigoriou, D. (2022). Social interaction with agents and avatars in immersive virtual environments: A survey. *Frontiers in Virtual Reality*, *2*, 786665. doi:10.3389/frvir.2021.786665

Pine, B. J., & Gilmore, J. H. (2011). *The experience economy.* Harvard Business Press.

Ritterbusch, G. D., & Teichmann, M. R. (2023). Defining the metaverse: A systematic literature review. *IEEE Access : Practical Innovations, Open Solutions, 11*, 12368–12377. doi:10.1109/ACCESS.2023.3241809

Verhoef, P. C., Broekhuizen, T., Bart, Y., Bhattacharya, A., Dong, J. Q., Fabian, N., & Haenlein, M. (2021). Digital transformation: A multidisciplinary reflection and research agenda. *Journal of Business Research, 122*, 889–901. doi:10.1016/j.jbusres.2019.09.022

Verhoef, P. C., Kannan, P., & Inman, J. (2015). From multi-channel retailing to omni-channel retailing: Introduction to the special issue on multi-channel retailing. *Journal of Retailing, 91*(2), 174–181. doi:10.1016/j.jretai.2015.02.005

KEY TERMS AND DEFINITIONS

Artificial Intelligence (AR): AI refers to the ability of a system to correctly interpret external data, learn from it, and use those learnings to achieve specific goals and tasks through flexible adaptation.

Augmented Reality (AR): AR is a technology that enhances the experience of customers by simulating physical control and embedding environments.

Chatbots: Chatbots are computer programs that interact with users using natural language.

Customer-Interfacing Retail Technologies: Customer-facing retail technologies are front-end offerings that inform the retail interface with current or potential customers.

Machine Learning: Machine learning is a powerful tool that enables systems to learn patterns from data, continuously improve performance, and make predictions based on those patterns.

Metaverse: The metaverse is a three-dimensional virtual environment accessed via a downloadable client program, and users can interact using virtual representations in the form of personalized avatars.

Service Robots: Service robots are physical machines embedded with AI technologies that can interact with one another and contribute to the dynamics of consumers' service experience.

Voice Commerce: Voice commerce refers to retail or shopping-related activities conducted through voice assistants.

Zero Consumers: Zero consumers are a consumer group that operates without traditional constraints or loyalty, actively seeking value in both cost and quality, and placing a high premium on convenience and sustainability in their purchasing decisions.

174

Chapter 7
Unleashing the Déjà Rêvé Effect in Marketing:
Empowering Customer Realities

Fatih Sahin

(iD) https://orcid.org/0000-0002-4760-4413
Bandirma Onyedi Eylul University, Turkey

ABSTRACT

Déjà rêvé, subjective sensation of re-experiencing a past dream, is a key concept in marketing. It involves the sensation of déjà vu, blurring the lines between reality and representation. The concept of simulacra, where replicas surpass their original sources, challenges the conventional understanding of reality. The metaverse, a concept that integrates digital experiences, raises concerns about the replacement of genuine reality with simulated ones. The convergence of VR, postmodernism, and innovative marketing strategies has reshaped how individuals interact with technology and perceive reality. The integration of VR and AR technologies with postmodern influences has led to immersive experiences that evoke a sense of déjà rêvé, blurring the boundaries between reality and the virtual world. This immersive experience can blur the boundaries between digital identities and real-life experiences, offering marketers a unique opportunity to engage with consumers authentically. By leveraging technologies, marketers can create familiarity, personalization, engagement, and consumer value.

DOI: 10.4018/979-8-3693-1594-1.ch007

Copyright © 2024, IGI Global. Copying or distributing in print or electronic forms without written permission of IGI Global is prohibited.

Unleashing the Déjà Rêvé Effect in Marketing

INTRODUCTION

The global population is growing, while the gap between different groups is narrowing. Individuals, consumers, sellers, governments, citizens, health practitioners, educators, and various other entities from diverse locations collaborate, surpassing spatial and cultural disparities. Mcluhan (1964) coined the term "global village" to refer to this phenomenon. A considerable amount of time has passed since the term was coined. Electronic media has undergone digitalization since that time. Mcluhan (1964) draws an analogy between media and the central nervous system. Our sensory organs shape our reality by influencing our perceptions. Furthermore, the media is considered an extension of human beings, allowing individuals to perceive and understand their self-image. In its capacity as a human extension, a medium enhances an organ, sense, or function. Mcluhan (1964) asserts that various forms of media have a profound impact on both humans and their surroundings. The term "extension" is a more advanced synonym for media. It pertains to the ability of humans to surpass their physical limitations through the creation of technological advancements. Media has become an indispensable and integral component of human existence. The current transformation offers proof that communication is unquestionably an essential social process, a crucial human requirement, and the basis of all social structures. The notion of being an essential component of the information society is regarded as fundamental (Mansell, 2005). The internet is widely recognized as a crucial element of contemporary communication and is universally acknowledged as a fundamental entitlement of individuals (Reglitz, 2023). Due to this progress, communication and subsequently the community underwent digitalization, resulting in an intensified state of hyperreality (Boyd, 2021). The term "digitalized global village" describes the transition from a traditional global village to a digitally connected one (Graham, 2013).

In the postmodern era, human needs undergo changes due to the absence of a universally acknowledged reality, resulting in variations in these needs based on individual perspectives. Nevertheless, the matter is more intricate than it appears. With the remarkable advancements in digital technologies, every new product brings individuals closer to experiencing their own reality. Brown, Bell, and Carson (1996) and Baudrillard (2010) illustrate the concept of hyperreality in postmodernism using an analogy involving Disney Land scenery. They explain how hyperreality can blur the lines between what is real and what is not. In the modern era, people can obtain the necessary resources to create their own version of reality. They no longer must physically visit or exist in a particular place to imagine and experience an alternate reality. Individuals who engage in the act of formulating and disseminating their own personal truths, while also attracting others who possess a profound alignment with these truths, possess the potential to construct novel realities. Marketing professionals

175

and academics should avoid categorizing clients by imposing rigid and abstract rules on them. Since individuals possess their own unique narratives and experiences. Marketers should deliver valuable offerings that meet the needs of consumers who aspire to create an environment in which they can achieve self-actualization.

In the postmodern world, the hierarchy of human needs is being reconstructed from a different perspective. For example, one approach is to associate the hierarchy of human needs with social media (Ghatak & Singh, 2019). The study replaced physiological needs with psychological needs and listed internet connectivity as one of the basic human needs. Search engines, antivirus software, digital map applications, and security measurements fulfill safety needs in the digital world. As in the previous version of Maslow's hierarchical needs of humans, the next ladder is belonging, and love needs; these needs are met by applications that provide connectivity with loved ones and a social environment. Humans have self-esteem needs; they try to reflect themselves via social media accounts to get the approval of others and prove their existence. The last step of the hierarchy of needs is self-actualization, which means that people try to realize themselves by reaching their full potential. In the digital era, individuals like to gather other people around, do what they do best, and create their own society. Applications like LinkedIn, YouTube, Discord, and similar ones make it possible for individuals to do that. Social media reconstructs the hierarchy of needs even in the postmodern world. Whether we are conscious of this fact or not, digital services and mediums are now an indispensable part of human life. Internet connectivity and internet-connected devices are now basic human needs, like water and food, which are physiological needs. Technological resources make it a lot easier than it was decades ago to turn dreams into reality. Therefore, existing in hyperreality is not an illusion; it is a postmodern reality. So, how does this relate to marketing? This could explain the glancing postmodern world through a modern-world lens. Humans sum up what they inspire or dream about. Hobson (1998) claims that dreams are more like films and "multimedia events" than language-based fiction. McGinn (2006) recently claimed that dreams and films liberate the body from material constraints and connect it with "our essential nature" as centers of awareness, presenting an altered world. This pertains to the facilitation of digitalization and the emergence of various technologies such as virtual reality, augmented reality, mixed reality, digital twin, cryptocurrencies, Web 3.0, artificial intelligence, and more. These technologies have, in some manner, disrupted the community's perception of reality. The modern understanding of reality is insufficient to accurately describe the reality of the postmodern world. Postmodernism acknowledges the possibility that reality may not be singular or unified. The concept of reality is subject to change, and there is no universally agreed-upon understanding of reality in the postmodern context. According to Woolley (1993), it is important to consider the possibility that reality may be rapidly transforming into a dream. Today, we are faced with the

Unleashing the Déjà Rêvé Effect in Marketing

challenge of determining whether we are currently asleep, with all our thoughts being a mere dream, or if we are awake and engaging in conversation in the state of wakefulness, as Plato questioned.

The concept of hyperreality is defined as a phenomenon in which simulations and virtual experiences surpass the level of reality itself (Barroso, 2022; Faulkner, 2022). Virtual reality and augmented reality have significantly contributed to the emergence of hyperreality within the digital realm. The shift towards hyperreality has consequences for how we perceive and experience things, as it blurs the distinctions between the virtual and the actual (Kama, 2018). Moreover, hyperreality has emerged as a prominent factor in diverse domains, such as tourism and multimedia systems (Crolla & Goepel, 2022). It is perceived as improving the overall user experience and generating immersive environments. Hyperreality can be defined as a novel manifestation of reality that is influenced by technological progress and significantly affects our perceptions and engagements with the world. This novel reality needs to be redefined; as stated in the postmodern stream, reality now holds an entirely novel meaning. Marketing studies in the field of postmodernism also suggest that there is no universal reality but that reality could be faked or simulated by using different factors. Instead, reality is subjective in nature and fragmented (Firat et al., 1995; Firat & Shultz, 1997). Especially the reality level of IMAX theaters, Disneyland, or shopping centers (Baudrillard, 2010; Brown, 1999b; Firat, 1992) is at the top, which depicts hyperreality. And as Firat, Dholakia, and Venkatesh (1995) proposed, there are five conditions of postmodern culture: hyperreality, fragmentation, reversal of consumption and production, decentering the subject, and paradoxical juxtaposition. One of the key conditions, among others, that indicates the constitution of social reality through hype or simulation in a way that is powerfully signified and represented is hyperreality. Brown (1997) points out the key role of this term in marketing since people cannot sense, interpret, and perceive the objective truth in the external world. From this perspective, individuals socially construct and give meaning to reality. Additionally, since the rise of postmodern studies, there have been significant advancements in technology, such as Augmented Reality (AR), Virtual Reality (VR), and Mixed Reality (MR). These technologies offer users highly immersive experiences that can either recreate real-life environments or create entirely fictional worlds. When people engage with these technologies, the sensory input, and the feeling of being there can be extremely persuasive, to the point where it may trigger a sense of déjà vu or a feeling of familiarity in a dreamlike state.

Dreams are one of the most mysterious phenomena known to humankind. Some researchers reveal that dreams determine the truth about individuals, or vice versa. That means that individuals' truths affect their dreams. So, one can assume that dreams tell us about more than what we anticipate; they provide clues about individuals. Dreams manifest in people's truth related to their world, and the truth lies in their dreams (Morewedge & Norton, 2009). As quoted from Gao Xingjian, "Dreams are more real than reality itself; they are closer to the self." This statement, also supported by Price (2009), postulates that we are the sum of what we dreamed of. Morewedge and Norton (2009) claims that dreams do influence people's decisions and attitudes. Besides that, people are dreaming, believing what they dreamed about, and living this reality. Most Greeks and Romans, both ancient and modern, held the view that dreams might foretell the future and provide insight into the present (Wamsley & Stickgold, 2010; Zhao, Li, & Li, 2018). Plato once said, "How can you prove whether at this moment we are sleeping and all our thoughts are a dream, or whether we are awake and talking to one another in the waking state?" The inclusion of déjà rêvé in this chapter serves to emphasize and assess its potential significance for marketing techniques and the theory of considering what people want. The future of reality lies in the fragmented dreams of individuals since humans take their dreams as guidelines and vice versa. Déjà rêvé is a French term that means "already dreamed". With the fact that individuals have enthusiasm to live their own reality in the postmodern world, they need to construct that reality. The degree of achievement of the goal that the process of creating their own truth is defining depends on the individual's ability to get closer to their own dream. Studies on human dreams classify the déjà rêvé into three groups. Episodic-like déjà rêve is the remembrance of a specific dream, according to studies. The individual who dreams spontaneously recalls the date. Familiarity-like déjà rêvé, unlike episodic déjà rêve, is like a foggy dream. The individual recalls a character, scenario, or place from a dream but cannot recall the date or dream. Dreamy state déjà rêvé, unlike the first two, depicts a dreamlike experience. With current technological resources, all these things can be turned into reality if people take their dreams as a reference point and do whatever and whenever they like to shape their utopian world. Marketing managers should have the skill to empower customers, enabling them to shape their own sense of reality. Additionally, they should provide support and analysis throughout this process to determine the optimal positioning of marketing value.

In a postmodern marketing perspective, the value of the market offering does not relate to a firm consumer or product-centric positioning. Their relationship is reciprocal, and both the consumer and the product can equally influence the market value. With the rapid integration of virtual reality into human life, there is a corresponding transformation in products, consumer relationships, and their definitions. This chapter utilizes the dream metaphor to underscore the significance of personal reality in the virtual world and its impact on consumer expectations and perceptions. The research emphasizes the examination of the truth and reality aspects of dreams, analyzing personal reality and truth through the lens of postmodern studies within the context of marketing.

Unleashing the Déjà Rêvé Effect in Marketing

DREAM THEORIES

Dreams are an important aspect of our lives that has interested and mystified people for decades, yet there is little agreement on their origin and role. Givrad (2016) expresses hat certain theories place emphasis on the independent function of the deeper brain regions and see dreaming as an epiphenomenon of rapid-eye movement (REM) sleep, lacking any obvious significance to interpret. Several other hypotheses propose that the function of dreaming involves emotional processing, memory consolidation, or evolutionary mechanisms that prepare individuals to confront potential risks when awake (Givrad, 2016).

Givrad (2016) examines the comprehension of dreams, with a specific focus on young individuals, and explores the phenomenological and neurological foundations associated with them. Even though we know more about how dreams work and what they mean, we still don't fully understand them. Givrad (2016) proposes that dreaming was once considered a REM sleep phenomenon without psychological significance, and new neuroscientific research has shown that REM sleep and dreaming are two separate things. Givrad (2016) claims that dreams have been regarded as an integral component of the spectrum of consciousness, exerting a substantial influence on the processes of memory and emotional regulation, and young individuals' dreams seem to follow a path that changes as they grow up, following their mental and emotional growth. It is possible that dreams have a substantial impact on the growth as well as the emotional and mental health of youngsters.

The theory posits that dreams serve to satisfy unconscious wants that emerge during sleep, stemming from instinctual impulses (Solms, 2015, p. 123). Freud postulated the existence of an intermediary process known as dream work, which included many processes, including "displacement," condensation, and regression, to convert unconscious desires into conscious dreams. This procedure included the distinction between the "manifest" and "latent" content of dreams, facilitating the conversion of unconscious desires into conscious dream experiences. The mind that is sleeping is cut off from the outside world, but not from its natural (instinctual) tendencies. During sleep, these inclinations are not affected by the limits that are imposed by the outside world (Solms, 2015, p. 123).

Lucidity in dreams, defined as the awareness of consciousness while dreaming, is associated with functions that aid in reality monitoring by distinguishing between memories generated internally and externally (Drinkwater, Denovan, & Dagnall, 2020) High-lucidity dreamers are better able to tell the difference between actual and imagined experiences, reducing the likelihood of reality monitoring mistakes (Yuill, 2015). Many cultures believe in dreams, and there are trends in how people experience, talk about, and use their dreams across communities (Laughlin, 2013). Neuroscience backs up the idea that there is a natural truth behind how we experience reality in all of our different states of awareness, even when we are dreaming (Evans, 2020). In accordance with virtual reality dream theory, people who have had diverse physiological sensations while awake will also have had varied sensory modality experiences while dreaming (Erdeniz et al., 2022). Dreams of physical self-consciousness are highly associated with waking dissociation. Morewedge and Norton (2009) claims that individuals tend to participate in some sort of interpretation of their dreams that is driven by personal motivations, and the study asserts that these interpretations have a significant influence on their day experiences. Revonsuo (1995) posits that dreams constitute authentic conscious experiences and proposes that investigating dreams empirically could help in the comprehension of awake consciousness.

Dreaming plays a crucial role in the human experience, exerting a profound impact on people's encounters and interpretations of the world around them. Some theories claim that dreams represent an emotional processing, memory consolidation, or evolutionary mechanism that occurs as a side effect of rapid-eye-movement (REM) sleep. As people become older, their dreams alter, which influences their mental and emotional well-being. Dreams play a significant role in fulfilling hidden needs and facilitating the process of differentiating between real and imagined events, particularly among those who possess a heightened level of lucidity throughout their dreams.

DÉJÀ RÊVÉ EFFECT

The concept of déjà rêvé refers to the occurrence in which a person dreams about a previous dream experience. Curot et al. (2018) maintain that the concept of déjà rêvé is characterized by its heterogeneity and distinctiveness from phenomena such as déjà vu and the historical notion of a "dreamy state," as well as other experienced phenomena. According to Funkhouser and Schredl (2010), the phenomenon of déjà rêvé was shown to be a prevalent occurrence, exhibiting a negative correlation with age. Additionally, this experience was discovered to be impacted by several variables, including the frequency of dream recall and individual personality features. In the study conducted by Pellegrini, Noffsinger, Caldwell, and Tutko (1993), an investigation was undertaken to examine the occurrence of déjà connu events in daily life. These experiences include situations when an individual encounters someone who triggers a sense of familiarity, reminiscent of another person. The idea of déjà rêvé has been confused with the notion of déjà vu. Déjà vu events are characterized by the subjective sensation of re-experiencing a past event. Frequently, individuals tend to link this phenomenon to a prior experience in dreams, and hence, it would be appropriate to refer to it as déjà rêve. Funkhouser and Schredl (2010) provide

Unleashing the Déjà Rêvé Effect in Marketing

convincing evidence that instances of déjà rêve are often reported, and their occurrence is associated with both the frequency of dream recollection and personality traits such as thin borders and absorption. Thompson, Moulin, Conway, and Jones (2004), the phenomenon of persistent déjà vu is examined as a condition affecting memory, with significant consequences for everyday functioning and potential involvement of cognitive impairments in brain regions such as the hippocampus and amygdala. The study conducted by Curot et al. (2018) examined the phenomenon of déjà rêvé that arises as a result of electrical brain stimulation. The research identified déjà rêvé as a separate entity with many subtypes and proposed a potential association with malfunction in the temporal lobe. The phenomenon of déjà rêvé potentially has ramifications for the cognitive processes of memory and brain functioning in individuals.

The concept of déjà rêvé refers to the subjective perception of a dreamer that they are re-experiencing a past dream while sleeping (Funkhouser & Schredl, 2010). However, the phenomenon known as déjà rêvé should not be seen as a mere straightforward remembrance of a dream, but rather as a more intricate encounter, much to how déjà vu is not merely a memory of past occurrences. According to the findings of Schredl, Goritz, and Funkhouser (2017), the phenomenon of déjà rêvé may be described as the occurrence of seeing a peculiar resemblance to a previously experienced dream, despite the inability to recall the dream prior to the encounter.

The studies indicate that several factors, such as age, gender, dream recall, and personality attributes, contribute to the frequency of déjà rêvé occurrences. The occurrence of déjà rêvé, also known as sensations of having previously dreamed, is subject to several factors, including age, gender, dream memory, and personality features. The occurrence of déjà rêvé events was seen to have a negative correlation with age, suggesting a higher frequency of such experiences among younger persons (Schredl et al., 2022). The frequency of déjà rêvé was shown to be influenced by personality traits, including thin borders, absorption, openness to experience, and neuroticism (Schredl et al., 2017). Furthermore, there was a favorable correlation between the frequency of dream recollection and the occurrence of déjà rêvé experiences (Settineri, Frisone, Alibrandi, & Merlo, 2019). Schredl et al. (2022) support that there exists a correlation between the frequency of dream recall and lucid dream experiences and the Big Five personality variables. Consequently, variations in dream-related measurements across individuals may be partially attributed to personality traits. The correlation between the tendency to remember dreams and openness to experience aligns with prior research (Schredl et al., 2017). Schredl et al. (2022) outline how these connections may contribute to the development of theoretical frameworks explaining the phenomenon of dream recall and/or lucid dreaming.

The studies suggest the Big Five personality characteristics have significance within the field of marketing. Sulehri, Awais, Dar, and Uzair (2021) revealed that agreeableness had a noteworthy and favorable influence on the achievement of projects inside marketing-oriented firms. There is also a favorable correlation between consumer empowerment in the retail business and the Big Five personality characteristics, namely conscientiousness, agreeableness, and neuroticism (Castillo, 2017). Consumers' Big Five personality qualities may serve as predictors of all relationship marketing preferences (Caliskan, 2019). Specifically, the traits of agreeableness and extroversion were found to be important predictors in this regard. The Big Five personality characteristics are crucial to explaining phenomena in several management domains, including job performance, motivation, leadership, collaboration, entrepreneurship, marketing, consumer behavior, and strategy.

DÉJÀ RÊVÉ EFFECT AND VIRTUAL REALITY

Technological advancements such as Virtual Reality (VR) and Augmented Reality (AR) provide users with deeply engaging experiences that can replicate real-life settings or construct wholly imaginative domains. When individuals interact with these technologies, the sensory stimuli, and the sensation of being present may be highly convincing, to the extent that it may elicit a perception of déjà vu or a sense of familiarity.

Virtual reality technology has the capability to mimic a greater number of images, therefore providing individuals with a specific kind of visual gratification. The utilization of virtual reality technology in the visual design of digital media technology has the potential to revolutionize conventional design practices. By leveraging virtual reality, developers can effectively extract and incorporate ecological environmental characteristics, thereby enhancing the quality of film and television production. This integration enables the enrichment of visual content and facilitates the utilization of diverse design approaches. The emergence of information technology can possibly be attributed to the demands of the era. The use of information technology has significantly transformed the lifestyle and functioning of a certain period. The use of virtual reality technology in the visual design of digital media has the potential to augment the sensory experience, enhance the creation of cinema and television, and enrich the visual content. The advancement of information technology has given rise to the advent of virtual reality technology and augmented reality technology, both of which provide a more immersive information experience and have significant practical application value.

The use of virtual reality technology has the potential to revolutionize conventional approaches to visual design, resulting in enhanced visual and audio experiences

Unleashing the Déjà Rêvé Effect in Marketing

and ultimately achieving a heightened degree of immersion. The emergence of 5th-generation networks and the introduction of ultra-low latency Internet, known as tactile Internet, has opened new applications such as Extended Reality (XR), holoportation, and remote control of machines. These technologies have the potential to revolutionize the future of factories, smart cities, and digital healthcare. While Virtual Reality (VR) provides realistic visual and auditory experiences, tactile sensation is important for perceiving and interacting with our surroundings (Sehad et al., 2023).

In contemporary times, Augmented Reality (AR), VR, and Mixed Reality (MR) technologies are becoming recognized as essential components within a diverse range of application fields. All these technologies are included under the range of XR. The application of XR technologies, specifically immersive experiences, is rapidly expanding across various domains. These domains include conventional sectors like entertainment and video game development, as well as emerging fields such as industry, healthcare, smart cities, and autonomous vehicles, among others. The proliferation of XR and VR is also propelled by technological breakthroughs that facilitate and, in some cases, enable novel modes of operation inside virtual environments. The use of "3D reconstructions," "digital twins," and "simulations" is facilitated by the accessibility of innovative hardware and software solutions. Furthermore, the incorporation of haptic feedback and tactile feeling into VR systems has the potential to augment the level of immersion and embodiment experienced in virtual worlds (Cannavò, Kapralos, Seinfeld, Prattico, & Zhang, 2023). The progress in hardware and software technologies has facilitated the development of high-fidelity digital objects and surroundings, hence enhancing the realism of virtual experiences (Wu, Wang, Sarker, & Srivastava, 2023).

In the realm of virtual reality, individuals may get deeply immersed in their digital personas to the extent that the experience closely approximates reality. The interactions that individuals have inside this digital realm can trigger a sense of familiarity, akin to a previously visualized scenario. This phenomenon occurs due to virtual environments often possessing dream-like characteristics, hence creating a heightened sense of realism in these encounters. Individuals who are fully involved in the virtual realm, where their simulated identities (simulacra) reside, may reach a level of immersion that leads them to perceive a feeling of realism comparable to that of the real world. The idea posits that occurrences taking place inside the virtual domain could trigger a sensation akin to déjà rêvé (already dreamt) owing to the dream-like attributes inherent in the virtual realm. When people have a strong sense of connection or disorientation because of their interactions inside the virtual realm, there is room for improvement in terms of clarity and coherence. From a similar perspective, it is plausible that persons who assume their digital identities in the virtual realm might get deeply absorbed, therefore blurring the boundary between their self-identified digital presence and actual reality. The experience of immersion in a virtual environment has the potential to elicit a feeling of familiarity like déjà rêvé. This is because the events that occur inside the virtual world often include dream-like qualities, which may significantly influence an individual's perception and experiences, resulting in an intensified sense of reality. The impact of virtual experiences on an individual's perspective and understanding of reality has similarities to the phenomenon known as the déjà rêvé effect. Individuals have the capacity to get extensively engaged in the virtual world, which may result in the blurring of boundaries between their digital life and the real world that they inhabit. Individuals who engage in experiences inside the virtual world might experience a sensation of familiarity akin to déjà rêvé, owing to the dream-like attributes inherent in the virtual environment.

SIMULACRA AND SIMULATION TO POSTMODERNISM

The concepts of simulacra and simulation have a substantial influence on our comprehension of reality. The studies debate the notion of genuineness and blur the boundary between reality and its depiction. Simulacra are often regarded as replicas derived from previous models, hence creating a state of hyperreality whereby the simulated entity obtains a heightened feeling of authenticity beyond that of its origin (Polasek, 2012). The phenomenon of simulation is evident across several disciplines, including but not limited to literature, banking, and cultural theme parks. Within the context of literature, adaptations function as simulations that solidify the underlying material into a cohesive and unified picture (Hossain, 2022). Fair value accounting in the field of finance is predicated on the use of simulacra as a fundamental measuring framework, hence presenting a challenge to the conventional notion of a market-based system (Bougen & Young, 2012). Cultural theme parks use replicas of historical locations and occurrences to generate simulacra that are consumed by tourists, so causing a blurring of boundaries between reality and representation (Ong & Jin, 2017). In general, the concept of simulacra and simulation serves to disturb our comprehension of reality by the replacement of authentic entities with symbols and the creation of hyperrealities (Schneider, Sklar, Azhar, Parsons, & Tuyls, 2015). Another idea that Baudrillard (2010 delineates in his explanation of simulation is that of simulacra. The term "simulacra" pertains to the creation of a representation that lacks an authentic genesis or genuine truth and is free of any connection with tangible reality. Fukuda (2023) offers an elucidation of the idea of simulacra, supported with a visual representation in the structure of a table, as seen below.

Unleashing the Déjà Rêvé Effect in Marketing

Table 1. Representation of the original, copy, and simulacrum

	Original	**Copy**	**Simulacrum**
Visual	Physical Body	Projected Body	Computer Graphics
Audio	Accoustic Sound	Prerecorded Sound	Synthesized Sounds

Source: Fukuda (2023)

Jean Baudrillard's profound influence on postmodern intellectuals and artists established his prominent position within the discipline. In the contemporary postmodern era, Baudrillard (1998) and Baudrillard (2010) define certain factors that contribute to the extinction of humanity. According to Baudrillard (2010) in his work "History: A Retro Scenario," he asserts that history serves as our faded point of reference, serving as a myth. Baudrillard (2010) asserts that the significant occurrence during this period, known as the epoch, is the diminishing presence of robust referentiality. This phenomenon, characterized by the disappearance of the real and rational, marks the beginning of the era dominated by simulation. Baudrillard (2010) posits that the persistent emphasis of the cinema industry and television (referred to as the media) on historical narratives and nostalgic recreations might be seen as a simple manifestation (according to Freud's concept of "response formation") of the erosion of historical consciousness. Television, movies, and the internet have the tendency to create a sense of isolation from reality, as they strive to replicate it with more precision and faithfulness. The concept of hyperrealism in communication and its relevance.

Literature often presents a lack of clarity in distinguishing between the notions of postmodernism and hyper modernism. However, it should be noted that these notions are distinct from one another. Pavlov and Erokhina (2019) conclude that hyper modernism is a "weak alternative" to postmodernism. The proposal of Gilles Lipovetsky, a French social philosopher, encompasses the concept of the "time of hypermodern" characterized by hyper individualism and hyper consumerism. The contemporary comprehension of hyper modernism is now being advanced by some sociologists in France, as well as within the English-speaking academic sphere. Nevertheless, despite its existence, this version of hyper-modernism failed to attain a significant level of impact (Pavlov & Erokhina, 2019). The studies of hyper modernism as a different idea from postmodernism has been undertaken by several researchers. According to Tapia (2012), hyper modernism may be seen as a collection of behaviors, attitudes, and accomplishments. Contrary to the previous statements, Trepczyński (2018) posits that hyper modernism signifies a departure from the postmodern epoch. Ferraz-Lorenzo (2018) highlights the need for a world that is grounded rather than speculation, and advocates for the adoption of new ethical principles. Tsibizova

Unleashing the Déjà Rêvé Effect in Marketing

(2023) expands upon the discourse by examining the vocabulary used in foreign policy, categorizing it as hyper-postmodern and highlighting its possible adverse consequences. The studies indicate that hyper modernism comprises a variety of socioeconomic and cultural transformations, hence establishing its distinctiveness from postmodernism. Hyper modernism is a distinct period in design that is different from postmodernism. While postmodernism encompasses hyper modernism, hyper modernism represents a new era. Hyper modernism is characterized by design trends rooted in modernism, such as orientation towards modernity, design for manufacturability, and the absence of aesthetic hierarchy. Flat design is a style that visually expresses these trends and reflects the basic request of hyper modernism - the democratization of mentality and the leveling of any differences, including aesthetic hierarchy (Martineau & Roult, 2021). Postmodernism, on the other hand, is associated with debates about society, religion, and social change, as well as feminist and post-colonial critiques of modernism (Tremlett, 2021). Therefore, while hyper modernism is a specific period in design, postmodernism encompasses a broader range of debates and critiques.

The reality concept in postmodernism is eliminated in a manner that is more genuine than tangible. According to Baudrillard (1998) analysis, our contemporary culture has become flooded with an overabundance of low-quality, tacky, mass-produced commodities. These products play a significant role in shaping our society, characterized by simulation and consumerism. Baudrillard argues that this abundance of popular culture is a result of industrial reproduction and the commodification of distinctive signs from various domains, such as the past, the new, the exotic, the traditional, and the futuristic. Furthermore, this profusion of "ready-made" signs contributes to the disorderly excess observed in our culture. The pervasive influence of a consumerist society has significantly shaped our cognitive processes, to the extent that our perception of reality is mostly filtered via the lens of exchange value and advertising. According to Baudrillard (1998), modern society perceives and characterizes itself as a civilization centered around consumption. Consumer culture and ideology, in their relentless pursuit of consumption, ultimately engulfs and exhausts itself. According to Baudrillard (1998), the notion that advertising serves as a triumphant tribute to this concept is put out. Furthermore, Baudrillard (1998) clarifies upon the notion of simulacra and simulation to illustrate the displacement of the actual by our perceptions of reality within postmodern society. The underlying principles of these cognitive processes have undergone development and gained more significance in contemporary times, mostly due to the improvements in sophisticated technologies that augment the entire consumer experience. Presently, contemporary society finds itself immersed in the latest iteration of the age of simulation.

With the prevalence of metaverse ideas among the wider public, some concerns emerged, as highlighted by the researchers. Since simulacra refers to simulated

Unleashing the Déjà Rêvé Effect in Marketing

experiences that may have been original but no longer have a clear connection to that reality, In the metaverse, the concern lies in the potential for these simulated experiences to replace genuine reality. Rospigliosi (2022) suggests that simulacra in the metaverse posits the danger of mistaking simulated digital experiences for actual reality, leading to a disconnect from authentic human interactions and the tangible world. This warning calls for a thoughtful approach to the metaverse's development, considering how these simulated experiences might impact societal norms, personal identities, and our understanding of reality.

UNDERSTANDING THE POSTMODERN MARKETING ENVIRONMENT

It has been a while since the debate over the scientific foundation of marketing was sparked by Taylor (1965) seminal study, which highlights the need to recognize marketing as a legitimate scientific discipline. The current debate is on the impact of postmodernism on the field of marketing, despite the little awareness among mainstream marketing scholars about this phenomenon. Postmodern society has seen significant changes in various aspects of individuals' social, economic, cultural, political, and technical domains, impacting marketing as a blend of arts and scientific disciplines. Marketing has shown resilience and adaptability through the adoption of flexible structures, but there are doubts about its viability in contemporary times. The impact of postmodernism on society has significant implications, as marketing serves a purpose beyond its commercial function and plays a crucial role in shaping and reflecting cultural values. To fully understand the future of marketing systems, it is essential to critically examine postmodernism, its fundamental tenets, and its impact on the field of marketing (Firat et al., 1995). Understanding the challenges and opportunities in postmodern society and marketing is crucial for gaining insight into the direction we are moving towards.

Postmodernism, a movement in art, architecture, literature, and cultural critique, emerged in the mid-20th century as a response to modernism. It rejects objective truth and emphasizes the social and cultural construction of knowledge. Postmodernism rejects traditional narrative frameworks and emphasizes the role of language and discourse in constructing meaning (Firat & Venkatesh, 1995). It is influenced by intellectual and cultural trends like existentialism, structuralism, and critical theory. Postmodernism contends that there is no objective reality, and all knowledge is the result of social and cultural forces. It emphasizes the individual's involvement in meaning and comprehension, the value of personal experience, and challenges power structures based on race, gender, social class, and other forms of social injustice. Baudrillard (2010) has significantly impacted postmodern thinkers and artists, highlighting the decline of strong referential and the rise of simulacra and simulation in postmodern society.

Postmodern culture is a response to the transformations in capitalist societies, characterized by a shift away from standardized functionalism and a focus on aesthetic and humanistic values. In postmodern society, the primary objective is shifting from economic prosperity to quality of life, with a growing acceptance of diverse individual choices in lifestyle and personal self-expression. This shift is part of a larger cultural transformation, with postmodern society embracing postmaterialist and postmodern principles, and decreasing the significance of legal and religious authority. Postmodern marketing and consumers have emerged as a result of this shift, with the rise of technology and mass production facilitating the emergence of consumer markets and retail frameworks. Postmodern marketing is a multifaceted concept that has influenced all aspects of society, culture, and academic discourse, with the advertising industry serving as a triumphant embodiment of this philosophical perspective. The emergence of postmodern marketing and consumers in postmodern society is a testament to the changing landscape of postmodern society and the impact of postmodern marketing on the world (Brown, 1997).

Postmodern marketing is a marketing approach that draws inspiration from postmodernism, a movement that emerged during the mid-20th century. This approach emphasizes the importance of human expression, self-construction, and audience participation in creating meaning and understanding. Postmodern marketing often employs tactics such as mimicry, satire, and intertextuality, as well as strategies like appropriation and deconstruction (Stern, 1993). It also considers socioeconomic and cultural factors that impact consumer behavior and employs new forms of media and technology to engage consumers in novel and interactive ways. Postmodern consumers are characterized by increased skepticism and relativism towards conventional authority and cultural narratives, placing a high importance on self-expression and creativity. They are less inclined to conform to established norms and expectations and are more prone to critical evaluation of marketing credibility and truthfulness (Firat & Shultz, 2001). Postmodern marketing research in consumer behavior adopts non-positivist approaches and adopts sociological/anthropological lenses, focusing on macro/cultural viewpoints.

Postmodern marketing, a paradigm shift in marketing philosophy, focuses on individuality, involvement, creativity, and cultural sensitivity in the postmodern culture and society (Firat et al., 1995). This approach enables the development of tailored marketing strategies that meet individual consumer needs and preferences, improving customer loyalty and brand support. However, challenges include the complexity of measuring efficacy, the willingness to take risks, and the constrained level of acceptance. The postmodern marketplace, characterized by increased fragmentation and unpredictability, is characterized by increased fragmentation and unpredictability (Firat & Shultz, 1997). The knowledge society, characterized by constant innovation and technological advancement, is essential for postmodern society. Education is also crucial in this knowledge society, providing individuals with the necessary skills to navigate the complex and ever-changing environment. However, the transformations and consequences of the postmodern age, marketplace, and consumer have yet to be acknowledged, posing significant challenges for financial services retailers and organizations.

Postmodern society is characterized by increased fragmentation and unpredictability, with postmodern consumers being more resistant to conventional marketing methods. This has led to the emergence of "authenticity," "experiential marketing," "post-advertising," and "socially responsible marketing" (Davidson, 2013). Postmodern consumers are more likely to be drawn to companies and goods that they consider true and authentic, focusing on the "realness" of their goods and brands. Postmodernism has also led to the proliferation of post-advertising strategies, such as "native advertising" and "content marketing," which aim to create more subtle and nuanced forms of marketing. As a result, the marketplace has become more sophisticated and nuanced, emphasizing authenticity, experience, and social responsibility.

Postmodern marketing has significantly influenced the way marketers craft customer value (Firat et al., 1995). Postmodern marketing emphasizes the importance of language and representation in determining meaning, resulting in a more diverse and individualized approach. This has led to a higher emphasis on the agency of the customer and the co-creation of value between marketers and consumers (Roberts, Baker, & Walker, 2005). Postmodern marketing also emphasizes the social and cultural backdrop of marketing techniques, allowing marketers to build more culturally sensitive advertisements that resonate with specific customer groups. This shift in marketing strategy has led to a more diverse, personalized, and culturally sensitive approach to crafting customer value, allowing businesses to differentiate new products and services and discover opportunities. This shift in marketing strategy is crucial for achieving a competitive advantage and maintaining long-term success.

Postmodern marketing is a crucial aspect of a changing society, characterized by fragmentation, de-differentiation, hyperreality, and pluralism (Firat & Shultz, 1997). This has led to a need for innovative products, services, and brands that cater to the evolving needs of consumers. The integration of these strategies, a postmodern mindset, and the effective use of digital media are essential for achieving market penetration and competitive expansion. The postmodern era has emphasized the importance of language and representation in the construction of meaning, enabling marketers to create unique and differentiated products and services. This shift in perspective has led to a more inclusive, innovative, and culturally attuned approach to creating goods, services, and brand identities.

Postmodern marketing has evolved significantly, focusing on sociocultural concerns and the role of consumers in shaping meaning (Firat, 2022). Marketers must be aware of the diversity of cultures, the agency of consumers, and the potential negative impacts of marketing on society. Postmodern marketing also emphasizes authenticity, privacy, and data protection. However, there is a growing awareness of the potential for deceptive practices, such as using irony and parody to manipulate consumer perceptions. Marketers must be cautious in their practices of data collection, preservation, and utilization. The emergence of postmodernism has also led to a greater awareness of the potential exploitation of personal data by marketers. The consumer's capacity to act with agency is also a significant concern, as marketers must be aware of the potential consequences of their marketing practices. Postmodern marketing is a dynamic and evolving field that requires marketers to consider their social and environmental obligations.

Postmodern marketing, a 20th-century movement, is gaining recognition due to globalization and technology, leading to increased trade and commerce. Postmodern consumers are characterized by skepticism, relativism, and a greater inclination towards self-expression and creativity. Postmodern marketing presents opportunities for individuality, involvement, creativity, and cultural sensitivity, but challenges include complexity in measuring efficacy, risk tolerance, and acceptance. Postmodern consumers are more resistant to conventional marketing methods and are more interested in authentic brands. Postmodern marketing has led to the emergence of authenticity, experiential marketing, post-advertising, and socially responsible marketing resulting in a more sophisticated and nuanced marketplace. Postmodernism has influenced marketers to adopt a more diverse, personalized, and culturally sensitive approach to crafting customer value and developing innovative products, services, and brands. It has also raised awareness of socio-cultural and ethical issues in marketing, requiring marketers to be more conscious and responsible in their practices (Firat & Venkatesh, 1993).

HARNESSING DÉJÀ RÊVÉ EFFECT TO UNLOCK CONSUMER VALUE IN THE POSTMODERN ERA

The contemporary landscape of the virtual epoch presents unprecedented opportunities that transcend the limitations of the physical world. In this realm, nearly boundless possibilities unfold through current technological capabilities. Individuals are empowered to craft and inhabit personalized, distinctive worlds, thereby curating unique experiences tailored to their preferences and desires. Such an expansive potential is a hallmark of the virtual epoch, enabling the realization of ambitions that elude realization within the constraints of physical reality.

Unleashing the Déjà Rêvé Effect in Marketing

This dynamic landscape, however, brings forth a significant dimension concerning the acquisition and utilization of neuroscientific data by marketers. Within the virtual sphere, marketers possess the means to access intricate neurological data streams of each consumer, leveraging this wealth of information to propel their commercial ventures. This access affords marketers the capability to shape their marketing strategies that transcend conventional paradigms. Through the integration of neuroscientific insights, businesses can curate immersive experiences evocative of déjà vu, engendering a sense of familiarity or anticipation within consumers. Consequently, this strategic utilization of neurological data holds the promise of cultivating compelling and impactful marketing campaigns within the virtual domain.

The fusion of technology and marketing strategies within the virtual epoch opens avenues for the creation of experiences that evoke sensations akin to déjà rêvé. This phenomenon hinges on the capacity of marketers to harness neuroscientific data, enabling the construction of immersive encounters that resonate profoundly with individuals. Such experiences, woven intricately within the fabric of the virtual realm, offer unprecedented potential for marketers to engage consumers on profound emotional and cognitive levels, promising transformative possibilities within the virtual landscape.

Déjà rêvé, a French term meaning "already dreamed," is a significant concept in the postmodern world. Dreams are a mysterious phenomenon that determines the truth about individuals and vice versa. In the postmodern world, the hierarchy of human needs is reconstructed from a different perspective, with hyperreality being a key condition. In the digital era, individuals use digital services and mediums to connect with loved ones, create their own society, and achieve their goals. The future of reality lies in the fragmented dreams of individuals, who take their dreams as guidelines and vice versa. Studies on human dreams classify déjà rêvé into three groups: episodic, familiarity, and dreamy state. Marketing managers should empower customers to create their own reality and analyze their journey to find marketing value.

In the postmodern world, individuals' needs and desires vary due to the lack of universally accepted reality. Virtual reality offers individuals the opportunity to construct their own reality, allowing them to share their own truth and create new realities. However, truth in the postmodern world is subjective and fragmented, and marketers should not impose abstract rules on clients. Dreams, an integral part of the spectrum of consciousness, play a significant role in shaping individuals' experiences and interpretations of the world. Dreams can serve as an emotional processing, memory consolidation, or evolutionary mechanism, and their lucidity in dreams aids monitoring. The déjà rêvé effect of dreams on individuals' experiences in virtual reality is a significant aspect of this postmodern world, as they help individuals navigate their experiences and understand their own reality.

Déjà rêvé, a phenomenon where individuals dream about a previous dream experience, is a significant aspect of postmodern society. It is influenced by factors such as age, gender, dream recall, and personality traits. The frequency of déjà rêvé events is negatively correlated with age, suggesting a higher frequency among younger individuals. The Big Five personality traits, such as agreeableness, conscientiousness, agreeableness, and neuroticism, have significant implications in marketing and other management domains. Simulacra and simulation, which are based on replicas of previous models, blur the boundaries between reality and representation, creating a state of hyperreality. This blurred understanding of reality is evident in various disciplines, such as literature, banking, and cultural theme parks. The concept of déjà rêvé has implications for cognitive processes, memory, and brain functioning in individuals.

The reality concept in postmodernism is eliminated in a more genuine manner than tangible, with the abundance of low-quality, mass-produced commodities shaping our society. The metaverse, a concept influenced by consumer culture and ideology, has raised concerns about the potential for simulated experiences to replace genuine reality. Virtual reality and augmented reality technologies offer immersive experiences that can elicit a sense of déjà rêvé, eliciting a sense of familiarity and familiarity in individuals. Virtual reality technology is revolutionizing visual design, enhancing immersive experiences and triggering a sensation similar to déjà rêvé. This phenomenon occurs due to the dream-like characteristics of virtual environments, creating a heightened sense of realism. The postmodern marketing environment has seen significant changes in individuals' social, economic, cultural, political, and technical domains, impacting marketing as a blend of arts and scientific disciplines. Postmodernism, a movement in art, architecture, literature, and cultural critique, rejects objective truth and emphasizes the social and cultural construction of knowledge. It challenges power structures based on race, gender, social class, and other forms of social injustice, emphasizing the individual's involvement in meaning and comprehension. Understanding the challenges and opportunities in postmodern society and marketing is crucial for gaining insight into the direction we are moving towards.

Postmodern culture is a response to the transformations in capitalist societies, focusing on aesthetic and humanistic values. It aims to shift from economic prosperity to the quality of life, with a growing acceptance of diverse individual choices in lifestyle and personal self-expression. Postmodern marketing, a paradigm shift in marketing philosophy, focuses on individuality, involvement, creativity, and cultural sensitivity in postmodern society. This approach enables the development of tailored marketing strategies that meet individual consumer needs and preferences, improving customer loyalty and brand support. Postmodern consumers are characterized by increased skepticism and relativism towards conventional authority and cultural

Unleashing the Déjà Rêvé Effect in Marketing

narratives, placing a high importance on self-expression and creativity. Postmodern marketing has significantly influenced the way marketers craft customer value, emphasizing language and representation in determining meaning. However, challenges include the complexity of measuring efficacy, the willingness to take risks, and the constrained level of acceptance.

The virtual epoch offers unprecedented opportunities for marketers to create personalized experiences and achieve their goals. By leveraging neuroscientific data, marketers can create immersive experiences that evoke a sense of déjà vu, engendering a sense of familiarity or anticipation. This strategic use of neurological data can lead to compelling and impactful marketing campaigns within the virtual domain. The fusion of technology and marketing strategies in the virtual epoch allows marketers to engage consumers on emotional and cognitive levels, presenting transformative possibilities in the virtual landscape.

DIGITAL TWIN TO UNLEASH A NEW ERA IN MARKETING PRACTICES

The Metaverse platform setting offers a safe environment for media and entertainment, enabling creative social change and spiritual growth, but also avoiding the shortcomings and shortcomings associated with postmodernism (Mohamed & Bukhari, 2023). The metaverse holds significant potential in enhancing internal staff communication and relationship marketing, as well as in revolutionizing conventional methods of training, teaching, and marketing within the domains of education, advertising, and communication (Mohamed & Bukhari, 2023). Mohamed and Bukhari (2023) critizes the Baudrillard (2010) simulacra theory and his pessimistic approach, and suggested that the metaverse offers potential for real-life tasks, training, and creative branding. It can improve productivity and culture through relationship marketing. Authors emphasize the metaverse's importance and the power of virtual reality and augmented reality to help marketers, educators, and others navigate the media simulacra trend. It is essential to acknowledge that Baudrillard (2010) does not just partake in assessing the apocalypse; Brown (1999a); Brown et al. (1996) also shares the same concern about marketing.

Several writers have conducted an evaluation of the early advantages of the virtual world, often referred to as the metaverse, which is characterized by its heightened precision in today's context. Additionally, authors have also offered critiques of Baudrillard's (2010) concept of simulation. As the use of metaverse technologies continues to expand, it becomes increasingly evident that these activities have become integral to human lifestyles and societal dynamics. Consequently, a significant number of tangible entities, including persons, are transitioning to the metaverse or other virtual realms. The advent of the metaverse has introduced a new paradigm into our society, namely the concept of the digital twin. IBM (2023) is desribing the digital twin as a virtual model that accurately represents a physical object, utilizing sensors to monitor performance aspects. This data is then applied to the digital copy, enabling simulations, performance studies, and potential improvements, ultimately reverting to the original physical object.

The utilization of digital twins is becoming more prevalent across various industries, resulting in significant transformations and the emergence of unique opportunities. Agriculture (Pylianidis, Osinga, & Athanasiadis, 2021), smart cities (Du et al., 2020), manufacturing (Kritzinger, Karner, Traar, Henjes, & Sihn, 2018).

The utilization of digital twin technology possesses the capacity to significantly influence society on a worldwide level. Various industries, including healthcare, life sciences, and fintech, are currently utilizing digital twin capabilities to propel advancements within their respective domains (Vasiliu-Feltes, 2023). The utilization of digital twins has the potential to facilitate the digital transformation of the daily lives of elderly individuals, thereby offering support functions and monitoring capabilities that contribute to the improvement of their overall well-being (Kobayashi, Fukae, Imai, & Arai, 2022). Digital twin technology serves as an interface between the physical and digital realms by generating a digital representation of tangible objects. This technology facilitates the provision of real-time, intelligent, and diverse services (Zhang, Fang, Deng, Qi, & Liang, 2023). The notion of digital twins is widely regarded as a potential remedy for societal issues across diverse domains such as health, wellness, security, transportation, energy, mobility, and communications (El Saddik, Laamarti, & Alja'Afreh, 2021). The research on and implementation of digital twin technology have sparked considerable interest and are projected to persistently expand in the foreseeable future. This advancement is anticipated to play a pivotal role in the advancement of intelligent urban areas and the enhancement of individuals' well-being. Grieves (2015) argues that digital twins synchronize the connection between physical and virtual product data, allowing for instantaneous comparison of manufacturing processes. Digital twin implications allow real-time or near-real-time comparison of the product's design specifications, enabling collaboration and visualization of manufacturing processes and ensuring product accuracy and up-to-date knowledge. Qi and Tao (2018) assess that digital twins and big data are crucial in promoting smart manufacturing. Digital twin allows real-time mapping between physical objects and digital representation, while big data enhances predictive capabilities. The reciprocal relationship between knowledge and production capabilities necessitates integrating effective marketing strategies that align with consumer expectations and enable the unhindered expression of consumer demand.

Unleashing the Déjà Rêvé Effect in Marketing

The increasing significance of familiarity in marketing strategies is evident, particularly within digital representations, automation, and the emergence of digital twins that encompass the interactions between clients and marketers. The significance of past experiences, whether acquired through physical interactions or digital representations, is growing in relevance for automated systems and individuals operating in mechanized capacities. Digital twins have become increasingly prominent in various industries, including marketing. These digital replicas serve as representations of entities or systems. The digital twin in question functions as symbolic embodiments of consumers and producers, facilitating a digital realm wherein interactions and transactions can occur. In the context of smart homes, an example can be observed in the capability to initiate product orders through diverse smart systems associated with different brands. This exemplifies the smooth exchange enabled by these digital representations, regardless of the presence of human intervention. The notion of personalization is emphasized as a pivotal element of forthcoming marketing strategies. The central theme is the increasing emphasis on enabling customers to assert their preferences and actively engage with products and services that are customized to their individual choices. There is a growing trend among brands to prioritize personalized experiences by tailoring their products and services to meet individual consumers' unique needs and desires. Nevertheless, the level of preparedness demonstrated by brands is a critical factor to consider. This state of preparedness encompasses many factors, including but not limited to technological readiness, data privacy, and security, adaptability to evolving consumer behaviors, and the capacity to generate seamless and personalized experiences across diverse digital platforms.

The impact of familiarity on marketing strategies increasingly extends to the domains of digital representations, automation, and personalized experiences. Brands that possess the ability to effectively navigate this dynamic environment, utilizing digital twins or representations while placing a high emphasis on personalization, are more likely to succeed in meeting the ever-changing demands of consumers and effectively involving them in their marketing initiatives.

CONCLUSION

The comprehensive exploration of dreams and their intersections with postmodern concepts such as hyperreality, personal reality construction, and the evolution of human needs in a digital era provides profound insights into the realm of marketing. Dreams are significant indicators of individual truths, intertwining personal aspirations with the shaping of reality. Dreams align with the notions presented in postmodernism about the construction of reality, as they are not just subconscious manifestations but potential guidelines influencing human behavior and decisions. The various dream theories offer divergent perspectives on the origin, function, and impact of dreams. From Freud's notion of dreams as a conduit for unconscious desires to the contemporary understanding of dreams' role in emotional regulation and memory consolidation, the discussion highlights the dynamic nature of dream-related research. The correlation between dreams and mental and emotional growth, as well as the differentiation between real and imagined experiences through lucidity in dreams, underscores the complex interplay between dreams and waking life.

The concept of déjà rêvé is characterized by the subjective sensation of re-experiencing a past dream. The multifaceted nature of déjà rêvé, segmented into episodic-like, familiarity-like, and dreamy state déjà rêvé, offers a nuanced understanding of how individuals recall and interpret their dreams. The correlation between déjà rêvé occurrences and factors like age, personality traits, and dream recall frequency illuminates the intricacies of this phenomenon and its potential implications for cognitive processes. Moreover, simulacra and simulation are fundamental concepts that challenge the conventional understanding of reality. The idea of simulacra, wherein replicas or representations surpass their original sources in authenticity, blurs the boundaries between reality and its depiction. Baudrillard (2010)'s perspective on simulation and hyperreality reinforces the notion of a world increasingly shaped by replicas and signs, transforming our perception of reality.

The metaverse is an emerging concept that integrates digital experiences and raises concerns about the replacement of genuine reality with simulated ones. The potential disconnect from authentic human interactions and tangible reality within the metaverse highlights the need for cautious consideration of the impact of simulated experiences on societal norms and personal identities. The convergence of virtual reality (VR), postmodernism's influence on society, and innovative marketing strategies has ushered in a transformative era, redefining the way individuals interact with technology, consume content, and perceive reality. VR and AR immerse individuals in experiences that blur the lines between the physical and digital realms, often evoking sensations of déjà vu or familiarity. VR's potential to revolutionize visual design, entertainment, and content creation offers compelling opportunities to enhance sensory experiences and enrich storytelling. The emergence of Extended Reality (XR) technologies has expanded beyond entertainment, infiltrating domains like healthcare, smart cities, and manufacturing, where these immersive technologies show promise in revolutionizing operational paradigms. In the realm of postmodernism, marketing has undergone a profound shift, emphasizing individuality, cultural sensitivity, and the subjective construction of meaning. This shift challenges conventional marketing approaches by acknowledging skepticism toward established narratives and highlighting the importance of personalized, diverse strategies that resonate with the individual.

Unleashing the Déjà Rêvé Effect in Marketing

The virtual epoch's implications for marketing are significant. Marketers, leveraging neuroscientific insights, are crafting immersive experiences within digital environments that evoke familiarity or anticipation, leveraging déjà rêvé-like sensations. This strategic fusion of technology and marketing not only engages consumers on emotional and cognitive levels but also blurs the boundaries between reality and representation. Furthermore, the rise of digital twin technology, which serves as virtual replicas of physical entities, permeates various industries, from healthcare to smart cities, enabling real-time simulations and solutions for societal issues. The concept bridges the physical and digital realms, offering insights, improvements, and services while catering to a technologically evolving landscape. The confluence of VR's immersive experiences, postmodernism's emphasis on subjective truths, and the rise of digital twins signifies a shift toward personalized, technology-driven encounters. As marketers continue to navigate this landscape, the emphasis on familiarity, personalization, and the innovative utilization of technology will define the future of consumer engagement and brand-consumer relationships. This era opens doors to unprecedented opportunities for crafting unique, immersive experiences, reimagining storytelling, and fostering deeper connections between brands and their audiences in an ever-evolving digital landscape.

The convergence of technological advancements, particularly in VR and AR, with postmodern influences has ushered in transformative shifts in various spheres, notably the realms of digital design, marketing, and societal interactions. The integration of VR and AR technologies has led to deeply immersive experiences that often evoke a sense of familiarity or déjà vu, blurring the boundaries between reality and the virtual world. VR's capacity to replicate numerous visual stimuli offers users a unique form of visual satisfaction. Its integration into digital media design has the potential to revolutionize conventional practices by enhancing the quality of film and television production through realistic environmental characteristics. Moreover, the advent of information technology has given rise to VR and AR, both promising immersive experiences and practical applications in various domains such as entertainment, healthcare, smart cities, and more. Additionally, the emergence of 5th-generation networks and ultra-low-latency Internet has introduced XR, holoportation, and remote-control applications. Industries like factories, smart cities, and digital healthcare are on the verge of a revolution with the emergence of these technologies, highlighting the importance of tactile sensation in perceiving and interacting with virtual environments. Within contemporary contexts, AR, VR, and MR technologies, encapsulated under XR, have expanded beyond conventional entertainment domains into emerging sectors like healthcare, smart cities, and autonomous vehicles. The proliferation of XR technologies has facilitated the creation of 3D reconstructions, digital twins, and simulations, leveraging sophisticated hardware and software solutions to enhance immersion and realism.

The immersive nature of virtual environments can induce a sensation akin to déjà rêvé, where individuals experience heightened realism due to the dream-like attributes inherent in these digital realms. This level of immersion might lead individuals to blur the boundaries between their digital identities and real-life experiences. Transitioning to postmodern marketing challenges traditional narratives by emphasizing subjective truths and individualistic cultural expressions. Postmodernism rejects objective reality, emphasizing the role of language and discourse in constructing meaning, challenging power structures, and celebrating individual expression. Postmodern marketing integrates these principles by emphasizing individuality, involvement, creativity, and cultural sensitivity. It employs tactics like mimicry, satire, and intertextuality to engage consumers in personalized, culturally sensitive ways. However, this shift poses challenges in measuring efficacy and navigating a fragmented, unpredictable marketplace. In the virtual epoch, the fusion of technology and marketing strategies enables the creation of immersive experiences that evoke a sense of déjà rêvé. Marketers leverage neuroscientific insights to craft campaigns that resonate deeply with individuals' emotions and cognitive perceptions within virtual landscapes. The introduction of digital twins in the metaverse era marks a significant transition, offering virtual models mirroring physical objects for performance monitoring, simulations, and potential improvements. These twins span various industries, from agriculture to smart cities, healthcare, and beyond, influencing societal advancements and individual well-being.

In summary, the exploration of dreams, déjà rêvé, simulacra, and the metaverse within the framework of postmodernism provides a rich tapestry of insights for marketing strategies. Understanding the nuances of how individuals construct their reality through dreams and simulated experiences offers a unique opportunity for marketers to engage with consumers authentically, catering to their personalized aspirations and fragmented truths in a digitally evolving world. By embracing the dynamic nature of reality, subjectivity, and the interplay between dreams and waking life, marketers can navigate the postmodern landscape to forge genuine connections and offer value that resonates with individual narratives and experiences. The integration of VR/AR technologies, postmodern principles in marketing, and the advent of digital twins in the virtual epoch signify an era where immersive experiences blur the lines between reality and the digital realm. Marketers can leverage these technologies to evoke sensations akin to déjà rêvé, providing consumers with deeply engaging experiences that bridge the gap between their digital and physical lives. This presents an opportunity for brands to create familiarity, personalization, and engagement, thereby unlocking consumer value in both the physical and digital realms.

REFERENCES

Barroso, P. (2022). From reality to the hyperreality of simulation. *Texto Livre, 15*.

Baudrillard, J. (1998). *The consumer society: Myths and structures*. Sage. doi:10.4135/9781526401502

Baudrillard, J. (2010). *Simulacra and Simulation* (S. F. Glaser, Trans.). The University of Michigan Press.

Bougen, P. D., & Young, J. J. (2012). Fair value accounting: Simulacra and simulation. *Critical Perspectives on Accounting, 23*(4-5), 390–402. doi:10.1016/j.cpa.2011.05.004

Boyd, D. (2021). A critical inquiry into the hyperreality of digitalization in construction. *Construction Management and Economics, 39*(7), 549–564. doi:10.1080/01446193.2021.1904515

Brown, S. (1997). Marketing science in a postmodern world: Introduction to the special issue. *European Journal of Marketing, 31*(3/4), 167–182. doi:10.1108/03090569710162308

Brown, S. (1999a). Postmodernism: the end of marketing. In D. Brownlie, M. Saren, R. Wensley, & R. Whittington (Eds.), *Rethinking Marketing: towards critical marketing accountings* (pp. 27–57). Sage. doi:10.4135/9781446280058.n3

Brown, S. (1999b). Retro-marketing: Yesterday's tomorrows, today! *Marketing Intelligence & Planning, 17*(7), 363–376. doi:10.1108/02634509910301098

Brown, S., Bell, J., & Carson, D. (1996). *Marketing apocalypse: eschatology, escapology and the illusion of the end* (Vol. 2). Psychology Press.

Caliskan, A. (2019). Applying the Right Relationship Marketing Strategy through Big Five Personality Traits. *Journal of Relationship Marketing, 18*(3), 196–215. doi:10.1080/15332667.2019.1589241

Cannavò, A., Kapralos, B., Seinfeld, S., Pratticò, F. G., & Zhang, C. (2023). *IEEE VR 2023 Workshops: Workshop: 3D Reconstruction, Digital Twinning, and Simulation for Virtual Experiences (ReDigiTS 2023)*. Paper presented at the 2023 IEEE Conference on Virtual Reality and 3D User Interfaces Abstracts and Workshops (VRW).

Castillo, J. (2017). *The Relationship between Big Five Personality Traits*. Customer Empowerment and Customer Satisfaction in the Retail Industry.

Crolla, K., & Goepel, G. (2022). Entering hyper-reality:"Resonance-in-sight," a mixed-reality art installation. *Frontiers in Virtual Reality*, *3*, 1044021. doi:10.3389/frvir.2022.1044021

Curot, J., Valton, L., Denuelle, M., Vignal, J.-P., Maillard, L., Pariente, J., Trébuchon, A., Bartolomei, F., & Barbeau, E. J. (2018). Déjà-rêvé: Prior dreams induced by direct electrical brain stimulation. *Brain Stimulation*, *11*(4), 875–885. doi:10.1016/j.brs.2018.02.016 PMID:29530448

Davidson, M. P. (2013). *The consumerist manifesto: Advertising in postmodern times*. Routledge. doi:10.4324/9781315002491

Drinkwater, K. G., Denovan, A., & Dagnall, N. (2020). Lucid Dreaming, Nightmares, and Sleep Paralysis: Associations With Reality Testing Deficits and Paranormal Experience/Belief. *Frontiers in Psychology*, *11*, 11. doi:10.3389/fpsyg.2020.00471 PMID:32256437

Du, J., Zhu, Q., Shi, Y., Wang, Q., Lin, Y., & Zhao, D. (2020). Cognition digital twins for personalized information systems of smart cities: Proof of concept. *Journal of Management Engineering*, *36*(2), 04019052. doi:10.1061/(ASCE)ME.1943-5479.0000740

El Saddik, A., Laamarti, F., & Alja'Afreh, M. (2021). The potential of digital twins. *IEEE Instrumentation & Measurement Magazine*, *24*(3), 36–41. doi:10.1109/MIM.2021.9436090

Erdeniz, B., Tekgün, E., Menteş, Ö., Çoban, A., Bilge, S., & Serin, E. K. (2022). Supplemental Material for Bodily Self-Consciousness in Dreams Questionnaire (BSD-Q) and Its Relation to Waking Dissociative Experiences. *Dreaming*.

Evans, G. J. (2020). The Dream and the Reality. *Global Responsibility to Protect*, *12*(4), 363–365. doi:10.1163/1875-984X-20200006

Faulkner, D. (2022). Hyper-Reality: A Dangerous Modern Phenomenon. In Creative Business Education: Exploring the Contours of Pedagogical Praxis (pp. 185-198). Springer. doi:10.1007/978-3-031-10928-7_11

Ferraz-Lorenzo, M. (2018). Modernity, postmodernity, hypermodernity and the ever uncertain (educational) future. *Educational Philosophy and Theory*, *50*(14), 1616–1617. doi:10.1080/00131857.2018.1461427

Firat, A. F. (1992). Postmodernism and the marketing organization. *Journal of Organizational Change Management*, *5*(1), 79–83. doi:10.1108/09534819210011006

Firat, A. F. (2022). Marketing and market. *Japan Marketing History Review*, *1*(1), 48–53.

Firat, A. F., Dholakia, N., & Venkatesh, A. (1995). Marketing in a postmodern world. *European Journal of Marketing*, *29*(1), 40–56. doi:10.1108/03090569510075334

Firat, A. F., & Shultz, C. J. (1997). From segmentation to fragmentation. *European Journal of Marketing*, *31*(3/4), 183–207. doi:10.1108/EUM0000000004321

Firat, A. F., & Shultz, C. J. II. (2001). Preliminary metric investigations into the nature of the "postmodern consumer". *Marketing Letters*, *12*(2), 189–203. doi:10.1023/A:1011173205199

Firat, A. F., & Venkatesh, A. (1993). Postmodernity: The age of marketing. *International Journal of Research in Marketing*, *10*(3), 227–249. doi:10.1016/0167-8116(93)90009-N

Firat, A. F., & Venkatesh, A. (1995). Liberatory postmodernism and the reenchantment of consumption. *The Journal of Consumer Research*, *22*(3), 239–267. doi:10.1086/209448

Fukuda, T. (2023). *Simulacra. (Doctoral)*. McGill University, Montr'eal, Qu'ebec.

Funkhouser, A. T., & Schredl, M. (2010). The frequency of déjà vu (déjà rêve) and the effects of age, dream recall frequency and personality factors. *International Journal of Dream Research*, *3*, 60–64.

Ghatak, S., & Singh, S. (2019). Examining Maslow's hierarchy need theory in the social media adoption. *FIIB Business Review*, *8*(4), 292–302. doi:10.1177/2319714519882830

Givrad, S. (2016). Dream Theory and Science: A Review. *Psychoanalytic Inquiry*, *36*(3), 199–213. doi:10.1080/07351690.2016.1145967

Graham, M. (2013). Geography/internet: Ethereal alternate dimensions of cyberspace or grounded augmented realities? *The Geographical Journal*, *179*(2), 177–182. doi:10.1111/geoj.12009

Grieves, M. (2015). *Digital Twin: Manufacturing Excellence through Virtual Factory Replication*. White Papers.

Hobson, J. A. (1998). *The Dreaming Brain: How the Brain Creates both the Sense and Nonsense of Dreams*. Basic Books.

Hossain, M. M. (2022). Simulation and Simulacra in Aldous Huxley's Brave New World: A Baudrillardian Appraisal. *J-Lalite: Journal of English Studies*.

IBM. (2023). *What is a digital twin?* Retrieved from https://www.ibm.com/topics/what-is-a-digital-twin

Kobayashi, T., Fukae, K., Imai, T., & Arai, K. (2022). *Digital Twin Agent for Super-Aged Society.* Paper presented at the 2022 IEEE International Conference on Consumer Electronics (ICCE). 10.1109/ICCE53296.2022.9730230

Kritzinger, W., Karner, M., Traar, G., Henjes, J., & Sihn, W. (2018). Digital Twin in manufacturing: A categorical literature review and classification. *IFAC-PapersOnLine*, *51*(11), 1016–1022. doi:10.1016/j.ifacol.2018.08.474

Laughlin, C. D. (2013). Dreaming and Reality: A Neuroanthropological Account. *International Journal of Transpersonal Studies*, *32*(1), 8. doi:10.24972/ijts.2013.32.1.64

Mansell, R. (2005). Human Rights and Equity in Cyberspace. In M. Klang & A. Murray (Eds.), Human Rights in the Digital Age. Academic Press.

Martineau, F., & Roult, R. (2021). L'art du flow et le développement spirituel dans la société hypermoderne. *Leisure/Loisir, 45*, 423 - 457.

McGinn, C. (2006). *The Power of Movies – How Screen and Mind Interact.* Pantheon.

Mcluhan, M. (1964). *Understanding Media: The Extensions of Man.* McGraw-Hill.

Mohamed, K., & Bukhari, S. (2023). The Media in Metaverse; Baudrillard's Simulacra, Is Metaverse that Begins the Apocalypse? *International Journal of Communication and Media Science*, *10*(1), 14–22. doi:10.14445/2349641X/IJCMS-V10I1P102

Morewedge, C. K., & Norton, M. I. (2009). When dreaming is believing: The (motivated) interpretation of dreams. *Journal of Personality and Social Psychology*, *96*(2), 249–264. doi:10.1037/a0013264 PMID:19159131

Ong, C.-E., & Jin, G. (2017). Simulacra and simulation: Double simulation at a North Song Dynasty theme park. *Tourism Geographies*, *19*(2), 227–243. doi:10.1 080/14616688.2016.1258431

Pavlov, A. V., & Erokhina, Y. V. (2019). Images of Modernity in the 21st Century: Altermodernism. *Russian Journal of Philosophical Sciences*, *62*(2), 7–25. doi:10.30727/0235-1188-2019-62-2-7-25

Pellegrini, R. J., Noffsinger, E. B., Caldwell, R. T., & Tutko, T. A. (1993). Exploring the Everyday Life Incidence of Déjà Connu Experiences in Impression Formation. *Perceptual and Motor Skills*, *76*(3_suppl), 1243–1250. doi:10.2466/pms.1993.76.3c.1243 PMID:8337071

Polasek, A. D. (2012). Sherlockian Simulacra: Adaptation and the Postmodern Construction of Reality. *Literature-film Quarterly, 40*, 191.

Price, M. (2009). You are what you dream. *Monitor on Psychology, 40*(4). https://www.apa.org/monitor/2009/04/dream

Pylianidis, C., Osinga, S., & Athanasiadis, I. N. (2021). Introducing digital twins to agriculture. *Computers and Electronics in Agriculture, 184*, 105942. doi:10.1016/j.compag.2020.105942

Qi, Q., & Tao, F. (2018). Digital twin and big data towards smart manufacturing and industry 4.0: 360 degree comparison. *IEEE Access : Practical Innovations, Open Solutions, 6*, 3585–3593. doi:10.1109/ACCESS.2018.2793265

Reglitz, M. (2023). The socio-economic argument for the human right to internet access. *Politics, Philosophy & Economics, 22*(4), 441–469. doi:10.1177/1470594X231167597

Revonsuo, A. (1995). Consciousness, dreams and virtual realities. *Philosophical Psychology, 8*(1), 35–58. doi:10.1080/09515089508573144

Roberts, D., Baker, S., & Walker, D. (2005). Can we learn together?: Co-creating with consumers. *International Journal of Market Research, 47*(4), 405–426. doi:10.1177/147078530504700401

Rospigliosi, P. a. (2022). *Metaverse or Simulacra? Roblox, Minecraft, Meta and the turn to virtual reality for education, socialisation and work* (Vol. 30). Taylor & Francis.

Schneider, E., Sklar, E., Azhar, M. Q., Parsons, S., & Tuyls, K. (2015). *Towards a methodology for describing the relationship between simulation and reality.* Paper presented at the European Conference on Artificial Life. 10.7551/978-0-262-33027-5-ch098

Schredl, M., Goritz, A., & Funkhouser, A. (2017). Frequency of déjà rêvé: Effects of age, gender, dream recall, and personality. *Journal of Consciousness Studies, 24*(7-8), 155–162.

Schredl, M., Remedios, A., Marin-Dragu, S., Sheikh, S., Forbes, A., Iyer, R. S., Orr, M., & Meier, S. (2022). Dream recall frequency, lucid dream frequency, and personality during the COVID-19 pandemic. *Imagination, Cognition and Personality, 42*(2), 113–133. doi:10.1177/02762366221104214

Sehad, N., Cherif, B., Khadraoui, I., Hamidouche, W., Bader, F., Jäntti, R., & Debbah, M. (2023). Locomotion-Based UAV Control Toward the Internet of Senses. *IEEE Transactions on Circuits and Wystems. II, Express Briefs*, *70*(5), 1804–1808. doi:10.1109/TCSII.2023.3257363

Settineri, S., Frisone, F., Alibrandi, A., & Merlo, E. M. (2019). Italian adaptation of the Mannheim Dream Questionnaire (MADRE): Age, Gender and Dream Recall effects. *International Journal of Dream Research*, 119–129.

Solms, M. (2015). Freudian dream theory today. In M. Solms (Ed.), *The Feeling Brain*. Karnac.

Stern, B. B. (1993). Feminist literary criticism and the deconstruction of ads: A postmodern view of advertising and consumer responses. *The Journal of Consumer Research*, *19*(4), 556–566. doi:10.1086/209322

Sulehri, N. A., Awais, A., Dar, I. B., & Uzair, A. (2021). *Big Five Personality Traits on Project Success in Marketing-Oriented Organizations: Moderation of Leader Member Exchange*. Academic Press.

Tapia, C. (2012). Modernity, Postmodernity, Hypermodernity. *ConneXions (Cupertino, Calif.)*, *97*(1), 15–25. doi:10.3917/cnx.097.0015

Taylor, W. J. (1965). "Is Marketing a Science?" Revisited. *Journal of Marketing*, *29*(3), 49–53. doi:10.1177/002224296502900309

Thompson, R. G., Moulin, C. J. A., Conway, M. A., & Jones, R. W. (2004). Persistent Déjà vu: A disorder of memory. *International Journal of Geriatric Psychiatry*, *19*(9), 19. doi:10.1002/gps.1177 PMID:15352150

Tremlett, P. F. (2021). Modernism and Postmodernism. *The Wiley Blackwell Companion to the Study of Religion*, 325-334.

Trepczyński, M. (2018). *Hypermodernism as Deceleration, Re-stabilisation and Reconciliation*. Edukacja Filozoficzna. doi:10.14394/edufil.2018.0021

Tsibizova, I. M. (2023). On the Foreign Policy Rhetoric of Hyper-Postmodernism. *The Bulletin of Irkutsk State University. Series Political Science and Religion Studies*.

Vasiliu-Feltes, I. (2023). Impact of Digital Twins on Smart Cities: Healthtech and Fintech Perspectives – opportunities, Challenges, and Future Directions. In I. Vasiliu-Feltes (Ed.), *Impact of Digital Twins in Smart Cities Development*. IGI Global.

Wamsley, E. J., & Stickgold, R. (2010). Dreaming and offline memory processing. *Current Biology*, *20*(23), R1010–R1013. doi:10.1016/j.cub.2010.10.045 PMID:21145013

Woolley, B. (1993). *Virtual Worlds: A Journey in Hype and Hyperreality*. Blackwell.

Wu, J., Wang, Z., Sarker, A., & Srivastava, M. B. (2023). Acuity: Creating Realistic Digital Twins Through Multi-resolution Pointcloud Processing and Audiovisual Sensor Fusion. *Proceedings of the 8th ACM/IEEE Conference on Internet of Things Design and Implementation*. 10.1145/3576842.3582363

Yuill, K. (2015). Between the dream and the reality. *Patterns of Prejudice*, *49*(5), 552–554. doi:10.1080/0031322X.2015.1103456

Zhang, Y., Fang, L., Deng, H., Qi, Z., & Liang, H. (2023). *Recent Advances and Future Perspectives of Digital Twins*. Paper presented at the 2023 IEEE International Conference on Control, Electronics and Computer Technology (ICCECT). 10.1109/ICCECT57938.2023.10140652

Zhao, H., Li, D., & Li, X. (2018). Relationship between dreaming and memory reconsolidation. *Brain Science Advances*, *4*(2), 118–130. doi:10.26599/BSA.2018.9050005

ADDITIONAL READING

Baudrillard, J. (1998). *The consumer society: Myths and structures*. Sage. doi:10.4135/9781526401502

Baudrillard, J. (2010). *Simulacra and Simulation* (S. F. Glaser, Trans.). The University of Michigan Press.

Brown, S. (1999). Postmodernism: the end of marketing. In D. Brownlie, M. Saren, R. Wensley, & R. Whittington (Eds.), *Rethinking Marketing: towards critical marketing accountings* (pp. 27–57). Sage. doi:10.4135/9781446280058.n3

Brown, S., Bell, J., & Carson, D. (1996). *Marketing apocalypse: eschatology, escapology and the illusion of the end* (Vol. 2). Psychology Press.

Davidson, M. P. (2013). *The consumerist manifesto: Advertising in postmodern times*. Routledge. doi:10.4324/9781315002491

Firat, A. F., & Venkatesh, A. (1993). Postmodernity: The age of marketing. *International Journal of Research in Marketing, 10*(3), 227–249. doi:10.1016/0167-8116(93)90009-N

Hobson, J. A. (1998). *The Dreaming Brain: How the Brain Creates both the Sense and Nonsense of Dreams*. Basic Books.

Vasiliu-Feltes, I. (2023). Impact of Digital Twins on Smart Cities: Healthtech and Fintech Perspectives – opportunities, Challenges, and Future Directions. In I. Vasiliu-Feltes (Ed.), *Impact of Digital Twins in Smart Cities Development*. IGI Global.

KEY TERMS AND DEFINITIONS

Customer Empowerment: The provision of information and tools to customers, enabling them to make informed decisions.

Déjà Rêvé Effect: Utilizing the concept of leveraging familiarity or recognition in marketing campaigns can effectively elicit emotional connections, enhance brand recall, and facilitate the creation of personalized experiences. This is achieved by capitalizing on the sensation of re-experiencing a past dream (virtual world) during consumers' interactions with brand content.

Digital Twins: Virtual replicas or digital representations of physical objects, systems, processes, or entities. These twins are created using real-time data, sensors, and simulations to mirror the physical counterpart's characteristics, behavior, and performance in a digital environment.

Postmodern Marketing Strategy: Set of approaches that prioritize individual experiences, subjective truths, and cultural sensitivity, challenging traditional marketing norms by emphasizing personalized, diverse, and creative engagement with consumers.

Simulacra: The representations or copies that replace the original, blurring the distinction between reality and its imitation, often leading to the perceived significance of the simulation over the actual object or concept it represents.

Simulacrum: The representation or imitation of something, often a person or an object, that may take the form of a copy or a likeness, blurring the distinction between the original and the reproduced version.

Simulation: The process of imitating or replicating the behavior, characteristics, or operations of a real-world system or process using models or computer programs to study, analyze, or predict its functioning without direct interaction with the actual system.

Chapter 8

Can Social Media Be a Transformative Tool for Building a Better Society?
The Case of YouTube Videos on Consumer Sustainability Perception

Neslihan Paker
https://orcid.org/0000-0001-8087-7758
Izmir Kavram Vocational School, Turkey

ABSTRACT

The study aims to evaluate consumers' perceptions of social marketing designed to enhance environmental awareness through social media platforms. The approach employed in this study is exploratory and interpretive. The data gathered from YouTube videos on the "Doğa İçin Çal" platform filmed during the 2019-2023 period were semiotically analyzed in terms of their content characteristics. Afterwards, the user comments were evaluated as well. During the analysis process, the consumer perception framework was used by utilizing the content analysis method through the Maxqda software program. The findings indicate that the videos effectively captured the target audience's attention and fostered social cohesion by promoting unity. However, the perception elements utilized in the videos indicate that the viewers pay greater attention to the aspects associated with musical performance, while the matter of environmental awareness remains in the background.

DOI: 10.4018/979-8-3693-1594-1.ch008

Copyright © 2024, IGI Global. Copying or distributing in print or electronic forms without written permission of IGI Global is prohibited.

INTRODUCTION

Social marketing involves using strategies that can affect human behavior, addressing socially complex issues such as promoting health and environmental sustainability, with a mission to provide greater benefits to individuals and communities (Andreasen, 2014). The primary objective of these strategies is to encourage the target audience to become active participants in shaping their own lives (Saunders et al., 2015). Nonetheless, the desired changes in behavior significantly rely on the individual's perception of stimuli, which contributes significantly to shaping their understanding of reality (Solomon, 2006). The process of perception begins with the reception of information through the five senses, whereas marketing communication plays a crucial role in concluding this process by capturing the individual's attention and subsequently interpreting the received information. In the contemporary era, these marketing communications are being held on through digitally produced commodities at an increasing pace, and social media products are a significant portion of this landscape. Furthermore, the utilization of social media by businesses has become increasingly favoured due to its numerous benefits, such as cost-effective reaching a wide-ranging audience, expeditious feedback for enhancing and advancing operations, as well as the capacity to cultivate customer satisfaction and facilitate the creation of value (Cheung et al., 2021; Li et al., 2021). As a result, in light of all these developments, businesses engage in marketing endeavours with the objective of fostering a shared awareness for a better society, employing social media platforms as a means to amplify their messages to a wider audience. Nonetheless, it is crucial to do a thorough follow-up and evaluation of the social marketing plan in order to ascertain the responses of the target market towards the social marketing activities, gauge the extent of awareness within the target audience, and determine whether the intended behavioural change has been achieved (Cheng et al., 2011). The research conducted to assess the effectiveness of these actions in shaping a meaningful consumer perception would ultimately contribute to the intended transformation in societal behaviour.

The primary aim of this study is to assess consumer perceptions of social marketing that seeks to promote environmental awareness via social media platforms. The study employed an exploratory and interpretive approach. "Doğa İçin Çal" platform was chosen as the research context, which got inspiration from "Playing for Change," platform established in the United States. Doğa İçin Çal has substantial views of more than 350 million and is primarily dedicated to fostering environmental awareness. In the study, firstly, data obtained from three YouTube videos on the platform shot between 2019-2023 were evaluated in a semiotic manner in terms of the characteristics utilized in the content. Thereafter, the user comments that received the maximum number of likes were analyzed. The consumer perception literature was used as the theoretical framework, and during the analysis process, the content analysis method was used through the Maxqda software application.

The following section presents the conceptual framework of the study, which encompasses the existing body of literature on social marketing, social media, perception, and the interconnections between these concepts. After providing a concise overview of the research context, data collection methods, and methodology employed, the parts that follow present the findings and results obtained. The research provided solutions and suggestions for improvement in the use of social marketing, especially for environmental awareness, through social media platforms, as well as recommendations for future research.

THEORETICAL BACKGROUND

Social Marketing for a Better World

Social marketing is a discipline focused on facilitating behavioral change and tackling complex societal issues, such as environmental conservation, injury prevention, and health promotion, in order to create substantial benefits for individuals and communities alike (Cheng et al., 2011; Andreasen, 2014; French and Russell-Bennett, 2015). The interventions associated with social marketing have the potential to facilitate the identification of several crucial factors in the development of programs on social concerns (Singaiah and Laskar, 2015) and, ultimately, contribute to the overall betterment of society (iSMA, 2023).

In the pursuit of this objective, social marketing employs "marketing principles and techniques to influence a target audience to voluntarily accept, reject, modify, or abandon a behavior for the benefit of individuals, groups, or society as a whole" (Kotler et al, 2002: 394), and so, like commercial marketing, encompasses product planning, price, communication, and distribution (Kotler and Zaltman, 1971). On the other hand, due to the distinct setting of social marketing, the principles and ideas of commercial marketing cannot always be seamlessly applied (Peattie and Peattie, 2009). For example, commercial marketing is primarily concerned with achieving the objectives of shareholders, whereas social marketing is primarily concerned with addressing society's aspiration to improve the overall quality of life for its members (Menegaki, 2012; Anker et al., 2022), and it also tries to persuade legislators (Grier and Bryant, 2005). Unlike traditional marketing, this one does not primarily target product or brand consumption or develop brand loyalty. Instead, its primary goal is to encourage desirable social behaviors by increasing public knowledge of challenges (Vallverdu-Gordi and Marine-Roig, 2023). Furthermore, it promotes a specific proposition rather than a social product. Given that social marketing mostly focuses on intangible items or ideas, it shares similarities with services marketing (Peattie and Peattie, 2009).

Along with the benefits of the concept to society, there exist specific critiques pertaining to the execution of social marketing, notably with regard to its inability to fulfill projected performance levels. One critique of social marketing pertains to its tendency to attribute responsibility to the person, thereby neglecting the fundamental environmental and societal factors that contribute to the issues it seeks to resolve (Grier and Bryant, 2005). Sutinen and Närvänen (2022) underline that many classic social marketing principles, such as customer centricity, exchange, and voluntary behavior modification, have limits when it comes to addressing sustainability problems because the focus is on the benefit to society or the environment rather than the person. On paper, the answer to some problems may appear to be relatively straightforward; however, the journey to this answer is complicated by a number of difficulties, including choices, motivation, influences, abilities, knowledge, and socio-cultural surroundings. Instead of placing responsibility on individuals, Peattie and Peattie (2009) advise taking into account the perspective of the audience, which may include any obstacles they encounter in their efforts toward change. Attempting to instill guilt in individuals regarding their lifestyles and consumption patterns yields only slight outcomes.

Several authors provide recommendations for managing these challenges. According to McKenzie-Mohr (2000), the development of an effective social marketing program must begin with the identification of barriers. For example, depending on whether a society is developed or developing, different barriers may exist. According to the studies, developing countries need to place a greater emphasis on education, incentives, and policies (Heydari et al., 2021; Issock et al., 2021). Also, despite individuals' willingness, there can be barriers to engaging in social marketing activities, primarily due to infrastructure limitations or economic constraints in developing countries. Even though approximately 80% of people in Türkiye are willing and eager to participate in separate collection programs (Metin et al., 2003), a recent study (Umut and Velioğlu, 2023) revealed that infrastructure and the dissemination of recycling knowledge to its residents is insufficient to encourage their participation in environmental activities. The findings of Akeke's (2022) study demonstrated a convincing association between sustainable behavior and social marketing, specifically the factors of price and place, which have the potential to encourage eco-friendly activities like individual home garbage disposal. Peattie and Peattie (2009) offered that segmentation can also be employed for individuals within the target demographic who exhibit varying levels of awareness and reactivity toward a certain issue or behavior. Furthermore, to be successful in social marketing, one must monitor the campaign to evaluate its efficacy and decide whether it should be continued. One must also identify activities that need to be revised midway through, educate the target audience, and seek assistance from the government via legislation (Grier and Bryant, 2005). McKenzie-Mohr (2000) suggests that community-based social marketing encourages sustainable behavior.

Social marketing is still in its early stages in Türkiye as in many developing or emerging countries, only a few investigations have been conducted on this topic. For example, the health aspects of social marketing, public service announcements, and educational short videos on the Turkish Ministry of Health's website were evaluated. Tobacco and tobacco products, as well as obesity, emerged as the most frequently discussed topics (İnci et al., 2021). Recently, Umut and Velioğlu (2023) designed a social marketing program to encourage recycling behaviour at the household level.

The Promotion of Social Marketing Through Social Media

Social media is the utilization of digital platforms, including customer blogs, online communities, and media-sharing platforms, to establish and cultivate connections, as well as disseminate information, between enterprises and customers (Li et al., 2021). Today, more than 4.2 billion people (Kemp, 2021) are social media users and mostly favorite Facebook, YouTube, and Instagram, boasting monthly active user counts of 3.0 million, 2.5 million, and 2.0 million, respectively (Statista, 2023). It has the great advantage of offering more cost-effective access to reach businesses' users (Amelia and Hidayatullah, 2020) and is a valuable tool for service development owing to its ability to facilitate active consumer engagement and foster brand loyalty (Seo and Park, 2018). Individuals choose to engage with social media platforms that respond to their needs, like the pursuit of knowledge, entertainment, leisure, or social interaction (Ko et al., 2005). In recent years, its role has extended beyond its traditional role of promoting and distributing services. Empirical data suggests that a considerable proportion of the populace is utilizing social media platforms as a means to disseminate news and information (Velichety and Shrivastava, 2022).

The essence of social marketing is promotion (Peattie and Peattie, 2009). Social media platforms are increasingly holding contemporary activities online, and the platforms have been extensively utilized to address a range of economic, societal, and environmental concerns. This includes promoting and fostering sustainable habits and lifestyles and shaping and strengthening individuals' environmental attitudes, ultimately leading to increased adoption of environmental behaviors. In a social media context, users engage in active participation in online discourse rather than only receiving messages from websites, which increases the efficacy of social media activism. This interaction includes a variety of behaviors, such as responding with likes and hearts, engaging with content with comments and responses, and sharing content with others with shares and retweets (Alsaad et al., 2023). Thus, the primary focus is to increase user engagement on social media and, in turn, responsible behaviour. Alam et al.' (2023) study results show that advertisement effectiveness, online interaction tendency, and environmental concerns positively affect customers' interactions with environmentally responsible behavior or pro-environmental campaigns. Customers who actively participate in pro-environmental initiatives are more likely to have pro-environmental consumption intentions.

The studies show that creativity, informativeness, and emotional appeal determine content attractiveness, which increases consumer interaction with social media content (Alam et al., 2023). The study conducted by Ummar et al. (2023) highlights the need to consider campaign qualities, such as informativeness and persuasiveness, in order to foster favorable attitudes towards green tourism. The impact of a green campaign on social media in terms of providing information has been found to have a beneficial influence on individuals' attitudes towards green tourism. Vallverdu-Gordi and Marine-Roig's (2023) study findings reveal that graphic design semiotics promote public environmental awareness and destination preservation by eliciting a sensitive, emotional, and cognitive response from the audience to the campaign. Florence et al. (2022) conducted a meta-analysis study to understand appropriate promotion frameworks for encouraging sustainable consumer behavior. According to the findings, message frame combinations such as positive-negative (benefits vs. costs) and self-other consequences (personal vs. societal) are more consistently convincing in encouraging the adoption of sustainable consumer behaviour.

Perception Mechanism and Social Media as a Transformative Tool for Sustainability Perception

Perception is a process in which individuals engage in the cognitive activities of selecting, organizing, and interpreting sensory stimuli (Hellriegel and Slocum, 2004; Schiffman and Kanuk, 2004). Its primary objective is to assign meaning to raw sensations through the incorporation of additional information (Solomon, 2018). The perceptual process has multiple stages, as seen in Figure 1.

The process starts with the reception of surrounding sensory stimuli, followed by an immediate response facilitated by our sensory receptors, namely the eyes, ears, nose, mouth, fingers, and skin. The perception of external sensory stimuli, such as hearing a song on the radio, has the potential to elicit internal sensory experiences. For example, a song may trigger a young man's memory of dancing and evoke memories of the scent of his date's perfume or the tactile sensation of her hair brushing against his cheek (Solomon, 2018). Attention, which is a significant part of this process, can be defined as a temporary and influential ability of the perceptual response (Berlyne, 1951: 141). Various factors contribute to the enhancement of attention, such as stimulus intensity, which affects the likelihood of a response. Additionally, attention can be influenced by motivation and value,

Figure 1.

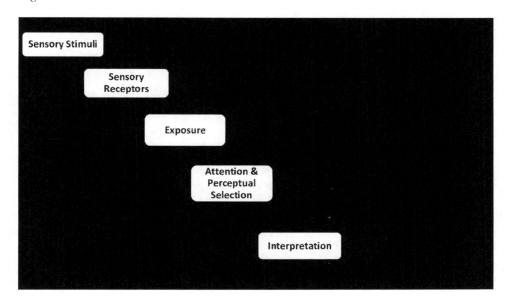

including enjoyable experiences and possibly damaging occurrences. Furthermore, the existence of novelty and curiosity also plays a role in improving attention. Color, size, position, motion, and sound are also among the stimulus selection factors, along with personal selection factors such as discrimination, exposure, and relevance. The findings of Spence's (2018) literature review study indicate that background color has a significant influence on consumer food choices, perception, and subsequent behavior. Additionally, the utilization of perceptual feedback and network learning allows individuals to discern certain visual elements while disregarding others within intricate visual environments. The mentioned mechanisms give rise to attentional blindness, a perceptual phenomenon characterized by individuals' inability to perceive and acknowledge irrelevant information (Janiszewski et al., 2013).

The philosopher Plato proposed the idea that the understanding of objects is achieved through the abilities of the senses but is ultimately influenced by the intellect. In a similar vein, Immanuel Kant also argued that perception is a crucial aspect of rational thought and cognitive processes, and dedicating excessive focus solely to studying the senses, would be an inefficient use of resources (Coren et al., 2003). According to Ferguson and Bargh (2004), individuals participate in a cognitive process referred to as "going beyond the information given" when making inferences and deriving additional information from a perceived stimulus, even if it is not explicitly provided. During the perceptual process, behavioral representations possess the capacity to be spontaneously triggered within memory. Once these representations are activated, they can subsequently exert influence and guide tangible behavior. Dijksterhuis and Bargh (2001) asserted that perception serves as a means for facilitating action. Nevertheless, perception inevitably elicits behavioral responses in certain animal species, whereas it does not have the same effect in others, such as human. Furthermore, the response can be reflected either covertly (attitudes, motivations, and feelings) or overtly (behaviour) (Hellriegel and Slocum, 2004) as a result of the perception process. There is no doubt that perception is the essential function of the domain of human psychology in comprehending and examining social behavior. Hence, justifying its incorporation as an intervening variable. Nevertheless, the understanding derived from a particular stimulus is not just determined by the existence of other stimuli but is also shaped by additional factors such as motivation and the influence of past experiences (Berlyne, 1951) and, further, cultural influences, which can moderate the link between perception and behavioral intention (Bond and Forgas, 1984).

The implementation of any significant transformation necessitates a corresponding shift in the attitudes and behaviors of individuals or the community. However, modifying behavior poses a formidable challenge due to the inherent cultural influence and inflexibility typically associated with behaviors. Social marketing aims to broaden individuals' perspectives and delve into the underlying psychological factors that directly influence their attitudes and value systems (Singaiah and Laskar, 2015). To effectively encourage individuals to embrace a change in behavior, it is imperative for social marketers to gain a comprehensive understanding of their customers' lifestyles and cognitive perspectives. In this context, it is imperative to possess comprehensive knowledge pertaining to the target population. This includes understanding their specific challenges, sources of motivation, obstacles encountered, influential figures, past experiences, social and cultural norms, as well as relevant demographic information (Singaiah and Laskar, 2015).

Environmentally responsible behavior pertains to the actions carried out by individuals with the explicit aim of promoting environmental well-being (Florence et al., 2022), which encompasses reducing resource and energy usage, employing non-toxic chemicals, and minimizing trash generation (Alsaad et al., 2023). Following this aforementioned logic, the achievement of environmental sustainability requires a fundamental change in human behaviour (Akeke, 2022). Individual age, gender, knowledge and education, beliefs, politics and worldview, objectives, responsibilities, childhood experiences, perceived environmental danger perception, environmental awareness, and so on all impact (pro)environmental behavior. Furthermore, one is driven by a combination of self-interest, social motivations, and even social norms. For instance, individuals may engage in such behavior to mitigate air pollution, which can have detrimental consequences for both society and the climate (Maartensson and Loi, 2021). Individuals also consider their hope, which is a subjective perception of one's ability to generate strategies or plans that lead to desired outcomes. For example, the findings of the study conducted by Maartensson and Loi (2021) demonstrate a positive relationship between constructive hope and pro-environmental behaviour. The strength of this link was more pronounced when levels of constructive hope were high, as opposed to when they were moderate or low.

Social media can be a transformer stimulator of perception, in turn, the behaviour of consumers. A recent study conducted by Walsh and Dodds (2022) found that the use of social marketing tools such as local tourist destination websites and social media had a significant statistical impact in promoting sustainable behavior. Furthermore, social media is becoming an increasingly important source of information that influences environmental actions by influencing the creation of norms (Han and Cheng, 2020). For example, the findings of Jans' (2021) study show that viewing a pro-environmental initiative as established by regular group members themselves allows for the establishment of a pro-environmental social identity, which in turn motivates behavior. Han and Cheng's (2020) study findings indicate that norm perception influences pro-environmental behaviour, and that social media has a favorable impact on regulating the link between subjective norm perception and pro-environmental behavior. Moreover, according to the findings of Alsaad et al.'s (2023) study, people who are supportively involved with pro-environmental initiatives prefer to assign meaning to their experiences, and engagement behavior entails meaning-attribution processes as well as a set of social media behaviors.

RESEARCH METHODOLOGY

Case Study: Playing for Nature (Doğa İçin Çal)

The "Doğa İçin Çal" platform is the research context that was inspired by "Playing for Change", which is a platform recognized in the United States. The platform aims to raise awareness about the importance of nature, and it became a member of the YouTube channel in 2009. The channel's content has garnered significant attention, with a cumulative viewership of over 350 million (DoğaİçinÇal,2023). The platform currently includes a collection of thirteen videos, and the songs used in the videos are traditional folk ballads of Turkish culture.

Data Collection and Data Analysis

The literature has paid little attention to social marketing through social media and the relationship between the concept and customer perception. According to Alsaad et al. (2023), there has been a lack of substantive research conducted to capture the method by which users observe and interpret their engagement behaviors, as well as the potential impact of these interpretations on environmental behaviors. As a result, a qualitative analysis was chosen for the study design, which allows for the use of an exploratory approach and an interpretive paradigm. Different methods can be used for qualitative analysis depending on the nature of the object of study, such as content analysis, discourse analysis, document analysis, historical analysis, narrative analysis, and semiotics. This research included two qualitative approaches by combining each other, which are semiotics and content analysis. The most recent videos, numbers 11, 12, and 13, which were filmed in 2019, 2022, and 2023, with 12, 19, and 1.2 million views, respectively, of YouTube videos on the platform, were selected as research samples. Secondary data was used for the research, which provides quick access to a sample, optimizes the use of resources, and has been previously collected by other individuals or organizations (Given, 2008).

In the first stage, the semiotic methodology was used to evaluate the content of the videos. Semiotics is an academic discipline that involves the methodical study of symbols or signs, which includes the study of how meaning is both constructed and understood. In essence, a sign can be defined as an entity that has the ability to represent or symbolize another entity. Almost any object or phenomenon that can be perceived has the potential to function as a sign, as long as it is capable of indicating or directing attention to something other than itself (Given, 2008). From a semiotic standpoint, it can be seen that any marketing communication comprises three fundamental elements: an object (the primary product of attention), a sign or symbol (a sensory image), and an interpretant (the associated meaning). The discipline of semiotics facilitates comprehending the utilization of symbols by marketers to generate meaning (Solomon, 2018), and the analysis of media visuals is a significant domain within the field of visual semiotics. Semiotics plays a crucial role in qualitative research, mostly as an associated field of study (Given, 2008). For example, the study conducted by Vallverdu-Gordi and Marine-Roig (2023) following semiotics shows that an awareness campaign's use of original graphic design strategies and familiar elements to attract attention has significant potential to generate changes in the audience through the cognitive experience.

Thereafter, in the second phase, 504 audience user comments garnered the highest number of likes for the 11th, 12th, and 13th numbered videos and were assessed. The process of data evaluation was deemed to have reached saturation when no more findings were noticed, leading to the conclusion that the procedure had ended. A directed content analysis approach was followed throughout the analysis process. In this particular approach of content analysis, the analysis process involves the creation of an initial code list derived from the underlying theoretical framework. Subsequently, the analysis proceeds by including newly identified codes or sub-codes that emerge throughout the analysis phase (Hsieh and Shannon, 2005:1281). The study employed a coding procedure that began with the identification of initial

Can Social Media Be a Transformative Tool?

codes, which were derived from stimulus selection and organization factors of the perceptual process offered by Solomon (2018), as seen in Figure 1. A deductive approach was followed because a structured code list was used during the analysis process and all the obtained main themes were in harmony with the given literature. The sub-themes were organized considering the context in question.

This was then followed by further stages of open and axial coding, as outlined by Neuman (2006). In the initial round of coding, pertinent keywords were established and example sentences were identified. At the axial coding stage, two main codes (sound and moving objects) and two sub-codes (impression type of song and number of songs) were obtained from the first stage, and two main codes (other social issues and environmental awareness) from the second phase were combined. Furthermore, the names of some of the subcodes were changed. In the first phase 323, and the second phase 535 coding, consequently a total of 838 codings were executed via the Maxqda 18.1.1. program. MaxQda is well recognized as a prominent software tool for qualitative data analysis, offering valuable support in the creation of a hierarchical code system and the building of a conceptual model for the phenomenon under investigation. At the end of the axial coding process; the final coding table has two main themes and six sub-themes for the first phase, which was named perceived object, and four primary codes and eleven sub-codes for the second phase, which was named interpretation of perceiver. The study's validity was attempted to be assured by raising its credibility. In this context, the code list was developed based on topics in the relevant literature, the derived codes were supported by examples of sentences containing direct citations and pictures taken from the videos, and transparency was attempted by detailing the research approach (Streubert and Carpenter, 2011).

The final themes and the analysis procedure are presented in Table 1 and Figure 2, respectively.

FINDINGS

The main and sub-codes obtained from the first and second phases of the research are explained in detail following part of the study, respectively.

Perceived Object

The videos, *perceived object*, are categorized into two primary dimensions: background, and sound and motion.

Can Social Media Be a Transformative Tool?

Table 1. The final research themes

Perceived Object (The First Phase)	Interpretation of Perceiver (The Second Phase)
1. Background	**1. Interest**
a. Venue	a. Musical performance
b. View	b. Celebrities
c. Other Object	**2. Culture and Value**
2. Sound & Motion	a. Patriotism
a. Song	b. Sympathy towards Turkish Culture
b. Musical Instruments	c. Cultural Heritage
c. Musicians	d. Solidarity
	e. Ethnocentrism
	3. Attitude toward Social Issues
	a. Environmental Sustainability
	b. Natural Disasters
	c. People with disabilities
	4. Nostalgia
	a. Childhood/youth memories
	b. Homesickness towards country

Figure 2.

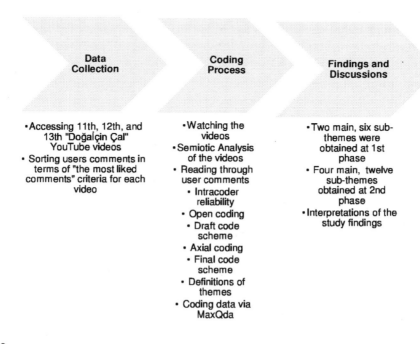

Background

Venue

Upon thorough review of the videos, it becomes evident that a diverse range of locations are utilized as venues, with a particular emphasis on cities within Türkiye. Additionally, a smaller number of the videos originate from foreign countries, including Azerbaijan and The United States of America. The videos captured between the years 2019 and 2023 featured a total of 26, 26, and 14 distinct locations.

View

The videos primarily focus on natural landscapes, specifically forests and coastal regions. The other content comprises scenes that have been recorded in residential or street environments. Conversely, the view of degraded nature, such as burned forests and dried or fallen trees, is infrequently observed.

Other object

All videos, however, just in a few scenes, feature cute cats wandering around beside other figures.

Sound and Motion

Song

Traditional famous folk ballads of Turkish culture were used in the videos. "Çarşamba'yı Sel Aldı" for the 11th, "Deniz Üstü Köpürür" and "Kağızman" for the 12th, "Hastane Önünde İncir Ağacı" for the 13th were used. Except for the 12th video, the others have just one song, which gives deep sadness. In the 12th video, while the first song was again blues-style, the video finished with an up-tempo and cheerful song.

Musical Instruments

The videos incorporate a diverse range of musical instruments as triggers for communication. There is a limited prevalence of Western instruments, such as the guitar and piano, compared to the extensive utilization of local musical instruments, including the tambourine, zurna, mute pipe, kemençe, tulum, and bağlama. The videos that were analyzed revealed the presence of 11, 14, and 6 distinct musical instruments, respectively.

Musicians

The musicians typically comprise individuals who are relatively unknown in the music field or are amateur practitioners. A limited presence of notable individuals from diverse domains or popular vocalists was also observed across all the videos. The eleventh video featured a deaf-mute artist, while the thirteenth video showcased the artistic contributions of a visually handicapped child.

Interpretation of Perceiver

Upon analysis of the audience comments that received the highest number of likes, it was observed that five distinct main themes emerged. The subsequent explanation of these themes is presented herein, arranged in accordance with their respective frequencies of appearance within the comments.

Interest

Musical Performance

The platform has been in service for more than 15 years and has garnered a dedicated following of enthusiastic members. They eagerly await the release of the videos, especially as a music product. Most probably because of the interest of the viewers in videos, user comments frequently pertain to the domain of music performance. The users commend the exceptional quality of the music and the attractiveness of the artists' vocal performances, frequently conveying their appreciation with heartfelt expressions of thanks.

"The whole series is great...I have listened to all the videos many times, I am impatiently waiting for new videos" (User comment, 13th video).

"I express my gratitude to each and every one of you directly. You possess exceptional qualities. Numerous unfavorable occurrences transpire in life, rendering me uncertain of the appropriate response to an exquisite musical event orchestrated by individuals of exceptional beauty" (User comment, 12th video)

Celebrities

Occasionally, well-known individuals also appeared as vocalists and received praise from users. Viewers expressed their delight and surprise in the comments when celebrities participated in music performances outside of their primary professional fields. Shiffman and Kanuk (2005) state that unexpected occurrences have the potential to heighten one's level of attentiveness.

"Levent Yuksel consistently demonstrated his distinctiveness" (User comment, 11th video)

"I didn't know Demet Evgar's voice was so beautiful, it was a great surprise and I loved it" (User comment, 12th video)

Culture and Value

Patriotism

The sentiment of patriotism was constantly underscored in the comments.

"...I would be a victim to my country...the people are beautiful, the music is beautiful, the nature is beautiful my dear homeland" (User comment, 13th video)

Sympathy Towards Turkish Culture

In the videos, viewer comments expressing sympathy or admiration for Turkish culture from different nations, especially Turkic Republics, are observed. Especially in the 12th video, an artist from Azerbaijan is featured, and probably the frequency of such comments is higher in this video due to this reason.

"Even though I am not a Turk, even though it has been more than 20 years since I graduated from university, I am a fan and lover of Turkish culture. My eyes get wet when I listen to Turkish folk music" (User comment, 12th video)

Cultural Heritage

The videos incorporate timeless and widely beloved folk songs, which have been shared in comments as a valued cultural heritage intended for generations to pass on.

"It is a great feeling to listen to those beautiful unique pieces of our culture with quality voices and various instruments in different styles" (User comment, 12th video)

Solidarity

The aspect of music that unites all people and strengthens the sense of solidarity was observed in the comments. Some comments emphasized this wish in a universal dimension, but it was mostly expressed in a national context.

"It is hard not to be touched when I see our nation in unity like this, this is how it should be, it is so beautiful" (User comment, 11th video)

Ethnocentrism

Some comments emphasizing the superiority of the Turkish nation are observed as well.

"We possess a wide array of aesthetically pleasing musical instruments and vocal abilities that are widely regarded as being among the most precious in the world" (User comment, 13th video)

Attitude Toward Social Issues

Environmental Sustainability

During the period when the videos were shot, there were many fire and flood disasters in Turkiye. When examining the comments, there are comments mentioning these natural degradations and their consequences. In the 12th video, the image of the Antalya Manavgat forests, which burned in 2022, was the subject of comments.

"The detail of the burnt forest was very painful; a bad image, an excellent message... congratulations" (User comment, 12th video)

Natural Disasters

Many flood and earthquake disasters frequently happen in Türkiye. In February 2023, there was an extremely sad earthquake disaster that affected the Eastern and Southern regions of Turkey, where many people died. In the comments, especially in the 13th video, the influence of the disaster is apparently seen.

"Just as I got chills when I saw the scene filmed in the burnt forest in Manavgat last year, I similarly felt terrible when I saw the city of Kahramanmaraş, which was hit by the earthquake, at the beginning of the song" (User comment, 13th video)

People with Disabilities

The 11th video included a deaf-mute artist, while the 13th video showed a visually impaired child's artistic contributions. The presence of disabled artists has been widely praised. Some impaired listeners claimed that they felt empowered as a result of this.

"Your inclusion of sign language is really appreciated" (User comment, 11th video)

"My dear İpek Nisa, I love you so much and appreciate you so much that I can't tell you this. I cannot tell you how happy I am that you crowned your countless achievements with such a group. As a disabled person, I am proud to see your achievements. May your piano never stop, İpek. You are hope for us" (User comment, 13th video)

Nostalgia

Childhood/Youth Memories

According to Solomon (2018), the reception of external sensory stimuli, such as the auditory experience of a song on the radio, possesses the capacity to evoke interior sensory encounters. During the course of watching a video, it was noted that individuals had sentiments of nostalgia for past times when they engaged with auditory content, as well as memories of loved ones who had passed away evoked by folk music.

"My geography teacher would always open at the end of the lesson, I miss his lessons very much" (User comment, 12th video)

"It was my dear grandmother's favorite folk song, she always sang it to me with her beautiful voice when I was little" (User comment, 13th video)

Homesickness Toward Country

Although they are rarely mentioned in the comments, it has been stated that folk songs are a means of satisfying the longing of Turks living abroad.

"I have been living abroad for 15 years. I discovered your channel today and listened to all the songs in one breath. I don't know if you have ever thought how meaningful your efforts are especially for us living abroad, but I felt Turkey in my heart for the first time" (User comment, 13th video)

Themes related to "Interpretation of Perceiver" are shown in Figure 3, along with their frequency of mention in the comments.

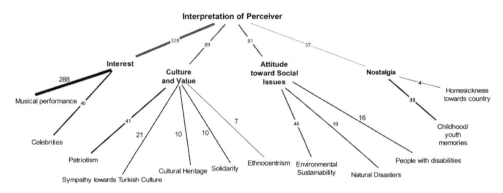

DISCUSSION, SOLUTIONS AND RECOMMENDATIONS

The process of perception starts with the reception of information through the five senses, whereas marketing communication serves to conclude this process by capturing the individual's attention and then interpreting it. According to Berlyne (1951), attention and perceptual selection play crucial roles in this process. Consequently, marketing operations are deemed unsuccessful if they do not effectively capture the attention of the target group (Solomon, 2018). The videos generously use the features mentioned in the literature in the context of stimulus selection factors, as shown by the findings of the study (Solomon, 2018; Schiffman and Kanuk, 2005; Hellriegel and Slocum, 2005) are used generously in the videos. The inclusion of various cities, artists, and instruments in the videos increases and maintains the viewer's attention by making the viewer curious about the next one, the intensity towards nature is increased by using primarily nature backgrounds in scenes, even by adding cat images to some pictures, and the contrast effect is created by using destroyed nature figures such as burnt forests in some scenes. The videos feature familiar faces, but some of them contribute by singing even though they are not in their field, blending familiarity and unexpectedness. Furthermore, patriotism

Can Social Media Be a Transformative Tool?

and solidarity feelings are apparent in the comments. A connection to the past is established, and social belonging is reinforced through the use of old and popular local folk songs. Thus, the videos effectively captured the attention of the intended viewers and influenced social dynamics by promoting a sense of cohesion.

Nevertheless, when we consider comments (interpretation of perceiver), it is seen that the audience directs their attention primarily toward the aspects associated with musical performance, relegating the matter of environmental consciousness to a secondary position. Shiffman and Kanuk (2005) underline that individuals often exhibit a proclivity to structure their cognitive processes by categorizing their perceptions into distinct figures and ground relationships. The figure under consideration should possess clear and unambiguous characteristics, exhibit a three-dimensional nature, and have a prominent position within the given context. The absence of clear delineation between figure and ground in marketing campaigns has the potential to generate confusion among consumers. Herein, we see the same problem. Musical performance became a figüre, and environmental awareness focusing on elements of natural degradation (such as forest fire) was perceived as ground. 62% of viewer comments are about music performance, while only 15% are about environmental awareness. Awareness of nature has remained in the background due to the prominence of other elements. The positioning of the artifact (promotion) does not fully correspond to the purpose of the platform.

In light of the problematic aspects observed in the videos, the present study draws upon relevant theoretical literature to propose a set of recommendations, which are outlined in Table 2.

LIMITATIONS AND FUTURE RESEARCH DIRECTIONS

The primary limitations of this study pertain to the utilization of qualitative methodologies and the inadequate size of the research sample. Furthermore, classifying this particular investigation as a case study limits the ability to make reliable judgments. The research has the potential for further expansion through the inclusion of diverse instances, greater sample sizes, and the incorporation of quantitative methodologies, which would yield more comprehensive and widely applicable findings. Furthermore, the study's limitation includes a lack of national diversity among the participants. It is worth mentioning that the majority of the comments involved in the study were of Turkish people origin. Consequently, the examination of various cultural perspectives on the subject matter can be fruitful. Periodical developments and modifications can be tracked and monitored over time. Further research can be undertaken to explore further areas within the realm of social marketing, such as raising awareness for disadvantaged people such as children, youth, the elderly, individuals with disabilities, immigrants, minority populations, former prisoners, women, single-parent families, and anyone experiencing poverty.

Table 2. Recommendations for social marketing on environmental awareness

	Recommendations
Perceived Objects	
Communication Message	• Make social awareness messages explicit and the most noticeable part of the promotion. The object and background should be obvious.
Background	• Nature disruptions including drought, fire, mucilage, and pollution might be highlighted.
Sound	• Folk songs that integrate the people can be rearranged by adapting social messages to the lyrics.
Color	• Backgrounds that evoke sadness and enthusiasm can be used appropriately. The wounding of the contrast of emotion will increase the perception.
Motion	• The sections on nature degradation can be supplemented with moving images taken from past events.
Celebrity	• Celebrities who are prominent in social aid activities can take part in the videos, even if they do not sing. Frequent appearances of surprise celebrities will increase attention.
Contrast	• Positive and negative images, such as beautiful nature and degraded nature images can be shared one after the other.
Grouping	• The cognitive process of perceiving stimuli as coherent sets of information enhances memory encoding and recall. The strategy of grouping to convey specific intended connotations in relation to their products can be employed.
Intensity	• More frequent videos or a concentration of videos raising environmental awareness on other platforms would increase reinforcement.
Perceiver	
Segmentation	• In order for the message to reach the target audience more efficiently and effectively; segmentation criteria can be determined; for example, based on different degrees of awareness, different values, different ages, and different motivations.
Monitoring	• The results of the campaign should be continuously monitored and updated according to the needs.
Encouraging	• Awareness can be raised by inviting people to activist movements on social media. There may be incentives for people to produce their own content. Slogan competitions can be organized.
Education	• Individuals can be educated on environmental sustainability.
Stakeholders	
	• Municipalities, associations, and provincial administrations can raise awareness through preventive and corrective measures as well as encouragement.

CONCLUSION

The foundational efficacy of social marketing, designed to enhance the well-being of individuals and society, relies on promotional initiatives that effectively engage and mobilize large numbers of people (Peattie and Peattie, 2009). Given that one in every two users is a user, social media is one of the most effective ways to reach communities nowadays (Kemp, 2021). One of these channels, YouTube, is great for social marketing efforts because it stimulates the perception system not just through images but also through sound, both of which are important for remembering and giving meaning to information (Winkler and Cowan, 2005). Thus, YouTube videos can be an extremely effective transformative tool for building a better society. However, it is critical that the social promotion in this media first reach the target population and attract attention. This strategy should aim to reposition their attitudes in a more positive light, which will have a significant impact on their desire to engage in action (Chin and Mansori, 2018). The effectiveness of these efforts in reaching the desired goal is dependent on the careful selection and strategic arrangement of communication stimuli. Some studies have shown that environmental behavior campaigns conducted through social media positively affect consumer behavior (Walsh and Dodds, 2022; Alam et al., 2023; Ummar et al., 2023). The findings of this study are consistent with the findings of previous studies in the context of raising environmental awareness. "Doğa İçin Çal" videos have made extensive use of the creativity and attractiveness features that social media users want (Alam et al., 2023). Previous studies show that users connect with the platform by watching numbers, comments, and likes, which is likely to lead to environmentally beneficial behavior (Alsaad et al., 2023). Furthermore, the videos are also very successful in developing the unifying aspects of the social movement through folk music. Nevertheless, due to the weight of the object and the background aspects, there are open areas for need development in terms of the platform directing attention to music performance rather than environmental awareness and therefore efficiently attaining the desired purpose in perception management. According to Sutinen and Närvänen (2022), while social marketing appears straightforward on paper, the path to this answer is difficult because of a number of issues. In future studies, producing social media content that takes into account the factors presented in the suggestions part of this study and continuing to develop social media platforms by taking into account the feedback provided by users will allow the desired success to be maintained, as well as the best for consumers, communities, and, moreover, nature.

REFERENCES

Akeke, O. (2022). Effect of social marketing on sustainable behaviour towards household waste disposal in Lagos State, Nigeria. *Modern Management Review*, *27*(2), 7–14. doi:10.7862/rz.2022.mmr.07

Alam, M. M., Lutfi, A., & Alsaad, A. (2023). Antecedents and consequences of customers' engagement with pro-environmental consumption-related content on social media. *Sustainability (Basel)*, *15*(5), 3974. doi:10.3390/su15053974

Amelia, R., & Hidayatullah, S. (2020). The effect of instagram engagement to purchase intention and consumers' luxury value perception as the mediator in the skylounge restaurant. *International Journal of Innovative Science and Research Technology*, *5*(4), 958–966.

Andreasen, A. R. (2014). Social marketing. The handbook of persuasion and social marketing. In D. W. Stewart (Ed.), *The Handbook of Persuasion and Social Marketing* (pp. 13–26). Praeger.

Anker, T. B., Gordon, R., & Zainuddin, N. (2022). Consumer-dominant social marketing: A definition and explication. *European Journal of Marketing*, *56*(1), 159–183. doi:10.1108/EJM-08-2020-0618

Berlyne, D. E. (1951). Attention, perception and behavior theory. *Psychological Review*, *58*(2), 137–146. doi:10.1037/h0058364 PMID:14834296

Bond, M. H., & Forgas, J. P. (1984). Linking person perception to behavior intention across cultures: The role of cultural collectivism. *Journal of Cross-Cultural Psychology*, *15*(3), 337–352. doi:10.1177/0022002184015003006

Cheng, H., Kotler, P., & Lee, N. R. (2011). *Social marketing for public health. The Handbook of Persuasion and Social Marketing*. Jones and Bartlett Publishers.

Cheung, M. L., Pires, G. D., Rosenberger, P. J. III, Leung, W. K., & Ting, H. (2021). Investigating the role of social media marketing on value co-creation and engagement: An empirical study in China and Hong Kong. *Australasian Marketing Journal*, *29*(2), 118–131. doi:10.1016/j.ausmj.2020.03.006

Chin, J. H., & Mansori, S. (2018). Social marketing and public health: A literature review. *Journal of Marketing Management and Consumer Behavior*, *2*(2), 48–66.

Coren, S., Porac, C., & Ward, L. (2003). Sensation and perception. In D. K. Freedheim & I. B. Weiner (Eds.), Handbook of psychology: Vol. 1. *history of psychology* (pp. 85–108). John Wiley & Sons, Inc.

Dijksterhuis, A., & Bargh, J. A. (2001). The perception-behavior expressway: Automatic effects of social perception on social behavior. *Advances in Experimental Social Psychology*, *33*, 1–40. doi:10.1016/S0065-2601(01)80003-4

Doğa İçin Çal. (2023). *Doğa İçin Çal*. https://www.youtube.com/@dogaicincal/about

Ferguson, M. J., & Bargh, J. A. (2004). How social perception can automatically influence behavior. *Trends in Cognitive Sciences*, *8*(1), 33–39. doi:10.1016/j.tics.2003.11.004 PMID:14697401

Florence, E. S., Fleischman, D., Mulcahy, R., & Wynder, M. (2022). Message framing effects on sustainable consumer behaviour: A systematic review and future research directions for social marketing. *Journal of Social Marketing*, *12*(4), 623–652. doi:10.1108/JSOCM-09-2021-0221

French, J., & Russell-Bennett, R. (2015). A hierarchical model of social marketing. *Journal of Social Marketing*, *5*(2), 139–159. doi:10.1108/JSOCM-06-2014-0042

Given, L. M. (2008). *The Sage Encyclopedia of Qualitative Research Methods*. Sage Publications, Inc. doi:10.4135/9781412963909

Grier, S., & Bryant, C. A. (2005). Social marketing in public health. *Annual Review of Public Health*, *26*(1), 319–339. doi:10.1146/annurev.publhealth.26.021304.144610 PMID:15760292

Han, R., & Cheng, Y. (2020). The influence of norm perception on pro-environmental behavior: A comparison between the moderating roles of traditional media and social media. *International Journal of Environmental Research and Public Health*, *17*(19), 7164. doi:10.3390/ijerph17197164 PMID:33007908

Hellriegel, D., & Slocum, J. W. Jr. (2005). *Organizational Behavior*. Thomson Learning.

Heydari, E., Solhi, M., & Farzadkia, M. (2021). Determinants of sustainability in recycling of municipal solid waste: Application of community-based social marketing (CBSM). *Challenges in Sustainability*, *9*(1), 16–27. doi:10.12924/cis2021.09010016

Hsieh, H.-F., & Shannon, S. E. (2005). Three approaches to qualitative content analysis. *Qualitative Health Research*, *15*(9), 1277–1288. doi:10.1177/1049732305276687 PMID:16204405

İnci, B., Sancar, O., & Bostancı, S. H. (2017). Usage of health-themed public service announcements as a social marketing communication tool: A content analysis related to public service announcements in the Republic of Turkey, Ministry of Health's web site. *Marketing and Branding Research*, *4*, 148–168. doi:10.33844/mbr.2017.60370 iSMA. (2023). *What is Social Marketing?* https://isocialmarketing.org/

Issock, P. B. I., Mpinganjira, M., & Roberts-Lombard, M. (2021). Investigating the relevance of the traditional marketing mix across different stages of change: Empirical evidence from household recycling. *Journal of Social Marketing, 11*(4), 489–506. doi:10.1108/JSOCM-11-2020-0221

Janiszewski, C., Kuo, A., & Tavassoli, N. T. (2013). The influence of selective attention and inattention to products on subsequent choice. *The Journal of Consumer Research, 39*(6), 1258–1274. doi:10.1086/668234

Jans, L. (2021). Changing environmental behaviour from the bottom up: The formation of pro-environmental social identities. *Journal of Environmental Psychology, 73*, 101531. doi:10.1016/j.jenvp.2020.101531

Kemp, S. (2021). *Digital 2021: The Latest Insights into The State of Digital.* https://wearesocial.com/uk/blog/2021/01/digital-2021-the-latest-insights-into-the-state-of-digital/

Ko, H., Cho, C.-H., & Roberts, M. S. (2005). Internet uses and gratifications: A structural equation model of interactive advertising. *Journal of Advertising, 34*(2), 57–70. doi:10.1080/00913367.2005.10639191

Kotler, P., Roberto, N., & Lee, N. (2002). *Social Marketing: Improving the Quality of Life* (2nd ed.). Sage.

Kotler, P., & Zaltman, G. (1971). Social marketing: An approach to planned social change. *Journal of Marketing, 35*(3), 3–12. doi:10.1177/002224297103500302 PMID:12276120

Li, F., Larimo, J., & Leonidou, L. C. (2021). Social media marketing strategy: Definition, conceptualization, taxonomy, validation, and future agenda. *Journal of the Academy of Marketing Science, 49*(1), 51–70. doi:10.1007/s11747-020-00733-3

Maartensson, H., & Loi, N. M. (2022). Exploring the relationships between risk perception, behavioural willingness, and constructive hope in pro-environmental behaviour. *Environmental Education Research, 28*(4), 600–613. doi:10.1080/135 04622.2021.2015295

McKenzie-Mohr, D. (2000). Fostering sustainable behavior through community-based social marketing. *The American Psychologist, 55*(5), 531–537. doi:10.1037/0003-066X.55.5.531 PMID:10842434

Menegaki, A. N. (2012). A social marketing mix for renewable energy in Europe based on consumer stated preference surveys. *Renewable Energy*, *39*(1), 30–39. doi:10.1016/j.renene.2011.08.042

Metin, E., Eröztürk, A., & Neyim, C. (2003). Solid waste management practices and review of recovery and recycling operations in Turkey. *Waste Management (New York, N.Y.)*, *23*(5), 425–432. doi:10.1016/S0956-053X(03)00070-9 PMID:12893015

Neuman, W. L. (2006). *Social Research Methods: Qualitative and Quantitative Approaches* (6th ed.). Allyn and Bacon.

Özbakır Umut, M., & Nurtanış Velioğlu, M. A recycling story: Developing recycling behavior in Turkey with social marketing program. *Journal of Public Affairs*, e2900.

Peattie, K., & Peattie, S. (2009). Social marketing: A pathway to consumption reduction? *Journal of Business Research*, *62*(2), 260–268. doi:10.1016/j.jbusres.2008.01.033

Saunders, S. G., Barrington, D. J., & Sridharan, S. (2015). Redefining social marketing: Beyond behavioural change. *Journal of Social Marketing*, *5*(2), 160–168. doi:10.1108/JSOCM-03-2014-0021

Schiffman, L. G., & Kanuk, L. L. (2004). *Consumer Behavior*. Pearson Education Limited.

Seo, E.-J., & Park, J.-W. (2018). A study on the effects of social media marketing activities on brand equity and customer response in the airline industry. *Journal of Air Transport Management*, *66*, 36–41. doi:10.1016/j.jairtraman.2017.09.014

Singaiah, G., & Laskar, S. R. (2015). Understanding of social marketing: A conceptual perspective. *Global Business Review*, *16*(2), 213–235. doi:10.1177/0972150914564282

Solomon, M., Bamossy, G., Askegaard, S., & Hogg, M. K. (2006). *Consumer Behavior: A European Perspective* (3rd ed.). Pearson Education Limited.

Solomon, M. R. (2018). *Consumer Behavior: Buying, Having, and Being* (12th ed.). Pearson Education Limited.

Spence, C. (2018). Background colour & its impact on food perception & behaviour. *Food Quality and Preference*, *68*, 156–166. doi:10.1016/j.foodqual.2018.02.012

Statista. (2023). *Most popular social networks worldwide as of October 2023, ranked by number of monthly active users*. https://www.statista.com/statistics/272014/global-social-networks-ranked-by-number-of-users/

Streubert, H. J., & Carpenter, D. R. (2011). *Qualitative research in nursing* (5th ed.). Lippincott Williams ve Wilkins.

Sutinen, U.-M., & Närvänen, E. (2022). Constructing the food waste issue on social media: A discursive social marketing approach. *Journal of Marketing Management, 38*(3-4), 219–247. doi:10.1080/0267257X.2021.1966077

Ummar, R., Shaheen, K., Bashir, I., Ul Haq, J., & Bonn, M. A. (2023). Green Social Media Campaigns: Influencing Consumers' Attitudes and Behaviors. *Sustainability (Basel), 15*(17), 12932. doi:10.3390/su151712932

Vallverdu-Gordi, M., & Marine-Roig, E. (2023). The Role of Graphic Design Semiotics in Environmental Awareness Campaigns. *International Journal of Environmental Research and Public Health, 20*(5), 4299. doi:10.3390/ijerph20054299 PMID:36901306

Velichety, S., & Shrivastava, U. (2022). Quantifying the impacts of online fake news on the equity value of social media platforms–Evidence from Twitter. *International Journal of Information Management, 64*, 102474. doi:10.1016/j.ijinfomgt.2022.102474

Walsh, P. R., & Dodds, R. (2022). The impact of intermediaries and social marketing on promoting sustainable behaviour in leisure travellers. *Journal of Cleaner Production, 338*, 130537. doi:10.1016/j.jclepro.2022.130537

Winkler, I., & Cowan, N. (2005). From sensory to long-term memory: Evidence from auditory memory reactivation studies. *Experimental Psychology, 52*(1), 3–20. doi:10.1027/1618-3169.52.1.3 PMID:15779526

ADDITIONAL READING:

Alam, M. M., Lutfi, A., & Alsaad, A. (2023). Antecedents and consequences of customers' engagement with pro-environmental consumption-related content on social media. *Sustainability (Basel), 15*(5), 3974. doi:10.3390/su15053974

Alsaad, A., Alam, M. M., & Lutfi, A. (2023). A sensemaking perspective on the association between social media engagement and pro-environment behavioural intention. *Technology in Society, 72*, 102201. doi:10.1016/j.techsoc.2023.102201

Andreasen, A. R. (2014). Social marketing. The handbook of persuasion and social marketing. In D. W. Stewart (Ed.), *The Handbook of Persuasion and Social Marketing* (pp. 13–26). Praeger.

Berlyne, D. E. (1951). Attention, perception and behavior theory. *Psychological Review, 58*(2), 137–146. doi:10.1037/h0058364 PMID:14834296

Hellriegel, D., & Slocum, J. W. Jr. (2005). *Organizational Behavior.* Thomson Learning.

Kotler, P., Roberto, N., & Lee, N. (2002). *Social Marketing: Improving the Quality of Life* (2nd ed.). Sage.

Peattie, K., & Peattie, S. (2009). Social marketing: A pathway to consumption reduction? *Journal of Business Research, 62*(2), 260–268. doi:10.1016/j.jbusres.2008.01.033

Schiffman, L. G., & Kanuk, L. L. (2004). *Consumer Behavior.* Pearson Education Limited.

Solomon, M. R. (2018). *Consumer Behavior: Buying, Having, and Being* (12th ed.). Pearson Education Limited.

Winkler, I., & Cowan, N. (2005). From sensory to long-term memory: Evidence from auditory memory reactivation studies. *Experimental Psychology, 52*(1), 3–20. doi:10.1027/1618-3169.52.1.3 PMID:15779526

KEY TERMS AND DEFINITIONS

Attention: Attention refers to the focused allocation of consciousness towards a certain phenomenon while disregarding other stimuli.

Environmental Behaviour: Environmental behaviour refers to individual behaviors conducted with the intentional goal of enhancing environmental well-being, such as reducing resource and energy consumption, waste reduction-management, forest degradation, wildlife protection, and water resource protection.

Ethnocentric: The concept of ethnocentrism refers to a belief held by individuals that their own culture is inherently superior to other cultures.

Patriotism: It is defined as love, dedication, and connection to one's nation. This connection might be a mix of sentiments for things like one's native tongue and its ethnic, cultural, political, or historical components.

Perception: Perception is a cognitive process in which individuals actively participate by engaging in the actions of selecting, organizing, and interpreting sensory stimuli.

Semiotics: Semiotics is the scholarly discipline concerned with the analysis and interpretation of signs and symbols, as well as their utilization in various contexts.

Sensory Stimuli: A sensory stimulus is any occurrence or something that triggers a reaction from a person's senses. The stimulus can take numerous forms, including light, heat, sound, and touch, as well as internal elements.

Social Marketing: Social marketing is a discipline that uses tactics to influence human behavior and address difficult societal concerns such as environmental conservation, injury prevention, and health promotion, with the goal of providing considerable benefits for individuals and communities.

Social Media: Social media is the use of digital channels, such as customer blogs, online forums, and media-sharing platforms, to develop and cultivate connections and disseminate information between businesses and customers.

Chapter 9
How Would You Like Your (Sustainability) Influencer?
A Cross-Cultural Discrete Choice Experiment on Preferred Influencer Characteristics

Moritz M. Botts

(iD) https://orcid.org/0000-0003-2514-5065
Turkish-German University, Turkey

Ömer Hurmacı

(iD) https://orcid.org/0000-0003-4213-0332
Turkish-German University, Turkey

ABSTRACT

Despite influencer marketing being among the most popular digital marketing tools in practice, there are still many research gaps, especially when it comes to specific influencer types. Though technology is converging worldwide, the perception of social influencers may differ between cultures. In this study, a model of influencer characteristics is applied to cases of sustainable and regular products. The optimal influencer for German and Turkish consumers is investigated via a discrete choice experiment (DCE). Findings suggest that female influencers are preferred over male influencers, and trustworthiness is especially required for promoting sustainable products, regardless of the respondent's involvement for sustainability. For German consumers, attractiveness plays a larger role than for Turkish consumers, who prefer high levels of trustworthiness and expertise. The applicability of this methodology for larger studies with multi-country samples is discussed.

DOI: 10.4018/979-8-3693-1594-1.ch009

Copyright © 2024, IGI Global. Copying or distributing in print or electronic forms without written permission of IGI Global is prohibited.

INTRODUCTION

This chapter takes a closer look on the preferred characteristics of social media influencers, especially focusing on the topic of sustainability. It identifies several important social media influencer characteristics and tests them in an online experimental setting. By collecting data from Turkish and German subjects, this study achieves an understanding of how cultural differences play a role in the preference of these characteristics. Results of this work are not only important for marketing managers and researchers but also for government executives who want to take advantage of sustainability influencers in their socially responsible and green campaigns.

With the wide proliferation of digital and mobile media that employ the internet, social influencers have become a widespread form of opinion leaders employed by companies to communicate new products and ideas (Hudders, De Jans, & De Veirman, 2021; Hudders & Lou, 2022). Whereas the concept of opinion leaders is not new (Vrontis, Makrides, Christofi, & Thrassou, 2021), during the last decade, user-based online marketing has become ubiquitous with the popularity of various forms of word-of-mouth communication via commenting or recommendation functions, online reviews (Christodoulides, Michaelidou, & Argyriou, 2012), and videos on platforms such as Instagram or YouTube. In this context, social influencers are defined as "individuals who create valuable content, have strong reputations in specific fields (…) and are followed by a large number of users on online social networks" (von Mettenheim & Wiedmann, 2021a, p. 366). Besides the academic literature, websites and practitioner-oriented books have not been shy with advice on how to best employ social (for a quasi-academic example, see for example Jahnke, 2018).

While there has been substantive research on the utility of influencer marketing, research gaps still exist (Abhishek & Srivastava, 2021; Vrontis et al., 2021; Ye, Hudders, De Jans, & De Veirman, 2021). Especially, effects of different media platforms and different types of influencers remain underresearched (Taylor, 2020). Types of influencers can include the celebrity status of the influencers or their topical focus (Jacobson & Harrison, 2022; Vrontis et al., 2021), such as fashion influencers or 'finfluencers', who are influencers perceived to be experts for financial products.

One type of influencer that has recently received more attention in the media and in research are influencers on social or sustainability issues (von Mettenheim & Wiedmann, 2021a), also known as Sinnfluencer in German (Baake et al., 2022), which can roughly be translated as "sense-fluencer", since their specific topic is seen as less commercial and rather idealist. This focus is also in line with a call for more research on sustainability influencers in the current literature (Hudders et al., 2021; Ye et al., 2021).

How Would You Like Your (Sustainability) Influencer?

Furthermore, there has been a lack of research on influencers in emerging and developing markets (Vrontis et al., 2021), especially with regards to sustainability topics (Chu, Chen, & Gan, 2020). This study therefore compares consumers in a developed country with a prominent public and academic discourse of sustainability issues, Germany (Schank & Lorch, 2019), and a transition economy, in which sustainability and corporate social responsibility are less prominent topics, Turkey (Cozannet, Rieper, & Gurgoz, 2007).

In the following study, a discrete choice experiment (DCE) was conducted regarding the selection of social influencers advertising a new t-shirt. While DCE and the related conjoint analyses are prominent in marketing research (Green & Srinivasan, 1978), they are usually employed concerning products or services. To our best knowledge, this is the first study in which DCE were used to evaluate the motives for the selection of an optimal social influencer.

Therefore, this chapter proceeds as follows. In the literature review, the concepts of influencer characteristics, sustainability influencers, and possible cultural differences of social influencers are derived from the literature. Hypotheses based on previous findings are outlined at the end of each subchapter. An extensive methodology follows, in which the initial manipulation (Experiment 1) and the discrete choice experiment (Experiment 2) are explained in detail. The findings section includes a statistical analysis of the data to answer the previously posed hypotheses. These findings are discussed in the following section. In the conclusion, limitations of this study are outlined and recommendations for future research are given.

BACKGROUND

Influencer Characteristics

Social influencers have been studied with a wide range of theories taken from psychology in general, and in marketing, from consumer behavior research in particular (Abhishek & Srivastava, 2021; Vrontis et al., 2021). This includes concepts such as social comparison theory, source credibility theory, the persuasion knowledge model, and attribution theory (Vrontis et al., 2021).

Among the most frequently employed concepts in influencer marketing research is source credibility theory (Jacobson & Harrison, 2022; Özbölük & Akdogan, 2022; Vrontis et al., 2021). According to this theory, the source of a message is regarded concerning their trustworthiness, expertise, and attractiveness (von Mettenheim & Wiedmann, 2021a; Wiedmann & von Mettenheim, 2021; Zhou, Barnes, McCormick, & Blazquez Cano, 2021). Trustworthiness refers to the reliability, honesty, and integrity of the source. Expertise considers the knowledge, experience, and professionalism of the social influencer. Finally, attractiveness covers both the personal status and the appearance of the source. (Kang, Choi, & Choi, 2019). These three characteristics are also called "sympathy attributes" by some authors (Berne-Manero & Marzo-Navarro, 2020).

While there have been some extensions of the nomological base of these source characteristics (Asan, 2022; Kang et al., 2019), to make a comparison in a discrete choice experiment possible, a simplified version of the source credibility model will be used. Based on these considerations, the following hypotheses were derived:

Hypothesis One (H1): The higher the level of a) trustworthiness, b) expertise, and c) attractiveness of a social influencer, the higher the preference for them.

Some studies have discussed these source characteristics in regards to a possible homophily between the source and target in some studies, that is whether it is desirable for an influencer to share traits with their audience (Vrontis et al., 2021; Xiao, Wang, & Chan-Olmsted, 2018). One finding is that influencers can be preferred over celebrities because they are seen as more relatable and credible (Schouten, Janssen, & Verspaget, 2020).

Hypothesis Two (H2): Social influencers who are similar to their audience are preferred over those who are not.

Sustainability Characteristics

While there is no unified definition of sustainability in marketing (Kemper & Ballantine, 2019; Lim, 2017), a general characteristic of sustainability is that it is difficult to show that a product or service is actually 'green' and not 'greenwashed' (Spelthahn, Fuchs, & Demele, 2009). Thus, in the context of information economics, the quality 'sustainability' can be described as a trust quality of a product that cannot be directly perceived or experienced by the customer (Schrader, 2008). This is also in line with research on social influencers that employs the elaboration likelihood model, in which under the condition of low involvement, the attractiveness of the influencer plays a larger role (von Mettenheim & Wiedmann, 2021a) and the expertise of the influence is less important (Wiedmann & von Mettenheim, 2021). At the same time, trustworthiness remains a meaningful characteristic under both central and peripheral routes of elaboration (Xiao et al., 2018). Therefore, for sustainable products and services, the trustworthiness of the social influencer would be their most important source characteristic. To the best of our knowledge, the level of involvement for sustainable products has not been systematically researched in the context of social influencers to this date.

Hypothesis Three (H3): Individuals cued with a sustainability topic judge the trustworthiness of an influencer as more important than individuals who were not cued.

Hypothesis Four (H4): Individuals judge the trustworthiness of an influencer as more important under higher (vs. lower) involvement in sustainability.

Cultural Differences of Social Influencers

Since the 1980s, there has been a wide consensus that cultural differences can play a significant role in management and marketing (Peterson, 2007). The literature on social influencers points to a number of possible variations in the perception and effect of social influencers across countries (Dang & Raska, 2022). This is due to the fact that even online, cultures differ on a number of elements, or 'dimensions' (Botts, 2021), such as the way messages are given and received or how easily the local language can be written on a keyboard (Straub, 1994). Relating to the function of social influencer marketing, word-of-mouth communication is especially relevant in more collectivist cultures, where peer recommendations play a larger role than in more individualist cultures (de Mooij & Hofstede, 2011). Not only are the characteristics of the social influencer crucial in such cultures (Chu et al., 2020), but homophily, or the preference of a match between influencer and target audience traits, tends to be more important in group-oriented societies than in individuum-oriented societies (Dang & Raska, 2022).

Concerning the countries investigated in this study, the topic of social influencer marketing has been well established in Germany, with a number of books on the topic (Jahnke, 2018) and a variety of empirical studies (e.g., Baake et al., 2022; von Mettenheim & Wiedmann, 2021a; von Mettenheim & Wiedmann, 2021b; Wiedmann & von Mettenheim, 2021). As a less researched location (Thomas, 1996), there have been some social influencer studies in Turkey (Acikgoz & Burnaz, 2021; Asan, 2022; Özbölük & Akdogan, 2022; Yılmaz, Sezerel, & Uzuner, 2020; Zengin Alp & Gündüz Öğüdücü, 2018). These studies have all been mono-cultural and mostly do not address particularities of their respective cultural context. In a comparative study conducted in Turkey, Poland, China, and the USA, Bartosik-Purgat (2018) found that Turkish and Polish respondents were more prone to voicing negative opinions about a product than their Chinese and US-American counterparts. Finally, it has to be kept in mind that social influencers addressing sustainability or corporate social responsibility is a new phenomenon in emerging markets (Chu et al., 2020), and might be understood differently in various cultures.

Hypothesis Five (H5): There is a difference between countries regarding the perceived importance of a) trustworthiness, b) expertise, and c) attractiveness of a social influencer.

METHODOLOGY

The joined experiments and survey questions were developed in three stages because of the different cultures of both the study subject and the authors. The native language of one of the authors is German and English, while it is Turkish for the other author. First, the experiments and survey questions were prepared in English by the authors, since it is the only common language both authors speak at a proficient level for research. Words, terms, and phrases were chosen meticulously in order not to lead to ambiguity or a loss in meaning. Second, the experiments and the survey questions were translated into German and Turkish by the authors. Lastly, the texts and items were parallel translated (Chidlow, Plakoyiannaki, & Welch, 2014; Douglas & Craig, 2007) by a trained translator who is fluent in Turkish, German, and English. Results were carefully compared by the authors to achieve a high degree of equivalency, including the concepts, functionality, translation, but also the measurements used (Usunier, 1998; Usunier, 2011).

There were two issues due to the nature of the German and Turkish languages. The first issue was the highly gendered nature of the German language, whereas English can be written in a gender-neutral way, and Turkish does not have any grammatical genders. For example, the term "influencer" can be written in a feminine or masculine form in German. It was chosen to use the full feminine and masculine forms in the German version of the questionnaire and not one of the different nonstandard gender-neutral forms. The second issue was the possibility of informal or formal forms of address in Turkish ('sen'/ 'siz') and German ('Du'/ 'Sie') compared to the general English 'you'. The research team decided on the formal form of address, because the survey was conducted with strangers and not with friends. Finally, as an example of a possible challenge to construct equivalence (van Herk, Poortinga, & Verhallen, 2005), this study used the word "sustainability" as a cue in the experiment for one group of subjects in either language. The concept of sustainability exists in all three languages that are used. However, there is a possibility that it can be understood in different ways by subjects who are from two different cultures, since the concepts of business ethics and CSR differ between countries (Palazzo, 2002). Thus, functional equivalence (van Herk, Poortinga, & Verhallen, 2005) might not be given, when for example the motives to consume sustainable products vary across cultures. Nevertheless, an effort was made to keep the variance in the understanding of the word as small as possible by including a short paragraph explaining the meaning of sustainability for the clothing sector in more detail.

Subjects of the study were informed that; a) the study aims to explore the role of influencers in the fashion sector, b) there are no right or wrong choices and c) they could leave the survey at any point.

How Would You Like Your (Sustainability) Influencer?

The experiment was conducted in two steps. Subjects in the experimental condition were cued with the words "a new sustainable t-shirt" whereas it was "a new t-shirt" for the control group. After this manipulation, they were presented with two influencers with different attributes and asked to make a choice between them. These steps are explained in detail in the following paragraphs.

In the first step of the experiment, all respondents are subjected to a short text about selecting the right social influencer for either a sustainable t-shirt in the experimental condition or a regular t-shirt in the control group. This means that the subjects were asked to select the influencer who they think would promote the t-shirt better. Subjects in the experimental condition received the following text with the cue "sustainable":

Imagine you will choose an influencer to promote a new sustainable t-shirt. This influencer will do the promotion on your preferred social media platform (please think of one platform). In the following sections, we will present a number of choices to you. You will pick one influencer from a selection of two. Please pick the influencer who you personally think would be the best choice to promote the sustainable t-shirt.

Subjects in the control condition received the following text:

Imagine you will choose an influencer to promote a new t-shirt. This influencer will do the promotion on your preferred social media platform (please think of one platform). In the following sections, we will present number of choices to you. You will pick one influencer from a selection of two. Please pick the influencer who you personally think would be the best choice to promote the t-shirt.

T-shirts were selected as products to be promoted, because they are everyday products bought by both women and men. Furthermore, the garment industry has been under scrutiny for ethical issues such as the sourcing of cotton or the working conditions of workers in the garment sector, and thus have a clear sustainability aspect (Jacobson & Harrison, 2022). In addition, previous research on social influencers often focused on fashion topics (Vrontis et al., 2021; Ye et al., 2021).

To keep cultural variance in the understanding of "sustainability" small, the text on the sustainable t-shirt included a short explanation on social and environmentally responsible production:

Sustainability means, that the t-shirt is made of organic cotton and that the people who made the t-shirt have been treated fairly.

In the second step, the discrete choice experiment was applied to subjects. Discrete choice experiments are based on random utility theory and are the more general case of conjoint analysis (Louviere, Flynn, & Carson, 2010). Subjects were asked to pick the social influencers best suited to promote a t-shirt on social media in five different choice sets. The experiment was created in the Qualtrics survey application with a Java Script that was created via a Python script programmed by Hainmueller and colleagues (Hainmueller, Hopkins, & Yamamoto, 2014) to produce randomly created social influencer profiles. With the help of this programming, two social influencer profiles with seven attributes were presented in writing for each choice set. The profiles of social influencers in the choice sets differed on the levels and order of these seven attributes. However, all social influencers were evaluated using the same seven attributes. Based on previous non-experimental studies on the attributes of successful social influencers (von Mettenheim & Wiedmann, 2021a; Wiedmann & von Mettenheim, 2021; Zhou et al., 2021), these seven attributes and their levels are as follows: the demographic attributes gender (female/male) and age (18/21/24/27), the social media metrics number of followers (5,000/10,000/15,000/20,000) and time spent watching the videos (1/3/5/7 minutes), and the influencer characteristics trustworthiness (low/average/high), expertise (low/average/high), and attractiveness (low/average/high).

Table 1 below demonstrates how the DCE is presented to respondents. Subjects see two different influencers at the same time. These influencers have the same levels for some attributes. However, they differ for some other. For example, in Table 1 they have the same level for all attributes except for age and time. This is how random utility theory understands the tradeoffs subjects make in their choices of attributes that are important for them.

Table 1. An example of a DCE as subjects see it on the screen

Attributes	Influencer 1	Influencer 2
Gender	Female	Female
Age	21	27
Attractiveness	average	average
Time	7	3
Followers	15,000	15,000
Expertise	high	high
Trustworthiness	average	average

How Would You Like Your (Sustainability) Influencer?

As the ordering of the attributes might imply their importance to the respondent, thereby introducing a priming effect to the experiment, DCE can be conducted in a way that the ordering is randomized across the different choices. This procedure makes sure that the influence of the ordering does not have systematic effect on the results. In Table 2, notice how attributes might be presented in a different order for another subject.

Table 2. A possible ordering of the seven attributes on another subject's screen

Attributes	Influencer 1	Influencer 2
Expertise	low	high
Age	18	18
Followers	10,000	10,000
Time	3	3
Attractiveness	high	high
Trustworthiness	high	average
Gender	Male	Female

Though more complex scales for source credibility exist (Wiedmann & von Mettenheim, 2021), they were not used in this study, since the number of attributes should be kept low to minimize survey fatigue. Unlike previous research, in which only high or low levels of influencer characteristics were compared, this discrete choice experiment used a three-level metric to make choices non-binary. To make the meaning of concepts such as influencer characteristics more clear, the respondents were shown a page with explanations for each attribute before the DCE. For example, expertise was defined as: "the knowledge of the influencer concerning the topics they promote".

Further questions included involvement on sustainability in general, employing an adaptation of the scale for fair trade involvement by Bezençon and Blili (2011). The items of that scale can be reviewed in Table 3.

For demographic questions, income levels (which were presented in brackets) were adapted to reflect average income levels of university students or junior employees. The experiments were distributed online to university students in Germany and Turkey in January 2023 as a pretest of this method, resulting in 31 German and 76 Turkish respondents. While students may lack external validity for the general population, they are in the right age bracket for heavy users of social media (Turner, 2015) and lead to a matched sample (van Herk et al., 2005).

Table 3. An adapted scale that is used to measure involvement on sustainability

Item Number	Adapted Item
1	I choose my clothes carefully between sustainable and non-sustainable.
2	Choosing between sustainable and non-sustainable clothes is an important decision for me.
3	The choice between sustainable and non-sustainable clothes is very important to me.

Source: Adapted from Bezençon and Blili (2011)

FINDINGS

The data was parallelly analyzed by both researchers with the statistical software IBM SPSS (Version 25) and R-Studio (Version 4.1.2) to ensure that results were computed correctly. The mean age was 21.98 for Turkish respondents and 22.65 for German respondents, with no significant differences between the two groups. Slightly over 75% of each sample was female. Whereas some countries have serious restrictions on the use of social media or in fact regionally distinct social media environments (Bartosik-Purgat, 2018), this was deemed as negligible between the two countries because of previous studies on social media use per country and the in-country experiences of the authors. For example, whereas the website formally known as Twitter was more popular in Turkey than in Germany during the time of the study (World Population Review, 2023), in fact around 95% of respondents in each sample gave Instagram as their preferred social medium, in line with the current popularity of the social media application (Lee, Sudarshan, Sussman, Bright, & Eastin, 2022; Lee, Sudarshan, Sussman, Bright, & Eastin, 2022). Income distributions were similar, with a skew towards lower income brackets, which is to be expected because the respondents were students.

Using a t-test on the means, answers on the three sustainability involvement items showed no significant differences between the two countries. An exploratory factor analysis on the items suggested a one-factorial solution in both samples explaining 82% of variance in the Turkish and 86% in the German sample respectively, with almost identical factor loadings. Hence, the role of involvement for sustainability can be interpreted as equivalent between both cultures (Usunier, 2011; van Herk et al., 2005).

The discrete choice experiment led to in 310 German and 760 Turkish cases respectively, which were analyzed with the help of a binomial logistic regression as a joined model (Model 1) and separately (Models 2 and 3). The results of these models can be reviewed in Table 4. In all models, the dependent variable is the respondents' selection of the social influencer they considered to be best suited for promoting a t-shirt.

How Would You Like Your (Sustainability) Influencer?

Table 4. Models comparing country samples

Variables	Model 1		Model 2		Model 3	
	Complete Sample		Turkish		German	
	Coeff.	*SE*	*Coeff.*	*SE*	*Coeff.*	*SE*
Intercept	2.703***	(0.386)	2.883***	(0.445)	1.871**	(0.696)
Gender M	-0.285†	(0.161)	-0.181	(0.191)	-0.669*	(0.336)
Age 1	-0.003	(0.235)	0.017	(0.279)	-0.151	(0.484)
Age 2	-0.236	(0.221)	-0.436†	(0.259)	0.364	(0.477)
Age 3	-0.062	(0.222)	-0.354	(0.268)	0.688	(0.430)
Follower 1	-1.351***	(0.251)	-1.335***	(0.275)	-0.688†	(0.401)
Follower 2	-0.773**	(0.245)	-0.806**	(0.268)	-0.199	(0.395)
Follower 3	-0.542*	(0.243)	-0.459†	(0.273)	-0.035	(0.031)
Time 1	-0.097	(0.229)	-0.035	(0.270)	-0.399	(0.487)
Time 2	0.289	(0.228)	0.135	(0.268)	0.902†	(0.471)
Time 3	0.069	(0.228)	0.058	(0.270)	0.109	(0.459)
Trust. 1	-1.661***	(0.211)	-1.972***	(0.257)	-0.946*	(0.426)
Trust. 2	-0.737***	(0.205)	-0.963***	(0.249)	-0.292	(0.403)
Exp. 1	-0.961***	(0.196)	-1.088***	(0.233)	-0.844*	(0.408)
Exp. 2	-0.415*	(0.201)	-0.405†	(0.237)	-0.355	(0.425)
Attr. 1	-1.028***	(0.199)	-0.840***	(0.232)	-1.757***	(0.432)
Attr. 2	-0.366†	(0.196)	-0.124	(0.233)	-0.896*	(0.402)
AIC	951.53		697.77		261.52	
χ^2	141.6***	df=16	123.65***	df=16	42.19***	df=15

Note: Coefficients are unstandardized. Significance levels are † $p < .10$, * $p < .05$, ** $p < .01$, *** $p < .001$

Confirming H1, all three source credibility characteristics had significant effects in the proposed direction. In the German sample, the item attractiveness played a larger role than in the Turkish sample, pointing to a possible cultural difference (H5c). A male social influencer was chosen less often than a female social influencer. In extended models with interaction effects between the gender of the influencer and the gender of the respondent, no meaningful effects could be found, hence if gender is taken as a cue for homophily, H2 cannot be confirmed.

There was a weak significant effect for the attribute Age 2 (i.e., 21 years) in the Turkish sample. A model including an interaction effect with the age of the respondent led to a meaningful effect (-0.138 at $p < 0.090$). Since the mean age of the Turkish sample is 21.98 years, this might be interpreted as a negative evaluation of social influencers being the same age as the target group. Respondents preferred

How Would You Like Your (Sustainability) Influencer?

social influencers with more followers, while time spent watching the influencer was not significant and non-linear, except for 3-minute videos which were evaluated positively in the German sample.

In Table 5, samples were separated into the experimental condition with a sustainable product (Model 4) and the control group (Model 5).

Concerning source credibility characteristics, trustworthiness was more important in the experimental condition. Therefore, H3 can be confirmed. There were no meaningful effects of age of the influencer or time spent watching the videos, while male influencers were seen negatively in the non-experimental condition. A larger number of followers was again considered favorable.

To test H4, variables derived from sustainability involvement were introduced to the models, with no meaningful results (not shown).

Table 5. Models comparing experimental conditions

Variables	Model 1		Model 4		Model 5	
	Complete Sample		sustainable cue		no cue	
	Coeff.	SE	Coeff.	SE	Coeff.	SE
Intercept	2.703***	(0.386)	2.619***	(0.567)	2.810***	(0.556)
Gender M	-0.285[†]	(0.161)	-0.201	(0.234)	-0.421[†]	(0.232)
Age 1	-0.003	(0.235)	-0.181	(0.344)	0.173	(0.332)
Age 2	-0.236	(0.221)	-0.335	(0.325)	-0.149	(0.312)
Age 3	-0.062	(0.222)	-0.197	(0.322)	0.070	(0.315)
Follower 1	-1.351***	(0.251)	-1.334***	(0.352)	-1.549***	(0.379)
Follower 2	-0.773**	(0.245)	-0.709*	(0.342)	-0.953*	(0.372)
Follower 3	-0.542*	(0.243)	-0.465	(0.346)	-0.675[†]	(0.361)
Time 1	-0.097	(0.229)	-0.272	(0.335)	0.123	(0.327)
Time 2	0.289	(0.228)	0.323	(0.335)	0.276	(0.318)
Time 3	0.069	(0.228)	0.473	(0.342)	-0.259	(0.315)
Trust. 1	-1.661***	(0.211)	-1.886***	(0.316)	-1.467***	(0.295)
Trust. 2	-0.737***	(0.205)	-0.865**	(0.301)	-0.594*	(0.288)
Exp. 1	-0.961***	(0.196)	-0.898**	(0.290)	-1.062***	(0.274)
Exp. 2	-0.415*	(0.201)	-0.343	(0.295)	-0.492[†]	(0.285)
Attr. 1	-1.028***	(0.199)	-0.796**	(0.304)	-1.207***	(0.272)
Attr. 2	-0.366[†]	(0.196)	-0.279	(0.286)	-0.460	(0.283)
AIC	951.53		471.03		503.93	
$\chi 2$	141.6***	df=16	70.35***	df=16	81.82***	df=16

Note: Coefficients are unstandardized. Significance levels are † $p < .10$, * $p < .05$, ** $p < .01$, *** $p < .001$

DISCUSSION

The study has shown that all three source credibility characteristics are important for sustainable and non-sustainable products that social influencers endorse. As expected, priming for a sustainable product has shown that trustworthiness is especially salient for goods with trust qualities.

Contrary to expectations, the evaluation of the influencer was independent of the involvement of the respondent, that is their previous interest in the topic. One possible explanation could be that being interested in a topic may actually make you more skeptical of marketing messages involving this topic, thus diminishing the involvement effect (Lee & Johnson, 2022).

Male influencers were in general chosen less often than female influencers, regardless of the gender of respondents. This might be because most sustainability influencers are female (Yıldırım, 2021) and both sustainability and fashion are feminine connoted topics (Baake et al., 2022; Jacobson & Harrison, 2022).

Age effects were inconclusive. While a weak negative effect for being the same age could be identified in the Turkish sample, it is not clear how to interpret this. Perhaps a social influencer who focuses on sustainability topics is expected to be relatively older to the audience to appear more knowledgeable on a complex topic.

The original set up of the study was to use 'time spent on watching a video' as the cost of the choice, but the time spent on a video had unclear results, with significant effect only for a 3-minute video in the German group. It is likely that this stems from too small differences in time intervals for the attribute values. The unclear results also point to the possibility that for social influencers, time can be a unsuitable indicator for costs. Watching a video of a social media influencer can be enjoyable instead of being considered as a waste of time. While opportunity costs of time are linear, the time spent watching a video can provide a non-linear utility in the form of enjoying to watch the video (Backhaus & Schneider, 2020).

Regarding the number of followers, the literature differentiates between various size categories of influencer popularity based on the number of people who follow the influencer, such as macro- and micro-influencers (Berne-Manero & Marzo-Navarro, 2020; Hudders et al., 2021; von Mettenheim & Wiedmann, 2021b; Zhou et al., 2021). Whereas macro-influencers can result in more trust because their popularity can be seen as a cue for respectability (Lee et al., 2022), those with less followers can have a higher homophily or stronger fit with the audience (Berne-Manero & Marzo-Navarro, 2020), in other words fit the needs of their audience more closely. The data points to clear preferences for many followers, which is not surprising given the task the respondents were given. They had been instructed to choose a social influencer for a company selling a product, thus they would have an incentive to pick those influencer with the largest audience.

Concerning cultural differences, no differences could be found concerning the answering pattern for sustainability involvement. Nevertheless, this does not reveal the content of what respondents associate with 'sustainability' or 'corporate social responsibility'. The concept of what is the right thing for a company to do can differ between cultures (Lin-Hi & Blumberg, 2018). Regarding the investigated cultural contexts, the Turkish notion of corporate social responsibility may differ from Western European expectations, being less legalistic and more dependent on individual motivations in a paternalistic management setting (Cozannet et al., 2007).

DCEs conducted in developing countries have used pretests to evaluate whether attributes and choices are meaningful within the cultural context (Mangham, Hanson, & McPake, 2009). In this experiment, pictures of social influencers were not used in order not to give ethnic cues, therefore preventing the issue of culturally specific beauty norms. The attractiveness of the social influencer played a larger role in the German sample. An explanation for this is that sustainability is seen with more reservation in Turkish society, being a comparatively recent and niche topic compared to discourses in Germany. Hence, the trustworthiness and expertise of the influencer should be more important for a Turkish audience, where the trust characteristic of 'sustainability' would play a stronger role than traditional advertising cues, such as the beauty of the presenter.

CONCLUSION

This study indicates that DCE is a viable method for understanding consumer preference for source credibility characteristics. There were differences in the answering patterns of respondents who were primed with a sustainable product versus those that were not. The research model could be successfully employed in two different cultures, with evidence of equivalence for a number of central concepts. A number of country differences remain, pointing to cultural differences in the understanding of sustainability.

For researchers, the findings show that the way consumers are affected by social influencers can be researched using experimental methods that can be relatively easily implemented using online questionnaires and analyzed using well-established statistical methods.[2] While the topic of social influencers is a growing field in the marketing literature (Hudders & Lou, 2022), there are still many theoretical gaps due to the rapidly development of influencer practice. This study shows that different kinds of products can require different influencer characteristics, supporting the notion of different influencer types.

For marketing managers, the idea of different influencer types shows that one person cannot be an influencer for any kind of product or service. These requirements

How Would You Like Your (Sustainability) Influencer?

towards influencers can vary between cultures, meaning that not only different languages or other cultural cues would need to be taken into account when selecting the right influencer, but also the importance of different source characteristics.

This study is not without a number of limitations, especially concerning the small student sample, which in this case was used to test the method. In future studies, larger and more representative samples from more than two countries should be used. Furthermore, respondents might not have read the priming text thoroughly. This could be amended by including a few test questions at the end of the text. Since social influencers mostly communicate via videos or pictures on social media platforms such as Instagram, visual cues instead of text cues would create a more realistic situation.[3] To increase external validity, further experiments resulting in respondents' actions could be included (Morales, Amir, & Lee, 2017), such as sharing a profile or following a link (Berne-Manero & Marzo-Navarro, 2020). Finally, the parasocial relationship between a user of social media and social influencer (Lee et al., 2022; Lee et al., 2022) was not considered for the study. It would have been more realistic to have included social influencers that were actually followed by the respondents, thus including the ongoing, though virtual relationship that a user of social media has with their role models. On the other hand, this set up would have severely limited the possibilities of a discrete choice experiment that enables the investigation of the role of different attributes.

For further studies using the discrete choice experiment method to investigate the function of source credibility characteristics, the samples should be expanded to other target groups and countries. It would be fruitful to compare more countries with public sustainability discourse to those in which the topic is less well known.

To avoid cultural imperialism in the sustainability discourse (Lin-Hi & Blumberg, 2017), a more thorough investigation of what respondents understand regarding the term 'sustainability' with the help of nomological frameworks and interviews with cultural experts could be carried out (Bhalla & Lin, 1987; van de Vijver & Tanzer, 2004). This points to the possibility of a strong institutional and cultural context of social influencers, which cannot be captured by quantitative studies alone. As suggested before, an in-depth study of each surveyed country would be necessary to make an experimental study of the kind conducted in this chapter comparable between cultures.

Furthermore, to increase external validity, experiments using picture or video cues should be conducted. While it would be possible to use artificially generated pictures to capture the random element of a discrete choice experiment, this would further complicate the study design. Since the present inquiry does not investigate the role of fake pictures, it is instead suggested to acquire a set of authentic influencer photographs or videos from different cultural contexts.

In summary, this study was a first step into experimental studies on the role of source characteristics concerning different influencer types. Since there appears to be no end to the role of social influencers in the current online environment, there is a wide space for further inquiries in this field.

ACKNOWLEDGMENT

The authors would like to thank M. Elif Botts for her support with the translation of the questionnaire.

This research received no specific grant from any funding agency in the public, commercial, or not-for-profit sectors.

REFERENCES

Abhishek, & Srivastava, M. (2021). Mapping the influence of influencer marketing: A bibliometric analysis. *Marketing Intelligence & Planning*, *39*(7), 979–1003. doi:10.1108/MIP-03-2021-0085

Acikgoz, F., & Burnaz, S. (2021). The influence of 'influencer marketing' on YouTube influencers. *International Journal of Internet Marketing and Advertising*, *15*(2), 201–219. doi:10.1504/IJIMA.2021.114331

Asan, K. (2022). Measuring the impacts of travel influencers on bicycle travellers. *Current Issues in Tourism*, *25*(6), 978–994. doi:10.1080/13683500.2021.1914004

Baake, J., Gensich, M., Kraus, T., Müller, C., Przyklenk, S., Rössler, P., Walpert, C., & Zang, A. M. (2022). Sinnfluencer*innen: Der Schlüssel zu mehr Glaubwürdigkeit in Social Media? - Ein Experiment zur Wahrnehmung von Nachhaltigkeitskommunikation auf Instagram ['Sense-fluencers': The key to more trustworthiness in social media? An experiment on the perception of sustainability communication on Instagram]. In A. S. Kümpel, C. Peter, A. Schnauber-Stockmann, & F. Mangold (Eds.), *Nachhaltigkeit als Gegenstand und Zielgröße der Rezeptions- und Wirkungsforschung - Aktuelle Studien und Befunde* [Sustainability as the object and performance indicator of reception and impact studies - Current research and findings] (Vol. 44, pp. 41–62). Nomos. doi:10.5771/9783748926436-41

Backhaus, K., & Schneider, H. (2020). *Strategisches Marketing* [Strategic Marketing] (3rd ed.). Schäffer-Poeschel. doi:10.34156/9783791046969

Bartosik-Purgat, M. (2018). International contexts of social media and e-WoM communication in the customer decision-making process. *Journal of Management and Business Administration. Central Europe*, *26*(2), 16–33.

Berne-Manero, C., & Marzo-Navarro, M. (2020). Exploring how influencer and relationship marketing serve corporate sustainability. *Sustainability (Basel)*, *12*(11), 1–19. doi:10.3390/su12114392

Bezençon, V., & Blili, S. (2011). Segmenting the market through the determinants of involvement: The case of fair trade. *Psychology and Marketing*, *28*(7), 682–708. doi:10.1002/mar.20407

Bhalla, G., & Lin, L. Y. S. (1987). Cross-cultural marketing research: A discussion of equivalence issues and measurement strategies. *Psychology and Marketing*, *4*(4), 275–285.

Botts, M. (2021). Understanding intercultural online communication via cultural tendencies. In S. Batuk Ünlü & A. Özer Torgalöz (Eds.), Remote and Hybrid Working: Variants, Determinants, Outcomes (pp. 241–262). Peter Lang. doi: 10.3726/b19135

Chidlow, A., Plakoyiannaki, E., & Welch, C. (2014). Translation in cross-language international business research: Beyond equivalence. *Journal of International Business Studies*, *45*(5), 562–582. doi:10.1057/jibs.2013.67

Christodoulides, G., Michaelidou, N., & Argyriou, E. (2012). Cross-national differences in e-WOM influence. *European Journal of Marketing*, *46*(11/12), 1689–1707. doi:10.1108/03090561211260040

Chu, S.-C., Chen, H.-T., & Gan, C. (2020). Consumers' engagement with corporate social responsibility (CSR) communication in social media: Evidence from China and the United States. *Journal of Business Research*, *110*, 260–271. doi:10.1016/j.jbusres.2020.01.036

Cozannet, N., Rieper, H., & Gurgoz, Y. (2007). *Corporate Social Responsibility in Turkey: Overview and Perspectives*. Working Paper 55, Agence Française de Développement.

Dang, A., & Raska, D. (2022). National cultures and their impact on electronic word of mouth: A systematic review. *International Marketing Review*, *39*(5), 1182–1225. doi:10.1108/IMR-12-2020-0316

de Mooij, M., & Hofstede, G. (2011). Cross-cultural consumer behavior: A review of research findings. *Journal of International Consumer Marketing*, *23*(3-4), 181–192.

Douglas, S. P., & Craig, C. S. (2007). Collaborative and iterative translation: An alternative approach to back translation. *Journal of International Marketing*, *15*(1), 30–43. doi:10.1509/jimk.15.1.030

Green, P. E., & Srinivasan, V. (1978). Conjoint analysis in consumer research: Issues and outlook. *The Journal of Consumer Research*, *5*(2), 103–123. doi:10.1086/208721

Hainmueller, J., Hopkins, D. J., & Yamamoto, T. (2014). Causal inference in conjoint analysis: Understanding multidimensional choices via stated preference experiments. *Political Analysis*, *22*(1), 1–30. doi:10.1093/pan/mpt024

Hudders, L., De Jans, S., & De Veirman, M. (2021). The commercialization of social media stars: A literature review and conceptual framework on the strategic use of social media influencers. *International Journal of Advertising*, *40*(3), 327–375. doi:10.1080/02650487.2020.1836925

Hudders, L., & Lou, C. (2022). A new era of influencer marketing: Lessons from recent inquires and thoughts on future directions. *International Journal of Advertising*, *41*(1), 1–5. doi:10.1080/02650487.2022.2031729

Jacobson, J., & Harrison, B. (2022). Sustainable fashion social media influencers and content creation calibration. *International Journal of Advertising*, *41*(1), 150–177. doi:10.1080/02650487.2021.2000125

Jahnke, M. (Ed.). (2018). *Influencer Marketing*. Springer. doi:10.1007/978-3-658-20854-7

Kang, M. Y., Choi, Y., & Choi, J. (2019). The effect of celebrity endorsement on sustainable firm value: Evidence from the Korean telecommunications industry. *International Journal of Advertising*, *38*(4), 563–576. doi:10.1080/02650487.2019.1601910

Kemper, J. A., & Ballantine, P. W. (2019). What do we mean by sustainability marketing? *Journal of Marketing Management*, *35*(3-4), 277–309. doi:10.1080/0267257X.2019.1573845

Lee, J. A., Sudarshan, S., Sussman, K. L., Bright, L. F., & Eastin, M. S. (2022). Why are consumers following social media influencers on Instagram? Exploration of consumers' motives for following influencers and the role of materialism. *International Journal of Advertising*, *41*(1), 78–100. doi:10.1080/02650487.2021.1964226

Lee, S. S., & Johnson, B. K. (2022). Are they being authentic? The effects of self-disclosure and message sidedness on sponsored post effectiveness. *International Journal of Advertising*, *41*(1), 30–53. doi:10.1080/02650487.2021.1986257

Lim, W. M. (2017). Inside the sustainable consumption theoretical toolbox: Critical concepts for sustainability, consumption, and marketing. *Journal of Business Research*, *78*, 69–80. doi:10.1016/j.jbusres.2017.05.001

Lin-Hi, N., & Blumberg, I. (2017). The power(lessness) of industry self-regulation to promote responsible labor standards: Insights from the Chinese toy industry. *Journal of Business Ethics*, *143*(4), 789–805. doi:10.1007/s10551-016-3075-0

Lin-Hi, N., & Blumberg, I. (2018). The link between (not) practicing CSR and corporate reputation: Psychological foundations and managerial implications. *Journal of Business Ethics*, *150*(1), 185–198. doi:10.1007/s10551-016-3164-0

Louviere, J. J., Flynn, T. N., & Carson, R. T. (2010). Discrete choice experiments are not conjoint analysis. *Journal of Choice Modelling*, *3*(3), 57–72. doi:10.1016/S1755-5345(13)70014-9

Mangham, L. J., Hanson, K., & McPake, B. (2009). How to do (or not to do). Designing a discrete choice experiment for application in a low-income country. *Health Policy and Planning*, *24*(2), 151–158. doi:10.1093/heapol/czn047 PMID:19112071

Morales, A. C., Amir, O., & Lee, L. (2017). Keeping it real in experimental research—Understanding when, where, and how to enhance realism and measure consumer behavior. *The Journal of Consumer Research*, *44*(2), 465–476. doi:10.1093/jcr/ucx048

Özbölük, T., & Akdogan, K. (2022). The role of online source credibility and influencer identification on consumers purchase decisions. *International Journal of Internet Marketing and Advertising*, *16*(1/2), 165–185. doi:10.1504/IJIMA.2022.120974

Palazzo, B. (2002). US-American and German business ethics: An intercultural comparison. *Journal of Business Ethics*, *41*(3), 195–216. doi:10.1023/A:1021239017049

Peterson, M. F. (2007). The heritage of cross cultural management research implications for the Hofstede chair in cultural diversity. *International Journal of Cross Cultural Management*, *7*(3), 359–377. doi:10.1177/1470595807083371

Schank, C., & Lorch, A. (2019). Sustainability citizenship through economics education? Contributions from the German debate on business ethics. *International Journal of Pluralism and Economics Education*, *10*(4), 401–417. doi:10.1504/IJPEE.2019.106125

Schouten, A. P., Janssen, L., & Verspaget, M. (2020). Celebrity vs. influencer endorsements in advertising: The role of identification, credibility, and product-endorser fit. *International Journal of Advertising*, *39*(2), 258–281. doi:10.1080/0 2650487.2019.1634898

Schrader, U. (2008). Transparenz über Corporate Social Responsibility (CSR) als Voraussetzung für einen Wandel zu nachhaltigerem Konsum [Transparency via corporate social responsibility (CSR) as a prerequisite for a change to more sustainable consumption]. In H. Lange (Ed.), *Nachhaltigkeit als radikaler Wandel* [Sustainability as radical change] (pp. 149–166). VS Verlag für Sozialwissenschaften. doi:10.1007/978-3-531-90956-1_7

Spelthahn, S., Fuchs, L., & Demele, U. (2009). Glaubwürdigkeit in der Nachhaltigkeitsberichterstattung [Trustworthiness in sustainability reporting]. *uwf - UmweltWirtschaftsForum, 17*(1), 61-68. doi:10.1007/s00550-008-0104-1

Straub, D. W. (1994). The effect of culture on IT diffusion: E-Mail and FAX in Japan and the U.S. *Information Systems Research*, *5*(1), 23–47. doi:10.1287/isre.5.1.23

Taylor, C. R. (2020). The urgent need for more research on influencer marketing. *International Journal of Advertising*, *39*(7), 889–891. doi:10.1080/02650487.202 0.1822104

Thomas, A. S. (1996). A call for research in forgotten locations. In B. J. Punnett & O. Shenkar (Eds.), *Handbook for International Management Research* (pp. 485–506). Blackwell.

Turner, A. (2015). Generation Z: Technology and social interest. *Journal of Individual Psychology*, *71*(2), 103–113. doi:10.1353/jip.2015.0021

Usunier, J.-C. (1998). International and Cross-Cultural Management Research. *Sage (Atlanta, Ga.)*.

Usunier, J.-C. (2011). Language as a resource to assess cross-cultural equivalence in quantitative management research. *Journal of World Business*, *46*(3), 314–319. doi:10.1016/j.jwb.2010.07.002

van de Vijver, F., & Tanzer, N. K. (2004). Bias and equivalence in cross-cultural assessment: An overview. *European Review of Applied Psychology*, *54*(2), 119–135. doi:10.1016/j.erap.2003.12.004

van Herk, H., Poortinga, Y. H., & Verhallen, T. M. M. (2005). Equivalence of survey data: Relevance for international marketing. *European Journal of Marketing*, *39*(3/4), 351–364. doi:10.1108/03090560510581818 von Mettenheim, W., & Wiedmann, K. (2021b). The complex triad of congruence issues in influencer marketing. *Journal of Consumer Behaviour*, *20*(5), 1277–1296. doi:10.1002/cb.1935

von Mettenheim, W., & Wiedmann, K.-P. (2021a). Social influencers and healthy nutrition – The challenge of overshadowing effects and uninvolved consumers. *Journal of Food Products Marketing*, *27*(8-9), 365–383. doi:10.1080/10454446.2 022.2028692

Vrontis, D., Makrides, A., Christofi, M., & Thrassou, A. (2021). Social media influencer marketing: A systematic review, integrative framework and future research agenda. *International Journal of Consumer Studies*, *45*(4), 617–644. doi:10.1111/ijcs.12647

Wiedmann, K.-P., & von Mettenheim, W. (2021). Attractiveness, trustworthiness and expertise – Social influencers' winning formula. *Journal of Product and Brand Management*, *30*(5), 707–725. doi:10.1108/JPBM-06-2019-2442

World Population Review. (2023). *Twitter users by country 2023*. https://worldpopulationreview.com/country-rankings/twitter-users-by-country

Xiao, M., Wang, R., & Chan-Olmsted, S. (2018). Factors affecting YouTube influencer marketing credibility: A heuristic-systematic model. *Journal of Media Business Studies*, *15*(3), 188–213. doi:10.1080/16522354.2018.1501146

Ye, G., Hudders, L., De Jans, S., & De Veirman, M. (2021). The value of influencer marketing for business: A bibliometric analysis and managerial implications. *Journal of Advertising*, *50*(2), 160–178. doi:10.1080/00913367.2020.1857888

Yıldırım, S. (2021). Do green women influencers spur sustainable consumption patterns? Descriptive evidences from social media influencers. *Ecofeminism and Climate Change*, *2*(4), 198–210. doi:10.1108/EFCC-02-2021-0003

Yılmaz, M., Sezerel, H., & Uzuner, Y. (2020). Sharing experiences and interpretation of experiences: A phenomenological research on Instagram influencers. *Current Issues in Tourism*, *23*(24), 3034–3041. doi:10.1080/13683500.2020.1763270

Zengin Alp, Z., & Gündüz Öğüdücü, Ş. (2018). Identifying topical influencers on Twitter based on user behavior and network topology. *Knowledge-Based Systems*, *141*, 211–221. doi:10.1016/j.knosys.2017.11.021

Zhou, S., Barnes, L., McCormick, H., & Blazquez Cano, M. (2021). Social media influencers' narrative strategies to create eWOM: A theoretical contribution. *International Journal of Information Management*, *59*, 102293. doi:10.1016/j.ijinfomgt.2020.102293

ADDITIONAL READING

Choi, Y. K., Zhang, R., & Sung, C. (2023). Attractiveness or expertise? Which is more effective in beauty product endorsement? Moderating role of social distance. *International Journal of Advertising*, *42*(7), 1201–1225. doi:10.1080/02650487.2023.2192111

Djafarova, E., & Rushworth, C. (2017). Exploring the credibility of online celebrities' Instagram profiles in influencing the purchase decisions of young female users. *Computers in Human Behavior*, *68*, 1–7. doi:10.1016/j.chb.2016.11.009

Hudders, L., De Jans, S., & De Veirman, M. (2021). The commercialization of social media stars: A literature review and conceptual framework on the strategic use of social media influencers. *International Journal of Advertising*, *40*(3), 327–375. doi:10.1080/02650487.2020.1836925

Leung, F. F., Gu, F. F., Li, Y., Zhang, J. Z., & Palmatier, R. W. (2022). Influencer marketing effectiveness. *Journal of Marketing*, *86*(6), 93–115. doi:10.1177/00222429221102889

Lou, C. (2022). Social media influencers and followers: Theorization of a trans-parasocial relation and explication of its implications for influencer advertising. *Journal of Advertising*, *51*(1), 4–21. doi:10.1080/00913367.2021.1880345

Lou, C., Kiew, S. T. J., Chen, T., Lee, T. J. M., Ong, J. E. C., & Phua, Z. X. (2023). Authentically fake? How consumers respond to the influence of virtual influencers. *Journal of Advertising*, *52*(4), 540–557. doi:10.1080/00913367.2022.2149641

Ohanian, R. (1990). Construction and validation of a scale to measure celebrity endorsers' perceived expertise, trustworthiness, and attractiveness. *Journal of Advertising*, *19*(3), 39–52. doi:10.1080/00913367.1990.10673191

Pradhan, B., Kishore, K., & Gokhale, N. (2023). Social media influencers and consumer engagement: A review and future research agenda. *International Journal of Consumer Studies*, *47*(6), 2106–2130. doi:10.1111/ijcs.12901

Zhang, Y., & Mac, L. (2023). Social media influencers: The formation and effects of affective factors during online interactions. *International Journal of Consumer Studies*, *47*(5), 1824–1837. doi:10.1111/ijcs.12957

KEY TERMS AND DEFINITIONS

Discrete Choice Experiment: A method that enables to evaluate the preferences of a respondent for a product, service, or person that differs on a number of attributes.

Elaboration Likelihood Model: A concept that includes a central and a peripheral route of processing information relevant for purchase decisions.

Information Economics: The concept that economic actors are affected by information asymmetry and thus cannot always perceive all qualities of a good. This is especially important in sustainability debates, because the quality 'sustainability' cannot be perceived.

Instagram: A social media site on which people can upload and share pictures and short videos.

Parasocial Relationship: A usually asymmetric relationship in which one side of the relationship is a celebrity, media character, or social media influencer, while the other side is an audience member, who feels a connection to the other.

Social Influencer: A person who produces content on social media that is viewed regularly by a large number of people.

Source Credibility: The level of credibility an audience attributes to a message, usually operationalized via the attractiveness, expertise, and trustworthiness of the message source.

Sustainability Influencer: A social influencer with a focus on sustainability topics. They are also called 'Sinnfluencer' in German.

Twitter: A social media site on which people can post or share short messages with attached pictures of short videos. It has officially been renamed in July 2023, but is still referred to by its former name in the literature.

Word-of-Mouth: Product information that is communicated not via advertisement but via personal recommendations.

ENDNOTES

[1] A previous version of this paper was presented at the 21st International Conference on Research in Advertising in July 2023. The authors would like to thank the audience and two anonymous reviewers for their helpful comments.

2. Tutorials on how to program the questionnaire and how to prepare the data can be found in Yevgen Bogodistov's excellent YouTube channel. It can be accessed here: https://www.youtube.com/@eugenleo

3. The authors would like to thank a member of the audience at ICORIA 2023 for pointing out this issue.

Chapter 10

Novel Forms of Consumption in the Postmodern Era

Myriam Ertz
LaboNFC, University of Quebec in Montreal, Canada

Walid Addar
LaboNFC, Université du Québec à Chicoutimi, Canada

Asmaah Sultan
LaboNFC, Université du Québec à Chicoutimi, Canada

ABSTRACT

This chapter discusses collaborative and creative consumption. Collaborative consumption is the exchange of goods and services between individuals and challenges the fundamental concept of ownership. It is closely linked to the circular economy, promoting product lifetime extension and resource mutualization, which contribute to reducing environmental impact. Companies are working to adapt to this trend by rethinking their business models. In contrast, creative consumption refers to the (mostly digital) ecosystem in which consumers use digital tools and services to become active creators of original content primarily disseminated across various online platforms. Creative consumption is also tangential to consumers' design, creation, marketing, remarketing, and reutilization of products using traditional approaches (e.g., production and self-production) or technologies such as 3D printing. The chapter also deals with co-creation, which involves consumers partnering with organizations throughout the product or service life cycle from design to disposal.

DOI: 10.4018/979-8-3693-1594-1.ch010

Copyright © 2024, IGI Global. Copying or distributing in print or electronic forms without written permission of IGI Global is prohibited.

INTRODUCTION

Collaborative and creative consumption reflects major societal changes that fit perfectly into the postmodern era (Kim, 2020). In this new era, rigid structures and traditional norms are giving way to greater flexibility, a questioning of hierarchies, and a search for authenticity. Collaborative and creative consumption embody these values by allowing individuals to actively participate in creating and exchanging goods, services, and content. They advocate a horizontal approach in which consumers are not simply recipients but key players. The movement is also rooted in postmodernist ideas that emphasize diversity, pluralism, and fragmentation. Collaborative and creative consumption celebrate this diversity by offering a variety of options, from product customization to content co-creation. They adapt to individual tastes and different needs and reflect the complexities of postmodernism.

The rise of collaborative and creative consumption marks an important turning point in the evolution of modern consumer behavior (Durif et al., 2016a). To place this development in context, it is important to look at the 20th century, often referred to as the "century of the self" (Curtis, 2002), during which the individual occupied a central place in society. According to Curtis (2002), The 20th century has been marked by the growth of consumption and materialism, both fertile grounds for the gradual fragmentation of historical social, workers', or religious communities and social relationships. In other words, the values of consumption and possession of material goods have deteriorated historical group membership, leading to a consumer society focused on material acquisition and the cult of personality, hence individualism. However, social, technological, economic, and even ecological shifts have eroded that movement in recent decades. Indeed, there has been a stark increase in loneliness and isolation in the social realm; powerful technologies connecting individuals – at least digitally – in the technological area; environmental degradation related to over-production and consumption in the ecological area; and global financial dysfunctions disrupting the economy and leading consumers to reunite to face financial hardships (e.g., children staying with parents; collective kitchens; swapping meets). Hence, manifestations of de-individualization in society include not only citizen movements focused on sustainability and environmental impact but also the rise of networks and systems of collective consumer exchange (Curtis, 2002).

More specifically, the changes in the consumption landscape have notably been driven by awareness of the environmental and social impacts of overconsumption and the desire to reduce these impacts (Fournier, 2020). In particular, collaborative consumption is based on the principle of sharing and exchanging goods and services between individuals. Short-term rental platforms like Airbnb or ride-hailing platforms like Uber have fundamentally changed how people access goods and services and challenged traditional ownership models (Slee, 2016). However, the environmental

Novel Forms of Consumption in the Postmodern Era

criterium does not predominantly lead consumers to opt for collaborative systems instead of conventional ones, as the economic motive is way more imperious in this regard (Durif et al., 2016b, 2017, 2018). Overall, it is nonetheless fair to say that consumer communities are growing, encouraging consumers to work together to meet their needs in a more sustainable and economically efficient way (Gensollen, 2003). The idea of environmental inefficiency inherent in traditional consumption patterns has been widely highlighted (Marchand et al., 2005). The environmental impact of producing, distributing, and disposing of consumer goods has led consumers to seek alternatives (Albinsson et al., 2012). Thus, alternative exchange systems have emerged that extend the lifespan of products and improve the overall response to consumer needs.

These changes in consumer behavior have important implications for market research and practice (Fournier, 2020). That is, businesses face the challenge of adapting to these new dynamics while meeting the changing needs of consumers and their increasingly (pro)active practices. Sustainability and eco-efficiency have become major concerns, forcing companies to rethink their services and processes (Laville, 2009). Collaborative and creative consumption offer a new vision of modern consumption that prioritizes efficiency and sustainability and meets the needs of individuals within consumer communities (Ertz and Quenum, forthcoming). This requires innovative market research and business management approaches to adapt to this new and ever-changing environment (Laville, 2009). Collaborative and creative consumption represent a fundamental change in the way we consume, shaped by the search for efficiency, sustainability, and community (Marchand et al., 2005). This shift redefines our understanding of consumption and has major implications for society and the economy. To better understand and benefit from these changes, it is important to better understand the fundamentals, forms, and current developments related to collaborative and creative consumption.

In the remainder of this discussion, we will explore several facets of collaborative and creative consumption. We will approach the topic starting with individualism versus collective approaches to life and consumption. Next, we will discuss the notion of "sharing" as a form of consumer behavior. Additionally, we will analyze collaborative consumption and the sharing and collaborative economy, as well as its implications for the circular economy. Finally, we will look at the role of technology in redistribution and collaboration, as well as the rise of the creator economy and creative consumption. These subjects are at the heart of current developments in the way we consume and interact with the world around us. We will examine each of these aspects in detail to better understand their impact on modern society.

The remainder of this chapter is organized as follows: a background section introduces the chapter by discussing modern individualism, sharing as a form of consumer behavior, and the evolution of sharing behavior. The next section covers the technological applet underpinning increasingly consumption and introducing the notion of co-creation. A third section elaborates more specifically on collaborative consumption and the sharing economy which rely heavily on enhanced consumer involvement. A fourth section explores the topic of the consumer as a producer, and the conclusion wraps up the chapter emphasizing its key points.

BACKGROUND

Collaborative and creative consumption are postmodern derivatives as they are closely linked to both individualistic and collective approaches to life and consumption, hence acknowledging this dual aspect inherent in consumption and life in general. From a modernist viewpoint, individuals are encouraged to develop their identities and assert themselves as individuals in a world that increasingly values individual achievement (Lee et al., 2010). Indeed, individualism promotes the idea that the satisfaction of individual needs and personal fulfillment are essential. Meanwhile, collaborative consumption emphasizes the notions of sharing and exchange and calls into question the notion of individual ownership (Perren and Grauerholz, 2015). It encourages people to join barter communities and lend, borrow, and share goods and services with others either directly or via intermediaries. This form of consumption promotes collaboration and cooperation and emphasizes the idea that living and consuming can be a collective experience. This calls for the necessity to decipher, more specifically, the notion of individualism in the context of our modern society.

Modern Individualism

Modern individualism emerged as a major social trend in the 20th century, marking a major break with the collective approaches to life and consumption that had dominated previous centuries (Cova, 1985). Alongside this change, the number of single-consumer households has increased, where individuals prioritize independence and autonomy and choose to live alone (Kaufmann and Widmer, 2005). This evolution can be explained through the influence of various factors, notably the emancipation of the individual from traditional ties such as religion, family, social class, and unions, among others, and economic and technological changes. Modern individualism encourages individuals to focus on their own personal needs, desires, and aspirations, and meanwhile, the number of single households and atomic families (parents with children) has increased significantly, particularly in Western societies (Kaufmann and Widmer, 2005). Thus, individuals sought to meet their needs independently and sometimes rejected traditional models of collective living, such as living within extended families or communities.

Novel Forms of Consumption in the Postmodern Era

To provide further explanation, this transition towards single-consumer households has a major impact on consumer behavior. Individuals sought to own their own goods rather than share them within a collective structure. A culture of ownership is reinforced, encouraging individuals to accumulate material goods as a sign of success and social status (Kaufmann and Widmer, 2005). However, this increase in personal consumption has a major impact on the environment. It is becoming increasingly clear that consumption models focused on individualism are relatively ineffective for the environment (Le Gall, 2002). Indeed, the production, distribution, and disposal process of consumer goods creates a significant environmental footprint. Overconsumption, waste, and planned obsolescence contribute significantly to current environmental problems such as climate change, environmental degradation, and the depletion of natural resources (Le Gall, 2002). Faced with these challenges, collaborative and creative consumption emerge as practical and innovative responses since they revolve around sharing, exchange, and sustainability principles (Ertz et al., 2017a, 2017b). They oppose individualism – at least on principle - by encouraging individuals to work together to meet their needs directly (user-to-user), more effectively, and resource-efficiently. Collaborative and creative consumption are also underpinned by the notion of sharing, which appears as a form of consumption behavior.

Sharing as a Form of Consumer Behavior

Although the concept "sharing" and the "sharing economy" are misnomers for characterizing many inherently profit-oriented business models (Belk, 2014), the concept of sharing has become generic to refer to resource circulation systems in which consumers are center stage due to their ability to provide resources and not merely consume them (Botsman and Rogers, 2010). Hence, collaborative and creative consumption are closely linked to sharing as a form of consumption behavior and overlap with it (Hamari et al., 2016). They encourage people to share goods, services, and ideas, promote a more efficient use of resources, and strengthen community ties. This trend is based on the idea that exclusive ownership is not necessarily helpful and that sharing can be a more sustainable and economical approach (Hamari et al., 2016). This creates a shared community where members can work together to meet their needs while reducing their impact on the environment. Thus, sharing has become a central act in how we consume and interact with our environment, highlighting the value of collaboration and community in today's society.

The Evolution of Sharing Behavior

The concept of "sharing" has evolved significantly to include acts such as bartering/swapping, reselling, and gift-giving as a form of consumption behavior within families and groups of friends (Matharu et al., 2020). These sharing behaviors were primarily rooted in the private sphere, where individuals shared resources and goods within their intimate circles. This reflects a tradition of solidarity and mutual assistance between parents, family, friends, and other acquaintances, and the nurturing of those ties often motivates the exchange of goods and services in the first place (Matharu et al., 2020). However, this private sharing behavior has fundamentally changed thanks to technological advancements. Online platforms, mobile applications, and social networks have created unprecedented opportunities to extend these sharing practices beyond intimate circles. We have witnessed the considerable evolution towards large-scale collaborative consumption, with the possibility of "sharing" with loved ones as well as with strangers (Perren and Grauerholz, 2015). For example, barter once only concerned people who were familiar with each other, but it has recently become an economic model in its own right thanks to online platforms where people come together wishing to exchange goods and services without spending money. Likewise, giving/donating, a practice deeply rooted in family and friendly interactions has transformed into a form of digital philanthropy that allows strangers to support causes and projects that are close to their hearts or give away preowned items. In addition, exchanging goods and services between foreigners is a pillar of the cooperative economy. Platforms like Airbnb and Uber have revolutionized the way people access temporary housing, vehicles, and other services (Degryse, 2016). These sharing systems among strangers have redefined consumption norms by allowing individuals to take advantage of unused resources "[...] and contribute to their more efficient use" (Degryse, 2016). The evolution of "sharing" as a consumer behavior shows how technology has changed our social and economic interactions.

Indeed, practices once limited to family and friendships have expanded to include strangers, creating new opportunities, challenges, and interactive dynamics. Global collaborative consumption now builds on these foundations, highlighting the potential of digital connectivity to transform the way we live and consume (Ertz et al., 2019). Technological shifts and the creation of online communities (e.g., brand communities) have dramatically contributed to that shift.

THE ROLE OF TECHNOLOGY IN REDISTRIBUTION AND COLLABORATION AND THE EMPOWERED CONSUMER BECOMING A BRAND COMMUNITY MEMBER AND CO-CREATOR

Collaborative and creative consumption are closely linked to dramatic technological changes for redistribution and collaboration purposes (Keymolen, 2013). Thanks

Novel Forms of Consumption in the Postmodern Era

to technological advances, online platforms have allowed individuals to exchange goods, services, and original works.

The Central Role of Platforms and Applications

Collaborative and creative consumption are evolving phenomena rooted in the redefinition of consumer behavior and technological advancements (Perren and Grauerholz, 2015). At the heart of this change are significant cultural and social shifts that have altered the way people interact with goods and services. Indeed, collaborative and creative consumption not only redefine attitudes towards ownership but also emphasizes redistribution, collaboration, and the growing role of technology. The emergence of digital platforms and dedicated applications plays an important role in facilitating collaborative consumption (Ramella and Manzo, 2020). Indeed, these technological tools have made it easier and more efficient for individuals to share, trade, give, and rent goods and services. Technology has created an ecosystem that fosters collaboration among consumers, from sharing rides on ride-sharing apps to renting homes on platforms like Airbnb to exchanging unwanted goods on redistribution sites (Ramella and Manzo, 2020). Meanwhile, creative consumption is inherently rooted within the digital realm and the development of brand communities herein. Some of these communities being notably preoccupied by sustainability issues.

Brand Communities and Sustainability

Brand communities play an important role in co-creation and promoting sustainable development. These communities bring together like-minded people, brand fans, loyal customers, and other engaged stakeholders. By interacting and exchanging ideas, experiences, and information, they help build the brand and promote its values, particularly in terms of sustainability.

Brand communities play a vital role in promoting sustainability and corporate social responsibility, both online and offline (Li et al., 2021). These communities are made up of consumers, fans, and supporters who share a common interest in a brand or company's products, values, and initiatives. They consist of spaces for members to interact, share experiences, and actively participate in brand activities. In addition, in terms of sustainability, brand communities have a huge impact (Li et al., 2021). Organizations may raise awareness among their fans and followers about environmental and social issues and encourage more responsible behavior. Members of these communities are often the first to support brands' sustainable efforts, such as reducing waste, adopting eco-friendly production practices, and promoting ethics in manufacturing. Online platforms such as social media play a central role in creating and developing these brand communities (Sridharan et al., 2018). Businesses can interact directly with their followers, share their sustainability success stories, and start discussions on important topics. Community members can express their opinions, ask questions, and influence the company's sustainability decisions. These communities also promote corporate transparency and accountability (Sridharan et al., 2018). Fans are increasingly attentive to brands' sustainable efforts and are not afraid to hold brands accountable when they fail to deliver on their promises. This allows brands to be more consistent in their sustainability efforts, increasing their credibility in the eyes of consumers.

Collaborative and creative consumption are at the heart of a social and economic revolution, with enormous implications for sustainability and brand communities (Selloni and Selloni, 2017). These trends are converging in significant ways to reinvent how consumers interact with products, brands and each other. Brand communities play an important role in promoting online and offline collaborative and sustainable consumption. Members of these communities share a common passion for a brand's products and values and increasingly engage in collaborative consumption practices. They exchange advice, information and even products with each other. For example, enthusiasts of high-tech products can help each other by exchanging ideas on online forums or by lending their devices. Brands want to encourage these interactions to strengthen relationships with consumers and contribute to their loyalty (Sahin et al., 2011). At the same time, sustainability is a central issue in this context. Collaborative and creative consumption extend the life of products and reduce waste (Binninger et al., 2015). For example, online redistribution marketplaces allow consumers to buy, sell, or trade used products (Ertz et al., 2018a). This avoids creating new products and promotes sustainability. Consumers are also increasingly aware of their impact on the environment, choosing sustainable brands and preferring second-hand goods (Liu et al.,2012). This constant interaction between consumers, brands and communities creates a feedback loop that encourages more ethical and responsible consumption. Brands want to integrate sustainable principles into their marketing and communication strategies to meet the expectations of these communities. Importantly, the recourse to communities further involves consumers and spurs their creative propensity, many of them turning into genuine co-creators of corporate value in cooperation with organizations.

Consumers as Co-Creators of Value Among Themselves and With Organizations

Based on what was said previously, it is obvious that collaborative and creative consumption are an element that redefines the way consumers interact with goods, services, and organizations. At the heart of this continuous development process is the idea of co-creation, where consumers play a key role in creating value within

Novel Forms of Consumption in the Postmodern Era

the economy (Nadeem et al., 2020). The concept of co-creation dates back to the beginning of the 2000s, and its objective was already, back then, to involve consumers in the process of design, development, and continuous improvement of products and services in order to create added value (Zhang et al., 2018). Indeed, consumers play a vital role as co-creators of the modern economy, determining how products and services are developed, personalized, and consumed (Bueno-Ravel and Gueudet, 2014). Consumer co-creators actively contribute to the value of a product or service. They are no longer just passive beneficiaries but actors involved in the development process. This involvement can take many forms, from customizing products to generating innovative ideas. Therefore, consumers directly influence the quality, relevance, and attractiveness of a company's products. Organizations have increasingly recognized the value of this collaboration, as it allows them to adapt to changing and evolving consumer needs and establish closer, more loyal relationships with their customer base (Zhang et al., 2018). This collaboration between consumers and organizations has a huge impact on value creation (Prahalad and Ramaswamy, 2004), sustainability (Roberts et al., 2005), and innovation (Zhang et al., 2018).

Value creation. Consumers have been recognized as being no longer just passive recipients but active partners in the value-creation process (Prahalad and Ramaswamy, 2004). An interesting example of co-creation is the personalization of products and services, as many companies have allowed consumers to personalize their products, whether clothing, shoes, beauty products, or even food products (Prahalad and Ramaswamy, 2004). This personalization goes beyond simple aesthetics and allows consumers to design products perfectly suited to their needs and preferences. This strengthens the emotional connection between consumers and brands. Yet, co-creation is not just limited to product design. It extends to content creation and enrichment. Social media and online platforms allow consumers to share their ideas, opinions, and experiences and create their own digital content (Alsubagh, 2015). Influencers are a great example of this as they create content enjoyed by millions, and businesses recognize the importance of working with them to reach their target audiences.

Sustainability co-creation. Today's consumers are increasingly concerned about environmental and social issues (Dagher et al., 2014). They want sustainable products and services, and co-creation can assist them in achieving these goals. For example, consumers can help design sustainable products, prioritize eco-friendly materials, and suggest ideas for reducing waste. Therefore, when it comes to sustainability, consumer co-creators are often more aware of environmental and social issues (Roberts et al., 2005). Their active participation can encourage organizations to adopt more sustainable practices to address the concerns of target groups. Consumer co-creators are also more likely to support brands that share their sustainability values (Lahtinen et al., 2020).

Innovation co-creation. Furthermore, co-creation promotes innovation (Boldrini, 2017). Consumer ideas and perspectives are a valuable source of inspiration for businesses. Organizations that actively incorporate customer feedback and ideas can develop products and services that better meet real-world needs, thereby reducing waste and promoting sustainability. Co-creation also strengthens the connection between consumers and organizations. Consumers who provide value feel more invested and engaged in the brand. This creates a more lasting and loyal relationship that benefits both parties (Boldrini, 2017).

For more precision on the matter, Table 1 summarizes all the different forms of co-creation involving consumer.

In sum, brand communities and co-creation have been a hotbed for the creation of a more active figure who has gradually become involved in digitally-mediated collaborative communities as consumers endorsed supplier roles. By empowering consumers and improving their agency over products and services, collaborative consumption and the sharing economy also have profound implications for sustainability by enabling more pronounced circularity.

COLLABORATIVE CONSUMPTION AND THE SHARING AND COLLABORATIVE ECONOMY: IMPLICATIONS FOR THE CIRCULAR ECONOMY

An aspect that needs to be discussed is the essential role of the consumers regarding their involvement as providers of resources by endorsing a merchant role.

The Consumer as a Provider and the Nuances of Collaborative Consumption

As a relatively renewed phenomenon, collaborative consumption has revolutionized how individuals perceive their role as consumers (Ertz et al., 2017a). This shift has given rise to the concept of the "consumer-merchant," in which the nuances of consumption extend far beyond purchasing goods and services (Upadhyaya et al., 2014). At the heart of this development are a variety of practices, from goods barter to services and goods swapping, from gifting to second-hand exchange, from rental to pooling, and from sharing to community lifestyles. Bartering/swapping and gift-giving are fundamental practices of community consumption. These measures often lie at the intersection of financial and sharing economics (Puschmann and Alt, 2016). Individuals exchange goods and services without necessarily spending money. The second-hand market, where second-hand goods have a second life, offers another perspective on community consumption (Strähle and Klatt, 2017). Meanwhile, the various forms of mutualization of resources, including community lifestyles, epitomize the sharing economy.

Novel Forms of Consumption in the Postmodern Era

Table 1. Identification and classification of value co-creation types

Steps	Forms of Co-Creation and Corresponding Definitions	Authors	Level of Participation	Return of the Company	Degree of Freedom	Participant Quality
Pre-design	*Open innovation* Involves the active participation of consumers in developing new products through the generation and evaluation of new product ideas, the elaboration of concepts, the discussion and improvement of prototypes, or the testing of products in simulations.	(Füller et al., 2006)	High	Yes	Open and creative freedom	Lead users and ordinary consumers
	Open source A massive online collaborative approach associated with the open-source movement that inspires that progress in the digital world is easily achievable through sharing intellectual property and allowing a large community of individuals to develop.	(Cooke and Buckley, 2008)	High	Yes	Open and creative freedom	Lead users and ordinary consumers
	Crowdsourcing An approach that enables a company to draw on the creativity, intelligence, and know-how of many individuals, most frequently Internet users, to generate new ideas and find solutions to specific problems.	(Rubel, 2006)	High	Yes	Open and creative freedom	Lead users and ordinary consumers
	Co-innovation It is a design method based on the contributions of several people involved in varying degrees of participation in the innovation process.	(Cova, 2008)	High	Yes	Open and creative freedom	Lead users and predefined targets
	Co-ideation The company invites consumers to submit innovative ideas, even providing resources such as toolkits, software, and beta versions to enhance their skills and knowledge and increase their participation in the co-ideation process.	(Von Hippel, 2001; Roser et al., 2013; Agrawal and Rahman, 2015)	High	Yes/No	Open and creative freedom	Lead users and predefined targets

continues on following page

Table 1. Continued

Steps	Forms of Co-Creation and Corresponding Definitions	Authors	Level of Participation	Return of the Company	Degree of Freedom	Participant Quality
Co-design	*Co-testing* Consumers, as co-testers, are involved in testing new offers prepared to be launched on the markets soon. Customer involvement as co-testers can increase the chances of product success.	(Agrawal and Rahman, 2015)	Low to High	Yes/No	Limited freedom	Lead-user consumers
	Mass customization This form allows consumers to configure their pre-purchase product, design part of the pre-purchase product, or customize part of the post-purchase product.	(Merle, 2010)	Low to High	Yes/No	Limited freedom	Lead users and ordinary consumers
	Customization The company adapts this product by recording customer profiles or preferences.	Moon (2002, 2004)	Low to High	Yes/No	Limited freedom	Lead users and ordinary consumers
	Co-design This technique involves interaction between the individual and the object during the pre-purchase product co-design process, using computer-assisted design software that enables the consumer to modify product components and visualize the result in real-time.	Merle et al., 2008)	Low to High	Yes/No	Limited freedom	Lead users and ordinary consumers
	Co-distribution Consumers are involved in the distribution service through the self-service mechanism.	(Agrawal and Rahman, 2015)	Low to High	No	Limited freedom	Lead users and ordinary consumers
	Co-evaluation Once submitted to the co-ideation process, ideas are evaluated to assess their potential value. A closed management circle first reviews evaluations and then opens to customer assessment.	(Agrawal and Rahman, 2015)	Low to High	Yes	Limited freedom	Lead users and ordinary consumers
	Co-promotion Involving a wide range of consumers in competitions to create visual images or films for advertising campaigns	(Muñiz and Schau, 2007)	Low to High	Yes	Limited freedom	Lead users and ordinary consumers
	Participatory operations Invite consumers to vote on the choice of a new product, take part in consumer castings, or compete to create new packaging or a new slogan.	(Reniou, 2009)	Low to High	Yes	Open and creative freedom	Lead users and ordinary consumers

Table 1. Continued

Steps	Forms of Co-Creation and Corresponding Definitions	Authors	Level of Participation	Return of the Company	Degree of Freedom	Participant Quality
Co-production	*Co-determination* The company encourages the development of cross-identification of its needs and those of consumers.	(Cova, 2008)	Moderate	Yes/No	Limited freedom	Lead-users and predefined target
	Co-production It involves consumer participation in the production and supply of services within the limits defined by the organization.	(Bendapudi and Leone, 2003; Bolton and Saxena-Iyer, 2009)	Low to moderate	No	Limited freedom	Lead users and ordinary consumers
	Co-consumption Results from sharing consumer experiences with other consumers	(Agrawal and Rahman, 2015)	Low	No	Open and creative freedom	Lead users and ordinary consumers
	Experience co-creation Companies can collaborate with customers, generating richer experiences for them and benefiting in return from access to and capitalization on their latent perceptions and preferences.	(Rahman, 2006)	Low to High	No	Open and creative freedom	Lead users and ordinary consumers
	Co-promotion Customers spread the experience of the service and goods they have consumed through word-of-mouth.	(Agrawal and Rahman, 2015)	Low	No	Limited freedom	Lead users and ordinary consumers
	Prosumption A set of value-creating activities consists of integrating physical activity, mental effort, and socio-psychological experiences undertaken by consumers, leading to the production of products that they eventually consume and which become their consumption experience.	(Xie et al., 2008)	High	No	Limited freedom	Lead users and ordinary consumers
	Self-production Consumers engage in self-production when they actively create finished products, such as preparing a meal or assembling a piece of furniture independently, using products, tools, and devices supplied by companies.	(Rifkin, 2011)	Moderate	No	Limited freedom	Lead users and ordinary consumers

Source: Ertz and Quenum (forthcoming).

Novel Forms of Consumption in the Postmodern Era

Online platforms facilitate these transactions, allowing consumers to sell or buy second-hand goods easily (Su and Jin, 2021). Besides, the rental of goods such as tools or experiences such as renting a vacation home is a common practice in online consumption communities (Botsman and Rogers, 2010). More and more people prefer to rent rather than buy goods, contributing to more efficient use of resources and reduced waste (Moeller and Wittkowski, 2010). Pooling or sharing resources is an important element of collaboration (Barnes and Mattsson, 2016). Individuals and businesses share resources such as jobs, vehicles, tools, and even community gardens (Barnes and Mattsson, 2016). This promotes the optimal use of products and allows individuals to reduce their environmental footprint. In this perspective, collaborative consumption is closely related to responsible consumption (Ertz et al., 2018b), which promotes the optimal use of products and allows individuals to reduce their environmental footprint. It is also important to consider the role of consumers as producers.

Consequently, collaborative consumption is formally defined as "the set of resource circulation schemes that enable consumers to both receive and provide, temporarily or permanently, valuable resources or services through direct interaction with other consumers or through an intermediary" (Ertz et al., 2019, p. 32). Past research has further differentiated between two major roles within the collaborative economy area, that of the receiver (the receiving pole) and that of the provider (the providing pole) (Ertz and Sarigöllü, 2019). Table 2 below summarizes the key defining features of each role.

In addition, consumers may engage in different types of collaboration, and Table 3 below summarizes the nuances of collaborative consumption.

Table 2. Consumer two-sided role

	Receiver	**Provider**
Function	The consumer seeks to receive a resource or service that is provided directly by another consumer (i.e., the provider) or indirectly through the mediation of an organization known as the mediator (for-profit or non-profit).	The consumer who provides a specific resource or service, either directly to a consumer (i.e., the receiver) or indirectly through a mediator (for-profit or non-profit).
Action	Reception entails second-hand purchase, free receiving, swapping, accessing resources for free or for compensation (excluding conventional consumption access), reconditioned/refurbished consumption.	Provision involves reselling, giving for free, swapping, providing access for free or in exchange for compensation, or trading in a product to an organization.

Source: Adapted from Ertz et al. (2019, p. 29).

Novel Forms of Consumption in the Postmodern Era

Table 3. Nuances of collaboration within the collaborative consumption framework

Collaborative Intensity	Pure Collaboration	Facilitated Collaboration	Mediated Collaboration	
			Sourcing Collaboration	Trading Collaboration
Process	Both the receiver and the provider are consumers who exchange a resource	Both the receiver and the provider are consumers who exchange a resource through a facilitator	The provider provides a resource or service to the receiver through a mediator.	The receiver obtains a resource or service from the provider through a mediator.
Process example	The second-hand purchase/sale of a pre-owned chair set at a flea market.	The second-hand purchase/sale of a pre-owned chair through an online classified ads website.	Resale of a pre-owned chair to a second-hand shop.	Purchase of a chair from a second-hand shop.
Exchange type	C2C	C2C	C2O	O2C
Consumer role	Receiver and provider	Receiver and provider	Provider	Receiver
Presence of intermediaries	No	Yes	Yes	Yes
Presence of mediator	No	No	Yes	Yes

Note: C2C consumer-to-consumer, C2O consumer-to-organization, O2C organization-to-consumer.
Source: Ertz et al. (2019, p. 31).

Pure collaboration can be defined as "direct P2P exchanges, in which consumers directly exchange a specific resource or service without any intermediary, whether facilitator or mediator. For example, through garage/yard sales, swap meets, or flea markets, consumers directly provide and receive resources or services" (Ertz et al., 2019, p. 30). In contrast, facilitated collaboration refers to direct P2P exchanges; however, these exchanges are facilitated by a facilitator, typically an online platform or an application. For example, [a carpooling platform] enables consumers who wish to obtain a ride to connect with consumers who are willing to offer a ride and to arrange between themselves the terms and conditions related to that ride, with the website acting merely as a facilitator, not as a mediator" (Ertz et al., 2019, p. 30). Finally, mediated collaboration involves more predominantly a mediating party called the mediator and consists in two applets. Formally, it is "a two-sided coin that mirrors the two-sided consumer role in collaborative consumption. Firstly, *sourcing collaboration* means that organizations do not themselves provide a resource or deliver a service to consumers but rely on providers (i.e., consumers) to do so [...] [and through] *trading collaboration*, the receiver enjoys a resource that was mediated by an organization but was originally provided by another consumer (i.e., provider) via sourcing collaboration" (Ertz et al., 2019, p. 31). In Table 2, the example of mediated collaboration involves a consumer who provides a chair to a secondhand shop (sourcing collaboration) before that shop resells the preowned chair to another consumer (trading collaboration), with the shop being the mediator. By becoming a provider, the consumer becomes an actor and contributes to product circularity which has profound implications for the circular economy.

Collaborative Consumption and the Sharing and Collaborative Economy and its Implications for the Circular Economy

Collaborative consumption is a phenomenon that changes the way we consume and produce goods and services (Nguyen et al., 2016). Traditional approaches to consumption are being redefined by encouraging sharing, exchange, and co-creation. Hence, by involving sharing and collaboration, the collaborative economy has a significant connection with the circular economy by promoting the optimal use of resources and significantly reducing the impact on the environment. This development opens new perspectives for understanding collaborative consumption within the sharing economy.

Collaborative Consumption Within the Broader Sharing Economy Ecosystem

Collaborative consumption and the sharing economy (to see how collaborative consumption and the collaborative economy are encapsulated in the broader sharing economy concept, see Ertz [2020]) are emerging as drivers of the postmodern economy, redefining the way we consume, share, and access goods and services. These practices have a profound impact on the circular economy, a concept aimed at minimizing waste and promoting environmental sustainability. According to Barros (2013), the sharing economy facilitates the reuse and bundling of goods, reducing the need to constantly produce new goods. Sharing platforms allow individuals to share vehicles, homes, tools, and many other resources, thereby extending the life of products. This approach helps reduce waste, conserve resources, and promote greener consumption models. In addition, the sharing economy is part of the circular economy by facilitating repair, refurbishment, and recycling (Georgantzis et al., 2021). Individuals can repair or upgrade existing items without throwing them away, reducing the amount of e-waste and used products. Additionally, sharing durable goods can help reduce demand for new products and reduce pressure on natural resources. As collaborative consumption is an essential part of the sharing economy (Georgantzis et al., 2021), it embodies a new way of consuming and living, highlighting the power of collaboration in postmodern society.

Novel Forms of Consumption in the Postmodern Era

At the heart of collaborative consumption are practices such as the exchange of goods, services, and experiences (Ertz and Durif, 2017). People share resources: shelter, vehicles, skills, and even food. This approach enables more efficient use of resources, reduces waste, and promotes stronger, more connected communities. Two essential elements worth exploring within the collaborative ecosystem are redistribution and mutualization.

Redistribution and the Secondhand Economy

The redistribution market plays a vital role in the quest to grant multiple lives to products and extend the lifespan of consumer goods (Paden and Stell, 2005). These markets not only provide a platform for exchange but also reflect the ideas of sustainability and responsible consumption. The basic idea is that instead of throwing away products that are no longer used, these can be put back on the market to find a new home. This extends the useful life of these products, reduces waste, and minimizes the environmental impact of their production (Paden and Stell, 2005). Recirculation markets encourage reuse, repurposing, and, notably, upcycling or downcycling, which contribute to a circular and sustainable economy (Briassoulis et al., 2021). These platforms facilitate transactions between product owners and those who need the products, creating an efficient exchange ecosystem. As shown in Table 4, redistribution markets involving free, monetized, or other compensation exchanges, give items a second life and keep them from ending up in landfills. By participating in these markets, consumers actively help extend the life of products while saving money and promoting a more sustainable lifestyle. This practice allows us to reshape views on end-of-life consumer goods by no longer considering them as waste but as resources that can be reused for as long as possible. Table 4 summarizes the three key activities of redistribution-based consumption systems.

Table 4. Redistribution-based consumption systems

Activities	Definitions	Examples
Secondhand market	Second-hand purchase: purchase of pre-acquired goods (used or not) by other consumers. Resale (or second-hand sale): Sale of pre-acquired goods (used or not) by other consumers.	Buying used clothing from another peer, Resale of unused clothing (e.g., wrong size) to another peer.
Donation	Transfer of goods between consumers without financial consideration.	Gift of toys to a peer. A peer receives a printer from another peer for free.
Barter	Bilateral exchange of goods between two consumers.	A peer trades their cup for another peer's sunglasses.

Sources: Adapted from Ertz and Quenum (forthcoming).

Mutualization and the Functional Economy

Issues related to access and ownership have evolved significantly in recent years. Historically, consumers asked themselves why they should rent if they can buy, but this question has gradually evolved into why they should buy if they could just rent. Multiple causes, ranging from financial constraints to space constraints (e.g., urbanization), but also cultural changes and influences with the calling into question of property, have led to this shift. Hence, some consumers have started, in specific consumption circumstances, to resort to the functional economy. Such an economy focuses on providing services rather than simply purchasing products (Stahel, 1997). Consumers resort to mutualization practices (adapted from Arnould and Rose's [2016] mutuality concept) shown in Table 5, such as leasing, renting, sharing, and pooling products rather than owning them. This approach is based on a "pay as you use" philosophy. This means individuals only pay for services and products when they need them, avoiding the upfront costs and long-term maintenance associated with ownership. In addition to the economic and practical benefits, this transition raises, however, questions of symbolism and ownership control. To be more precise, owning properties has long been associated with social status, security, and control over consumers' lives. However, as consumers consider that owning properties is a burden, possibly a waste of resources, and a dependence on material goods, the functional economy challenges this perception by emphasizing flexibility, access, and reduction in environmental impacts (Stahel, 1997). The functional economy has given rise to the emergence of business models focused on service delivery, which, in turn, have started to affect consumers' relationships with goods and services, challenging traditional norms and offering new perspectives for future consumption. Table 5 summarizes the four key activities of mutualization-based consumption systems.

Just as for redistribution and the secondhand market, mutualization and the functional economy benefited greatly from technological advances as well as the rise of consumption and brand communities. Yet, so did the creative economy and creative consumption.

THE CONSUMER AS PRODUCER

Another crucial albeit less covered aspect that needs elaboration is the essential role of consumers as providers of resources by endorsing a self-producer role.

Novel Forms of Consumption in the Postmodern Era

Table 5. Mutualization-based consumption systems

Activities	Definitions	Examples
Leasing	The user pays regular compensation for an unlimited number and individual use of the resource made available by a peer.	Payment of recurring compensation to a peer for the unlimited and individual use of his woodlot for the felling of trees.
Renting (court/long term)	The user makes use of the resource of a peer individually for a predetermined (short/long) period.	Rental of a peer's bike for a weekend.
Sharing	Different consumers sequentially or simultaneously use a peer's resource.	A peer shares the journey in their vehicle with other peers (ridesharing).
Pooling	Peers simultaneously use resources that they or others have pooled.	Peers pool funds for the realization of a project (crowdfunding).

Sources: Adapted from Ertz and Quenum (forthcoming).

Note: The classification uses the categorizations developed by the authors mentioned above to adapt them to collaborative consumption, as theorized in this chapter.

Creative Consumption and the Creative Economy

The creator economy is a growing ecosystem where individuals can grow their audiences and earn income by creating and sharing content, products, and services on digital platforms. From content creators to independent artists, this phenomenon is changing how individuals work, consume, and interact, opening new perspectives on consumption and creativity.

Alongside the rise of the collaborative economy, the creator economy has expanded (Schram, 2020). This economy relies on generating income with an emphasis on individual skills, artistic talent, and creativity. Content creators, artists, artisans, and freelancers share their work with global audiences through online platforms (Schram, 2020). This form of creative consumption allows consumers to purchase unique and personalized products while directly supporting creators. The impact of creative consumption goes well beyond the simple act of consumption. It also stimulates the economy by creating new opportunities for self-employed workers and entrepreneurs.

Platforms and applications play a central role in the dynamics of creative consumption (Oliveira et al., 2020), possibly even more so than in the case of collaborative consumption. The technological tools underpinning the creator economy create an ecosystem that promotes collaboration, redistribution, and creativity, providing numerous benefits to both consumers and creators. These platforms allow people with similar interests and needs to connect quickly and efficiently. Platforms and apps make it easier to connect people (Oliveira et al., 2020) who want to create, disseminate, and access creative content, whether it be text, music, video, or other formats. As such, digital platforms expand the reach of creators and artists, allowing them to share their work with a global audience and break down traditional geographic barriers. Content creators, artisans, and freelancers thus envision a potential global market for their products and services. The ease of use and flexibility of creative consumption applications allow users to participate in shared transactions informally. Importantly, these platforms integrate online payment systems and simplify transactions between participants. This ensures creators are paid for their work, thus supporting all the more the growth of the creative economy.

To summarize, the various aspects of this creative economy cover a wide range of areas. What we're seeing now is that social media influencers, podcasters, video creators, bloggers, and music producers are leveraging the digital age to make a huge impact. Additionally, generative artificial intelligence, such as text and image generation, plays an increasing role in the creation of innovative content (Acquatella et al., 2022). The ever-expanding metaverse offers new spaces for creativity and interaction, paving the way for new forms of content and virtual experiences. In addition to content creation, consumers are also able to engage in more active forms of production such as self-production.

Self-Production

The role of the consumer is not limited to that of a simple buyer but increasingly extends to the role of the producer. The concept of self-production underlines this change. Self-production is an increasingly popular practice within the framework of creative consumption and sustainable lifestyles (Trębska, 2020). Indeed, self-production consists of consumers producing their own goods and services rather than purchasing them on traditional markets, although organizations may facilitate that process or empower consumers to self-produce (Cova et al., 2013). This can take many forms, such as making crafts or generating solar energy at home, for example. Self-production reflects consumers' growing desire to regain control of their consumption, reduce their dependence on large corporations, and contribute to environmental sustainability (Atakan et al., 2014). Self-production is part of a broader trend towards sustainable lifestyles. Individuals increasingly seek to minimize their environmental impact by producing locally, reducing waste, and promoting environmentally friendly practices (Carney and Déméné, 2022). Self-production plays a key role in this approach, as it allows consumers to consciously design products, use sustainable materials, and reduce overconsumption. Self-production is not only an expression of collective consumption but also a means of expressing one's own creativity and individuality. Self-producing consumers can personalize their products, adapt them to their specific needs, and share their knowledge with other members of their community (Cova et al., 2013). This form of creative consumption is an act that expresses autonomy, responsibility, and commitment to a more sustainable lifestyle

Novel Forms of Consumption in the Postmodern Era

(Carney and Déméné, 2022). By viewing consumers as producers, we can better understand how they actively contribute to shaping the consumption environment. This development is closely linked to collaborative consumption and the sharing and collaboration economy and has a significant impact on the development of the circular economy. Table 6 below summarizes the nuances in self-production.

Table 6. Forms of self-production by individuals

Self-Production Categories	Definitions	Examples
Not facilitated or empowered by the organization	The consumer delimits a set of activities to be carried out and performs them, possibly with other consumers but without organizational input.	Gardening DIY
Facilitated by the organization	The organization delimits a set of activities to be carried out autonomously by consumers so that they are able to carry out/organize activities autonomously.	Bla-Bla Car eBay Warhammer
Empowered by the organization	The organization allows a set of activities performed independently by consumers so that consumers can independently perform/arrange activities.	Fan-club Lego Brickfairs Klikobil

Note: DIY = do-it-yourself.
Source: Cova et al. (2013).

Figure 1 summarizes the different forms of consumer involvement discussed so far in this chapter. Consumer may engage in co-creative behaviour with organizations. Second, the red arrows and boxes represent the redistribution applet of collaborative consumption and the sharing economy and this practice can take place at two levels. Either consumer-to-consumer (C2C) when consumers directly interact with each other or with organizations (C2O2C) who act as mediators. While interacting with each other, consumers also create (brand communities). The same applies to the mutualization applet in blue in Figure 1. Finally, each consumer can engage in self-production at an individual level or in collaboration with other consumers. This is represented by the light grey boxes for individual self-production and by the black arrows for collaborative production.

Figure 1. Summary of novel forms of consumption in the postmodern era

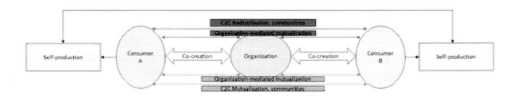

CONCLUSION

In the current postmodern era, collaborative and creative consumption have profoundly changed the way we live, work, and consume. This has given individuals the power to be creators, influencers, and consumers all at once, creating a new dynamic in the world of consumption. This revolution paved the way for the emergence of the so-called "metaconsumer" (Ertz, forthcoming). Meta-consumers are the pioneers of this new era, embodying the future of consumption by combining these roles in new ways. They are both content creators and influencers who share their experiences and informed consumers looking for innovative products and services. They are the driving force behind this development, shaping trends and inspiring other consumers. Meta-consumerism reflects an era in which creativity, collaboration, and innovation are at the heart of interactions and consumption decisions. This demonstrates consumers' ability to constantly adapt to new technologies and continually redefine our understanding of consumption. Metaconsumers embody this change by simultaneously endorsing user and provider roles, thus challenging the modernist conception of a divide between consumption and production, as well as of the consumer as a passive agent (Ertz, forthcoming). Instead, metaconsumers pave the way for new forms of expression and interaction. The future of collaboration and creative consumption looks promising as it continues to evolve with metaconsumers at the forefront. They will shape the next trends, explore new opportunities for creativity and innovation, and contribute to the constant redefinition of the way we live, work, and consume. With the advancement of novel technologies underpinned by artificial intelligence, virtual reality, and the metaverse, but also 3D Printing, which will generalize among the broad public, collaborative and creative consumption may ultimately collapse into meta-consumption, which promises us a future in which consumption is an interactive and participatory experience, characterized by more creativity and collaboration than ever before. For managers, the exploration of these novel forms of consumption offers promising avenues. The perspective offered in this chapter demonstrates the broader network in which organizations are typically placed and which comprises all of their consumers who are directly related to organizations through conventional consumption and co-creation but also other more alternative forms of consumption including redistribution and mutualization. Consumers work also independently from organization whether through C2C initiatives or through self-production activities. Organizations may therefore craft strategies and potentially even rebrand themselves as enabler and facilitators of those interactions whether with consumers or between consumers themselves. This entails organizing collaborative marketplaces, encouraging consumers to hand in their pre-owned goods (swap, resale, gift-giving/donation) and any type of resource. Incidentally while creating avenues for alternative value creation, such initiatives may also contribute to heightened product circularity and hence, the circular economy and sustainability.

REFERENCES

Acquatella, F., Fernandez, V., & Houy, T. (2022). A technical-economic perspective of the central role of artificial intelligence in platform markets. *Information Systems Management*, (4), 51–73.

Agrawal, A. K., & Rahman, Z. (2015). Roles and resource contributions of customers in value co-creation. *International Strategic Management Review*, *3*(1-2), 144–160. doi:10.1016/j.ism.2015.03.001

Albinsson, P. A., & Yasanthi Perera, B. (2012). Alternative marketplaces in the 21st century: Building community through sharing events. *Journal of Consumer Behaviour*, *11*(4), 303–315. doi:10.1002/cb.1389

Alsubagh, H. (2015). The impact of social networks on consumers' behaviors. *International Journal of Business and Social Science*, *6*(1), 209–216.

Arnould, E. J., & Rose, A. S. (2016). Mutuality: Critique and substitute for Belk's "sharing.". *Marketing Theory*, *16*(1), 75–99. doi:10.1177/1470593115572669

Atakan, S. S., Bagozzi, R. P., & Yoon, C. (2014). Consumer participation in the design and realization stages of production: How self-production shapes consumer evaluations and relationships to products. *International Journal of Research in Marketing*, *31*(4), 395–408. doi:10.1016/j.ijresmar.2014.05.003

Barnes, S. J., & Mattsson, J. (2016). Understanding current and future issues in collaborative consumption: A four-stage Delphi study. *Technological Forecasting and Social Change*, *104*, 200–211. doi:10.1016/j.techfore.2016.01.006

Barros, P. (2013). Collaborative consumption and the sharing economy in developing markets. *Sustainable Brands*, *23*(02), 2014.

Belk, R. (2014). You are what you can access: Sharing and collaborative consumption online. *Journal of Business Research*, *67*(8), 1595–1600. doi:10.1016/j. jbusres.2013.10.001

Bendapudi, N., & Leone, R. P. (2003). Psychological implications of customer participation in co-production. *Journal of Marketing*, *67*(1), 14–28. doi:10.1509/ jmkg.67.1.14.18592

Binninger, A. S., Ourahmoune, N., & Robert, I. (2015). Collaborative Consumption And Sustainability: A Discursive Analysis Of Consumer Representations And Collaborative Website Narratives. *Journal of Applied Business Research*, *31*(3), 969–986. doi:10.19030/jabr.v31i3.9229

Boldrini, J. C. (2017). Co-creation of value in a collaborative innovation project: a case of transition towards the circular economy 1. *Innovations*, (0).

Bolton, R., & Saxena-Iyer, S. (2009). Interactive services: A framework, synthesis and research directions. *Journal of Interactive Marketing*, *23*(1), 91–104. doi:10.1016/j.intmar.2008.11.002

Botsman, R., & Rogers, R. (2010). *What's mine is yours. The rise of collaborative consumption*. Penguin Press.

Briassoulis, D., Pikasi, A., & Hiskakis, M. (2021). Recirculation potential of post-consumer/industrial bio-based plastics through mechanical recycling-Techno-economic sustainability criteria and indicators. *Polymer Degradation & Stability*, *183*, 109217. doi:10.1016/j.polymdegradstab.2020.109217

Bueno-Ravel, L., & Gueudet, G. (2014). *Quelles ressources pour les professeurs des écoles et leurs formateurs? Apports de la recherche en didactique. In Conférence au 41e colloque Copirelem, 18-20 June*. Mont de Marsan.

Carney, L., & Déméné, C. (2022). Towards patterns of responsible consumption and production: An exploration of do-it-yourself practitioners through motivations, designs, and manufacturing processes. *Journal of Desert Research*, *20*(3), 179–208.

Cooke, M., & Buckley, N. (2008). Web 2.0, social networks and the future of market research. *International Journal of Market Research*, *50*(2), 267–292. doi:10.1177/147078530805000208

Cova, B. (1985). Beyond the market when the connection matters more than the good. *Beyond the market when the link matters more than the good*, 1-174.

Cova, B. (2008). Consumer made: quand le consommateur devient producteur. Décisions Marketing, 19–27.

Cova, B., Ezan, P., & Fuschillo, G. (2013). Zoom sur l'autoproduction du consommateur. *Revue Française de Gestion*, *5*(234), 115–133. doi:10.3166/rfg.234.115-133

Curtis, A. (2002). *The Century of the Self*. Full Adam Curtis Documentary.

Dagher, G. K., & Itani, O. (2014). Factors influencing green purchasing behavior: Empirical evidence from the Lebanese consumers. *Journal of Consumer Behaviour*, *13*(3), 188–195. doi:10.1002/cb.1482

Degryse, C. (2016). *Social impacts of the digitalization of the economy*. Box.

Durif, F., Arcand, M., Ertz, M., & Connolly, M. (2017). *Kijiji secondhand economy index: 2017 report*. http://secondhandeconomy.kijiji.ca/

Durif, F., Arcand, M., Ertz, M., & Connolly, M. (2018). *Kijiji secondhand economy index: 2018 report*. https://www.kijiji.ca/kijijicentral/app/uploads/2016/08/Kijiji-Index-Report-2018_EN_Final_web-2.pdf

Durif, F., Arcand, M., Tedds, L., Boivin, C., & Ertz, M. (2016b). *Kijiji secondhand economy index: 2016 report*. https://www.kijiji.ca/kijijicentral/app/uploads/2016/08/Kijiji-Index-Report-2016-1.pdf

Durif, F., Ertz, M., & Bigot, A. (2016a). Collaborative economy: towards a new socio-economic model - Clé Vie Numérique. In A. Poitras (Ed.), *The State of Quebec 2016* (pp. 95–101). Éditions du Boréal.

Ertz, M. (2020). Collaborative consumption, a buzzword that has gone conceptual: Three shades of the sharing economy. *Oikonomics*, *14*(14), 1–14. doi:10.7238/o.n14.2011

Ertz, M. (forthcoming). The metaconsumer: Beyond the consumer. *International Review of Retail, Distribution and Consumer Research*.

Ertz, M., & Durif, F. (2017). Definition of collaborative consumption and associated concepts. In A. Decrop (Ed.), *Collaborative consumption: Issues and challenges of the new sharing society* (pp. 33–54). De Boeck. doi:10.3917/dbu.decro.2017.01.0031

Ertz, M., Durif, F., & Arcand, M. (2017b). Life after death? Study of goods multiple lives practices. *Journal of Consumer Marketing*, *34*(2), 108–118. doi:10.1108/JCM-07-2015-1491

Ertz, M., Durif, F., & Arcand, M. (2018a). Business at the fingertips of consumers: A scale for measuring resale motivations in online settings. *International Review of Retail, Distribution and Consumer Research*, *28*(1), 92–114. doi:10.1080/0959 3969.2017.1334692

Ertz, M., Durif, F., & Arcand, M. (2019). A conceptual perspective on collaborative consumption. *AMS Review*, *9*(1-2), 27–41. doi:10.1007/s13162-018-0121-3

Ertz, M., Durif, F., Lecompte, A., & Boivin, C. (2018b). Does "sharing" mean "socially responsible consuming"? Exploration of the relationship between collaborative consumption and socially responsible consumption. *Journal of Consumer Marketing*, *35*(4), 392–402. doi:10.1108/JCM-09-2016-1941

Ertz, M., Lecompte, A., & Durif, F. (2017a). Dual roles of consumers: Towards an insight into collaborative consumption motives. *International Journal of Market Research*, *59*(6), 725–748. doi:10.2501/IJMR-2017-040

Ertz, M., & Quenum, G. G. Y. (forthcoming). Collaborative and creative consumption: A review. In K. Peattie, R. de Angelis, N. Koenig-Lewis, & C. Strong (Eds.), *The Routledge Companion to Marketing and Sustainability*. Routledge.

Ertz, M., & Sarigöllü, E. (2019). Assessing the potential of sustainable value chains in the collaborative economy. *Sustainability (Basel)*, *11*(2), 390. doi:10.3390/su11020390

Fournier, I. (2020). Environmental impact of overconsumption on the ecosystems of Quebec science fiction: "increase the level of wealth while respecting the environment" (Legault 2018). *The American Review of Canadian Studies*, *50*(3), 386–399. doi:10.1080/02722011.2020.1811584

Füller, J., Bartl, M., Ernst, H., & Mühlbacher, H. (2006). Community based innovation: How to integrate members of virtual communities into new product development. *Electronic Commerce Research*, *6*(1), 57–73. doi:10.1007/s10660-006-5988-7

Gensollen, M. (2003). Informational assets and mediated communities. *Political Economy Review*, *113*(9).

Georgantzis Garcia, D., Kipnis, E., Vasileiou, E., & Solomon, A. (2021). Consumption in the circular economy: Learning from our mistakes. *Sustainability (Basel)*, *13*(2), 601. doi:10.3390/su13020601

Hamari, J., Sjöklint, M., & Ukkonen, A. (2016). The sharing economy: Why people participate in collaborative consumption. *Journal of the Association for Information Science and Technology*, *67*(9), 2047–2059. doi:10.1002/asi.23552

Jin, J., & Klatt, L.M. (2017). The second hand market for fashion products. *Green Fashion Retail*, 119-134.

Kaufmann, V., & Widmer, E. (2005). The acquisition of motility within families: State of the question and research hypotheses. *Spaces and Societies*, *120*(1), 199–217.

Keymolen, E. (2013). Trust and technology in collaborative consumption. Why it is not just about you and me. *Bridging Distances in Technology and Regulation*, *135*, 135-150.

Kim, J. (2020). Collaborative fashion consumption in the sharing economy: Philosophical and aesthetic perspectives. *Journal of Global Fashion Marketing*, *11*(3), 289–305. doi:10.1080/20932685.2020.1724815

Lahtinen, S., & Närvänen, E. (2020). Co-creating sustainable corporate brands: A consumer framing approach. *Corporate Communications*, *25*(3), 447–461. doi:10.1108/CCIJ-11-2019-0121

Laville, É. (2009). *The company green: sustainable development changes business to change the world*. Pearson Education France.

Le Gall, M. (2002). From concern for the environment to sustainable consumption. *Proceedings of the 2nd congress on Marketing trends in Europe ESCP-EAP*, 25-26.

Lee, M., Pant, A., & Ali, A. (2010). Does the individualist consume more? The interplay of ethics and beliefs that governs consumerism across cultures. *Journal of Business Ethics*, *93*(4), 567–581. doi:10.1007/s10551-009-0240-8

Li, M., Hua, Y., & Zhu, J. (2021). From interactivity to brand preference: The role of social comparison and perceived value in a virtual brand community. *Sustainability (Basel)*, *13*(2), 625. doi:10.3390/su13020625

Liu, Z. L., Anderson, T. D., & Cruz, J. M. (2012). Consumer environmental awareness and competition in two-stage supply chains. *European Journal of Operational Research*, *218*(3), 602–613. doi:10.1016/j.ejor.2011.11.027

Marchand, A., De Coninck, P., & Walker, S. (2005). Responsible consumption: New perspectives in the fields of product design. *New Social Practices*, *18*(1), 39–56.

Matharu, M., Jain, R., & Kamboj, S. (2020). Understanding the impact of lifestyle on sustainable consumption behavior: A sharing economy perspective. *Management of Environmental Quality*, *32*(1), 20–40. doi:10.1108/MEQ-02-2020-0036

Merle, A., Chandon, J. L., & Roux, E. (2008). Understanding the perceived value of mass customization: The distinction between product value and experiential value of co-design. [English Edition]. *Recherche et Applications en Marketing*, *23*(3), 27–50. doi:10.1177/076737010802300301

Merle, A., Chandon, J. L., Roux, E., & Alizon, F. (2010). Perceived value of the mass-customized product and mass customization experience for individual consumers. *Production and Operations Management, 19*(5), 503–514. doi:10.1111/j.1937-5956.2010.01131.x

Moeller, S., & Wittkowski, K. (2010). The burdens of ownership: Reasons for preferring renting. *Managing Service Quality, 20*(2), 176–191. doi:10.1108/09604521011027598

Muñiz, A. M. Jr, & Schau, H. J. (2007). Vigilante marketing and consumer-created communications. *Journal of Advertising, 36*(3), 35–50. doi:10.2753/JOA0091-3367360303

Nadeem, W., Juntunen, M., Shirazi, F., & Hajli, N. (2020). Consumers' value co-creation in sharing economy: The role of social support, consumers' ethical perceptions and relationship quality. *Technological Forecasting and Social Change, 151*, 119786. doi:10.1016/j.techfore.2019.119786

Nguyen Tran Ba, T., & Nguyen Thuong, B. (2016). *The Creative Industry in the Age of Collaborative Consumption*. Laurea University of Applied Sciences. https://www.theseus.fi/handle/10024/113459

Oliveira, T., Tomar, S., & Tam, C. (2020). Evaluating collaborative consumption platforms from a consumer perspective. *Journal of Cleaner Production, 273*, 123018. doi:10.1016/j.jclepro.2020.123018

Paden, N., & Stell, R. (2005). Consumer product redistribution: Disposition decisions and channel options. *Journal of Marketing Channels, 12*(3), 105–123. doi:10.1300/J049v12n03_06

Perren, R., & Grauerholz, L. (2015). Collaborative consumption. International Encyclopedia of the Social & Behavioral Sciences, 4(2), 139-144.

Prahalad, C. K., & Ramaswamy, V. (2004). Co-creating unique value with customers. *Strategy and Leadership, 32*(3), 4–9. doi:10.1108/10878570410699249

Puschmann, T., & Alt, R. (2016). Sharing economy. *Business & Information Systems Engineering, 58*(1), 93–99. doi:10.1007/s12599-015-0420-2

Rahman, Z. (2006). Customer experience management—A case study of an Indian bank. *Journal of Database Marketing & Customer Strategy Management, 13*(3), 203–221. doi:10.1057/palgrave.dbm.3240298

Ramella, F., & Manzo, C. (2020). *The economy of collaboration: The new digital platforms of production and consumption*. Routledge. doi:10.4324/9780429355936

Novel Forms of Consumption in the Postmodern Era

Reniou, F. (2009). *Opérations participatives des marques: pourquoi et comment faire participer les consommateurs? De la compréhension des opérations participatives et des motivations des consommateurs à s'y engager à l'analyse de leurs effets sur la marque.* University Paris Dauphine.

Rifkin, J. (2011). *The third industrial revolution: how lateral power is transforming energy, the economy, and the world.* Palgrave Macmillan.

Roberts, D., Baker, S., & Walker, D. (2005). Can we learn together? Co-creating with consumers. *International Journal of Market Research, 47*(4), 405–426. doi:10.1177/147078530504700401

Roser, T., DeFillippi, R., & Samson, A. (2013). Managing your co-creation mix: Co-creation ventures in distinctive contexts. *European Business Review, 25*(1), 20–41. doi:10.1108/09555341311287727

Rubel, S. (2006). Who's Ready to Crowdsource? Check Your Egos at the Door, and Tap Into the Collective Wisdom of Millions for Solutions [Preprint]. *Advertising Age.*

Sahin, A., Zehir, C., & Kitapçı, H. (2011). The effects of brand experiences, trust and satisfaction on building brand loyalty; an empirical research on global brands. *Procedia: Social and Behavioral Sciences, 24,* 1288–1301. doi:10.1016/j.sbspro.2011.09.143

Schram, R. (2020). The state of the creator economy. *Journal of Brand Strategy, 9*(2), 152–162.

Selloni, D., & Selloni, D. (2017). New forms of economies: sharing economy, collaborative consumption, peer-to-peer economy. *Codesign for public-interest services,* 15-26.

Slee, T. (2016). *What's yours is mine: Against Airbnb, Uber and other avatars of the "sharing economy.".* Lux publisher. doi:10.2307/j.ctt1bkm65n

Sridharan, S., Bondy, M., Nakaima, A., & Heller, R. F. (2018). The potential of an online educational platform to contribute to achieving sustainable development goals: A mixed-methods evaluation of the Peoples-uni online platform. *Health Research Policy and Systems, 16*(1), 1–14. doi:10.1186/s12961-018-0381-2 PMID:30419943

Stahel, W. R. (1997). *The functional economy: cultural and organizational change* (Vol. 1). National Academy Press.

Su, Y., & Jin, L. (2021). The impact of online platforms' revenue model on consumers' ethical inferences. *Journal of Business Ethics,* 1–15.

Trębska, P. (2020). Food self-supply in new consumer trends. *Zeszyty Naukowe Szkoły Głównej Gospodarstwa Wiejskiego w Warszawie. Polityki Europejskie. Finance i Marketing, 23*(72), 237–246.

Upadhyaya, S., Vann, R. J., Camacho, S., Baker, C. N., Leary, R. B., Mittelstaedt, J. D., & Rosa, J. A. (2014). Subsistence consumer-merchant marketplace deviance in marketing systems: Antecedents, implications, and recommendations. *Journal of Macromarketing, 34*(2), 145–159. doi:10.1177/0276146713504107

Von Hippel, E. (2001). User toolkits for innovation. *Journal of Product Innovation Management, 18*(4), 247–257. doi:10.1111/1540-5885.1840247

Xie, C., Bagozzi, R. P., & Troye, S. V. (2008). Trying to prosume: Toward a theory of consumers as co-creators of value. *Journal of the Academy of Marketing Science, 36*(1), 109–122. doi:10.1007/s11747-007-0060-2

Zhang, T. C., Jahromi, M. F., & Kizildag, M. (2018). Value co-creation in a sharing economy: The end of price wars? *International Journal of Hospitality Management, 71*, 51–58. doi:10.1016/j.ijhm.2017.11.010

ADDITIONAL READING

Ertz, M., & Boily, E. (2019). The rise of the digital economy: Thoughts on blockchain technology and cryptocurrencies for the collaborative economy. *International Journal of Innovation Studies, 3*(4), 84–93. doi:10.1016/j.ijis.2019.12.002

Ertz, M., Boily, É., Sun, S., & Sarigöllü, E. (2022). Role Transitions at the prosumer level: Spillover Effects in the Collaborative Economy. *European Journal of Marketing, 56*(10), 2721–2748. doi:10.1108/EJM-10-2021-0828

Ertz, M., Deschênes, J., & Sarigöllü, E. (2021). From user to provider: Switchover effects in the collaborative economy. *Sustainability (Basel), 13*(10), 5662. doi:10.3390/su13105662

Ertz, M., & Sarigöllü, E. (2022). Consumer intentions to use collaborative economy platforms: A meta-analysis. *International Journal of Consumer Studies, 46*(5), 1859–1876. doi:10.1111/ijcs.12840

Sarigöllü, E., Hou, C., & Ertz, M. (2021). Sustainable product disposal: Consumer redistributing behaviors versus hoarding and throwing away. *Business Strategy and the Environment, 30*(1), 340–356. doi:10.1002/bse.2624

Novel Forms of Consumption in the Postmodern Era

Scarano, M. C., & Ertz, M. (2023). Consumption systems: Unveiling bi-residential and delegated consumption. *Journal of Consumer Behaviour*, cb.2246. Advance online publication. doi:10.1002/cb.2246

Sun, S., & Ertz, M. (2021). Theory-based roadmap for assessing sustainability in the collaborative economy. *Frontiers in Psychology*, *12*, 752867. doi:10.3389/fpsyg.2021.752867 PMID:34690898

Sun, S., & Ertz, M. (2021). Dynamic evolution of ride-hailing from a systemic perspective: Forecasting financial sustainability. *Transportation Research Part C, Emerging Technologies*, *125*, 103003. doi:10.1016/j.trc.2021.103003

Sun, S., & Ertz, M. (2021). Environmental impact of mutualized mobility: Evidence from a life cycle perspective. *The Science of the Total Environment*, *772*, 145014. doi:10.1016/j.scitotenv.2021.145014 PMID:33581535

Sun, S., & Ertz, M. (2022). Can shared micromobility programs fight climate change for smart cities and sustainability: Global evidence from transportation big data. *Sustainable Cities and Society*, *85*, 104045. doi:10.1016/j.scs.2022.104045

Torrent-Sellens, J. X., Escofet, N., & Ertz, M. (2020). Motivations of collaborative obtainers and providers in Europe. *Behaviour & Information Technology*, *41*(5), 1065–1079. doi:10.1080/0144929X.2020.1851770

KEY TERMS AND DEFINITIONS

Co-Creation: A process where consumers are not only end-users but also contributors to the value creation process.

Collaborative Economy: A category within the sharing economy encompassing the economic and social systems in which individuals both obtain and provide resources either directly to other consumers or through an intermediary.

Creative Consumption: The (mostly digital) ecosystem in which consumers use digital tools and services to become active creators of original content primarily disseminated across various online platforms.

Creative Economy: The creative economy encompasses industries that are based on individual creativity, skill, and talent. These industries have the potential to create wealth and jobs through the generation and exploitation of intellectual property.

Sharing Economy: The sharing economy is a socio-economic system built around the sharing of resources. It includes the shared creation, production, distribution, trade, and consumption of goods and services by different people and organizations.

Compilation of References

Abhishek, & Srivastava, M. (2021). Mapping the influence of influencer marketing: A bibliometric analysis. *Marketing Intelligence & Planning*, *39*(7), 979–1003. doi:10.1108/MIP-03-2021-0085

Acikgoz, F., & Burnaz, S. (2021). The influence of 'influencer marketing' on YouTube influencers. *International Journal of Internet Marketing and Advertising*, *15*(2), 201–219. doi:10.1504/IJIMA.2021.114331

Acquatella, F., Fernandez, V., & Houy, T. (2022). A technical-economic perspective of the central role of artificial intelligence in platform markets. *Information Systems Management*, (4), 51–73.

Adriatico, J. M., Cruz, A., Tiong, R. C., & Racho-Sabugo, C. R. (2022). An analysis on the impact of choice overload to consumer decision paralysis. *Journal of Economics, Finance and Accounting Studies*, *4*(1), 55–75. doi:10.32996/jefas.2022.4.1.4

Agile Transformation. (2014). *Marketing at the speed of agile A CMO's guide to applying agile methodologies to transform marketing.* PWC. https://www.pwc.com/us/en/advisory/business-strategy-consulting/assets/agile-marketing.pdf

Agrawal, A. K., & Rahman, Z. (2015). Roles and resource contributions of customers in value co-creation. *International Strategic Management Review*, *3*(1-2), 144–160. doi:10.1016/j.ism.2015.03.001

Akben, İ., & Ös, M. (2019). Akıllı ve Veriye Dayalı Tedarik Zincirleri. 3rd International EMI Entrepreneurship & Social Sciences Congress, 28-30.

Akben, İ., & Avşar, İ. İ. (2018). Endüstri 4.0 ve Karanlık Üretim: Genel Bir Bakış. *Türk Sosyal Bilimler Araştırmaları Dergisi*, *3*(1), 26–37.

Akeke, O. (2022). Effect of social marketing on sustainable behaviour towards household waste disposal in Lagos State, Nigeria. *Modern Management Review*, *27*(2), 7–14. doi:10.7862/rz.2022.mmr.07

Akter, S., Taufique Hussain, T. M., & Strong, C. (2021). What omnichannel really means? *Journal of Strategic Marketing*, *29*(7), 567–573. doi:10.1080/0965254X.2021.1937284

Compilation of References

Alam, M. M., Lutfi, A., & Alsaad, A. (2023). Antecedents and consequences of customers' engagement with pro-environmental consumption-related content on social media. *Sustainability (Basel)*, *15*(5), 3974. doi:10.3390/su15053974

Albinsson, P. A., & Yasanthi Perera, B. (2012). Alternative marketplaces in the 21st century: Building community through sharing events. *Journal of Consumer Behaviour*, *11*(4), 303–315. doi:10.1002/cb.1389

Alexander, S. (2011). The voluntary simplicity movement: Reimagining the good life beyond consumer culture. *Int. J. Environ. Cult. Econ. Soc. Sustain.*, *7*.

Alexander, S., & Ussher, S. (2012). The voluntary simplicity movement: A multi-national survey analysis in theoretical context. *Journal of Consumer Culture*, *1*(12), 66–86. doi:10.1177/1469540512444019

Alsubagh, H. (2015). The impact of social networks on consumers' behaviors. *International Journal of Business and Social Science*, *6*(1), 209–216.

Amelia, R., & Hidayatullah, S. (2020). The effect of instagram engagement to purchase intention and consumers' luxury value perception as the mediator in the skylounge restaurant. *International Journal of Innovative Science and Research Technology*, *5*(4), 958–966.

Amirkhanpour, M., & Vrontis, D. (2017). Mobile Marketing: A Contemporary Strategic Perspective. *International Journal of Technology Marketing*, *9*(3), 252–269.

Anastasiadou, E., Chrissos Anestis, M., Karantza, I., & Vlachakis, S. (2020). The coronavirus' effects on consumer behavior and supermarket activities: Insights from Greece and Sweden. *The International Journal of Sociology and Social Policy*, *40*(9/10), 893–907. doi:10.1108/IJSSP-07-2020-0275

Andhyka, B. (2020). Marketing 4.0 a Literature Review. *Journal of Business and Management*, *22*(4), 49–52.

Andreasen, A. R. (2014). Social marketing. The handbook of persuasion and social marketing. In D. W. Stewart (Ed.), *The Handbook of Persuasion and Social Marketing* (pp. 13–26). Praeger.

Anker, T. B., Gordon, R., & Zainuddin, N. (2022). Consumer-dominant social marketing: A definition and explication. *European Journal of Marketing*, *56*(1), 159–183. doi:10.1108/EJM-08-2020-0618

Ao, L., Bansal, R., Pruthi, N., & Khaskheli, M. B. (2023, February 2). Impact of Social Media Influencers on Customer Engagement and Purchase Intention: A Meta-Analysis. *Sustainability (Basel)*, *15*(3), 2744. Advance online publication. doi:10.3390/su15032744

Aramamotoru. (2023). https://www.aramamotoru.com/icerik-pazarlamasi-ve-2023-yili-trendleri/

Armstrong, G., Kotler, P., Harker, M., & Brennan, R. (2015). *Marketing: An Introduction* (3rd ed.). Pearson.

Arndt, J., Solomon, S., Kasser, T., & Sheldon, K. M. (2004a). The Urge to Splurge: A Terror Management Account of Materialism and Consumer Behavior. *Journal of Consumer Psychology*, *14*(3), 198–212. doi:10.1207/s15327663jcp1403_2

Arndt, J., Solomon, S., Kasser, T., & Sheldon, K. M. (2004b). The Urge to Splurge Revisited: Further Reflections on Applying Terror Management Theory to Materialism and Consumer Behavior. *Journal of Consumer Psychology*, *14*(3), 225–229. doi:10.1207/s15327663jcp1403_5

Arnould, E. J., & Rose, A. S. (2016). Mutuality: Critique and substitute for Belk's "sharing.". *Marketing Theory*, *16*(1), 75–99. doi:10.1177/1470593115572669

Arora, S., & Sahney, S. (2017). Webrooming behaviour: A conceptual framework. *International Journal of Retail & Distribution Management*, *45*(7/8), 762–781. Advance online publication. doi:10.1108/IJRDM-09-2016-0158

Artun, O., & Levin, D. (2015). *Predictive marketing: Easy ways every marketer can use customer analytics and big data*. John Wiley & Sons. doi:10.1002/9781119175803

Asan, K. (2022). Measuring the impacts of travel influencers on bicycle travellers. *Current Issues in Tourism*, *25*(6), 978–994. doi:10.1080/13683500.2021.1914004

Aslam, S., Jadoon, E. K., Zaman, K., & Gondal, S. (2011, September 1). Effect of Word of Mouth on Consumer Buying Behavior. *Mediterranean Journal of Social Sciences*. Advance online publication. doi:10.5901/mjss.2011.v2n3p497

Asmare, A., & Zewdie, S. (2021). Omnichannel retailing strategy: A systematic review. *International Review of Retail, Distribution and Consumer Research*, *32*(1), 59–79. doi:10.108 0/09593969.2021.2024447

Asshidin, N. H. N., Abidin, N., & Borhan, H. B. (2016). Perceived Quality and Emotional Value that Influence Consumer's Purchase Intention towards American and Local Products. *Procedia Economics and Finance*, *35*, 639–643. doi:10.1016/S2212-5671(16)00078-2

Atakan, S. S., Bagozzi, R. P., & Yoon, C. (2014). Consumer participation in the design and realization stages of production: How self-production shapes consumer evaluations and relationships to products. *International Journal of Research in Marketing*, *31*(4), 395–408. doi:10.1016/j. ijresmar.2014.05.003

Atasoy, O., & Morewedge, C. K. (2018). Digital goods are valued less than physical goods. *The Journal of Consumer Research*, *44*(6), 1343–1357. doi:10.1093/jcr/ucx102

Ayman, U. (2023). *A New Era of Consumer Behavior-In and Beyond the Pandemic*. IntechOpen. doi:10.5772/intechopen.100829

Compilation of References

Baake, J., Gensich, M., Kraus, T., Müller, C., Przyklenk, S., Rössler, P., Walpert, C., & Zang, A. M. (2022). Sinnfluencer*innen: Der Schlüssel zu mehr Glaubwürdigkeit in Social Media? - Ein Experiment zur Wahrnehmung von Nachhaltigkeitskommunikation auf Instagram ['Sense-fluencers': The key to more trustworthiness in social media? An experiment on the perception of sustainability communication on Instagram]. In A. S. Kümpel, C. Peter, A. Schnauber-Stockmann, & F. Mangold (Eds.), *Nachhaltigkeit als Gegenstand und Zielgröße der Rezeptions- und Wirkungsforschung - Aktuelle Studien und Befunde* [Sustainability as the object and performance indicator of reception and impact studies - Current research and findings] (Vol. 44, pp. 41–62). Nomos. doi:10.5771/9783748926436-41

Bacher, N. (2022). *Metaverse Retailing* [Unpublished master thesis]. Universita Di Pavia.

Backhaus, K., & Awan, A. (2019). *The Paradigm Shift in Customer Analysis: Marketing or IT-Driven? The Art of Structuring.* doi:10.1007/978-3-030-06234-7_32

Backhaus, K., & Schneider, H. (2020). *Strategisches Marketing* [Strategic Marketing] (3rd ed.). Schäffer-Poeschel. doi:10.34156/9783791046969

Baker, J., Levy, M., & Grewal, D. (1992). An experimental approach to making retail store environmental decisions. *Journal of Retailing*, *68*(4), 445.

Balis, J. (2022). How brands can enter the metaverse. *HBR Online*, 1-6.

Bandura, A. (1977). Self-efficacy: Toward a Unifying Theory of Behavioral Change. *Psychological Review*, *2*(84), 191–215. doi:10.1037/0033-295X.84.2.191 PMID:847061

Bardhi, F., & Eckhardt, G. M. (2017). Liquid consumption. *The Journal of Consumer Research*, *44*(3), 582–597. doi:10.1093/jcr/ucx050

Barnes, S. J., & Mattsson, J. (2016). Understanding current and future issues in collaborative consumption: A four-stage Delphi study. *Technological Forecasting and Social Change*, *104*, 200–211. doi:10.1016/j.techfore.2016.01.006

Barrera, K. G., & Shah, D. (2023). Marketing in the Metaverse: Conceptual understanding, framework, and research agenda. *Journal of Business Research*, *155*, 113420. doi:10.1016/j.jbusres.2022.113420

Barroso, P. (2022). From reality to the hyperreality of simulation. *Texto Livre, 15*.

Barros, P. (2013). Collaborative consumption and the sharing economy in developing markets. *Sustainable Brands*, *23*(02), 2014.

Barta, S., Gurrea, R., & Flavián, C. (2023). The double side of flow in regret and product returns: Maximizers versus satisficers. *International Journal of Information Management*, *71*(4), 102648. doi:10.1016/j.ijinfomgt.2023.102648

Bartosik-Purgat, M. (2018). International contexts of social media and e-WoM communication in the customer decision-making process. *Journal of Management and Business Administration. Central Europe*, *26*(2), 16–33.

Batat, W. (2021). How augmented reality (AR) is transforming the restaurant sector: Investigating the impact of "Le Petit Chef" on customers' dining experiences. *Technological Forecasting and Social Change, 172*(C), 3–10. doi:10.1016/j.techfore.2021.121013

Batat, W. (2022). What does phygital really mean? A conceptual introduction to the phygital customer experience (PH-CX) framework. *Journal of Strategic Marketing*, 10–18. doi:10.1080 /0965254X.2022.2059775

Baudrillard, J. (1998). *The consumer society: Myths and structures.* Sage. doi:10.4135/9781526401502

Baudrillard, J. (2010). *Simulacra and Simulation* (S. F. Glaser, Trans.). The University of Michigan Press.

Bauman, Z. (2001). *The Individualized Society*. Polity Press.

Bauman, Z. (2007). *Liquid times: Living in an Age of Uncertainty*. Polity Press.

Bauman, Z. (2008). *The art of life*. Polity Press.

Bauman, Z. (2013). *Liquid modernity*. John Wiley & Sons.

Becker, E. (1973). *The denial of death*. Free Press.

Begley, S., Coggins, B., Green, C., Hamdan, J., Kuijpers, D., & Laizet, F. (2023). Retail reset: A new playbook for retail leaders. *The McKinsey Quarterly.*

Belk, R. (2014). You are what you can access: Sharing and collaborative consumption online. *Journal of Business Research, 67*(8), 1595–1600. doi:10.1016/j.jbusres.2013.10.001

Belk, R. (2020). Resurrecting marketing. *AMS Review, 10*(3), 168–171. doi:10.1007/s13162-020-00182-9

Belk, R. W. (1985). Materialism: Trait aspects of living in the material world. *The Journal of Consumer Research, 12*(3), 265–280. doi:10.1086/208515

Belz, F., & Peattie, K. J. (2013). *Sustainability marketing: A global perspective* (2nd ed.). Wiley.

Bendapudi, N., & Leone, R. P. (2003). Psychological implications of customer participation in co-production. *Journal of Marketing, 67*(1), 14–28. doi:10.1509/jmkg.67.1.14.18592

Beretta, E., Miniero, G., & Ricotta, F. (2021). Consumers' journey between liquid and solid consumption. *Sustainability (Basel), 13*(24), 13730. doi:10.3390/su132413730

Berlyne, D. E. (1951). Attention, perception and behavior theory. *Psychological Review, 58*(2), 137–146. doi:10.1037/h0058364 PMID:14834296

Bernard, M., & Parker, L. (2021, May 24). *The effect of conscious consumerism on purchasing behaviours: the example of greenwashing in the cosmetics industry.* Academic Press.

Compilation of References

Berne-Manero, C., & Marzo-Navarro, M. (2020). Exploring how influencer and relationship marketing serve corporate sustainability. *Sustainability (Basel), 12*(11), 1–19. doi:10.3390/su12114392

Bertacchini, F., Bilotta, E., & Pantano, P. (2017). Shopping with a robotic companion. *Computers in Human Behavior, 77,* 382–395. doi:10.1016/j.chb.2017.02.064

Bezençon, V., & Blili, S. (2011). Segmenting the market through the determinants of involvement: The case of fair trade. *Psychology and Marketing, 28*(7), 682–708. doi:10.1002/mar.20407

Bhalla, G., & Lin, L. Y. S. (1987). Cross-cultural marketing research: A discussion of equivalence issues and measurement strategies. *Psychology and Marketing, 4*(4), 275–285.

Bhandari, R., Singer, M., & van der Scheer, H. (2014). Using Marketing Analytics to Drive Superior Growth. *The McKinsey Quarterly.*

Binninger, A. S., Ourahmoune, N., & Robert, I. (2015). Collaborative Consumption And Sustainability: A Discursive Analysis Of Consumer Representations And Collaborative Website Narratives. *Journal of Applied Business Research, 31*(3), 969–986. doi:10.19030/jabr.v31i3.9229

Bitner, M. J. (1992). Servicescapes: The impact of physical surroundings on customers and employees. *Journal of Marketing, 56*(2), 57–71. doi:10.1177/002224299205600205

Blackburn, R., Leviston, Z., Walker, I., & Schram, A. (2023). Could a minimalist lifestyle reduce carbon emissions and improve wellbeing? A review of minimalism and other low consumption lifestyles. *Wiley Interdisciplinary Reviews: Climate Change, 865,* e865. Advance online publication. doi:10.1002/wcc.865

Black, I. R., & Cherrier, H. (2010). Anti-consumption as part of living a sustainable lifestyle: Daily practices, contextual motivations and subjective values. *Journal of Consumer Behaviour, 9*(6), 437–453. doi:10.1002/cb.337

Blackshaw, T. (2016). Bauman on consumerism–living the market-mediated life. In *The Sociology of Zygmunt Bauman* (2nd ed., pp. 117–136). Routledge.

Blake, D. (2020). *Covid-19 has almost doubled e-commerce sales.* Available. https://insideretail.co.nz/2020/04/22/covid-19-has-almost-doubled-e-commerce-sales/

Błoński, K., & Witek, J. (2019). Minimalism in consumption. *Annales Universitatis Mariae Curie-Skłodowska, Sectio H – Oeconomia, 53*(2), 7. doi:10.17951/h.2019.53.2.7-15

Bloomberg. J. (2018). Digitization, digitalization, and digital transformation: confuse them at your peril. *Forbes.* https://moniquebabin.com/wp content/uploads/articulate_ uploads/Going Digital4/story_content/external_files /Digitization% 20Digitalization %20and% 20Digital%20 Transformation%20Confusion.pdf

Böhm, E., Eggert, A., Garnefeld, I., Holzmüller, H. H., Schaefers, T., Steinhoff, L., & Woisetschläger, D. M. (2022). Exploring the Customer Journey of Voice Commerce: A Research Agenda. *SMR-Journal of Service Management Research, 6*(4), 216–231. doi:10.5771/2511-8676-2022-4-216

Boldrini, J. C. (2017). Co-creation of value in a collaborative innovation project: a case of transition towards the circular economy 1. *Innovations*, (0).

Bolton, R. N. (2020). First steps to creating high impact theory in marketing. *AMS Review*, *10*(3), 172–178. doi:10.1007/s13162-020-00181-w

Bolton, R., & Saxena-Iyer, S. (2009). Interactive services: A framework, synthesis and research directions. *Journal of Interactive Marketing*, *23*(1), 91–104. doi:10.1016/j.intmar.2008.11.002

Bond, M. H., & Forgas, J. P. (1984). Linking person perception to behavior intention across cultures: The role of cultural collectivism. *Journal of Cross-Cultural Psychology*, *15*(3), 337–352. doi:10.1177/0022002184015003006

Botsman, R., & Rogers, R. (2010). *What's mine is yours. The rise of collaborative consumption.* Penguin Press.

Botts, M. (2021). Understanding intercultural online communication via cultural tendencies. In S. Batuk Ünlü & A. Özer Torgalöz (Eds.), Remote and Hybrid Working: Variants, Determinants, Outcomes (pp. 241–262). Peter Lang. doi: 10.3726/b19135

Bougen, P. D., & Young, J. J. (2012). Fair value accounting: Simulacra and simulation. *Critical Perspectives on Accounting*, *23*(4-5), 390–402. doi:10.1016/j.cpa.2011.05.004

Boujbel, L., & D'Astous, A. (2012). Voluntary simplicity and life satisfaction: Exploring the mediating role of consumption desires. *Journal of Consumer Behaviour*, *11*(6), 487–494. doi:10.1002/cb.1399

Bourlakis, M., Papagiannidis, S., & Li, F. (2009). Retail spatial evolution: Paving the way from traditional to metaverse retailing. *Electronic Commerce Research*, *9*(1-2), 135–148. doi:10.1007/s10660-009-9030-8

Boyd, D. (2021). A critical inquiry into the hyperreality of digitalization in construction. *Construction Management and Economics*, *39*(7), 549–564. doi:10.1080/01446193.2021.1904515

Braig, B. M., & Witt, H. (2023, June 19). Developing empathy as a strategic and tactical skill in the context of innovating for transgender consumers. *Marketing Education Review*, 1–17. doi:10.1080/10528008.2023.2226124

Brasel, S. A., & Gips, J. (2014). Tablets, touchscreens, and touchpads: How varying touch interfaces trigger psychological ownership and endowment. *Journal of Consumer Psychology*, *24*(2), 226–233. doi:10.1016/j.jcps.2013.10.003

Brassington, F., & Pettitt, S. (2003). *Principles of Marketing* (3rd ed.). Financial Times.

Briassoulis, D., Pikasi, A., & Hiskakis, M. (2021). Recirculation potential of post-consumer/industrial bio-based plastics through mechanical recycling-Techno-economic sustainability criteria and indicators. *Polymer Degradation & Stability*, *183*, 109217. doi:10.1016/j.polymdegradstab.2020.109217

Compilation of References

Bridle, J. (2018). *New Dark Age: Technology and the End of the Future*. Verso Books.

Brown, R. (2017). Location-based marketing: the pitfalls and promise of retail campaigns. *Mobile Marketer*. Available from: https://www.mobilemarketer.com/news/location-based-marketing-the-pitfalls-and-promise-of-retail-campaigns/440927/

Brown, S. (1997). Marketing science in a postmodern world: Introduction to the special issue. *European Journal of Marketing*, *31*(3/4), 167–182. doi:10.1108/03090569710162308

Brown, S. (1999a). Postmodernism: the end of marketing. In D. Brownlie, M. Saren, R. Wensley, & R. Whittington (Eds.), *Rethinking Marketing: towards critical marketing accountings* (pp. 27–57). Sage. doi:10.4135/9781446280058.n3

Brown, S. (1999b). Retro-marketing: Yesterday's tomorrows, today! *Marketing Intelligence & Planning*, *17*(7), 363–376. doi:10.1108/02634509910301098

Brown, S., Bell, J., & Carson, D. (1996). *Marketing apocalypse: eschatology, escapology and the illusion of the end* (Vol. 2). Psychology Press.

Bueno-Ravel, L., & Gueudet, G. (2014). *Quelles ressources pour les professeurs des écoles et leurs formateurs? Apports de la recherche en didactique. In Conférence au 41e colloque Copirelem, 18-20 June*. Mont de Marsan.

Burroughs, J. E., & Rindfleisch, A. (2002). Materialism and Well-Being: A Conflicting Values Perspective. *The Journal of Consumer Research*, *29*(3), 348–370. doi:10.1086/344429

Caboni, F., & Hagberg, J. (2019). Augmented reality in retailing: A review of features, applications and value. *International Journal of Retail & Distribution Management*, *47*(11), 1125–1140. doi:10.1108/IJRDM-12-2018-0263

Çalış Duman, M. (2022). Toplum 5.0: İnsan odaklı dijital dönüşüm. *Sosyal Siyaset Konferansları Dergisi*, *82*, 309–336. doi:10.26650/jspc.2022.82.1008072

Çalışkan, G., & Erdoğan, Y. (2023). Marketing 5.0. In The Essentials of Today's Marketing (pp. 87-102). Efe Akademi.

Caliskan, A. (2019). Applying the Right Relationship Marketing Strategy through Big Five Personality Traits. *Journal of Relationship Marketing*, *18*(3), 196–215. doi:10.1080/1533266 7.2019.1589241

Cannavò, A., Kapralos, B., Seinfeld, S., Prattlcò, F. G., & Zhang, C. (2023). *IEEE VR 2023 Workshops: Workshop: 3D Reconstruction, Digital Twinning, and Simulation for Virtual Experiences (ReDigiTS 2023)*. Paper presented at the 2023 IEEE Conference on Virtual Reality and 3D User Interfaces Abstracts and Workshops (VRW).

Carney, L., & Déméné, C. (2022). Towards patterns of responsible consumption and production: An exploration of do-it-yourself practitioners through motivations, designs, and manufacturing processes. *Journal of Desert Research*, *20*(3), 179–208.

Castillo, J. (2017). *The Relationship between Big Five Personality Traits*. Customer Empowerment and Customer Satisfaction in the Retail Industry.

Cayla, J., & Arnould, E. J. (2008, December). A Cultural Approach to Branding in the Global Marketplace. *Journal of International Marketing*, *16*(4), 86–112. doi:10.1509/jimk.16.4.86

Chaffey, D., & Ellis-Chadwick, F. (2015). *Digital Marketing* (6th ed.). Pearson.

Chakrabarti, A., & Chaudhuri, A. K. (2017). Blockchain and its scope in retail. *International Research Journal of Engineering and Technology*, *4*(7), 3053–3056.

Chandrasekar, K. S., & Raj, R. V. (2013, July 1). *Family and Consumer behaviour*. ResearchGate. https://www.researchgate.net/publication/331319721_Family_and_Consumer_behaviour

Chatzidakis, A., & Lee, M. S. W. (2013). Anti-Consumption as the Study of Reasons against. *Journal of Macromarketing*, *33*(3), 190–203. doi:10.1177/0276146712462892

Chaveesuk, S., Khalid, B., & Chaiyasoonthorn, W. (2021). Digital payment system innovations: A marketing perspective on intention and actual use in the retail sector. *Innovative Marketing*, *17*(3), 109–123. doi:10.21511/im.17(3).2021.09

Cheah, J. H., Lim, X. J., Ting, H., Liu, Y., & Quach, S. (2022). Are privacy concerns still relevant? Revisiting consumer behavior in omnichannel retailing. *Journal of Retailing and Consumer Services*, *65*, 102242. Advance online publication. doi:10.1016/j.jretconser.2020.102242

Cheek, N. N., & Schwartz, B. (2016). On the meaning and measurement of maximization. *Judgment and Decision Making*, *11*(2), 126–146. doi:10.1017/S1930297500007257

Cheng, C., Eagan, J. T., & Yurko, A. (2022). ChicagoLand Popcorn®—Examining Online Retailer Nexus Following Wayfair Using Data Visualization and Robotics Process Automation. *Journal of Emerging Technologies in Accounting*, *19*(1), 133–164. doi:10.2308/JETA-2020-044

Cheng, H., Kotler, P., & Lee, N. R. (2011). *Social marketing for public health. The Handbook of Persuasion and Social Marketing*. Jones and Bartlett Publishers.

Chen, S., Kou, S., & Lv, L. (2023). Stand out or fit in: Understanding consumer minimalism from a social comparison perspective. *Journal of Business Research*, *170*, 114307. doi:10.1016/j.jbusres.2023.114307

Chen, W., & Liu, J. (2023). When less is more: Understanding consumers' responses to minimalist appeals. *Psychology and Marketing*, *40*(10), 2151–2162. doi:10.1002/mar.21869

Cherrier, H. (2009). Anti-consumption discourses and consumer-resistant identities. *Journal of Business Research*, *62*(2), 181–190. doi:10.1016/j.jbusres.2008.01.025

Cherrier, H., Black, I. R., & Lee, M. (2011). Intentional non-consumption for sustainability: Consumer resistance and/or anti-consumption? *European Journal of Marketing*, *45*(11/12), 1757–1767. doi:10.1108/03090561111167397

Compilation of References

Cheung, M. L., Pires, G. D., Rosenberger, P. J. III, Leung, W. K., & Ting, H. (2021). Investigating the role of social media marketing on value co-creation and engagement: An empirical study in China and Hong Kong. *Australasian Marketing Journal*, *29*(2), 118–131. doi:10.1016/j.ausmj.2020.03.006

Chidlow, A., Plakoyiannaki, E., & Welch, C. (2014). Translation in cross-language international business research: Beyond equivalence. *Journal of International Business Studies*, *45*(5), 562–582. doi:10.1057/jibs.2013.67

Chin, J. H., & Mansori, S. (2018). Social marketing and public health: A literature review. *Journal of Marketing Management and Consumer Behavior*, *2*(2), 48–66.

Chohan, R., & Paschen, J. (2021). What marketers need to know about non-fungible tokens (NFTs). *Business Horizons*, *66*(1), 43–50. doi:10.1016/j.bushor.2021.12.004

Chong, T., Yu, T., Keeling, D. I., & de Ruyter, K. (2021). AI-chatbots on the services frontline addressing the challenges and opportunities of agency. *Journal of Retailing and Consumer Services*, *63*, 102735. doi:10.1016/j.jretconser.2021.102735

Chopik, W. J., & Edelstein, R. S. (2014). Death of a salesman: Webpage-based manipulations of mortality salience. *Computers in Human Behavior*, *31*, 94–99. doi:10.1016/j.chb.2013.10.022

Christodoulides, G., Michaelidou, N., & Argyriou, E. (2012). Cross-national differences in e-WOM influence. *European Journal of Marketing*, *46*(11/12), 1689–1707. doi:10.1108/03090561211260040

Chu, S.-C., Chen, H.-T., & Gan, C. (2020). Consumers' engagement with corporate social responsibility (CSR) communication in social media: Evidence from China and the United States. *Journal of Business Research*, *110*, 260–271. doi:10.1016/j.jbusres.2020.01.036

Clingingsmith, D., & Sheremeta, R. M. (2018). Status and the demand for visible goods: Experimental evidence on conspicuous consumption. *Experimental Economics*, *21*(4), 877–904. doi:10.1007/s10683-017-9556-x

Coba, L., Zanker, M., Rook, L., & Symeonidis, P. (2018). Decision making of maximizers and satisficers based on collaborative explanations. *arXiv preprint arXiv*:1805.11537.

Colicev, A., Malshe, A., Pauwels, K., & O'Connor, P. (2018). Improving consumer mindset metrics and shareholder value through social media: The different roles of owned and earned media. *Journal of Marketing*, *82*(1), 37–56. doi:10.1509/jm.16.0055

Cong, L. W., Li, B., & Zhang, Q. T. (2021). Internet of Things: Business Economics and Applications. *Review of Business*, *41*(1).

Consumer Behavior Archives. (n.d.). American Marketing Association. https://www.ama.org/topics/consumer-behavior/

Cooke, M., & Buckley, N. (2008). Web 2.0, social networks and the future of market research. *International Journal of Market Research*, *50*(2), 267–292. doi:10.1177/147078530805000208

Coren, S., Porac, C., & Ward, L. (2003). Sensation and perception. In D. K. Freedheim & I. B. Weiner (Eds.), Handbook of psychology: Vol. 1. *history of psychology* (pp. 85–108). John Wiley & Sons, Inc.

Cova, B. (1985). Beyond the market when the connection matters more than the good. *Beyond the market when the link matters more than the good*, 1-174.

Cova, B. (2008). Consumer made: quand le consommateur devient producteur. Décisions Marketing, 19–27.

Cova, B., Ezan, P., & Fuschillo, G. (2013). Zoom sur l'autoproduction du consommateur. *Revue Française de Gestion*, *5*(234), 115–133. doi:10.3166/rfg.234.115-133

Cova, B., Maclaran, P., & Bradshaw, A. (2013). *Rethinking consumer culture theory from the postmodern to the communist horizon. In Marketing Theory*. SAGE Publishing. doi:10.1177/1470593113477890

Cozannet, N., Rieper, H., & Gurgoz, Y. (2007). *Corporate Social Responsibility in Turkey: Overview and Perspectives*. Working Paper 55, Agence Française de Développement.

Crespo, C. F., Ferreira, A. G., & Cardoso, R. M. (2022, January 23). *The influence of storytelling on the consumer–brand relationship experience*. Journal of Marketing Analytics. doi:10.1057/s41270-021-00149-0

Crolla, K., & Goepel, G. (2022). Entering hyper-reality:"Resonance-in-sight," a mixed-reality art installation. *Frontiers in Virtual Reality*, *3*, 1044021. doi:10.3389/frvir.2022.1044021

Cunow, S., Desposato, S., Janusz, A., & Sells, C. (2021). Less is more: The paradox of choice in voting behavior. *Electoral Studies*, *69*(1), 102230. doi:10.1016/j.electstud.2020.102230

Curot, J., Valton, L., Denuelle, M., Vignal, J.-P., Maillard, L., Pariente, J., Trébuchon, A., Bartolomei, F., & Barbeau, E. J. (2018). Déjà-rêvé: Prior dreams induced by direct electrical brain stimulation. *Brain Stimulation*, *11*(4), 875–885. doi:10.1016/j.brs.2018.02.016 PMID:29530448

Curtis, A. (2002). *The Century of the Self*. Full Adam Curtis Documentary.

Czech, S. (2016). Choice overload paradox and public policy design. The case of swedish pension. *Equilibrium*, *11*(3), 559–584. doi:10.12775/EQUIL.2016.025

Dabholkar, P. A. (1996). Consumer evaluations of new technology-based self-service options: An investigation of alternative models of service quality. *International Journal of Research in Marketing*, *13*(1), 29–51. doi:10.1016/0167-8116(95)00027-5

Dagher, G. K., & Itani, O. (2014). Factors influencing green purchasing behavior: Empirical evidence from the Lebanese consumers. *Journal of Consumer Behaviour*, *13*(3), 188–195. doi:10.1002/cb.1482

Compilation of References

Dang, A., & Raska, D. (2022). National cultures and their impact on electronic word of mouth: A systematic review. *International Marketing Review*, *39*(5), 1182–1225. doi:10.1108/IMR-12-2020-0316

Dar-Nimrod, I., Rawn, C. D., Lehman, D. R., & Schwartz, B. (2009). The maximization paradox: The costs of seeking alternatives. *Personality and Individual Differences*, *46*(5-6), 631–635. doi:10.1016/j.paid.2009.01.007

Das, R., Kalia, S., & Kuijpers, D. (2023). Zero consumers': What they want and why it matters. *McKinsey*. https://www.mckinsey.com/industries/retail/our-insights/zero-consumers-what-they-want-and-why-it-matters#/

Davidson, M. P. (2013). *The consumerist manifesto: Advertising in postmodern times*. Routledge. doi:10.4324/9781315002491

Dawson, J. (2000). Retailing at century end: Some challenges for management and research. *International Review of Retail, Distribution and Consumer Research*, *10*(2), 119–148. doi:10.1080/095939600342325

de Mooij, M., & Hofstede, G. (2011). Cross-cultural consumer behavior: A review of research findings. *Journal of International Consumer Marketing*, *23*(3-4), 181–192.

De Regt, A., & Barnes, S. J. (2019). V-commerce in retail: nature and potential impact. *Augmented reality and virtual reality: The power of AR and VR for business*, 17-25. doi:10.1007/978-3-030-06246-0_2

Degryse, C. (2016). *Social impacts of the digitalization of the economy*. Box.

Deighton, J. A., Mela, C. F., & Moorman, C. (2021). Marketing thinking and doing. *Journal of Marketing*, *85*(1), 1–6. doi:10.1177/0022242920977093

Del Chiappa, G., Serravalle, F., & Viassone, M. (2019). Perceiving a haptic experience: how augmented reality could increase willingness to buy without physically touching products. In Atti del XVI Convegno annuale della Società Italiana di Marketing. Marketing 4.0: le sfide della multicanalità (pp. 1-6). Academic Press.

Deloitte Insights. (2022). *2022 Global Marketing Trends, Thriving through customer centricity*. https://www2.deloitte.com/content/dam/insights/articles/us164911_gmt_2022_master/DI_2022-Global-Marketing-Trends.pdf

Deloitte. (2017). *Disruptions in Retail through Digital Transformation Reimagining the Store of the Future*. https://www2.deloitte.com /content/dam/Deloitte/in/Documents/CIP/in-cip-disruptions-in-retail-noexp. pdf

Dennis, C., Brakus, J., & Alamanos, E. (2013). The wallpaper matters: Digital signage as customer-experience provider at the Harrods (London, UK) department store. *Journal of Marketing Management*, *29*(3-4), 338–355. doi:10.1080/0267257X.2013.766628

Dijksterhuis, A., & Bargh, J. A. (2001). The perception-behavior expressway: Automatic effects of social perception on social behavior. *Advances in Experimental Social Psychology, 33*, 1–40. doi:10.1016/S0065-2601(01)80003-4

Doğa İçin Çal. (2023). *Doğa İçin Çal.* https://www.youtube.com/@dogaicincal/about

Donthu, N., Kumar, S., Pattnaik, D., & Lim, W. M. (2021). A bibliometric retrospection of marketing from the lens of psychology: Insights from Psychology & Marketing. *Psychology and Marketing, 38*(5), 834–865. doi:10.1002/mar.21472

Dopierala, R. (2017). Minimalism – a new mode of consumption? *Przegląd Socjologiczny, 66*(4), 67–83. doi:10.26485/PS/2017/66.4/4

Dos Remedios, L. (2023). The influence of the Metaverse on Brand Management: A study. *Communities, 2*(2), 5.

Douglas, S. P., & Craig, C. S. (2007). Collaborative and iterative translation: An alternative approach to back translation. *Journal of International Marketing, 15*(1), 30–43. doi:10.1509/jimk.15.1.030

Drinkwater, K. G., Denovan, A., & Dagnall, N. (2020). Lucid Dreaming, Nightmares, and Sleep Paralysis: Associations With Reality Testing Deficits and Paranormal Experience/Belief. *Frontiers in Psychology, 11*, 11. doi:10.3389/fpsyg.2020.00471 PMID:32256437

Du, J., Zhu, Q., Shi, Y., Wang, Q., Lin, Y., & Zhao, D. (2020). Cognition digital twins for personalized information systems of smart cities: Proof of concept. *Journal of Management Engineering, 36*(2), 04019052. doi:10.1061/(ASCE)ME.1943-5479.0000740

Dunning, D. (2007, October). Self-Image Motives and Consumer Behavior: How Sacrosanct Self-Beliefs Sway Preferences in the Marketplace. *Journal of Consumer Psychology, 17*(4), 237–249. doi:10.1016/S1057-7408(07)70033-5

Duong, T. T.-T., Ngo, L. V., Surachartkumtonkun, J., Tran, M. D., & Northey, G. (2023). Less is more! A pathway to consumer's transcendence. *Journal of Retailing and Consumer Services, 72*, 103294. doi:10.1016/j.jretconser.2023.103294

Đurđević, N., Labus, A., Barać, D., Radenković, M., & Despotović-Zrakić, M. (2022). An approach to assessing shopper acceptance of beacon triggered promotions in smart retail. *Sustainability (Basel), 14*(6), 3256. doi:10.3390/su14063256

Durif, F., Arcand, M., Ertz, M., & Connolly, M. (2017). *Kijiji secondhand economy index: 2017 report.* http://secondhandeconomy.kijiji.ca/

Durif, F., Arcand, M., Ertz, M., & Connolly, M. (2018). *Kijiji secondhand economy index: 2018 report.* https://www.kijiji.ca/kijijicentral/app/uploads/2016/08/Kijiji-Index-Report-2018_EN_Final_web-2.pdf

Compilation of References

Durif, F., Arcand, M., Tedds, L., Boivin, C., & Ertz, M. (2016b). *Kijiji secondhand economy index: 2016 report*. https://www.kijiji.ca/kijijicentral/app/uploads/2016/08/Kijiji-Index-Report-2016-1.pdf

Durif, F., Ertz, M., & Bigot, A. (2016a). Collaborative economy: towards a new socio-economic model - Clé Vie Numérique. In A. Poitras (Ed.), *The State of Quebec 2016* (pp. 95–101). Éditions du Boréal.

Edelman. (2021). Edelman Trust Barometer Special Report 2021. *Trust the New Brand Equity*, 7-15. https://www.edelman.com/sites/g/files/aatuss191/files/2021-06/2021%20Edelman%20Trust%20Barometer%20Specl%20Report%20Trust%20The%20New%20Brand%20Equity.pdf

El Saddik, A., Laamarti, F., & Alja'Afreh, M. (2021). The potential of digital twins. *IEEE Instrumentation & Measurement Magazine*, *24*(3), 36–41. doi:10.1109/MIM.2021.9436090

Elliott, A. (Ed.). (2019). *Routledge Handbook of Identity Studies* (2nd ed.). Taylor & Francis. doi:10.4324/9781315626024

Erdeniz, B., Tekgün, E., Menteş, Ö., Çoban, A., Bilge, S., & Serin, E. K. (2022). Supplemental Material for Bodily Self-Consciousness in Dreams Questionnaire (BSD-Q) and Its Relation to Waking Dissociative Experiences. *Dreaming*.

Erragcha, N., & Romdhane, V. (2014). New Faces of Marketing In The Era of The Web: From Marketing 1.0 To Marketing 3.0. *Journal of Research in Marketing*, *2*(2), 137–142. doi:10.17722/jorm.v2i2.46

Ertz, M. (2020). Collaborative consumption, a buzzword that has gone conceptual: Three shades of the sharing economy. *Oikonomics*, *14*(14), 1–14. doi:10.7238/o.n14.2011

Ertz, M. (forthcoming). The metaconsumer: Beyond the consumer. *International Review of Retail, Distribution and Consumer Research*.

Ertz, M., & Durif, F. (2017). Definition of collaborative consumption and associated concepts. In A. Decrop (Ed.), *Collaborative consumption: Issues and challenges of the new sharing society* (pp. 33–54). De Boeck. doi:10.3917/dbu.decro.2017.01.0031

Ertz, M., Durif, F., & Arcand, M. (2017b). Life after death? Study of goods multiple lives practices. *Journal of Consumer Marketing*, *34*(2), 108–118. doi:10.1108/JCM-07-2015-1491

Ertz, M., Durif, F., & Arcand, M. (2018a). Business at the fingertips of consumers: A scale for measuring resale motivations in online settings. *International Review of Retail, Distribution and Consumer Research*, *28*(1), 92–114. doi:10.1080/09593969.2017.1334692

Ertz, M., Durif, F., & Arcand, M. (2019). A conceptual perspective on collaborative consumption. *AMS Review*, *9*(1-2), 27–41. doi:10.1007/s13162-018-0121-3

Ertz, M., Durif, F., Lecompte, A., & Boivin, C. (2018b). Does "sharing" mean "socially responsible consuming"? Exploration of the relationship between collaborative consumption and socially responsible consumption. *Journal of Consumer Marketing*, *35*(4), 392–402. doi:10.1108/JCM-09-2016-1941

Ertz, M., Lecompte, A., & Durif, F. (2017a). Dual roles of consumers: Towards an insight into collaborative consumption motives. *International Journal of Market Research*, *59*(6), 725–748. doi:10.2501/IJMR-2017-040

Ertz, M., & Quenum, G. G. Y. (forthcoming). Collaborative and creative consumption: A review. In K. Peattie, R. de Angelis, N. Koenig-Lewis, & C. Strong (Eds.), *The Routledge Companion to Marketing and Sustainability*. Routledge.

Ertz, M., & Sarigöllü, E. (2019). Assessing the potential of sustainable value chains in the collaborative economy. *Sustainability (Basel)*, *11*(2), 390. doi:10.3390/su11020390

European Commission. (2021). *Special Eurobarometer 508 on Values and Identities of EU citizens* (508 – Wave EB94.1). Publications Office of the European Union.

Evans, G. J. (2020). The Dream and the Reality. *Global Responsibility to Protect*, *12*(4), 363–365. doi:10.1163/1875-984X-20200006

Faulkner, D. (2022). Hyper-Reality: A Dangerous Modern Phenomenon. In Creative Business Education: Exploring the Contours of Pedagogical Praxis (pp. 185-198). Springer. doi:10.1007/978-3-031-10928-7_11

Faulkner, P., & Runde, J. (2011, July). The social, the material, and the ontology of non-material technological objects. In European Group for Organizational Studies (EGOS) Colloquium, Gothenburg (Vol. 985, pp. 4-8). Academic Press.

Ferguson, M. J., & Bargh, J. A. (2004). How social perception can automatically influence behavior. *Trends in Cognitive Sciences*, *8*(1), 33–39. doi:10.1016/j.tics.2003.11.004 PMID:14697401

Ferraz-Lorenzo, M. (2018). Modernity, postmodernity, hypermodernity and the ever uncertain (educational) future. *Educational Philosophy and Theory*, *50*(14), 1616–1617. doi:10.1080/00131857.2018.1461427

Firat, A. F. (1992). Postmodernism and the marketing organization. *Journal of Organizational Change Management*, *5*(1), 79–83. doi:10.1108/09534819210011006

Firat, A. F. (2022). Marketing and market. *Japan Marketing History Review*, *1*(1), 48–53.

Firat, A. F., & Dholakia, N. (2006). Theoretical and philosophical implications of postmodern debates: Some challenges to modern marketing. *Marketing Theory*, *6*(2), 123–162. doi:10.1177/1470593106063981

Firat, A. F., Dholakia, N., & Venkatesh, A. (1995). Marketing in a postmodern world. *European Journal of Marketing*, *29*(1), 40–56. doi:10.1108/03090569510075334

Compilation of References

Firat, A. F., & Shultz, C. J. (1997). From segmentation to fragmentation. *European Journal of Marketing*, *31*(3/4), 183–207. doi:10.1108/EUM0000000004321

Firat, A. F., & Shultz, C. J. II. (2001). Preliminary metric investigations into the nature of the "postmodern consumer". *Marketing Letters*, *12*(2), 189–203. doi:10.1023/A:1011173205199

Firat, A. F., & Venkatesh, A. (1993). Postmodernity: The age of marketing. *International Journal of Research in Marketing*, *10*(3), 227–249. doi:10.1016/0167-8116(93)90009-N

Firat, A. F., & Venkatesh, A. (1995). Liberatory postmodernism and the reenchantment of consumption. *The Journal of Consumer Research*, *22*(3), 239–267. doi:10.1086/209448

Fitzmaurice, J., & Comegys, C. (2006). Materialism and Social Consumption. *Journal of Marketing Theory and Practice*, *14*(4), 287–299. doi:10.2753/MTP1069-6679140403

Florence, E. S., Fleischman, D., Mulcahy, R., & Wynder, M. (2022). Message framing effects on sustainable consumer behaviour: A systematic review and future research directions for social marketing. *Journal of Social Marketing*, *12*(4), 623–652. doi:10.1108/JSOCM-09-2021-0221

Fournier, I. (2020). Environmental impact of overconsumption on the ecosystems of Quebec science fiction: "increase the level of wealth while respecting the environment" (Legault 2018). *The American Review of Canadian Studies*, *50*(3), 386–399. doi:10.1080/02722011.2020.1811584

Fransen, M. L., Arendsen, J., & Das, E. (2019). Consumer Culture as Worldview Defense. In *Handbook of Terror Management Theory* (pp. 485–512). Elsevier. doi:10.1016/B978-0-12-811844-3.00020-2

French, J., & Russell-Bennett, R. (2015). A hierarchical model of social marketing. *Journal of Social Marketing*, *5*(2), 139–159. doi:10.1108/JSOCM-06-2014-0042

Fucui, M., & Dumitrescu, L. (2018). From Marketing 1.0 To Marketing 4.0 – The Evolution Of The Marketing Concept In The Context Of The 21st Century. *International Conference Knowledge-Based Organization, 24*(2), 43-48.

Fukuda, T. (2023). *Simulacra. (Doctoral).* McGill University, Montr'eal, Qu'ebec.

Füller, J., Bartl, M., Ernst, H., & Mühlbacher, H. (2006). Community based innovation: How to integrate members of virtual communities into new product development. *Electronic Commerce Research*, *6*(1), 57–73. doi:10.1007/s10660-006-5988-7

Funkhouser, A. T., & Schredl, M. (2010). The frequency of déjà vu (déjà rêve) and the effects of age, dream recall frequency and personality factors. *International Journal of Dream Research*, *3*, 60–64.

Gardiner, B. (2020, June 18). *Why COVID-19 will end up harming the environment.* Science. https://www.nationalgeographic.com/science/article/why-covid-19-will-end-up-harming-the-environment

Gensollen, M. (2003). Informational assets and mediated communities. *Political Economy Review, 113*(9).

Georgantzis Garcia, D., Kipnis, E., Vasileiou, E., & Solomon, A. (2021). Consumption in the circular economy: Learning from our mistakes. *Sustainability (Basel), 13*(2), 601. doi:10.3390/su13020601

GFK. (2023). *Global retailer report 2023 executive summary.* https://www.gfk.com/state-of-tech-and-durables/global-retailer-report-2023-executive-summary

Ghatak, S., & Singh, S. (2019). Examining Maslow's hierarchy need theory in the social media adoption. *FIIB Business Review, 8*(4), 292–302. doi:10.1177/2319714519882830

Given, L. M. (2008). *The Sage Encyclopedia of Qualitative Research Methods.* Sage Publications, Inc. doi:10.4135/9781412963909

Givrad, S. (2016). Dream Theory and Science: A Review. *Psychoanalytic Inquiry, 36*(3), 199–213. doi:10.1080/07351690.2016.1145967

Gök, Ö. A. (2020). How does omnichannel transform consumer behavior? In Managing Customer Experiences in an Omnichannel World: Melody of Online and Offline Environments in the Customer Journey. Emerald Publishing Limited. doi:10.1108/978-1-80043-388-520201005

Gollnhofer, J. F., & Schouten, J. W. (2017). Complementing the Dominant Social Paradigm with Sustainability. *Journal of Macromarketing, 37*(2), 143–152. doi:10.1177/0276146717696892

Gong, S., Suo, D., & Peverelli, P. (2023). Maintaining the order: How social crowding promotes minimalistic consumption practice. *Journal of Business Research, 160*, 113768. doi:10.1016/j.jbusres.2023.113768

Graham, M. (2013). Geography/internet: Ethereal alternate dimensions of cyberspace or grounded augmented realities? *The Geographical Journal, 179*(2), 177–182. doi:10.1111/geoj.12009

Grandhi, B., Patwa, N., & Saleem, K. (2021). Data-driven marketing for growth and profitability. *EuroMed Journal of Business, 16*(4), 381–398. doi:10.1108/EMJB-09-2018-0054

Graves, P. (2013). *Consumer.ology. The Truth about Consumers and the Psychology of Shopping* (2nd ed.). Nicholas Brealey Publishing.

Greenberg, J., & Arndt, J. (2012). Terror Management Theory. In P. A. M. Van Lange, A. W. Kruglanski, & E. T. Higgins (Eds.), *Handbook of Theories of Social Psychology* (Vol. 1, pp. 398–415). SAGE Publications Ltd. doi:10.4135/9781446249215.n20

Greenberg, J., Solomon, S., & Pyszczynski, T. (1997). Terror Management Theory of Self-Esteem and Cultural Worldviews: Empirical Assessments and Conceptual Refinements. In Advances in Experimental Social Psychology (Vol. 29, pp. 61–139).. Elsevier. doi:10.1016/S0065-2601(08)60016-7

Compilation of References

Green, P. E., & Srinivasan, V. (1978). Conjoint analysis in consumer research: Issues and outlook. *The Journal of Consumer Research*, *5*(2), 103–123. doi:10.1086/208721

Grewal, D., Gauri, D. K., Das, G., Agarwal, J., & Spence, M. T. (2021). Retailing and emergent technologies. *Journal of Business Research*, *134*, 198–202. doi:10.1016/j.jbusres.2021.05.004

Grewal, D., Hulland, J., Kopalle, P., & Karahanna, E. (2020). The future of technology and marketing: A multidisciplinary perspective. *Journal of the Academy of Marketing Science*, *48*(1), 1–8. doi:10.1007/s11747-019-00711-4

Grewal, D., Iyer, G. R., & Levy, M. (2004). Internet retailing: Enablers, limiters and market consequences. *Journal of Business Research*, *57*(7), 703–713. doi:10.1016/S0148-2963(02)00348-X

Grewal, D., Lindsey-Mullikin, J., & Munger, J. (2004). Loyalty in e-tailing: A conceptual framework. *Journal of Relationship Marketing*, *2*(3-4), 31–49. doi:10.1300/J366v02n03_03

Grier, S., & Bryant, C. A. (2005). Social marketing in public health. *Annual Review of Public Health*, *26*(1), 319–339. doi:10.1146/annurev.publhealth.26.021304.144610 PMID:15760292

Grieves, M. (2015). *Digital Twin: Manufacturing Excellence through Virtual Factory Replication.* White Papers.

Guha, A., Grewal, D., Kopalle, P. K., Haenlein, M., Schneider, M. J., Jung, H., Moustafa, R., Hegde, D. R., & Hawkins, G. (2021). How artificial intelligence will affect the future of retailing. *Journal of Retailing*, *97*(1), 28–41. doi:10.1016/j.jretai.2021.01.005

Gupta, M. S. (2020). What is Digitization, Digitalization, and Digital Transformation? *ARC Advisory Group.* https://www.arcweb.com/blog/what-digitization-digitalization-digital-transformation

Gupta, S., & Ramachandran, D. (2021). Emerging market retail: transitioning from a product-centric to a customer-centric approach. *Journal of Retailing, 97*(4), 597-620. https://doi.org/.2021.01.008 doi:10.1016/j.jretai

Hagberg, J., Sundstrom, M., & Egels-Zandén, N. (2016). The digitalization of retailing: An exploratory framework. *International Journal of Retail & Distribution Management*, *44*(7), 694–712. doi:10.1108/IJRDM-09-2015-0140

Hainmueller, J., Hopkins, D. J., & Yamamoto, T. (2014). Causal inference in conjoint analysis: Understanding multidimensional choices via stated preference experiments. *Political Analysis*, *22*(1), 1–30. doi:10.1093/pan/mpt024

Hamari, J., Sjöklint, M., & Ukkonen, A. (2016). The sharing economy: Why people participate in collaborative consumption. *Journal of the Association for Information Science and Technology*, *67*(9), 2047–2059. doi:10.1002/asi.23552

Hamouda, M., & Gharbi, A. (2013). The Postmodern Consumer: An Identity Constructor? *International Journal of Marketing Studies*, *5*(2), 41–47. doi:10.5539/ijms.v5n2p41

Han, R., & Cheng, Y. (2020). The influence of norm perception on pro-environmental behavior: A comparison between the moderating roles of traditional media and social media. *International Journal of Environmental Research and Public Health*, *17*(19), 7164. doi:10.3390/ijerph17197164 PMID:33007908

Har, L. L., Rashid, U. K., Te Chuan, L., Sen, S. C., & Xia, L. Y. (2022). Revolution of retail industry: From perspective of retail 1.0 to 4.0. *Procedia Computer Science*, *200*, 1615–1625. doi:10.1016/j.procs.2022.01.362

Hassouneh, D., & Brengman, M. (2015). *Retailing in social virtual worlds: developing a typology of virtual store atmospherics*. Academic Press.

Hausen, J. E. (2019). Minimalist life orientations as a dialogical tool for happiness. *British Journal of Guidance & Counselling*, *47*(2), 168–179. doi:10.1080/03069885.2018.1523364

Hayes, O., & Kelliher, F. (2022). The emergence of B2B omnichannel marketing in the digital era: A systematic literature review. *Journal of Business and Industrial Marketing*, *37*(11), 2156–2168. doi:10.1108/JBIM-02-2021-0127

Hedström, P., & Stern, Ch. (2017). Rational Choice Theory. In B. S. Turner, Ch. Kyung-Sup, C. F. Epstein, P. Kivisto, J. M. Ryan, & W. Outhwaite (Eds.), *The Wiley-Blackwell Encyclopedia of Social Theory* (pp. 1925–1931). Wiley-Blackwell. doi:10.1002/9781118430873.est0305

Heinze, A., Fletcher, G., Rashid, T., & Cruz, A. (2017). *Digital and Social Media Marketing: A Results-Driven Approach*. Routledge Taylor and Francis Group.

Hellriegel, D., & Slocum, J. W. Jr. (2005). *Organizational Behavior*. Thomson Learning.

Helm, S., Serido, J., Ahn, S. Y., Ligon, V., & Shim, S. (2019). Materialist values, financial and pro-environmental behaviors, and well-being. *Young Consumers*, *20*(4), 264–284. doi:10.1108/YC-10-2018-0867

Heydari, E., Solhi, M., & Farzadkia, M. (2021). Determinants of sustainability in recycling of municipal solid waste: Application of community-based social marketing (CBSM). *Challenges in Sustainability*, *9*(1), 16–27. doi:10.12924/cis2021.09010016

Hobson, J. A. (1998). *The Dreaming Brain: How the Brain Creates both the Sense and Nonsense of Dreams*. Basic Books.

Hoehle, H., Aloysius, J. A., Chan, F., & Venkatesh, V. (2018). Customers' tolerance for validation in omnichannel retail stores: Enabling logistics and supply chain analytics. *International Journal of Logistics Management*, *29*(2), 704–722. doi:10.1108/IJLM-08-2017-0219

Hogberg, K. (2017). Challenges of Social Media Marketing – An Explorative International Study of Hotels. *International Journal of Technology Marketing*, *12*(2), 127–141. doi:10.1504/IJTMKT.2017.083372

Hokkanen, H., Walker, C., & Donnelly, A. (2020). Business model opportunities in brick and mortar retailing through digitalization. *Journal of Business Models*, *8*(3), 33–61.

Compilation of References

Hollinshead, M. (1996). Retailing: Historical patterns and Future Trends. *Plan Canada*, 12-18.

Holt, D. B. (1995). How Consumers Consume: A Typology of Consumption Practices. *The Journal of Consumer Research*, *22*(1), 1. doi:10.1086/209431

Hook, J. N., Hodge, A. S., Zhang, H., Van Tongeren, D. R., & Davis, D. E. (2023). Minimalism, voluntary simplicity, and well-being: A systematic review of the empirical literature. *The Journal of Positive Psychology*, *18*(1), 130–141. doi:10.1080/17439760.2021.1991450

Hopkins, J., & Turner, J. (2012). Go Mobile. John Wiley and Sons, Inc.

Hossain, M. M. (2022). Simulation and Simulacra in Aldous Huxley's Brave New World: A Baudrillardian Appraisal. *J-Lalite: Journal of English Studies*.

Howarth, C., Lane, M., & Slevin, A. (2022). *Addressing the Climate Crisis: Local Action in Theory and Practice*. Springer Nature. doi:10.1007/978-3-030-79739-3

Hoyer, W. D., Kroschke, M., Schmitt, B., Kraume, K., & Shankar, V. (2020). Transforming the customer experience through new technologies. *Journal of Interactive Marketing*, *51*(1), 57–71. doi:10.1016/j.intmar.2020.04.001

Hsieh, H.-F., & Shannon, S. E. (2005). Three approaches to qualitative content analysis. *Qualitative Health Research*, *15*(9), 1277–1288. doi:10.1177/1049732305276687 PMID:16204405

Hudders, L., De Jans, S., & De Veirman, M. (2021). The commercialization of social media stars: A literature review and conceptual framework on the strategic use of social media influencers. *International Journal of Advertising*, *40*(3), 327–375. doi:10.1080/02650487.2020.1836925

Hudders, L., & Lou, C. (2022). A new era of influencer marketing: Lessons from recent inquires and thoughts on future directions. *International Journal of Advertising*, *41*(1), 1–5. doi:10.108 0/02650487.2022.2031729

Huneke, M. E. (2005). The Face of the Un-Consumer: An Empirical Examination of the Practice of Voluntary Simplicity in the United States. *Psychology and Marketing*, *7*(22), 527–550. doi:10.1002/mar.20072

Hunt, S. D. (2020). Indigenous theory development in marketing: The foundational premises approach. *AMS Review*, *10*(1), 8–17. doi:10.1007/s13162-020-00165-w

Hüttel, A., Balderjahn, I., & Hoffmann, S. (2020). Welfare Beyond Consumption: The Benefits of Having Less. *Ecological Economics*, *176*, 106719. doi:10.1016/j.ecolecon.2020.106719

IBM. (2023). *What is a digital twin?* Retrieved from https://www.ibm.com/topics/what-is-a-digital-twin

Iglesias-Pradas, S., & Acquila-Natale, E. (2023). The future of E-commerce: Overview and prospects of multichannel and omnichannel retail. *Journal of Theoretical and Applied Electronic Commerce Research*, *18*(1), 656–667. doi:10.3390/jtaer18010033

İnci, B., Sancar, O., & Bostancı, S. H. (2017). Usage of health-themed public service announcements as a social marketing communication tool: A content analysis related to public service announcements in the Republic of Turkey, Ministry of Health's web site. *Marketing and Branding Research, 4*, 148–168. doi:10.33844/mbr.2017.60370

iSMA. (2023). *What is Social Marketing?* https://isocialmarketing.org/

Issock, P. B. I., Mpinganjira, M., & Roberts-Lombard, M. (2021). Investigating the relevance of the traditional marketing mix across different stages of change: Empirical evidence from household recycling. *Journal of Social Marketing, 11*(4), 489–506. doi:10.1108/JSOCM-11-2020-0221

Iyengar, S. (2010). *The Art of Choosing.* Little Brown.

Iyer, R., & Muncy, J. A. (2009). Purpose and object of anti-consumption. *Journal of Business Research, 62*(2), 160–168. doi:10.1016/j.jbusres.2008.01.023

Jackson, G., & Ahuja, V. (2016). Dawn of the digital age and the evolution of the marketing mix. *Journal of Direct, Data and Digital Marketing Practice, 17*(3), 170–186. doi:10.1057/dddmp.2016.3

Jacobson, J., & Harrison, B. (2022). Sustainable fashion social media influencers and content creation calibration. *International Journal of Advertising, 41*(1), 150–177. doi:10.1080/02650 487.2021.2000125

Jahnke, M. (Ed.). (2018). *Influencer Marketing.* Springer. doi:10.1007/978-3-658-20854-7

Jain, K., Bearden, J. N., & Filipowicz, A. (2013). Do maximizers predict better than satisficers? *Journal of Behavioral Decision Making, 26*(1), 41–50. doi:10.1002/bdm.763

Jain, V. K., Gupta, A., & Verma, H. (2023). Goodbye materialism: Exploring antecedents of minimalism and its impact on millennials well-being. *Environment, Development and Sustainability.* Advance online publication. doi:10.1007/s10668-023-03437-0 PMID:37363025

Jaiswal, S., & Singh, A. (2015). Customer Experience Management: A Paradigm Shift in e-Retailing. *VIMARSH - A Bi-Annual Peer-Reviewed Refereed Journal, 9*(2).

Janiszewski, C., Kuo, A., & Tavassoli, N. T. (2013). The influence of selective attention and inattention to products on subsequent choice. *The Journal of Consumer Research, 39*(6), 1258–1274. doi:10.1086/668234

Jans, L. (2021). Changing environmental behaviour from the bottom up: The formation of pro-environmental social identities. *Journal of Environmental Psychology, 73*, 101531. doi:10.1016/j.jenvp.2020.101531

Järvinen, J., & Karjaluoto, H. (2015). The use of Web analytics for digital marketing performance measurement. *Industrial Marketing Management, 50*, 117–127. doi:10.1016/j.indmarman.2015.04.009

Compilation of References

Jessen, A., Hilken, T., Chylinski, M., Mahr, D., Heller, J., Keeling, D. I., & de Ruyter, K. (2020). The playground effect: How augmented reality drives creative customer engagement. *Journal of Business Research*, *116*, 85–98. doi:10.1016/j.jbusres.2020.05.002

Jin, J., & Klatt, L.M. (2017). The second hand market for fashion products. *Green Fashion Retail*, 119-134.

Jin, P. (2023, September 13). *Research on Confirmation Bias and Its Influences on Purchase Decision-making*. Advances in Economics Management and Political Sciences. https://doi.org/ doi:10.54254/2754-1169/10/20230471

Jin, B., Kim, G., Moore, M., & Rothenberg, L. (2021). Consumer store experience through virtual reality: Its effect on emotional states and perceived store attractiveness. *Fashion and Textiles*, *8*(1), 1–21. doi:10.1186/s40691-021-00256-7

Jobber, D., & Ellis-Chadwick, F. (2016). *Principles and Practice of Marketing* (8th ed.). McGraw Hill Higher Education.

Johnson, M., & Barlow, R. (2021). Defining the Phygital Marketing Advantage. *Journal of Theoretical and Applied Electronic Commerce Research*, *16*(6), 2365–2385. doi:10.3390/ jtaer16060130

Jovin. (2023, June 6). The psychology of consumer behaviour: Understanding how customer make decision. *International Journal of Creative Research Thoughts, 11*.

Kaczorowska-Spychalska, D. (2019). How chatbots influence marketing. *Management*, *23*(1), 251–270. doi:10.2478/manment-2019-0015

Kahneman, D. (2011). *Thinking, Fast and Slow*. Farrar, Straus and Giroux.

Kamoonpuri, S. Z., & Sengar, A. (2023). Hi, May AI help you? An analysis of the barriers impeding the implementation and use of artificial intelligence-enabled virtual assistants in retail. *Journal of Retailing and Consumer Services*, *72*, 103258. doi:10.1016/j.jretconser.2023.103258

Kang, J., Martinez, C. M. J., & Johnson, C. (2021). Minimalism as a sustainable lifestyle: Its behavioral representations and contributions to emotional well-being. *Sustainable Production and Consumption*, *27*, 802–813. doi:10.1016/j.spc.2021.02.001

Kang, M. Y., Choi, Y., & Choi, J. (2019). The effect of celebrity endorsement on sustainable firm value: Evidence from the Korean telecommunications industry. *International Journal of Advertising*, *38*(4), 563–576. doi:10.1080/02650487.2019.1601910

Kasser, T. (2009). Psychological Need Satisfaction, Personal Well-Being, and Ecological Sustainability. *Ecopsychology*, *1*(4), 175–180. doi:10.1089/eco.2009.0025

Kastanakis, M. N., & Balabanis, G. (2015). Explaining Variation in Conspicuous Consumption: An Empirical Examination. In L. Robinson (Ed.), *Marketing Dynamism & Sustainability: Things Change, Things Stay the Same...* (pp. 248–248). Springer International Publishing. doi:10.1007/978-3-319-10912-1_81

Kaufmann, V., & Widmer, E. (2005). The acquisition of motility within families: State of the question and research hypotheses. *Spaces and Societies*, *120*(1), 199–217.

Kazancoglu, I., & Demir, B. (2021). Analysing flow experience on repurchase intention in e-retailing during COVID-19. *International Journal of Retail & Distribution Management*, *49*(11), 1571–1593. doi:10.1108/IJRDM-10-2020-0429

Keita, K., & Ebina, T. (2015). Paradox of choice and consumer nonpurchase behavior. *AI & Society*, *30*(2), 291–297. doi:10.1007/s00146-014-0546-7

Kemp, S. (2021). *Digital 2021: The Latest Insights into The State of Digital*. https://wearesocial.com/uk/blog/2021/01/digital-2021-the-latest-insights-into-the-state-of-digital/

Kemper, J. A., & Ballantine, P. W. (2019). What do we mean by sustainability marketing? *Journal of Marketing Management*, *35*(3-4), 277–309. doi:10.1080/0267257X.2019.1573845

Kemper, J. A., Hall, C., & Ballantine, P. (2019). Marketing and Sustainability: Business as Usual or Changing Worldviews? *Sustainability (Basel)*, *11*(3), 780. doi:10.3390/su11030780

Kenny, D., & Marshall, J. (2020). Contextual Marketing: The Real Business of the Internet. *Harvard Business Review*. https://hbr.org/2000/11/contextual-marketing-the-real-business-of-the-internet

Keymolen, E. (2013). Trust and technology in collaborative consumption. Why it is not just about you and me. *Bridging Distances in Technology and Regulation*, *135*, 135-150.

Khan, N. (2022). The cost of living crisis: How can we tackle fuel poverty and food insecurity in practice? *The British Journal of General Practice*, *72*(720), 330–331. doi:10.3399/bjgp22X719921 PMID:35773000

Khare, A., Chowdhury, T. G., & Morgan, J. (2021). Maximizers and satisficers: Can't choose and can't reject. *Journal of Business Research*, *135*(5), 731–748. doi:10.1016/j.jbusres.2021.07.008

Kida, T., Moreno, K. K., & Smith, J. F. (2010). Investment decision making: Do experienced decision makers fall prey to the paradox of choice? *Journal of Behavioral Finance*, *11*(1), 21–30. doi:10.1080/15427561003590001

Kilbourne, W. E., & LaForge, M. C. (2010). Materialism and its relationship to individual values. *Psychology and Marketing*, *27*(8), 780–798. doi:10.1002/mar.20357

Kim, J. (2020). Collaborative fashion consumption in the sharing economy: Philosophical and aesthetic perspectives. *Journal of Global Fashion Marketing*, *11*(3), 289–305. doi:10.1080/20932685.2020.1724815

Kim, K., & Miller, E. G. (2017). Vulnerable maximizers: The role of decision difficulty. *Judgment and Decision Making*, *12*(5), 516–526. doi:10.1017/S1930297500006537

Kirk, C. P., & Swain, S. D. (2018). Consumer psychological ownership of digital technology. *Psychological ownership and consumer behavior*, 69-90. doi:10.1007/978-3-319-77158-8_16

Compilation of References

Kishen, R., Upadhyay, S., Jaimon, F., Suresh, S., Kozlova, N., Bozhuk, S., ... Matchinov, V. A. (2021). Prospects for artificial intelligence implementation to design personalized customer engagement strategies. *Journal of Legal, Ethical and Regulatory Issues, 24*(1).

Kobayashi, T., Fukae, K., Imai, T., & Arai, K. (2022). *Digital Twin Agent for Super-Aged Society.* Paper presented at the 2022 IEEE International Conference on Consumer Electronics (ICCE). 10.1109/ICCE53296.2022.9730230

Ko, H., Cho, C.-H., & Roberts, M. S. (2005). Internet uses and gratifications: A structural equation model of interactive advertising. *Journal of Advertising, 34*(2), 57–70. doi:10.1080/00913367.2005.10639191

Koles, B., Wells, V., & Tadajewski, M. (2018). Compensatory consumption and consumer compromises: A state-of-the-art review. *Journal of Marketing Management, 34*(1–2), 96–133. doi:10.1080/0267257X.2017.1373693

Kotler, P. A. G. O. M., Armstrong, G., & Opresnik, M. O. (2021). Principles of Marketing (18e Global). Harlow: Pearson Education Limited.

Kotler, P., Kartajaya, H., & Setiawan, I. (2010). *Marketing 3.0.* John Wiley & Sons, Inc. doi:10.1002/9781118257883

Kotler, P., Kartajaya, H., & Setiawan, I. (2017). *Marketing 4.0.* John Wiley & Sons, Inc.

Kotler, P., Kartajaya, H., & Setiawan, I. (2021). *Marketing 5.0.* John Wiley & Sons, Inc.

Kotler, P., Kartajaya, H., & Setiawan, I. (2021). *Marketing 5.0: Technology For Humanity.* John Wiley & Sons.

Kotler, P., & Keller, K. (2017). *Marketing Management* (15th Global Edition). Pearson Education Limited.

Kotler, P., Roberto, N., & Lee, N. (2002). *Social Marketing: Improving the Quality of Life* (2nd ed.). Sage.

Kotler, P., & Zaltman, G. (1971). Social marketing: An approach to planned social change. *Journal of Marketing, 35*(3), 3–12. doi:10.1177/002224297103500302 PMID:12276120

Kozinets, R. V., Handelman, J. M., & Lee, M. S. W. (2010). Don't read this; or, who cares what the hell anti-consumption is, anyways? *Consumption Markets & Culture, 13*(3), 225–233. doi:10.1080/10253861003786918

Kritzinger, W., Karner, M., Traar, G., Henjes, J., & Sihn, W. (2018). Digital Twin in manufacturing: A categorical literature review and classification. *IFAC-PapersOnLine, 51*(11), 1016–1022. doi:10.1016/j.ifacol.2018.08.474

Kumar, S., Sharma, G., Kejriwal, N., Jain, S., Kamra, M., Singh, B., & Chauhan, V. K. (2014, April). *Remote retail monitoring and stock assessment using mobile robots. In 2014 IEEE international conference on technologies for practical robot applications (TePRA).* IEEE.

Kumar, V., Zhang, X., & Luo, A. (2014). Modeling customer opt-in and opt-out in a permission-based marketing context. *JMR, Journal of Marketing Research*, *51*(4), 403–419. doi:10.1509/jmr.13.0169

Kyrlitsias, C., & Michael-Grigoriou, D. (2022). Social interaction with agents and avatars in immersive virtual environments: A survey. *Frontiers in Virtual Reality*, *2*, 786665. doi:10.3389/frvir.2021.786665

Labrecque, L. I., vor dem Esche, J., Mathwick, C., Novak, T., & Hofacker, C. F. (2013). Consumer power: Evolution in the digital age. *Journal of Interactive Marketing*, *27*(4), 257–269. doi:10.1016/j.intmar.2013.09.002

Lahtinen, S., & Närvänen, E. (2020). Co-creating sustainable corporate brands: A consumer framing approach. *Corporate Communications*, *25*(3), 447–461. doi:10.1108/CCIJ-11-2019-0121

Lamberton, C. & Stephen, A. T. (2016). A thematic exploration of digital, social media, and mobile marketing: research evolution from 2000 to 2015 and an agenda for future inquiry. *Journal of Marketing, 80,* 146-172. doi:10.1509/jm.15.0415

Lapavitsas, C., Meadway, J., & Nicholls, D. (2023). *The Cost of Living Crisis: (and how to get out of it)*. Verso Books.

Laughlin, C. D. (2013). Dreaming and Reality: A Neuroanthropological Account. *International Journal of Transpersonal Studies*, *32*(1), 8. doi:10.24972/ijts.2013.32.1.64

Laville, É. (2009). *The company green: sustainable development changes business to change the world*. Pearson Education France.

Le Gall, M. (2002). From concern for the environment to sustainable consumption. *Proceedings of the 2nd congress on Marketing trends in Europe ESCP-EAP*, 25-26.

LeCun, Y., Bengio, Y., & Hinton, G. (2015). Deep learning. *Nature, 521*(7553), 436-444. doi:10.1038/nature14539

Lee, H., & Leonas, K. (2018). Consumer experiences, the key to survive in an omni-channel environment: Use of virtual technology. *Journal of Textile and Apparel, Technology and Management, 10*(3).

Lee, J. A., Sudarshan, S., Sussman, K. L., Bright, L. F., & Eastin, M. S. (2022). Why are consumers following social media influencers on Instagram? Exploration of consumers' motives for following influencers and the role of materialism. *International Journal of Advertising*, *41*(1), 78–100. doi:10.1080/02650487.2021.1964226

Lee, K. S., & Tan, S. J. (2003). E-retailing versus physical retailing: A theoretical model and empirical test of consumer choice. *Journal of Business Research*, *56*(11), 877–885. doi:10.1016/S0148-2963(01)00274-0

Lee, M. S. W. (2022a). Anti-consumption research: A foundational and contemporary overview. *Current Opinion in Psychology*, *45*, 101319. doi:10.1016/j.copsyc.2022.101319 PMID:35325808

Compilation of References

Lee, M. S. W., & Ahn, C. S. Y. (2016). Anti-consumption, Materialism, and Consumer Well-being. *The Journal of Consumer Affairs*, *50*(1), 18–47. doi:10.1111/joca.12089

Lee, M., Pant, A., & Ali, A. (2010). Does the individualist consume more? The interplay of ethics and beliefs that governs consumerism across cultures. *Journal of Business Ethics*, *93*(4), 567–581. doi:10.1007/s10551-009-0240-8

Lee, S. S., & Johnson, B. K. (2022). Are they being authentic? The effects of self-disclosure and message sidedness on sponsored post effectiveness. *International Journal of Advertising*, *41*(1), 30–53. doi:10.1080/02650487.2021.1986257

Leonard-Barton, D. (1981). Voluntary Simplicity Lifestyles and Energy Conservation. *The Journal of Consumer Research*, *8*(3), 243. doi:10.1086/208861

Leonhard, G. (2016). *Technology vs. Humanity: The Coming Clash Between Man and Machine.* FutureScapes.

Leung, C. H., & Yan Chan, W. T. (2020). Retail chatbots: The challenges and opportunities of conversational commerce. *Journal of Digital & Social Media Marketing*, *8*(1), 68–84.

Librová, H., Pelikán, V., Galčanová, L., & Kala, L. (2016). *Věrní a rozumní. Kapitoly o ekologické zpozdilosti* [The Faithful and the Reasonable: Chapters on Ecological Foolishness]. Masarykova univerzita.

Li, F., Larimo, J., & Leonidou, L. C. (2021). Social media marketing strategy: Definition, conceptualization, taxonomy, validation, and future agenda. *Journal of the Academy of Marketing Science*, *49*(1), 51–70. doi:10.1007/s11747-020-00733-3

Li, M., Hua, Y., & Zhu, J. (2021). From interactivity to brand preference: The role of social comparison and perceived value in a virtual brand community. *Sustainability (Basel)*, *13*(2), 625. doi:10.3390/su13020625

Lim, W. M. (2017). Inside the sustainable consumption theoretical toolbox: Critical concepts for sustainability, consumption, and marketing. *Journal of Business Research*, *78*, 69–80. doi:10.1016/j.jbusres.2017.05.001

Lin-Hi, N., & Blumberg, I. (2017). The power(lessness) of industry self-regulation to promote responsible labor standards: Insights from the Chinese toy industry. *Journal of Business Ethics*, *143*(4), 789–805. doi:10.1007/s10551-016-3075-0

Lin-Hi, N., & Blumberg, I. (2018). The link between (not) practicing CSR and corporate reputation: Psychological foundations and managerial implications. *Journal of Business Ethics*, *150*(1), 185–198. doi:10.1007/s10551-016-3164-0

Lipovetsky, G. (2007). Paradoxní štěstí [Paradoxal Happiness]. *Prostor.*

Littler, J. (2011). What's wrong with ethical consumption? In T. Lewis & E. Potter (Eds.), Ethical Consumption: A Critical Introduction (pp. 27–37). Routledge Taylor and Francis Group.

Liu, Y. J., Du, H., Niyato, D., Feng, G., Kang, J., & Xiong, Z. (2022). Slicing4Meta: An intelligent integration framework with multi-dimensional network resources for Metaverse-as-a-service in Web 3.0. *arXiv preprint arXiv:2208.06081*.

Liu, Y. (2023). How and why a touchscreen interface impacts psychological ownership and its downstream consequences. *Journal of Retailing and Consumer Services, 70*, 103182. doi:10.1016/j.jretconser.2022.103182

Liu, Z. L., Anderson, T. D., & Cruz, J. M. (2012). Consumer environmental awareness and competition in two-stage supply chains. *European Journal of Operational Research, 218*(3), 602–613. doi:10.1016/j.ejor.2011.11.027

Li, X., Zhao, X., & Pu, W. (2020). Measuring ease of use of mobile applications in e-commerce retailing from the perspective of consumer online shopping behaviour patterns. *Journal of Retailing and Consumer Services, 55*, 102093. doi:10.1016/j.jretconser.2020.102093

Lloyd, K., & Pennington, W. (2020). Towards a Theory of Minimalism and Wellbeing. *International Journal of Applied Positive Psychology, 5*(3), 121–136. doi:10.1007/s41042-020-00030-y

Loewenstein, G. F., & Prelec, D. (1993). Preferences for sequences of outcomes. *Psychological Review, 100*(1), 91–108. doi:10.1037/0033-295X.100.1.91

Loiacono, E. T., Watson, R. T., & Goodhue, D. L. (2002). WebQual: A measure of website quality. American Marketing Association. *Conference Proceedings, Suppl.2002 AMA Winter Educators' Conference, 13*, 432. https://www.proquest.com/scholarly-journals/webqual-measure-website-quality/docview/199486360/se-2

Louviere, J. J., Flynn, T. N., & Carson, R. T. (2010). Discrete choice experiments are not conjoint analysis. *Journal of Choice Modelling, 3*(3), 57–72. doi:10.1016/S1755-5345(13)70014-9

Loxton, M., Truskett, R., Scarf, B., Sindone, L., Baldry, G., & Zhao, Y. (2020). Consumer behaviour during crises: Preliminary research on how coronavirus has manifested consumer panic buying, herd mentality, changing discretionary spending and the role of the media in influencing behaviour. *Journal of Risk and Financial Management, 13*(8), 166. doi:10.3390/jrfm13080166

Luangrath, A. W., Peck, J., Hedgcock, W., & Xu, Y. (2022). Observing product touch: The vicarious haptic effect in digital marketing and virtual reality. *JMR, Journal of Marketing Research, 59*(2), 306–326. doi:10.1177/00222437211059540

Lury, C. (2011). *Consumer Culture* (2nd ed.). Polity Press.

Maartensson, H., & Loi, N. M. (2022). Exploring the relationships between risk perception, behavioural willingness, and constructive hope in pro-environmental behaviour. *Environmental Education Research, 28*(4), 600–613. doi:10.1080/13504622.2021.2015295

Mangham, L. J., Hanson, K., & McPake, B. (2009). How to do (or not to do). Designing a discrete choice experiment for application in a low-income country. *Health Policy and Planning, 24*(2), 151–158. doi:10.1093/heapol/czn047 PMID:19112071

Compilation of References

Manolică, A., Guță, A. S., Roman, T., & Dragăn, L. M. (2021). Is consumer overchoice a reason for decision paralysis? *Sustainability (Basel)*, *13*(11), 5920. doi:10.3390/su13115920

Mansell, R. (2005). Human Rights and Equity in Cyberspace. In M. Klang & A. Murray (Eds.), Human Rights in the Digital Age. Academic Press.

Marchand, A., De Coninck, P., & Walker, S. (2005). Responsible consumption: New perspectives in the fields of product design. *New Social Practices*, *18*(1), 39–56.

MariA. (2019). Voice Commerce:Understanding Shopping-Related Voice Assistants and their Effect on Brands. In *IMMAA Annual Conference*. Northwestern University in Qatar. doi:10.5167/uzh-197725

Markets and Markets. (2020). *Service robotics market*. Available at: https://www.marketsandmarkets.com/Market-Reports/service-robotics-market-681.html

Martineau, F., & Roult, R. (2021). L'art du flow et le développement spirituel dans la société hypermoderne. *Leisure/Loisir, 45*, 423 - 457.

Martin-Woodhead, A. (2022). Limited, considered and sustainable consumption: The (non) consumption practices of UK minimalists. *Journal of Consumer Culture*, *22*(4), 1012–1031. doi:10.1177/14695405211039608

Mary, P., & Ming-Ming, L. (2022). Minimalism Lifestyles Promote Well-Being: The New Paradigm. In A. Asmawi (Ed.), *Proceedings of the International Conference on Technology and Innovation Management (ICTIM 2022)* (*Vol. 228*, pp. 145–153). Atlantis Press International BV. 10.2991/978-94-6463-080-0_12

Masatlioglu, Y., & Suleymanov, E. (2021). Decision Making within a Product Network. *Economic Theory*, *71*(1), 185–209. doi:10.1007/s00199-019-01238-z

Matharu, M., Jain, R., & Kamboj, S. (2020). Understanding the impact of lifestyle on sustainable consumption behavior: A sharing economy perspective. *Management of Environmental Quality*, *32*(1), 20–40. doi:10.1108/MEQ-02-2020-0036

Mathur, P. (2019). Overview of Machine Learning in Retail. In *Machine Learning Applications Using Python*. Apress. doi:10.1007/978-1-4842-3787-8_7

Matte, J., Fachinelli, A. C., De Toni, D., Milan, G. S., & Olea, P. M. (2021). Relationship between minimalism, happiness, life satisfaction, and experiential consumption. *SN Social Sciences*, *1*(7), 166. doi:10.1007/s43545-021-00191-w

Mayol, A., & Staropoli, C. (2021). Giving consumers too many choices: A false good idea? A lab experiment on water and electricity tariffs. *European Journal of Law and Economics*, *51*(2), 383–410. doi:10.1007/s10657-021-09694-6

McDonald, S., Oates, C. J., Young, C. W., & Hwang, K. (2006). Toward sustainable consumption: Researching voluntary simplifiers. *Psychology and Marketing*, *23*(6), 515–534. doi:10.1002/mar.20132

McGinn, C. (2006). *The Power of Movies – How Screen and Mind Interact*. Pantheon.

McKenzie-Mohr, D. (2000). Fostering sustainable behavior through community-based social marketing. *The American Psychologist*, *55*(5), 531–537. doi:10.1037/0003-066X.55.5.531 PMID:10842434

Mcluhan, M. (1964). *Understanding Media: The Extensions of Man*. McGraw-Hill.

Meissner, M. (2019). Against accumulation: Lifestyle minimalism, de-growth and the present post-ecological condition. *Journal of Cultural Economics*, *12*(3), 185–200. doi:10.1080/17530 350.2019.1570962

Melnyk, V., Carrillat, F. A., & Melnyk, V. (2021, October 8). The Influence of Social Norms on Consumer Behavior: A Meta-Analysis. *Journal of Marketing*, *86*(3), 98–120. doi:10.1177/00222429211029199

Menegaki, A. N. (2012). A social marketing mix for renewable energy in Europe based on consumer stated preference surveys. *Renewable Energy*, *39*(1), 30–39. doi:10.1016/j.renene.2011.08.042

Merle, A., Chandon, J. L., & Roux, E. (2008). Understanding the perceived value of mass customization: The distinction between product value and experiential value of co-design. [English Edition]. *Recherche et Applications en Marketing*, *23*(3), 27–50. doi:10.1177/076737010802300301

Merle, A., Chandon, J. L., Roux, E., & Alizon, F. (2010). Perceived value of the mass-customized product and mass customization experience for individual consumers. *Production and Operations Management*, *19*(5), 503–514. doi:10.1111/j.1937-5956.2010.01131.x

Metin, E., Eröztürk, A., & Neyim, C. (2003). Solid waste management practices and review of recovery and recycling operations in Turkey. *Waste Management (New York, N.Y.)*, *23*(5), 425–432. doi:10.1016/S0956-053X(03)00070-9 PMID:12893015

Mittal, B. (2016). The maximizing consumer wants even more choices: How consumers cope with the marketplace of overchoice. *Journal of Retailing and Consumer Services*, *31*(6), 361–370. doi:10.1016/j.jretconser.2016.05.003

Mittal, M., & Manocha, S. (2023). Alexa! What is Voice Commerce?" Examining Consumer Behavior towards Voice Assistants. *International Management Review*, *19*(2).

Moeller, S., & Wittkowski, K. (2010). The burdens of ownership: Reasons for preferring renting. *Managing Service Quality*, *20*(2), 176–191. doi:10.1108/09604521011027598

Mohamed, K., & Bukhari, S. (2023). The Media in Metaverse; Baudrillard's Simulacra, Is Metaverse that Begins the Apocalypse? *International Journal of Communication and Media Science*, *10*(1), 14–22. doi:10.14445/2349641X/IJCMS-V10I1P102

Mondol, E. P. (2021). The impact of block chain and smart inventory system on supply chain performance at retail industry. *International Journal of Computations, Information and Manufacturing*, *1*(1). Advance online publication. doi:10.54489/ijcim.v1i1.30

Compilation of References

Morales, A. C., Amir, O., & Lee, L. (2017). Keeping it real in experimental research—Understanding when, where, and how to enhance realism and measure consumer behavior. *The Journal of Consumer Research, 44*(2), 465–476. doi:10.1093/jcr/ucx048

Morewedge, C. K., & Norton, M. I. (2009). When dreaming is believing: The (motivated) interpretation of dreams. *Journal of Personality and Social Psychology, 96*(2), 249–264. doi:10.1037/a0013264 PMID:19159131

Muñiz, A. M. Jr, & Schau, H. J. (2007). Vigilante marketing and consumer-created communications. *Journal of Advertising, 36*(3), 35–50. doi:10.2753/JOA0091-3367360303

Mustajbasic, A. (2018). *Introducing an E-Marketplace and Phygital Store to the Swiss Market: The Key Success Factors for the Fashion Industry in Switzerland.* Haute Ecole de Gestion de Genève, Bachelor Project.

Nadeem, W., Juntunen, M., Shirazi, F., & Hajli, N. (2020). Consumers' value co-creation in sharing economy: The role of social support, consumers' ethical perceptions and relationship quality. *Technological Forecasting and Social Change, 151,* 119786. doi:10.1016/j.techfore.2019.119786

Nanda, A., Xu, Y., & Zhang, F. (2021). How would the COVID-19 pandemic reshape retail real estate and high streets through acceleration of E-commerce and digitalization? *Journal of Urban Management, 10*(2), 110–124. doi:10.1016/j.jum.2021.04.001

Nan, X., & Faber, R. J. (2004). Advertising theory: Reconceptualizing the building blocks. *Marketing Theory, 4*(1-2), 7–30. doi:10.1177/1470593104044085

Narang, U. & Shankar, V. (2019). Mobile marketing 2.0: state of the art and research agenda. *Marketing in a Digital World, 16,* 97-119. doi:10.1108/S1548-643520190000016008

Narin, N. G. (2021). A content analysis of the metaverse articles. *Journal of Metaverse, 1*(1), 17–24.

Nazlan, N. H., Tanford, S., & Montgomery, R. J. V. (2018, July 13). The effect of availability heuristics in online consumer reviews. *Journal of Consumer Behaviour, 17*(5), 449–460. Advance online publication. doi:10.1002/cb.1731

Neslin, S. A. (2022). The omnichannel continuum: Integrating online and offline channels along the customer journey. *Journal of Retailing, 98*(1), 111–132. doi:10.1016/j.jretai.2022.02.003

Neuman, W. L. (2006). *Social Research Methods: Qualitative and Quantitative Approaches* (6th ed.). Allyn and Bacon.

Newport, C. (2019). *Digital minimalism: On living better with less technology.* Portfolio/Penguin.

Ngo, L. V., & O'Cass, A. (2013). Innovation and business success: The mediating role of customer participation. *Journal of Business Research, 66*(8), 1134–1142. doi:10.1016/j.jbusres.2012.03.009

Nguyen Tran Ba, T., & Nguyen Thuong, B. (2016). *The Creative Industry in the Age of Collaborative Consumption.* Laurea University of Applied Sciences. https://www.theseus.fi/handle/10024/113459

Nguyen, H., Mladenow, A., Strauss, C., & Auer-Srnka, K. (2021, November). Voice commerce: Anthropomorphism using voice assistants. In *The 23rd International Conference on Information Integration and Web Intelligence* (pp. 434-442). Academic Press.

Nguyen, A., McClelland, R., Thuan, N. H., & Hoang, T. G. (2022). Omnichannel Marketing: Structured Review, Synthesis, and Future Directions. *International Review of Retail, Distribution and Consumer Research*, *32*(3), 221–265. doi:10.1080/09593969.2022.2034125

Nguyen, D. T., Pham, M., Chovancová, M., & Duc hoang, S. (2023). How service operations, perceived benefit, and psychological ownership enhance customer retention in retail-evidence in Vietnam supermarkets. *Cogent Business & Management*, *10*(2), 2200519. doi:10.1080/2331 1975.2023.2200519

Nikolaev, B., & Bennett, D. L. (2016). Give me liberty and give me control: Economic freedom, control perceptions and the paradox of choice. *European Journal of Political Economy*, *45*, 39–52. doi:10.1016/j.ejpoleco.2015.12.002

Noble, S. M., Mende, M., Grewal, D., & Parasuraman, A. (2022). The Fifth Industrial Revolution: How harmonious human–machine collaboration is triggering a retail and service [r] evolution. *Journal of Retailing*, *98*(2), 199–208. doi:10.1016/j.jretai.2022.04.003

O'Leary, D. E. (2023). Digitization, digitalization, and digital transformation in accounting, electronic commerce, and supply chains. *International Journal of Intelligent Systems in Accounting Finance & Management*, *30*(2), 101–110. doi:10.1002/isaf.1524

Oancea, O., & Mihaela, E. (2015). The Influence of the Integrated Marketing Communication on the Consumer Buying Behavior. *Procedia Economics and Finance, 2nd Global Conference on Business, Economics, Management and Tourism*, 23, 1446-1450.

OECD. (2020). *OECD Policy Responses to Coronavirus (COVID-19) E-commerce in the time of COVID-19*. Available at: https://www.oecd.org/coronavirus/policy-responses/e-commerce-in-the-time-of-covid-19-3a2b78e8/#section-d1e102

Oh, S., & Syn, S. Y. (2015). Motivations for sharing information and social support in social media: A comparative analysis of Facebook, Twitter, Delicious, YouTube, and Flickr. *Journal of the Association for Information Science and Technology*, *66*(10), 2045–2060. doi:10.1002/asi.23320

Oishi, S., Tsutsui, Y., Eggleston, C., & Galinha, I. C. (2014). Are maximizers unhappier than satisficers? A comparison between Japan and the USA. *Journal of Research in Personality*, *49*, 14–20. doi:10.1016/j.jrp.2013.12.001

Ok, Ş., & Kağıtçı Candan, S. (2023). Endüstri 5.0'a Doğru Pazarlama 5.0. In İnsan ve Teknoloji, Sanayi Yönetiminde Gelecek yaklaşımları Dijitalleşme ve Yetenekler (pp. 59-82). Nobel Yayınevi.

Okazaki, S. (2012). *Fundamentals of Mobile Marketing Theories and Practices*. Peter Lang Publishing, Inc.

Compilation of References

Oliveira, T., Tomar, S., & Tam, C. (2020). Evaluating collaborative consumption platforms from a consumer perspective. *Journal of Cleaner Production, 273*, 123018. doi:10.1016/j.jclepro.2020.123018

Olsson, T., Lagerstam, E., Kärkkäinen, T., & Väänänen-Vainio-Mattila, K. (2013). Expected user experience of mobile augmented reality services: A user study in the context of shopping centres. *Personal and Ubiquitous Computing, 17*(2), 287–304. doi:10.1007/s00779-011-0494-x

Ong, C.-E., & Jin, G. (2017). Simulacra and simulation: Double simulation at a North Song Dynasty theme park. *Tourism Geographies, 19*(2), 227–243. doi:10.1080/14616688.2016.1258431

Oulasvirta, A., Hukkinen, J. P., & Schwartz, B. (2009). When More is Less: The Paradox of Choice in Search Engine Use. In *Proceedings of the 32nd international ACM SIGIR conference on Research and development in information retrieval*. Association for Computing Machinery. 10.1145/1571941.1572030

Özbakır Umut, M., & Nurtanış Velioğlu, M. A recycling story: Developing recycling behavior in Turkey with social marketing program. *Journal of Public Affairs*, e2900.

Özbölük, T., & Akdogan, K. (2022). The role of online source credibility and influencer identification on consumers purchase decisions. *International Journal of Internet Marketing and Advertising, 16*(1/2), 165–185. doi:10.1504/IJIMA.2022.120974

Paden, N., & Stell, R. (2005). Consumer product redistribution: Disposition decisions and channel options. *Journal of Marketing Channels, 12*(3), 105–123. doi:10.1300/J049v12n03_06

Palafox, C. L. (2020). When Less is More: Minimalism and the Environment. *Earth Jurisprudence & Envtl. Just, 10*.

Palazzo, B. (2002). US-American and German business ethics: An intercultural comparison. *Journal of Business Ethics, 41*(3), 195–216. doi:10.1023/A:1021239017049

Pandey, A. K., & Desai, J. (2020). Analysing the paralysis: Inquiry into the paradox of choices in online apparel shopping. *Our Heritage, 68*(22), 101–123.

Pangarkar, A., Shukla, P., & Taylor, C. R. (2021). Minimalism in consumption: A typology and brand engagement strategies. *Journal of Business Research, 127*, 167–178. doi:10.1016/j.jbusres.2021.01.033

Pantano, E., Pizzi, G., Scarpi, D., & Dennis, C. (2020). Competing during a pandemic? Retailers' ups and downs during the COVID-19 outbreak. *Journal of Business Research, 116*, 209–213. doi:10.1016/j.jbusres.2020.05.036 PMID:32501307

Papagiannidis, S., & Bourlakis, M. A. (2010). Staging the New Retail Drama: At a Metaverse Near You! *Journal of Virtual Worlds Research, 2*(5), 425-446.

Papagiannidis, S., Pantano, E., See-To, E. W., Dennis, C., & Bourlakis, M. (2017). To immerse or not? Experimenting with two virtual retail environments. *Information Technology & People, 30*(1), 163–188. doi:10.1108/ITP-03-2015-0069

Par, T. (2021). Materialism to Minimalism. *Healt, Wellnes, and Life Sciences, BU WELL, 1*(6).

Paul, J., & Barari, M. (2022). Meta-analysis and traditional systematic literature reviews – What, why, when, where and how? *Psychology and Marketing*, *39*(6), 1099–1115. Advance online publication. doi:10.1002/mar.21657

Pavlov, A. V., & Erokhina, Y. V. (2019). Images of Modernity in the 21st Century: Altermodernism. *Russian Journal of Philosophical Sciences*, *62*(2), 7–25. doi:10.30727/0235-1188-2019-62-2-7-25

Pazarlama. (2023). https://pazarlamailetisimi.com/2023-pazarlama-trendleri-ve-pazarlama-dunyasini-bekleyen-riskler/

Pazarlama30. (2023). https://www.pazarlama30.com/2023-yili-icerik-pazarlama-trendleri/

Peattie, K., & Peattie, S. (2009). Social marketing: A pathway to consumption reduction? *Journal of Business Research*, *62*(2), 260–268. doi:10.1016/j.jbusres.2008.01.033

Pellegrini, R. J., Noffsinger, E. B., Caldwell, R. T., & Tutko, T. A. (1993). Exploring the Everyday Life Incidence of Déjà Connu Experiences in Impression Formation. *Perceptual and Motor Skills*, *76*(3_suppl), 1243–1250. doi:10.2466/pms.1993.76.3c.1243 PMID:8337071

Perren, R., & Grauerholz, L. (2015). Collaborative consumption. International Encyclopedia of the Social & Behavioral Sciences, 4(2), 139-144.

Peterson, M. F. (2007). The heritage of cross cultural management research implications for the Hofstede chair in cultural diversity. *International Journal of Cross Cultural Management*, *7*(3), 359–377. doi:10.1177/1470595807083371

Peyer, M., Balderjahn, I., Seegebarth, B., & Klemm, A. (2017). The role of sustainability in profiling voluntary simplifiers. *Journal of Business Research*, *70*, 37–43. doi:10.1016/j.jbusres.2016.07.008

Pillai, R., Sivathanu, B., & Dwivedi, Y. K. (2020). Shopping intention at AI-powered automated retail stores (AIPARS). *Journal of Retailing and Consumer Services*, *57*, 102207. doi:10.1016/j.jretconser.2020.102207

Polasek, A. D. (2012). Sherlockian Simulacra: Adaptation and the Postmodern Construction of Reality. *Literature-film Quarterly*, *40*, 191.

Polman, E. (2010). Why are maximizers less happy than satisficers? Because they maximize positive and negative outcomes. *Journal of Behavioral Decision Making*, *23*(2), 179–190. doi:10.1002/bdm.647

Prahalad, C. K., & Ramaswamy, V. (2004). Co-creating unique value with customers. *Strategy and Leadership*, *32*(3), 4–9. doi:10.1108/10878570410699249

Price, M. (2009). You are what you dream. *Monitor on Psychology*, *40*(4). https://www.apa.org/monitor/2009/04/dream

Compilation of References

Prothero, A., McDonagh, P., & Dobscha, S. (2010). Is Green the New Black? Reflections on a Green Commodity Discourse. *Journal of Macromarketing*, *30*(2), 147–159. doi:10.1177/0276146710361922

Purcarea, T. (2019). Modern Marketing, CX, CRM, Customer Trust and Identity. *Holistic Marketing Management Journal*, *9*(1), 8.

Puschmann, T., & Alt, R. (2016). Sharing economy. *Business & Information Systems Engineering*, *58*(1), 93–99. doi:10.1007/s12599-015-0420-2

Pylianidis, C., Osinga, S., & Athanasiadis, I. N. (2021). Introducing digital twins to agriculture. *Computers and Electronics in Agriculture*, *184*, 105942. doi:10.1016/j.compag.2020.105942

Pyszczynski, T., Lockett, M., Greenberg, J., & Solomon, S. (2021). Terror Management Theory and the COVID-19 Pandemic. *Journal of Humanistic Psychology*, *61*(2), 173–189. doi:10.1177/0022167820959488

Qi, Q., & Tao, F. (2018). Digital twin and big data towards smart manufacturing and industry 4.0: 360 degree comparison. *IEEE Access : Practical Innovations, Open Solutions*, *6*, 3585–3593. doi:10.1109/ACCESS.2018.2793265

Quinones, M., Gomez-Suarez, M., Cruz-Roche, I., & Díaz-Martín, A. M. (2023). Technology: A strategic imperative for successful retailers. *International Journal of Retail & Distribution Management*, *51*(4), 546–566. doi:10.1108/IJRDM-03-2022-0088

Quintana, M., Menendez, J. M., Alvarez, F., & Lopez, J. P. (2016). *Improving retail efficiency through sensing technologies*. Pattern Recognition Letters, Elsevier B. V. doi:10.1016/j.patrec.2016.05.027

Rafailidis, D., & Manolopoulos, Y. (2019, June). Can virtual assistants produce recommendations? In *Proceedings of the 9th International Conference on Web Intelligence, Mining and Semantics* (pp. 1-6). 10.1145/3326467.3326468

Rahman, Z. (2006). Customer experience management—A case study of an Indian bank. *Journal of Database Marketing & Customer Strategy Management*, *13*(3), 203–221. doi:10.1057/palgrave.dbm.3240298

Ramadan, Z. (2023). Marketing in the metaverse era: Toward an integrative channel approach. *Virtual Reality (Waltham Cross)*, *27*(3), 1–14. doi:10.1007/s10055-023-00783-2 PMID:37360809

Ramella, F., & Manzo, C. (2020). *The economy of collaboration: The new digital platforms of production and consumption*. Routledge. doi:10.4324/9780429355936

RaneN. L. (2023, October 17). Multidisciplinary collaboration: key players in successful implementation of ChatGPT and similar generative artificial intelligence in manufacturing, finance, retail, transportation, and construction industry. doi:10.31219/osf.io/npm3d

Reglitz, M. (2023). The socio-economic argument for the human right to internet access. *Politics, Philosophy & Economics*, *22*(4), 441–469. doi:10.1177/1470594X231167597

Reniou, F. (2009). *Opérations participatives des marques: pourquoi et comment faire participer les consommateurs? De la compréhension des opérations participatives et des motivations des consommateurs à s'y engager à l'analyse de leurs effets sur la marque.* University Paris Dauphine.

Rese, A., Ganster, L., & Baier, D. (2020). Chatbots in retailers' customer communication: How to measure their acceptance? *Journal of Retailing and Consumer Services*, 56, 102176. doi:10.1016/j.jretconser.2020.102176

Retail Customer Experience. (2020). *COVID-19 spurring impulse spending, reveals survey.* Available at: https://www.retailcustomerexperience.com/news/covid-19-spurring-impulse-spending-reveals-survey/

Revonsuo, A. (1995). Consciousness, dreams and virtual realities. *Philosophical Psychology*, 8(1), 35–58. doi:10.1080/09515089508573144

Richardson, K., Steffen, W., Lucht, W., Bendtsen, J., Cornell, S. E., Donges, J. F., Drüke, M., Fetzer, I., Bala, G., von Bloh, W., Feulner, G., Fiedler, S., Gerten, D., Gleeson, T., Hofmann, M., Huiskamp, W., Kummu, M., Mohan, C., Nogués-Bravo, D., ... Rockström, J. (2023). Earth beyond six of nine planetary boundaries. *Science Advances*, 9(37), 1–16. doi:10.1126/sciadv.adh2458 PMID:37703365

Richins, M. L. (1994). Special Possessions and the Expression of Material Values. *The Journal of Consumer Research*, 21(3), 522. doi:10.1086/209415

Richins, M. L., & Dawson, S. (1992). A Consumer Values Orientation for Materialism and Its Measurement: Scale Development and Validation. *The Journal of Consumer Research*, 19(3), 303. doi:10.1086/209304

Rifkin, J. (2011). *The third industrial revolution: how lateral power is transforming energy, the economy, and the world.* Palgrave Macmillan.

Ritter, D. (2023). *The 36 key chatbot statistics: how chatbots help businesses grow in 2023.* https://www.dashly.io/blog/chatbot-statistics/

Ritzer, G., & Rey, P. J. (2016). From 'Solid' Producers and Consumers to 'Liquid 'Prosumers. In M. Davis (Ed.), Liquid Sociology. Metaphor in Zygmunt Bauman's Analysis of Modernity (pp. 157-176). Routledge.

Roberts, D., Baker, S., & Walker, D. (2005). Can we learn together?: Co-creating with consumers. *International Journal of Market Research*, 47(4), 405–426. doi:10.1177/147078530504700401

Roberts, P. (2014). *The Impulse Society: America in the Age of Instant Gratification.* Bloomsbury Publishing USA.

Rode, H. (2016). To Share or not to Share: The Effects of Extrinsic and Intrinsic Motivations on Knowledge-sharing in Enterprise Social Media Platforms. *Journal of Information Technology*, 31(2), 152–165. doi:10.1057/jit.2016.8

Compilation of References

Rodriguez, J. (2018). The US Minimalist Movement: Radical Political Practice? *The Review of Radical Political Economics*, *50*(2), 286–296. doi:10.1177/0486613416665832

Roggeveen, A. L., & Sethuraman, R. (2020). Customer-interfacing retail technologies in 2020 & beyond: An integrative framework and research directions. *Journal of Retailing*, *96*(3), 299–309. doi:10.1016/j.jretai.2020.08.001

Roggeveen, A. L., & Sethuraman, R. (2020). How the COVID-19 pandemic may change the world of retailing. *Journal of Retailing*, *96*(2), 169–171. doi:10.1016/j.jretai.2020.04.002

Roser, T., DeFillippi, R., & Samson, A. (2013). Managing your co-creation mix: Co-creation ventures in distinctive contexts. *European Business Review*, *25*(1), 20–41. doi:10.1108/09555341311287727

Rospigliosi, P. a. (2022). *Metaverse or Simulacra? Roblox, Minecraft, Meta and the turn to virtual reality for education, socialisation and work* (Vol. 30). Taylor & Francis.

Roubal, O. (2012). Éra nejistoty a nástup „lovecko-hráčské" společnosti [Era of Uncertainty and Accession into the Age of „Hunter-gamer"Society]. *Communication Today*, *3*(1), 6–20.

Roubal, O. (2018). Maximizers and satisficers in consumer culture changes. *Communication Today*, *9*(2), 38–54.

Roubal, O. (2022). The ethical consumer and the religious nature of environmental thinking. *European Journal of Science and Theology*, *18*(1), 113–124.

Roubal, O. (2023). Consumer Culture and Abundance of Choices: Having More, Feeling Blue. In U. Ayman (Ed.), *A New Era of Consumer Behavior - In and Beyond the Pandemic* (pp. 3–21). IntechOpen. doi:10.5772/intechopen.105607

Roy, S. K., Balaji, M. S., Sadeque, S., Nguyen, B., & Melewar, T. C. (2017). Constituents and consequences of smart customer experience in retailing. *Technological Forecasting and Social Change*, *124*, 257–270. doi:10.1016/j.techfore.2016.09.022

Rubel, S. (2006). Who's Ready to Crowdsource? Check Your Egos at the Door, and Tap Into the Collective Wisdom of Millions for Solutions [Preprint]. *Advertising Age*.

Ruby, D. (2023, April 6). *65 Voice Search Statistics For 2023 (Updated Data)*. https://www.demandsage.com/voice-search-statistics/

Ryan, R. M., & Deci, E. L. (2000a). Intrinsic and Extrinsic Motivations: Classic Definitions and New Directions. *Contemporary Educational Psychology*, *25*(1), 54–67. doi:10.1006/ceps.1999.1020 PMID:10620381

Ryan, R. M., & Deci, E. L. (2000b). Self-Determination Theory and the Facilitation of Intrinsic Motivation, Social Development, and Well-Being. *The American Psychologist*, *1*(55), 68–78. doi:10.1037/0003-066X.55.1.68 PMID:11392867

Rzepka, C., Berger, B., & Hess, T. (2020). Why another customer channel? Consumers' perceived benefits and costs of voice commerce. *Proceedings of the 53rd Hawaii International Conference on System Sciences*, 4079-4088.

Sahin, A., Zehir, C., & Kitapçı, H. (2011). The effects of brand experiences, trust and satisfaction on building brand loyalty; an empirical research on global brands. *Procedia: Social and Behavioral Sciences*, *24*, 1288–1301. doi:10.1016/j.sbspro.2011.09.143

Sajidan, S. Saputro, R. Perdana, I. R., Atmojo W. & Nugraha D. A. (2020). Development of science learning model towards Society 5.0: A conceptual model. *Journal of Physics: Conference Series, 1511*, 2. . doi:10.1088/1742-6596/1511/1/012124

Saruchera, F., & Mthombeni, L. (2023). Antecedents to the conspicuous consumption of luxury fashion brands by middle-income black South Africans. *Journal of Fashion Marketing and Management*, *27*(6), 1–21. doi:10.1108/JFMM-06-2022-0126

Sassatelli, R. (2019). Consumer Identities. In A. Elliott (Ed.), *Routledge Handbook of Identity Studies* (pp. 237–255). Routledge. doi:10.4324/9781315626024-14

Satish, K., Venkatesh, A., & Manivannan, A. S. R. (2021). Covid-19 is driving fear and greed in consumer behaviour and purchase pattern. *South Asian Journal of Marketing*, *2*(2), 113–129. doi:10.1108/SAJM-03-2021-0028

Saunders, S. G., Barrington, D. J., & Sridharan, S. (2015). Redefining social marketing: Beyond behavioural change. *Journal of Social Marketing*, *5*(2), 160–168. doi:10.1108/JSOCM-03-2014-0021

Saura, J., Reyes-Menendez, A., Matos, N., Correia, M., & Palos-Sanchez, P. (2020). Consumer Behavior in the Digital Age. *Journal of Spatial and Organizational Dynamics.*, *8*, 190–194.

Schank, C., & Lorch, A. (2019). Sustainability citizenship through economics education? Contributions from the German debate on business ethics. *International Journal of Pluralism and Economics Education*, *10*(4), 401–417. doi:10.1504/IJPEE.2019.106125

Scheibehenne, B., Greifeneder, R., & Todd, P. M. (2010). Can there ever be too many options? A meta-analytic review of choice overload. *The Journal of Consumer Research*, *37*(3), 409–425. doi:10.1086/651235

Schiffman, L. G., & Kanuk, L. L. (2004). *Consumer Behavior*. Pearson Education Limited.

Schiffman, L. G., & Wisenblit, J. (2019). *Consumer behavior* (12th ed.). Pearson.

Schneider, E., Sklar, E., Azhar, M. Q., Parsons, S., & Tuyls, K. (2015). *Towards a methodology for describing the relationship between simulation and reality.* Paper presented at the European Conference on Artificial Life. 10.7551/978-0-262-33027-5-ch098

Scholz, J., & Smith, A. N. (2016). Augmented reality: Designing immersive experiences that maximize consumer engagement. *Business Horizons*, *59*(2), 149–161. doi:10.1016/j.bushor.2015.10.003

Compilation of References

Schouten, A. P., Janssen, L., & Verspaget, M. (2020). Celebrity vs. influencer endorsements in advertising: The role of identification, credibility, and product-endorser fit. *International Journal of Advertising*, *39*(2), 258–281. doi:10.1080/02650487.2019.1634898

Schrader, U. (2008). Transparenz über Corporate Social Responsibility (CSR) als Voraussetzung für einen Wandel zu nachhaltigerem Konsum [Transparency via corporate social responsibility (CSR) as a prerequisite for a change to more sustainable consumption]. In H. Lange (Ed.), *Nachhaltigkeit als radikaler Wandel* [Sustainability as radical change] (pp. 149–166). VS Verlag für Sozialwissenschaften. doi:10.1007/978-3-531-90956-1_7

Schram, R. (2020). The state of the creator economy. *Journal of Brand Strategy*, *9*(2), 152–162.

Schredl, M., Goritz, A., & Funkhouser, A. (2017). Frequency of déjà rêvé: Effects of age, gender, dream recall, and personality. *Journal of Consciousness Studies*, *24*(7-8), 155–162.

Schredl, M., Remedios, A., Marin-Dragu, S., Sheikh, S., Forbes, A., Iyer, R. S., Orr, M., & Meier, S. (2022). Dream recall frequency, lucid dream frequency, and personality during the COVID-19 pandemic. *Imagination, Cognition and Personality*, *42*(2), 113–133. doi:10.1177/02762366221104214

Schulman, G. I. (1967, March). Asch Conformity Studies: Conformity to the Experimenter and/or to the Group? *Sociometry*, *30*(1), 26. doi:10.2307/2786436 PMID:6037868

Schwartz, S. H. (1994). Beyond Individualism-Collectivism: New Cultural Dimensions of Values. In U. Kim, H. C. Triandis, C. Kagitcibasi, S-C. Choi & G. Yoon (Eds.), Individualism and Collectivism: Theory, Method, and Applications (pp. 85-119). Sage Publications.

Schwartz, B. (2004). *The Paradox of Choice: Why More is Less*. Harper Perennial.

Schwartz, B. (2015). The Paradox of Choice. In S. Joseph (Ed.), *Positive Psychology in Practice: Promoting Human Flourishing in Work, Health, Education, and Everyday Life* (pp. 121–138). Wiley. doi:10.1002/9781118996874.ch8

Scott, J. (2000). Rational Choice Theory. In G. Browning, A. Halcli A. & F. Webster (Eds.) Understanding Contemporary Society: Theories of the Present (pp. 126-138). Sage Publications Ltd. doi:10.4135/9781446218310.n9

Seegebarth, B., Peyer, M., Balderjahn, I., & Wiedmann, K. (2016). The Sustainability Roots of Anticonsumption Lifestyles and Initial Insights Regarding Their Effects on Consumers' Well-Being. *The Journal of Consumer Affairs*, *50*(1), 68–99. doi:10.1111/joca.12077

Segev, S., Shoham, A., & Gavish, Y. (2015). A closer look into the materialism construct: The antecedents and consequences of materialism and its three facets. *Journal of Consumer Marketing*, *32*(2), 85–98. doi:10.1108/JCM-07-2014-1082

Sehad, N., Cherif, B., Khadraoui, I., Hamidouche, W., Bader, F., Jäntti, R., & Debbah, M. (2023). Locomotion-Based UAV Control Toward the Internet of Senses. *IEEE Transactions on Circuits and Wystems. II, Express Briefs*, *70*(5), 1804–1808. doi:10.1109/TCSII.2023.3257363

Selloni, D., & Selloni, D. (2017). New forms of economies: sharing economy, collaborative consumption, peer-to-peer economy. *Codesign for public-interest services*, 15-26.

Seo, E.-J., & Park, J.-W. (2018). A study on the effects of social media marketing activities on brand equity and customer response in the airline industry. *Journal of Air Transport Management, 66*, 36–41. doi:10.1016/j.jairtraman.2017.09.014

Settineri, S., Frisone, F., Alibrandi, A., & Merlo, E. M. (2019). Italian adaptation of the Mannheim Dream Questionnaire (MADRE): Age, Gender and Dream Recall effects. *International Journal of Dream Research*, 119–129.

Shafqat, T., Ishaq, M. I., & Ahmed, A. (2023). Fashion consumption using minimalism: Exploring the relationship of consumer well-being and social connectedness. *Journal of Retailing and Consumer Services, 71*, 103215. doi:10.1016/j.jretconser.2022.103215

Shankar, V., Inman, J. J., Mantrala, M., Kelley, E., & Rizley, R. (2011). Innovations in shopper marketing: Current insights and future research issues. *Journal of Retailing, 87*(No. S1), 29–42. doi:10.1016/j.jretai.2011.04.007

Shankar, V., Kalyanam, K., Setia, P., Golmohammadi, A., Tirunillai, S., Douglass, T., Hennessey, J., Bull, J. S., & Waddoups, R. (2021). How technology is changing retail. *Journal of Retailing, 97*(1), 13–27. doi:10.1016/j.jretai.2020.10.006

Sharma, A., & Nair, S. K. (2017). Switching behaviour as a function of number of options: How much is too much for consumer choice decisions? *Journal of Consumer Behaviour, 16*(6), 153–160. doi:10.1002/cb.1670

Sharma, P., Ueno, A., Dennis, C., & Turan, C. P. (2023). Emerging digital technologies and consumer decision-making in retail sector: Towards an integrative conceptual framework. *Computers in Human Behavior, 148*, 107913. doi:10.1016/j.chb.2023.107913

Shawar, B. A., & Atwell, E. (2007). Chatbots: are they really useful? *LDV-Forum, 22*(1), 29–49. https://jlcl.org/content/2-allissues/20-Heft1-2007/Bayan_Abu-Shawar_and_Eric_Atwell.pdf

Sherry, J. F., & Storm, D. (2001). Being in the zone: Staging retail theater at ESPN Zone Chicago. *Journal of Contemporary Ethnography, 30*(4), 465–510. doi:10.1177/089124101030004005

Shrum, L. J., Lowrey, T. M., Pandelaere, M., Ruvio, A. A., Gentina, E., Furchheim, P., Herbert, M., Hudders, L., Lens, I., Mandel, N., Nairn, A., Samper, A., Soscia, I., & Steinfield, L. (2014). Materialism: The good, the bad, and the ugly. *Journal of Marketing Management, 30*(17–18), 1858–1881. doi:10.1080/0267257X.2014.959985

Shukla, Y., Mishra, S., Chatterjee, R., & Arora, V. (2023). Consumer minimalism for sustainability: Exploring the determinants of rental consumption intention. *Journal of Consumer Behaviour*, cb.2219. doi:10.1002/cb.2219

Silverman, A. (2019). Breaking the paralysis of choice. *Twice, 34*(13), 9–9.

Compilation of References

Singaiah, G., & Laskar, S. R. (2015). Understanding of social marketing: A conceptual perspective. *Global Business Review, 16*(2), 213–235. doi:10.1177/0972150914564282

Singh, R., Paste, M., Shinde, N., Patel, H., & Mishra, N. (2018). Chatbot using TensorFlow for small Businesses. *Proceedings of the 2018 Second International Conference on Inventive Communication and Computational Technologies (ICICCT),* 1614–1619.

Siradisidigital. (2023). https://siradisidigital.com/blog/2023-dijital-pazarlama-trendleri

Slee, T. (2016). *What's yours is mine: Against Airbnb, Uber and other avatars of the "sharing economy.".* Lux publisher. doi:10.2307/j.ctt1bkm65n

Smith, P. R. (2018). SOSTAC Guide to your Perfect Digital Marketing Plan 2018. PR Smith Marketing Success.

Smith, S. (2017). A brief look at multichannel vs omnichannel marketing. *Customer Think.* Available from: https://customerthink.com/a-brief-look-at-multichannel-vs-omnichannel-marketing/

Smith, A., & Machová, V. (2021). Consumer tastes, sentiments, attitudes, and behaviors related to COVID-19. *Analysis and Metaphysics, 20*(0), 145–158. doi:10.22381/AM20202110

Smith, J. (2019). The Power of User-Generated Content: How UGC Impacts Consumer Behaviour. *Journal of Marketing Trends, 6*(2), 45–56.

Solms, M. (2015). Freudian dream theory today. In M. Solms (Ed.), *The Feeling Brain.* Karnac.

Solomon, M. R. (2018). *Consumer Behavior: Buying, Having, and Being* (12th ed.). Pearson Education Limited.

Solomon, M., Bamossy, G., Askegaard, S., & Hogg, M. K. (2006). *Consumer Behavior: A European Perspective* (3rd ed.). Pearson Education Limited.

Soper, K. (2023). *Post-growth living: For an alternative hedonism.* Verso Books.

Sorescu, A., Frambach, R. T., Singh, J., Rangaswamy, A., & Bridges, C. (2011). Innovations in retail business models. *Journal of Retailing, 87*, S3–S16. doi:10.1016/j.jretai.2011.04.005

Spelthahn, S., Fuchs, L., & Demele, U. (2009). Glaubwürdigkeit in der Nachhaltigkeitsberichterstattung [Trustworthiness in sustainability reporting]. *uwf - UmweltWirtschaftsForum, 17*(1), 61-68. doi:10.1007/s00550-008-0104-1

Spence, C. (2018). Background colour & its impact on food perception & behaviour. *Food Quality and Preference, 68*, 156–166. doi:10.1016/j.foodqual.2018.02.012

Spry, A., Figueiredo, B., Gurrieri, L., Kemper, J. A., & Vredenburg, J. (2021). Transformative Branding: A Dynamic Capability To Challenge The Dominant Social Paradigm. *Journal of Macromarketing, 41*(4), 531–546. doi:10.1177/02761467211043074

Sridharan, S., Bondy, M., Nakaima, A., & Heller, R. F. (2018). The potential of an online educational platform to contribute to achieving sustainable development goals: A mixed-methods evaluation of the Peoples-uni online platform. *Health Research Policy and Systems*, *16*(1), 1–14. doi:10.1186/s12961-018-0381-2 PMID:30419943

Srinivasan, S. S., Anderson, R., & Ponnavolu, K. (2002). Customer loyalty in e-commerce: An exploration of its antecedents and consequences. *Journal of Retailing*, *78*(1), 41–50. doi:10.1016/S0022-4359(01)00065-3

Stahel, W. R. (1997). *The functional economy: cultural and organizational change* (Vol. 1). National Academy Press.

Statista. (2023). *Luxury Goods—Worldwide | Statista Market Forecast*. Statista. https://www.statista.com/outlook/cmo/luxury-goods/worldwide

Statista. (2023). *Most popular social networks worldwide as of October 2023, ranked by number of monthly active users*. https://www.statista.com/statistics/272014/global-social-networks-ranked-by-number-of-users/

Stern, B. B. (1993). Feminist literary criticism and the deconstruction of ads: A postmodern view of advertising and consumer responses. *The Journal of Consumer Research*, *19*(4), 556–566. doi:10.1086/209322

Straub, D. W. (1994). The effect of culture on IT diffusion: E-Mail and FAX in Japan and the U.S. *Information Systems Research*, *5*(1), 23–47. doi:10.1287/isre.5.1.23

Streubert, H. J., & Carpenter, D. R. (2011). *Qualitative research in nursing* (5th ed.). Lippincott Williams ve Wilkins.

Sulehri, N. A., Awais, A., Dar, I. B., & Uzair, A. (2021). *Big Five Personality Traits on Project Success in Marketing-Oriented Organizations: Moderation of Leader Member Exchange*. Academic Press.

Sutinen, U.-M., & Närvänen, E. (2022). Constructing the food waste issue on social media: A discursive social marketing approach. *Journal of Marketing Management*, *38*(3-4), 219–247. doi:10.1080/0267257X.2021.1966077

Su, Y., & Jin, L. (2021). The impact of online platforms' revenue model on consumers' ethical inferences. *Journal of Business Ethics*, 1–15.

Taleb, N. N. (2014). *Antifragile: Things that gain from disorder* (3rd ed.). Random House Trade Paperbacks.

Talukdar, N., & Yu, S. (2021). Breaking the psychological distance: The effect of immersive virtual reality on perceived novelty and user satisfaction. *Journal of Strategic Marketing*, *12*, 1–25. Advance online publication. doi:10.1080/0965254X.2021.1967428

Tang, Q. (2021). Consumerism in the Digital Age. *2021 World Automation Congress (WAC)*, 97–99. 10.23919/WAC50355.2021.9559559

Compilation of References

Tapia, C. (2012). Modernity, Postmodernity, Hypermodernity. *ConneXions (Cupertino, Calif.)*, *97*(1), 15–25. doi:10.3917/cnx.097.0015

Taylor, C. R. (2020). The urgent need for more research on influencer marketing. *International Journal of Advertising*, *39*(7), 889–891. doi:10.1080/02650487.2020.1822104

Taylor, W. J. (1965). "Is Marketing a Science?" Revisited. *Journal of Marketing*, *29*(3), 49–53. doi:10.1177/002224296502900309

Thaichon, P., Quach, S., Barari, M., & Nguyen, M. (2023). Exploring the Role of Omnichannel Retailing Technologies: Future Research Directions. *Australasian Marketing Journal*. Advance online publication. doi:10.1177/14413582231167664

Thinkwithgoogle. (2023). https://www.thinkwithgoogle.com/intl/tr-tr/icgoruler/tuketici-trendleri/2023-dijital-pazarlama-trendleri/

Thomas, A. S. (1996). A call for research in forgotten locations. In B. J. Punnett & O. Shenkar (Eds.), *Handbook for International Management Research* (pp. 485–506). Blackwell.

Thompson, R. G., Moulin, C. J. A., Conway, M. A., & Jones, R. W. (2004). Persistent Déjà vu: A disorder of memory. *International Journal of Geriatric Psychiatry*, *19*(9), 19. doi:10.1002/gps.1177 PMID:15352150

Trębska, P. (2020). Food self-supply in new consumer trends. *Zeszyty Naukowe Szkoły Głównej Gospodarstwa Wiejskiego w Warszawie. Polityki Europejskie. Finance i Marketing*, *23*(72), 237–246.

Tremlett, P. F. (2021). Modernism and Postmodernism. *The Wiley Blackwell Companion to the Study of Religion*, 325-334.

Trepczyński, M. (2018). *Hypermodernism as Deceleration, Re-stabilisation and Reconciliation.* Edukacja Filozoficzna. doi:10.14394/edufil.2018.0021

Tsibizova, I. M. (2023). On the Foreign Policy Rhetoric of Hyper-Postmodernism. *The Bulletin of Irkutsk State University. Series Political Science and Religion Studies.*

Tueanrat, Y., Papagiannidis, S., & Alamanos, E. (2021). A conceptual framework of the antecedents of customer journey satisfaction in omnichannel retailing. *Journal of Retailing.*

Turner, A. (2015). Generation Z: Technology and social interest. *Journal of Individual Psychology*, *71*(2), 103–113. doi:10.1353/jip.2015.0021

Uggla, Y. (2019). Taking back control: Minimalism as a reaction to high speed and overload in contemporary society. *Sociologisk Forskning*, *56*(3–4), 233–252. doi:10.37062/sf.56.18811

Ummar, R., Shaheen, K., Bashir, I., Ul Haq, J., & Bonn, M. A. (2023). Green Social Media Campaigns: Influencing Consumers' Attitudes and Behaviors. *Sustainability (Basel)*, *15*(17), 12932. doi:10.3390/su151712932

Upadhyaya, S., Vann, R. J., Camacho, S., Baker, C. N., Leary, R. B., Mittelstaedt, J. D., & Rosa, J. A. (2014). Subsistence consumer-merchant marketplace deviance in marketing systems: Antecedents, implications, and recommendations. *Journal of Macromarketing, 34*(2), 145–159. doi:10.1177/0276146713504107

Usunier, J.-C. (1998). International and Cross-Cultural Management Research. *Sage (Atlanta, Ga.)*.

Usunier, J.-C. (2011). Language as a resource to assess cross-cultural equivalence in quantitative management research. *Journal of World Business, 46*(3), 314–319. doi:10.1016/j.jwb.2010.07.002

Vaishnav, B., & Ray, S. (2023). A thematic exploration of the evolution of research in multichannel marketing. *Journal of Business Research, 157*, 113564. Advance online publication. doi:10.1016/j.jbusres.2022.113564

Vallverdu-Gordi, M., & Marine-Roig, E. (2023). The Role of Graphic Design Semiotics in Environmental Awareness Campaigns. *International Journal of Environmental Research and Public Health, 20*(5), 4299. doi:10.3390/ijerph20054299 PMID:36901306

van de Vijver, F., & Tanzer, N. K. (2004). Bias and equivalence in cross-cultural assessment: An overview. *European Review of Applied Psychology, 54*(2), 119–135. doi:10.1016/j.erap.2003.12.004

van Herk, H., Poortinga, Y. H., & Verhallen, T. M. M. (2005). Equivalence of survey data: Relevance for international marketing. *European Journal of Marketing, 39*(3/4), 351–364. doi:10.1108/03090560510581818

Van Tichelen, B. (2019). *The Role and Opportunities of Phygital in the Digital Omni-Channel Strategy*. Louvain School of Management, Université Catholique de Louvain. http://hdl.handle.net/2078.1/thesis:21074

Vanessa, N., & Japutra, A. (2021). Contextual Marketing Based on Customer Buying Pattern in Grocery E-Commerce: The Case of Bigbasket.com (India). *ASEAN Marketing Journal, 9*(1). Advance online publication. doi:10.21002/amj.v9i1.9286

Varadarajan, R., Srinivasan, R., Vadakkepatt, G. G., Yadav, M. S., Pavlou, P. A., Krishnamurthy, S., & Krause, T. (2010). Interactive technologies and retailing strategy: A review, conceptual framework and future research directions. *Journal of Interactive Marketing, 24*(2), 96-110. doi:10.1016/j.intmar.2010.02.004

Varnali, K., Toker, A., & Yilmaz, C. (2011). *Mobile Marketing Fundamentals and Strategy* (1st ed.). McGraw Hill.

Vasiliu-Feltes, I. (2023). Impact of Digital Twins on Smart Cities: Healthtech and Fintech Perspectives – opportunities, Challenges, and Future Directions. In I. Vasiliu-Feltes (Ed.), *Impact of Digital Twins in Smart Cities Development*. IGI Global.

Velichety, S., & Shrivastava, U. (2022). Quantifying the impacts of online fake news on the equity value of social media platforms–Evidence from Twitter. *International Journal of Information Management, 64*, 102474. doi:10.1016/j.ijinfomgt.2022.102474

Compilation of References

Verdugo, G. B., & Ponce, H. R. (2023). Gender Differences in Millennial Consumers of Latin America Associated with Conspicuous Consumption of New Luxury Goods. *Global Business Review, 24*(2), 229–242. doi:10.1177/0972150920909002

Villegas-Ch, W., Amores-Falconi, R., & Coronel-Silva, E. (2023). Design Proposal for a Virtual Shopping Assistant for People with Vision Problems Applying Artificial Intelligence Techniques. *Big Data and Cognitive Computing, 7*(2), 96. doi:10.3390/bdcc7020096

Von Hippel, E. (2001). User toolkits for innovation. *Journal of Product Innovation Management, 18*(4), 247–257. doi:10.1111/1540-5885.1840247

von Mettenheim, W., & Wiedmann, K. (2021b). The complex triad of congruence issues in influencer marketing. *Journal of Consumer Behaviour, 20*(5), 1277–1296. doi:10.1002/cb.1935

von Mettenheim, W., & Wiedmann, K.-P. (2021a). Social influencers and healthy nutrition – The challenge of overshadowing effects and uninvolved consumers. *Journal of Food Products Marketing, 27*(8-9), 365–383. doi:10.1080/10454446.2022.2028692

Vrontis, D., Makrides, A., Christofi, M., & Thrassou, A. (2021). Social media influencer marketing: A systematic review, integrative framework and future research agenda. *International Journal of Consumer Studies, 45*(4), 617–644. doi:10.1111/ijcs.12647

Walczak, R. B., Gerymski, R., & Filipkowski, J. (2018). Would you fancy a premium five o'clock after the funeral? Application of Terror Management Theory in daily shopping decisions. *Acta Universitatis Lodziensis. Folia Psychologica, 22*(22), 5–15. doi:10.18778/1427-969X.22.01

Walsh, P. R., & Dodds, R. (2022). The impact of intermediaries and social marketing on promoting sustainable behaviour in leisure travellers. *Journal of Cleaner Production, 338*, 130537. doi:10.1016/j.jclepro.2022.130537

Wamsley, E. J., & Stickgold, R. (2010). Dreaming and offline memory processing. *Current Biology, 20*(23), R1010–R1013. doi:10.1016/j.cub.2010.10.045 PMID:21145013

Wan Hussain, W. M. H., & Aziz, N. (2022). Mobile marketing in business sustainability: A bibliometric analysis. *TEM Journal, 11*(1), 111–119. doi:10.18421/TEM111-13

Wang, X. S., Ryoo, J. H. J., Bendle, N., & Kopalle, P. K. (2021). The role of machine learning analytics and metrics in retailing research. *Journal of Retailing, 97*(4), 658–675. doi:10.1016/j.jretai.2020.12.001

Weaver, K., Daniloski, K., Schwarz, N., & Cottone, K. (2015). The role of social comparison for maximizers and satisficers: Wanting the best or wanting to be the best? *Journal of Consumer Psychology, 25*(3), 372–388. doi:10.1016/j.jcps.2014.10.003

Web. (2023). *Gartner Trends 2023: How a Retailer Can Turn Them Into Growth*. Available at: https://blog.contactpigeon.com/gartner-trends-2023/

Wei, J., Wang, Z., Hou, Z., & Meng, Y. (2022, March 30). The Influence of Empathy and Consumer Forgiveness on the Service Recovery Effect of Online Shopping. *Frontiers in Psychology*, *13*, 842207. Advance online publication. doi:10.3389/fpsyg.2022.842207 PMID:35432063

Welschen, J., Todorova, N., & Mills, A. M. (2012). An Investigation of the Impact of Intrinsic Motivation on Organizational Knowledge Sharing. *International Journal of Knowledge Management*, *8*(2), 23–42. doi:10.4018/jkm.2012040102

Wiedmann, K.-P., & von Mettenheim, W. (2021). Attractiveness, trustworthiness and expertise – Social influencers' winning formula. *Journal of Product and Brand Management*, *30*(5), 707–725. doi:10.1108/JPBM-06-2019-2442

Wilson, A. V., & Bellezza, S. (2022). Consumer Minimalism. *The Journal of Consumer Research*, *48*(5), 796–816. doi:10.1093/jcr/ucab038

Winkler, I., & Cowan, N. (2005). From sensory to long-term memory: Evidence from auditory memory reactivation studies. *Experimental Psychology*, *52*(1), 3–20. doi:10.1027/1618-3169.52.1.3 PMID:15779526

Wolfinbarger, M., & Gilly, M. C. (2003). eTailQ: Dimensionalizing, measuring and predicting etail quality. *Journal of Retailing*, *79*(3), 183–198. doi:10.1016/S0022-4359(03)00034-4

Wong An Kee, A., & Yazdanifard, R. (2015). The Review of Content Marketing as a New Trend in Marketing Practices. *International Journal of Management. Accounting and Economics*, *2*(9), 1055–1064.

Woolley, B. (1993). *Virtual Worlds: A Journey in Hype and Hyperreality*. Blackwell.

World Population Review. (2023). *Twitter users by country 2023*. https://worldpopulationreview.com/country-rankings/twitter-users-by-country

Wu, J., Wang, Z., Sarker, A., & Srivastava, M. B. (2023). Acuity: Creating Realistic Digital Twins Through Multi-resolution Pointcloud Processing and Audiovisual Sensor Fusion. *Proceedings of the 8th ACM/IEEE Conference on Internet of Things Design and Implementation*. 10.1145/3576842.3582363

Xiao, M., Wang, R., & Chan-Olmsted, S. (2018). Factors affecting YouTube influencer marketing credibility: A heuristic-systematic model. *Journal of Media Business Studies*, *15*(3), 188–213. doi:10.1080/16522354.2018.1501146

Xie, C., Bagozzi, R. P., & Troye, S. V. (2008). Trying to prosume: Toward a theory of consumers as co-creators of value. *Journal of the Academy of Marketing Science*, *36*(1), 109–122. doi:10.1007/s11747-007-0060-2

Ye, G., Hudders, L., De Jans, S., & De Veirman, M. (2021). The value of influencer marketing for business: A bibliometric analysis and managerial implications. *Journal of Advertising*, *50*(2), 160–178. doi:10.1080/00913367.2020.1857888

Compilation of References

Yıldırım, S. (2021). Do green women influencers spur sustainable consumption patterns? Descriptive evidences from social media influencers. *Ecofeminism and Climate Change*, *2*(4), 198–210. doi:10.1108/EFCC-02-2021-0003

Yılmaz, M., Sezerel, H., & Uzuner, Y. (2020). Sharing experiences and interpretation of experiences: A phenomenological research on Instagram influencers. *Current Issues in Tourism*, *23*(24), 3034–3041. doi:10.1080/13683500.2020.1763270

Yoo, K., Welden, R., Hewett, K., & Haenlein, M. (2023). The merchants of meta: A research agenda to understand the future of retailing in the metaverse. *Journal of Retailing*, *99*(2), 173–192. Advance online publication. doi:10.1016/j.jretai.2023.02.002

Yuill, K. (2015). Between the dream and the reality. *Patterns of Prejudice*, *49*(5), 552–554. doi :10.1080/0031322X.2015.1103456

Zalewska, J., & Cobel-Tokarska, M. (2016). Rationalization of Pleasure and Emotions: The Analysis of the Blogs of Polish Minimalists. *Polish Sociological Review*, *196*(4).

Zavestoski, S. (2002). Guest editorial: Anticonsumption attitudes. *Psychology and Marketing*, *19*(2), 121–126. doi:10.1002/mar.10005

Zengin Alp, Z., & Gündüz Öğüdücü, Ş. (2018). Identifying topical influencers on Twitter based on user behavior and network topology. *Knowledge-Based Systems*, *141*, 211–221. doi:10.1016/j. knosys.2017.11.021

Zengin, S. (2022). Çevik Pazarlama Yapısının İşletmelerde Uygulanmasına İlişkin Öneriler. *Beykent Üniversitesi Sosyal Bilimler Dergisi*, *15*(2), 98–111. doi:10.18221/bujss.1140640

Zhang, J. (2020). *A systematic review of the use of augmented reality (AR) and virtual reality (VR) in online retailing.* https://hdl.handle.net/10292/13339 doi:10.1057/s41270-022-00161-y

Zhang, Y., Fang, L., Deng, H., Qi, Z., & Liang, H. (2023). *Recent Advances and Future Perspectives of Digital Twins.* Paper presented at the 2023 IEEE International Conference on Control, Electronics and Computer Technology (ICCECT). 10.1109/ICCECT57938.2023.10140652

Zhang, T. C., Jahromi, M. F., & Kizildag, M. (2018). Value co-creation in a sharing economy: The end of price wars? *International Journal of Hospitality Management*, *71*, 51–58. doi:10.1016/j. ijhm.2017.11.010

Zhao, H., Li, D., & Li, X. (2018). Relationship between dreaming and memory reconsolidation. *Brain Science Advances*, *4*(2), 118–130. doi:10.26599/BSA.2018.9050005

Zhou, S., Barnes, L., McCormick, H., & Blazquez Cano, M. (2021). Social media influencers' narrative strategies to create eWOM: A theoretical contribution. *International Journal of Information Management*, *59*, 102293. doi:10.1016/j.ijinfomgt.2020.102293

About the Contributors

Fatih Sahin currently works at Bandirma Onyedi Eylul University, where he conducts research in consumer behavior, social media marketing, relationship marketing, complaint management, and branding. He holds a graduate degree from the Statistics Department at Yıldız Technical University, completed his undergraduate studies in business administration at Bahcesehir University, and earned a Ph.D. from Dumlupınar University.

* * *

Monaliz Amirkhanpour is a certified digital marketer from the Digital Marketing Institute (DMI Ireland) and Microsoft Certified Professional. She holds a Postgraduate Certificate in Business IT from Middlesex University London (UK), an MBA (with Distinction) in Management of Information Systems (MIS) from the University of Nicosia (Cyprus), a BSc in Computer Engineering from the University of Nicosia (Cyprus), and a BSc in Computer Science from the University of Indianapolis (USA). Currently, She is a PhD researcher in Business & Enterprise Management programme at the School of Business and Technology, University of Gloucestershire, UK. Her research is focused on the effective application of smartphone-based mobile and digital marketing tools within the retail industry. Monaliz has a number of publications in outstanding academic journals in addition to book chapter contributions and co-editing books related to business and management disciplines. She has received a number of academic awards including: the industry award of being the Best Graduate in Computer Engineering from Cyprus Telecommunications Authority (CYTA) in 2009, an industry award for the Best MBA Thesis in E-Learning practices within Cyprus public and private universities from the Tseriotis Group of Companies (Cyprus) in 2011.

Vedika Bhargaw is a student pursuing BSc Psychology (Hons.) at PES University, Bengaluru, India. Her research interests include Criminal Psychology, Cross-cultural Studies and Personality Psychology.

About the Contributors

Moritz Botts studied economics and management with a minor in media sciences at Leibniz University Hannover in Germany and Poznań University of Economics in Poland. He received his doctorate from European University Viadrina in Frankfurt an der Oder, Germany. He currently holds the position of assistant professor for marketing at Turkish-German University in Istanbul. His research focuses on international marketing, cross-cultural research and business ethics, with forthcoming publications in these fields.

Myriam Ertz is Associate Professor of Marketing at University of Quebec at Chicoutimi, Director of LaboNFC, Tier-2 Canada Research Chair in Technology, Sustainability, and Society, and co-responsible for Axis 1 of the Research Network on the circular economy of Quebec (RRECQ). Recipient of MDPI's Social Sciences 2020 Young Investigator Award and the University of Quebec's 2022 Research Succession Award, she has published over 90 research articles on product lifetime extension, responsible marketing, pro-environmental behavior, and the collaborative economy in top-tier journals including Renewable and Sustainable Energy Reviews, Journal of Cleaner Production, Resources Conservation & Recycling, Science of the Total Environment, Sustainable Cities & Society, Journal of Environmental Management, Business Strategy & the Environment, Journal of Consumer Behaviour, Journal of Business Research, Industrial Marketing Management, and European Journal of Marketing among others, and has extensive editorial experience, as author (author of the first handbook on responsible marketing in French language: Marketing responsable, JFD Editions), book (co-)editor (e.g., Handbook of research on the platform economy and the evolution of e-commerce, IGI Global), journal associate editor (Frontiers in Psychology, Frontiers in Sustainability), and special issue guest editor (Sustainability, Discover Sustainability, Revue Organisations & Territoires).

Ömer Hurmacı received his bachelor's degree in tourism administration from Boğaziçi University and master's in production management and marketing from Marmara University. He works as a research assistant at the department of management at Turkish-German University, while pursuing his PhD in Management at İstanbul Technical University. His current research interest is in psychological ownership and technology acceptance models.

Zidan Kachhi is a Consultant Counselling Psychologist. He is currently associated with the Department of Psychology at PES University, RR Campus, Bengaluru, India as an Assistant Professor. He has authored two books and presented papers at various international conferences. His research interests include gender and sexuality studies, media representation of marginalized communities, biases in science, behavioral finance, and sustainability.

About the Contributors

Neslihan Paker is an Assistant Professor in the Logistics Department at Izmir Kavram Vocational School in Izmir, Turkey. She holds an MBA degree and a Ph.D. in Business Administration, and two undergraduate degrees; an Industrial Engineering, and a second bachelor degree in Sociology. She worked in the supply chain management and marketing departments of several companies before joining academia. Her research interests are in services marketing, marine tourism, consumer behavior, and logistics.

Ondřej Roubal, Ph.D. is Associate Professor of Sociology, the Vice-Rector for the Development and Research and the guarantor of the Marketing Communication study programme at the University of Finance and Administration in Prague, Czech Republic. Through lecturing and his research work, he tries to discuss and further develop sociological, anthropological and psychological knowledge on the life of society in terms of marketing communication practice. His aim is to create a profile of the sociology of marketing communication via interdisciplinary approaches. He regularly publishes in the field of current problems of late modernity related to consumer culture and consumer decision making, individualism, hedonism, construction of identities and seeking happiness within the conditions of material abundance.

Astha Singh is a student pursuing BSc Psychology (Hons.) at PES University, Bengaluru, India. Her research interests include Clinical Psychology, Rehabilitation Psychology, and Gender and Relationship studies.

Index

2D Barcodes 111
3D Printing 259, 280

A

Ambivalence 52, 65, 85
Anchoring Bias 1, 10-11, 14, 22
Anti-Consumerism 26-29
Anti-Consumption 23, 25, 27-30, 40, 50
Artificial Intelligence (AR) 52, 113, 115, 119-120, 122, 124-125, 128, 130, 133, 138, 141, 147, 149-153, 159, 173, 176, 278, 280
Attractiveness 64-65, 212, 220, 227, 235, 237-239, 242, 245, 248, 257, 267
Augmented Reality (AR) 111, 113, 141, 147, 154, 161, 173, 177, 182-183
Availability Heuristics 12, 22

B

Beacon Technology 112
Brand Communities 264-266, 268, 276, 279

C

Chatbots 113, 125, 128, 141, 146, 150-153, 173
Co-Creation 189, 259-260, 262, 265-268, 274, 280, 289
Cognitive Biases 1-2, 10, 13-15, 19, 22
Collaborative Consumption 259-262, 264-266, 268, 272-275, 277, 279
Collaborative Economy 261, 268, 272, 274, 277, 289
Confirmation Bias 1, 9-10, 13, 15, 19, 22

Conscious Consumerism 3, 22
Consumer Culture 24, 27-29, 51-53, 56-57, 62-63, 65, 67-68, 70, 76-78, 85, 186, 192
Consumer Perception 207-208
Consumerism 3, 22, 25, 28-29, 50, 53, 58, 70-71, 76, 185-186
Content Analysis 207, 209, 216
Content Marketing 98, 113, 117-118, 123, 138, 189
Creative Consumption 259-266, 276-278, 280, 289
Creative Economy 276-278, 289
Customer Empowerment 206
Customer-Interfacing Retail Technologies 173

D

Déjà Rêvé Effect 174, 180, 182, 184, 190-191, 206
Delayed Gratification 51, 57, 71, 73-76, 78
Digital Engagement 18
Digital Marketing 86-88, 90-92, 95-98, 102, 104, 106, 115, 128, 132-133, 235
Digital Retailing 139, 141-147, 161
Digital Twins 183, 194-195, 197-198, 206
Digitalization 5, 25, 52, 69, 120, 131-132, 139-143, 147, 156, 159, 175-176
Direct Marketing 87, 92-93
Discrete Choice Experiment 235, 237-238, 242-244, 249, 257
Doğa İçin Çal 207-208, 215, 227
Downshifting 27, 31-32, 50
Dream Theories 179, 196

Index

E

Elaboration Likelihood Model 238, 257
Endowment Effect 10, 12-14, 22
Environmental Behaviour 233
Ethnocentric 233
Experimental Study 249

H

Hedonism 53, 70-76, 78, 85, 117

I

Individualization 51-52, 57-58, 77
Influencer Marketing 15-16, 113, 128, 138, 235-237, 239
Information Economics 238, 257
Instagram 25, 154, 211, 236, 244, 249, 257

L

Location-Based Services (LBS) 90, 112

M

Machine Learning 113, 122, 124, 128, 138, 141, 147, 150, 153, 173
Marketing 5.0 24, 113, 115, 118, 120, 122, 124, 126-127, 138
Marketing Communications 66, 87-88, 90-92, 95, 102, 104-106, 208
Marketing Strategy 10, 12, 86, 97-99, 104-106, 128, 138, 189, 206
Marketing Trends 98, 104, 113-114
Materialism 23-24, 30-31, 33, 37-40, 50, 260
Materialist Consumption 23-26
Maximizer 85
Maxqda 207, 209, 217
Mentality 53, 57-58, 62-64, 67, 70-71, 73-78, 186
Metaverse 130-131, 138-139, 141-142, 144, 147, 156-162, 173-174, 186-187, 192-194, 196, 198, 278, 280
Metaverse Retailing 139, 141-142, 147, 156, 158-160

Minimalist Consumption 23, 25, 27, 29
Minimalist Lifestyle 24-26, 29-34, 36, 41
Mobile Advertising 102, 128, 138
Mobile Marketing 86-90, 92, 95-107, 112, 124

N

Near-Field Communications (NFC) 90, 112

O

Online Retail 101

P

Paradox of Choice 51, 53-58, 69, 73-75, 77, 85
Parasocial Relationship 249, 257
Patriotism 221, 224, 233
Peer Influence 1, 17-18, 22
Permission-Based Marketing 94-95
Phygital Marketing 115-116, 138
Predatory Hedonism 73, 76, 85
Promotional Mix 87, 92-93

Q

QR Code Marketing 112

S

Satisficer 75, 85
Semiotics 212, 216, 233
Sensory Stimuli 182, 212, 223, 233-234
Service Robots 152, 173
Sharing Economy 36, 74, 120, 262-263, 268, 274, 279, 289
Simulacra 174, 183-184, 186-188, 192-193, 196, 198, 206
Simulacrum 206
Smartphones 3, 7, 86, 90, 92, 96, 98, 101, 104, 112, 138, 144, 153-154, 159
Social Identity 1, 9, 17-19, 22, 215
Social Influencer 237-239, 241-242, 244, 247-249, 257

340

Index

Social Marketing 27, 50, 207-211, 214-215, 225, 227, 234
Social Media 1, 3-9, 15-19, 25, 30, 86-87, 90, 92, 95, 97-99, 105-106, 118-120, 128, 131, 138, 141-142, 144, 153, 159, 176, 207-209, 211-212, 215, 227, 234, 236, 241-244, 247, 249, 257, 265, 267, 278
Social Media Marketing 92, 128
Source Credibility 237-238, 243, 245-249, 257
Sustainability Influencer 257
Sustainable Consumption 26-28, 40, 50, 266

T

Terror Management Theory 26, 39-40, 50
Transformation in Retailing 142
Trustworthiness 235, 237-239, 242, 246-248, 257
Twitter 244, 257

V

Virtual Reality (VR) 112-113, 141, 147, 154, 177, 182-183, 196
Voice Commerce 141, 153, 173
Voluntary Simplicity 24, 26-36, 40-41, 50-51, 57, 71-72, 75-76, 85

W

Word-of-Mouth 1, 5, 16, 18-19, 236, 239, 257

Y

YouTube 25, 176, 207-208, 211, 215-216, 227, 236

Z

Zero Consumers 141, 156, 173

Recommended Reference Books

IGI Global's reference books are available in three unique pricing formats:
Print Only, E-Book Only, or Print + E-Book.
Order direct through IGI Global's Online Bookstore at **www.igi-global.com** or through your preferred provider.

ISBN: 9781799887096
EISBN: 9781799887119
© 2022; 413 pp.
List Price: US$ **250**

ISBN: 9781799874157
EISBN: 9781799874164
© 2022; 334 pp.
List Price: US$ **240**

ISBN: 9781668440230
EISBN: 9781668440254
© 2022; 320 pp.
List Price: US$ **215**

ISBN: 9781799889502
EISBN: 9781799889526
© 2022; 263 pp.
List Price: US$ **240**

ISBN: 9781799885283
EISBN: 9781799885306
© 2022; 587 pp.
List Price: US$ **360**

ISBN: 9781668455906
EISBN: 9781668455913
© 2022; 2,235 pp.
List Price: US$ **1,865**

Do you want to stay current on the latest research trends, product announcements, news, and special offers?
Join IGI Global's mailing list to receive customized recommendations, exclusive discounts, and more.
Sign up at: **www.igi-global.com/newsletters**.

Publisher of Timely, Peer-Reviewed Inclusive Research Since 1988

www.igi-global.com   Sign up at www.igi-global.com/newsletters   facebook.com/igiglobal   twitter.com/igiglobal

Ensure Quality Research is Introduced to the Academic Community

Become an Evaluator for IGI Global Authored Book Projects

   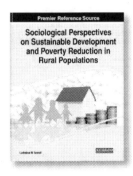

The overall success of an authored book project is dependent on quality and timely manuscript evaluations.

Applications and Inquiries may be sent to:
development@igi-global.com

Applicants must have a doctorate (or equivalent degree) as well as publishing, research, and reviewing experience. Authored Book Evaluators are appointed for one-year terms and are expected to complete at least three evaluations per term. Upon successful completion of this term, evaluators can be considered for an additional term.

If you have a colleague that may be interested in this opportunity, we encourage you to share this information with them.

IGI Global OnDemand

Easily Identify, Acquire, and Utilize Published Peer-Reviewed Findings in Support of Your Current Research

Purchase Individual IGI Global OnDemand Book Chapters and Journal Articles

For More Information:
www.igi-global.com/e-resources/ondemand/

Browse through 150,000+ Articles and Chapters!

Find specific research related to your current studies and projects that have been contributed by international researchers from prestigious institutions, including:

- Accurate and Advanced Search
- Affordably Acquire Research
- Instantly Access Your Content
- Benefit from the InfoSci Platform Features

« It really provides an excellent entry into the research literature of the field. It presents a manageable number of highly relevant sources on topics of interest to a wide range of researchers. The sources are scholarly, but also accessible to 'practitioners'. »

- Ms. Lisa Stimatz, MLS, University of North Carolina at Chapel Hill, USA

Interested in Additional Savings?

Subscribe to
IGI Global OnDemand *Plus*

Learn More

Acquire content from over 126,000+ research-focused book chapters and 33,000+ scholarly journal articles for as low as US$ 5 per article/chapter (original retail price for an article/chapter: US$ 37.50).

7,300+ E-BOOKS.
ADVANCED RESEARCH.
INCLUSIVE & AFFORDABLE.

IGI Global e-Book Collection

- Flexible Purchasing Options (Perpetual, Subscription, EBA, etc.)
- Multi-Year Agreements with No Price Increases Guaranteed
- No Additional Charge for Multi-User Licensing
- No Maintenance, Hosting, or Archiving Fees
- Continually Enhanced & Innovated Accessibility Compliance Features (WCAG)

Handbook of Research on Digital Transformation, Industry Use Cases, and the Impact of Disruptive Technologies
ISBN: 9781799877127
EISBN: 9781799877141

Handbook of Research on New Investigations in Artificial Life, AI, and Machine Learning
ISBN: 9781799886860
EISBN: 9781799886877

Handbook of Research on Future of Work and Education
ISBN: 9781799882756
EISBN: 9781799882770

Research Anthology on Physical and Intellectual Disabilities in an Inclusive Society (4 Vols.)
ISBN: 9781668435427
EISBN: 9781668435434

Innovative Economic, Social, and Environmental Practices for Progressing Future Sustainability
ISBN: 9781799895909
EISBN: 9781799895923

Applied Guide for Event Study Research in Supply Chain Management
ISBN: 9781799889694
EISBN: 9781799889717

Mental Health and Wellness in Healthcare Workers
ISBN: 9781799888130
EISBN: 9781799888147

Clean Technologies and Sustainable Development in Civil Engineering
ISBN: 9781799898108
EISBN: 9781799898122

Request More Information, or Recommend the IGI Global e-Book Collection to Your Institution's Librarian

For More Information or to Request a Free Trial, Contact IGI Global's e-Collections Team: eresources@igi-global.com | 1-866-342-6657 ext. 100 | 717-533-8845 ext. 100

Printed in the United States
by Baker & Taylor Publisher Services